The New Sabin

Entries 23829-25946

\ The New Sabin;

Books Described by Joseph Sabin and His

Successors, Now Described Again on the

Basis of Examination of Originals,

and Fully Indexed by Title, Subject,

Joint Authors, and Institutions and Agencies

by

Lawrence S. Thompson
111

Entries 23829-25946

Volume X

The Whitston Publishing Company
Troy, New York
1984

PREFACE

The tenth volume of The New Sabin contains material relating
to slavery, mainly in the United States, but also in the West Indies,
Brazil, and other parts of the world, and in antiquity and modern
times. It supplements Lawrence S. Thompson, The Southern Black,
Slave and Free (1970). Both volumes represent the microfiche
collections of the Lost Cause Press, Louisville, one of the largest
collections, if not the largest, on this subject. The originals of
a great proportion of the titles in The Southern Black are in the
Oberlin College collection, and of those in the present volume in
the Library of Congress, but there is a substantial group held by
one library and not by the other. Further, a considerable number of
scarce titles have been copied from other sources, some in quite
unlikely repositories but owning the material as part of other
collections. The microform publication of this material is a conti-
nuing project, and the ultimate objective is to bring back to avail-
ability in one collection as much of the vast corpus of the literature
of slavery as can be located.

It will be noted that a list of numbers of entries which relate
to slavery and are recorded in the first nine volumes is appended.
It is characteristic of the literature of slavery that much signifi-
cant material is found in travel literature, theological works,
treatises on economics and commerce, creative literature (e.g.,
Uncle Tom and its progeny), ethnological studies, and works in many
other fields. The student of the economic structure of the Roman
Empire or of the sources of poverty in modern Brazil and the West
Indies, to cite but two of many examples, will neglect the literature
of slavery at his peril.

The broad importance of the literature of slavery to scholars
in a wide variety of fields will be obvious from the cumulative index
to the first ten volumes of The New Sabin. (There will be no separate index to this volume.) The index has been cumulated after each
volume, but the time required to prepare copy and proofread this very
large index may not permit its appearance before that of the eleventh
volume, now in preparation.

Finally, it should be noted that there have always been and still
are varieties of enforced human labor and even bondage on which there
is an enormous literature not included in this collection. Although

there is only a tenuous line of distinction between legally sanctioned proprietary ownership of another human and the conditions of
the labor force on a modern sugar plantation in the Caribbean or in
labor camps in totalitarian countries (right and left), all is a
part of the sordid story of man's almost congenital inhumanity to
man. Those who delve into the texts of the literature about slavery
up to the formal emancipations in the Americas may find something
here which will identify those noxious genes in the human race which
have persisted from the evil pimps of the New Comedy through Simon
Legree and into our own times.

Lawrence S. Thompson
Lexington, Kentucky

To

Whitney Moore Young, Jr., 1921-1971,
Humanitarian and Kentuckian

23829 Abel, Annie Heloise, 1873-
       The American Indian as slaveholder and secessionist;
       an omitted chapter in the diplomatic history of the
       Southern Confederacy, by Annie Heloise Abel, Ph.D.
       Cleveland, The Arthur H. Clark company, 1915.
           394 p. incl. front., ports., maps, plan.   24½ cm.
       (Her The slaveholding Indians, v. 1)

23830 La abolición de la esclavitud y el proyecto del señor
       Moret. Madrid, Estab. tip. de T. Fortanet, 1870.
           116 p.   21 cm.

23831 El Abolicionista español... año 1-   [Madrid, Imp.
       de T. Fortanet, 18   ]
               v.   29 cm.   monthly.
           Caption title. Organ of the Sociedad abolicionista
       española. Editor: J. L. Vizcarrondo.

23832 Abolition a sedition, by a Northern man. Philadelphia,
       George W. Donohue, 1839.
           187 p.   15 cm.

23833 The abolition conspiracy to destroy the union; or,
       A ten years' record of the "Republican" party. The
       opinions of William Lloyd Garrison, Wendell Phillips,
       Abraham Lincoln, William H. Seward... &c. New York,
       Van Evrie, Horton & company, 1866.
           31 p.   22½ cm.   (Anti-abolition tracts, no. 3)

23834 ... Abolition is national death; or, The attempt to
       equalize races the destruction of society. New York,
       Van Evrie, Horton & co., 1866.
           1 p.l., [5]-30 p.   22½ cm.   (Anti-abolition
       tracts, no. 1)
           Published New York, 1862, with title: Abolition and
       secession; or, Cause and effect...

23835 Abolitionism exposed, corrected. By a physician,
       formerly resident of the South. With A plan for
       abolishing the American anti-slavery society and its
       auxiliaries. By a Tennesseean. Philadelphia,

J. Sharp, 1838.
   40 p.   22 cm.

23838 L'Abolitioniste français, bulletin mensuel de la Société
       instituée en 1834 pour l'abolition de l'esclavage. t. 1-
       jan./fév. 1844-   Paris, Au bureau du journal
       [1844-   ]
            v.   20½ cm.

23837 Adams, Alice Dana, 1864-
       ... The neglected period of anti-slavery in America
       (1808-1831) by Alice Dana Adams, A.M.   Boston and
       London, Ginn and company, 1908.
            xi, 307 p.   23½ cm.   (Radcliffe College monographs,
       no. 14)

23838 Adams, John Quincy, pres. U.S., 1767-1848.
            Speech of the Hon. John Quincy Adams, in the House of
       Representatives, on the State of the Nation: delivered
       May 25, 1836. New York, H. R. Piercy, 1836.
            18 p.   22½ cm.

23839 Adams, Robert, sailor.
            The narrative of Robert Adams, an American sailor,
       who was wrecked on the western coast of Africa, in the
       year 1810; was detained three years in slavery by the
       Arabs of the great desert, and resided several months
       in the city of Tombuctoo [!] With a map, notes, and an
       appendix. Boston, Wells and Lilly, 1817.
            xxviii, [29]-200 p.   front. (fold. map)   23 cm.
            Ed. by S. Cock. Cf. Introductory details and
       Dedication.

23840 Address of the Peterboro State Convention to the slaves,
       and its vindication. Cazenovia [N.Y.] R. L. Myrick,
       1842.
            23 p.   13 cm.
            Vindication: Extract from a letter from Gerrit Smith
       to Rev. Wm. H. Brisbane.

23841 The address of Southern delegates in Congress, to their
       constituents. [Washington] Towers, printer [1848?]
            15 p.   24 cm..
            Caption title. Signed: R.M.T. Hunter and 47 other
       members of both branches of the 30th Congress.

23842 An address on slavery, and against immediate emancipation;
       with a plan of their being gradually emancipated &
       colonized, in 32 years. By a citizen of New York.

New York, S. B. White, 1834.
16 p.   23 cm.

23843   Address to the Democracy of Missouri. [St. Louis? 1850?]
14 p.   20 cm.
Caption title. Signed by M. Blair and 37 others.
Principally on the question of the legality of slavery
in the territories.

23844   An address to ministers and Christian masters. [n.p., 1829]
27 p.   18 cm.
"Inquiry into the meaning of the word δοῦλος in the
New Testament", p. [3]-13.

23845   An address to the people of Great Britain, on the
consumption of West-India produce. The 2d ed. [London]
L. Phillips [etc., 17--]
12 p.   17½ cm.

23846   Address to the people of Maryland, by a farmer and land-
holder, of Jessup's Cut, Maryland. [Baltimore] Printed
by Bull & Tuttle, 1863.
8 p.   23 cm.

23847   ... An address to the respectable people of every colour,
and others if you please. n.p. [1829]
21 p.   20½ cm.
Signed: A messenger.

23848   Adrain, Garnett Bowditch, 1816-1878.
State of the Union. Speech of Hon. Garnett B. Adrain,
of New Jersey, in the House of Representatives, January 15,
1861. [Washington, Printed at the office of the
Congressional Globe, 1861]
8 p.   23 cm.
Caption title.

23849   The Age [a southern monthly eclectic magazine] Wm. M.
Burwell & Ernest Lagarde, editors. v. 1, no. 1-5;
Jan. 1864-Jan. 1865. Richmond, E. Lagarde & co.,
proprietors, 1864-65.
cover-title, 400 p.   23 cm.
Caption title: The Richmond age, a southern eclectic
magazine. Publication suspended, May-Dec. 1864.

23850   The agitation of slavery. Who commenced! and Who can
end it!! Buchanan and Fillmore compared from the
record. [n.p., 1850?]
32 p.   22 cm.

23851   [Aguilera, Francisco Vicente] 1821-1877.
            Notes about Cuba... [New York, 1872]
            54 p.   23½ cm.
            Preface Signed: Francisco V. Aguilera, Ramon Cespedes,
        commissioners of the republic of Cuba.

23852   Ahumada y Centurión, José de.
            La abolición de la esclavitud en países de colonización
        europea. Exposición de disposiciones, compiladas por
        d. José Ahumada y Centurión. Madrid, Imp. de F. Lopez
        Vizcaino, 1870.
            vii, [9]-176 p.   18 cm.

23853   Aimes, Hubert Hillary Suffern.
            Coartación: A Spanish institution for the advancement
        of slaves into freedmen. [n.p., 1909]
            412-431 p.   22 cm.
            Reprinted from Yale review, v. 17, Feb. 1909.

23854   Aimes, Hubert Hillary Suffern.
            A history of slavery in Cuba, 1511 to 1868, by Hubert
        H. S. Aimes... New York and London, G. P. Putnam's sons,
        1907.
            xi, 298 p.   21 cm.

23855   Albertario, Emilio, 1885-
            ... Un interessante testo di Giavoleno (D. 41, 2, 24
        ex 1. 14 epist.)   Roma, Athenaeum, 1916.
            12 p.   25 cm.
            "Estratto dagli Annali della Facoltà di giurisprudenza
        della Università di Perugia, vol. XXX-1915, ser. III,
        vol. XIII."

23856   Alcalá y Henke, Agustín.
            ... La esclavitud de los negros en la América
        española... Madrid, Impr. de J. Pueyo, 1919.
            110 p.   24 cm.
            Tesis - Madrid.

23857   [Alexander, Ann Tuke)] 1767-1849.
            An address to the inhabitants of Charleston, South
        Carolina. Philadelphia, Printed by Kimber, Conrad, &
        co., 1805.
            7 p.   22 cm.

23858   Alexander, Archibald, 1772-1851.
            A history of colonization on the western coast of
        Africa. By Archibald Alexander... Philadelphia,

4

W. S. Martien, 1846.
xii, [5]-603 p.   front. (fold. map)   23 cm.

23859   Alexander, William T
          History of the colored race in America. Containing
        also their ancient and modern life in Africa... the
        origin and development of slavery in the Old World,
        and its introduction on the American continent; the
        slave trade; slavery, and its abolition in Europe and
        America. The civil war, emancipation, education and
        advancement of the colored race, their civil and poli-
        tical rights. Prepared and arranged by Wm. T. Alexander...
        Kansas City, Mo., Palmetto publishing co., 1887.
          2 p.l., 600 p.   11 pl., ports. (incl. front.)   23 cm.

23860   Alford, Julius C
          Speech of Mr. J. C. Alford, of Georgia, on abolition
        petitions. Delivered in the House of Representatives,
        January 22, 1840. Washington, Printed by Gales and
        Seaton, 1840.
          14 p. $24\frac{1}{2}$ cm.

23861   Alger, William Rounseville, 1822-1905.
          The historic purchase of freedom. An oration
        delivered before the fraternity, in the Music Hall,
        Boston, Dec. 22, 1859, the two hundred and thirty-ninth
        anniversary of the landing of the Pilgrims at Plymouth.
        By William Rounseville Alger. 2d ed. Boston, Walker,
        Wise and company, 1859.
          2 p.l., [3]-44 p. $22\frac{1}{2}$ cm.

23862   The Algerine slaves; a poem. By a citizen of Newburyport...
        Newburyport, Printed by A. March, 1798.
          [175]-189 p. $18\frac{1}{2}$ cm.
          (In Foss, John. A journal of the captivity and
        sufferings of John Foss... Newburyport [1798?])
          Signed: Juvenis.

23863   Allard, Paul, 1841-1916.
          Les ésclaves chrétiens, depuis les premiers temps de
        l'église jusqu'à la fin de la domination romaine en
        Occident, par Paul Allard... 3. éd., rev. et augm.
        Paris, V. Lecoffre, 1900.
          4 p.l., xv, 494 p. $18\frac{1}{2}$ cm.

23864   Allard, Paul, 1841-1916.
          ... Les origines du servage en France. Paris,
        J. Gabalda, 1913.
          2 p.l., 332 p. $18\frac{1}{2}$ cm.

23865   [Allen, Joseph Henry] 1820-1898.
        The great controversy of states and people. Boston,
        W. Crosby and H. P. Nichols, 1851.
        45 p.   19 cm.

23866   Allen, Joseph Henry, 1820-1895.
        A reign of terror. A sermon preached in Union Street
        Church, Bangor, on Sunday evening, June 1, 1856. By
        Joseph Henry Allen... Bangor, Printed by S. S. Smith,
        1856.
        16 p. $21\frac{1}{2}$ cm.

23867   Allen, Stephen Merrill, 1819-1894.
        Democrat and Republican. Slavery and freedom. Past
        and present crises. An historical address in behalf
        of the veteran founders of the Republican Party upon
        the pending dangers of political corruption, anarchical
        disorganization, and increasing intemperance of the
        present day. By Hon. Stephen M. Allen... Duxbury,
        June 17, 1888. Boston, A. C. Getchell, printer, 1888.
        44 p. $22\frac{1}{2}$ cm.

23868   Allen, Thomas Newton, 1839-
        Chronicles of Oldfields, by Thomas N. Allen. Seattle,
        Washington, The Alice Harriman company, 1909.
        157 p. incl. front. (port.)   21 cm.

23869   Allison, John, 1812-1878.
        The slavery question. Speech of Hon. John Allison,
        of Pa., delivered in the House of Representatives,
        April 1, 1856. [Washington, D.C., Buell & Blanchard,
        printers, 1856]
        8 p. $22\frac{1}{2}$ cm.

23870   Almada, José de.
        ... Comparative essay on indentured labour at St. Thomé
        and Principe, by José de Almada, head-section in the
        Colonial office, private secretary to the minister for
        foreign affairs. Lisbon, National printing office, 1913.
        81 p., 1 l.   25 cm.

23871   Alonso y Sanjurjo, Eugenio.
        Apuntes sobre los proyectos de abolición de la
        esclavitud en las islas de Cuba y Puerto Rico, por
        d. Eugenio Alonso y Sanjurjo. Madrid, Impr. de la
        Biblioteca de instrucción y recreo [1874?]
        68 p.   17 cm.

23872   Alston, William Jeffreys, 1800-1876.
        The slavery question. Speech of Hon. Wm. J. Alston,

of Alabama, in the House of Representatives, April 18, 1850, in Committee of the Whole on the State of the Union, on the President's message transmitting the constitution of California. [Washington, Printed at the Congressional globe office, 1850]
8 p.   23 cm.
Caption title.

23873 Alvarado, Hermógenes.
... Segunda conferencia histórica de propaganda patriótica, por el doctor Don Hermogenes Alvarado h. San Salvador, El Salvador, Tip. La Unión, 1920.
cover-title, 25 p.   port.   21 cm.
Half-title: Tema: José Simeón Cañas y la abolición de la esclavitud en Centro América.

23874 Alves Rocadas, José Augusto.
... La main d'oeuvre indigène à Angola, par J. A. Alves Rocadas... Lisbonne, Impr. "A Editora limitada," 1914.
55 p.   26 cm.
At head of title: III° Congrès international d'agriculture tropicale, Londres - 1914.

23875 Alvord, Clarence Walworth, 1868-1928, ed.
... Governor Edward Coles; ed. with introduction and notes by Clarence Walworth Alvord... Springfield, Ill., The Trustees of the Illinois State Historical Library, 1920.
4 p.l., iii-viii, 435 p.   front. (port.)   facsims. (part fold.)   23 cm.   (Collections of the Illinois State Historical Library, vol. 15. Biographical ser., v. I)

23876 America's misfortune; or, A practical view of slavery. By an American. Buffalo, Thomas & Lathrops' steam presses, 1856.
91 p.   19 cm.

23877 American and foreign anti-slavery reporter. New York, 1840-45.
2 v.   illus.   32 cm.

23878 [American and Foreign Anti-Slavery Society]
An address to the anti-slavery Christians of the United States. New-York, Printed by J. A. Gray, 1852.
cover-title, 16 p.   22½ cm.

23879 American and Foreign Anti-Slavery Society.
Address to the inhabitants of New Mexico and California,

on the omission by Congress to provide them with
territorial governments, and on the social and
political evils of slavery. New York, The Am. & For.
Anti-Slavery Society, 1849.
56 p.   18½ cm.

23880 [American and Foreign Anti-Slavery Society]
The Fugitive slave bill: its history and unconstitu-
tionality; with an account of the seizure and enslave-
ment of James Hamlet, and his subsequent restoration
to liberty. 3d ed. New-York, W. Harned, 1850.
36 p.   19 cm.
Preface signed: Lewis Tappan, cor. sec.

23881 American Anti-Slavery Society.
Commemoration of the fiftieth anniversary of the
organization of the American Anti-Slavery Society, in
Philadelphia... Philadelphia, T. S. Dando & co., 1884.
65 p.   front. (port.)   22½ cm.

23882 American Anti-Slavery Society.
... Declaration of sentiments of the American Anti-
Slavery Society. Adopted at the formation of said
Society, in Philadelphia, on the 4th day of December,
1833. [New York, American Anti-Slavery Society, n.d.]
4 p.   23 cm.   (Penny tracts, no. 1)
Caption title.

23883 American Anti-Slavery Society.
[Erklärung] und Constitution der Amerikanischen
Gegensclaverey-Gesellschaft... Harrisburg, Pa.,
1836.
24 p.   17½ cm.

23884 American Anti-Slavery Society.
Platform of the American Anti-Slavery Society and
its auxiliaries. New York, N. Y. Anti-Slavery Society,
1836.
35, [1] p.   19 cm.

23885 American Anti-Slavery Society.
Platform of the American Anti-Slavery Society and
its auxiliaries. New York, N. Y. Anti-Slavery Society,
1853.
35, [1] p.   19 cm.

23886 American Anti-Slavery Society.
Platform of the American Anti-Slavery Society and
its auxiliaries. New York, N. Y. Anti-Slavery Society,

1855.
     36 p.   18 cm.

23887   American Anti-Slavery Society.
          Prejudice against color. New York [n.d.]
          16 p.   11 cm.

23888   American Anti-Slavery Society.
          ... To the people of the United States; or, To such
          Americans as value their rights, and dare to maintain
          them. [New York, American Anti-Slavery Society, 1836]
          8 p.   23 cm.   (The Anti-slavery examiner, vol. 1,
          August, 1836, no. 1)
          Caption title. On the right of petition.

23889   [American Board of Commissioners for Foreign Missions]
          On receiving donations from holders of slaves.
          Boston, Printed by Perkins and Marvin [1840?]
          cover-title, 20 p. $18\frac{1}{2}$ cm.

23890   American slavery. Demonstrations in favor of Dr. Cheever,
          in Scotland. Letter of sympathy from distinguished
          clergymen and other gentlemen. Speeches at meetings
          in Edinburgh and Glasgow, by Drs. Candlish, Guthrie,
          Alexander, Buchanan, and Smyth. And a statement of
          Dr. Cheever's case, by Rev. H. Batchelor. Letter of
          Dr. Guthrie to the Presbyterian. New-York, J. A. Gray,
          printer, 1860.
          vii, [9]-77 p.   15 cm.

23891   American slavery. A protest against American slavery,
          by one hundred and seventy-three Unitarian ministers.
          Boston, B. H. Greene, 1845.
          20 p. $13\frac{1}{2}$ cm.
          Approved and published by the Rhode Island and
          Massachusetts Christian Conference in New Bedford.
          Authorship attributed by Cushing to James Freeman Clarke.

23892   American slavery. Report of a meeting of members of a
          Unitarian body, held at the Freemasons' tavern,
          June 13th, 1851, to deliberate on the duty of English
          Unitarians in reference to slavery in the United
          States. Rev. Dr. Huttin in the chair. [London]
          E. T. Whitfield, 1851.
          23, [1] p. $19 \times 9\frac{1}{2}$ cm.

23893   American Union for the Relief and Improvement of the
          Colored Race.
          Report of the Executive Committee of the American

Union, at the annual meeting of the society, May 25,
1836. Boston, Printed by Perkins & Marvin, 1836.
39 p.   22 cm.

23894 [Amicus] pseud.
Slavery among the Puritans. A letter to the Rev.
Moses Stuart. Boston, C. C. Little and J. Brown, 1850.
42 p.   21 cm.

23895 Analyse e commentario critico da proposta do governo
imperial ás camaras legislativas sobre o elemento servil,
por um magistrado. Rio de Janeiro, Typographia nacional,
1871.
67 p.   22 cm.

23896 Annesley, James, 1715-1760.
Memoirs of an unfortunate young nobleman, return'd
from a thirteen years slavery in America, where he had
been sent by the wicked contrivances of his cruel uncle.
A story founded on truth, and address'd equally to
the head and heart. London, J. Freeman, 1743-47.
3 v. $17\frac{1}{2}$ cm.

23897 Anti-Slavery Conference, Paris, 1867.
Special report of the Anti-Slavery Conference, held
in Paris in the Salle Herz, on the twenty-sixth and
twenty-seventh August, 1867, hon. president. M. le duc
de Broglie. President. Mons. Édouard Laboulaye...
London, Committee of the British and Foreign Anti-
Slavery Society [1867]
1 p.l., ii, 166 p.   24 cm.

23898 Anti-Slavery Convention of American Women. 1st, New York,
1837.
An appeal to the women of the nominally free states,
issued by an Anti-Slavery Convention of American Women,
held by adjournments from the 9th to the 12th of May,
1837... New York, W. S. Dorr, printer, 1837.
68 p. $17\frac{1}{2}$ cm.

23899 Anti-Slavery Convention of American Women. 1st, New York,
1837.
Proceedings of the Anti-Slavery Convention of American
Women, held in the city of New York, May 9th, 10th,
11th, and 12th, 1837. New-York, Printed by W. S. Dorr,
1837.
23 p.   22 cm.

23900 Anti-Slavery Convention of American Women. 2nd, Philadelphia, 1838.

Proceedings of the Anti-Slavery Convention of American Women, held in Philadelphia. May 15th, 16th, 17th and 18th, 1838. Philadelphia, Printed by Merrihew and Gunn, 1838.
18 p.   22 cm.

23901   Anti-Slavery Convention of American Women. 3d, Philadelphia, 1839.
An address from the Convention of American Women, to the Society of Friends, on the subject of slavery. Philadelphia: printed. Bristol [Eng.] Reprinted, J. Wright, 1840.
8 p.   16 cm.

23902   Anti-Slavery Convention of American Women. 3d, Philadelphia, 1839.
Proceedings of the third Anti-Slavery Convention of American Women, held in Philadelphia, May 1st, 2d and 3d, 1839. Philadelphia, Printed by Merrihew and Thompson, 1839.
28 p.   22½ cm.

23903   Anti-slavery crisis. Policy of ministers. Reprinted from the Eclectic review, for April, 1838. With a postcript on the debate and division in the House of Commons, on the 29th and 30th of March. London, W. Ball [etc., etc.] 1838.
32 p.   front.   21 cm.

23904   Anti-slavery nominations. [n.p., 1839]
[1] p.   61 cm.
Broadside.

23905   The Anti-slavery record... v. 1-3; Jan. 1835-Dec. 1837. New York, American Anti-Slavery Society, 1835-38.
3 v.   18½ cm.

23906   Anti-Slavery Society, London.
Slavery in Europe; a letter to neutral governments from the Anti-Slavery Society. London, New York [etc.] Hodder & Stoughton, 1917.
7, [1] p.   18½ cm.

23907   Anti-Slavery Society of Salem and Vicinity, Salem, Mass.
Constitution of the Anti-Slavery Society of Salem and Vicinity. The society organized January 27, A.D. 1834. - Salem, Mass. Salem, Printed by W. & S. B. Ives, 1834.
8 p.   22 cm.

23908 ... The anti-slavery struggle. Boston, Old South Meeting-
House, 1897.
cover-title, [198] p.   18 cm.   (Old South leaflets,
ser. 15, 1897)
Various pagings.
Contents. - [1] The Liberator, vol. I, no. 1, Jan. 1,
1831 [a reprint of p. 1-3] - [2] Phillips, W. William
Lloyd Garrison; eulogy at the funeral of Garrison, May
28, 1879. Phillips, W. The murder of Lovejoy; first
speech in Faneuil hall, Dec. 8, 1837. - [3] Parker, T.
The dangers from slavery; from a sermon, 1854. Emerson,
R. W. Theodore Parker, from the address, 1860. -
[4] Whittier, J. G. The anti-slavery convention of
1833 [etc.] - [5] Stowe, H. B. The story of "Uncle
Tom's cabin." - [6] Sumner, C. The crime against Kansas,
1856. - [7] Brown, J. Words of John Brown. - [8] The
first Lincoln and Douglas debate, 1858.

23909 An Appeal on the subject of slavery; addressed to the
members of the New England and New Hampshire Conferences
of the Methodist Episcopal church. Together with a
defence of said appeal, in which is shown the sin of
holding property in man. Boston, D. H. Ela, 1835.
48 p.   20½ cm.
Signed: Shipley W. Willson, Abram D. Merrill, La Roy
Sunderland, George Storrs, Jared Perkins.

23910 Appel en faveur des esclaves aux États-Unis. [Paris,
lmpr. de C. Meyrueis et Ce, 1855]
4 p.   23 cm.
Caption title. Signed: Mmes. André Walther...
Frédéric Monod... Edmond de Pressensé... J. J. Keller.

23911 Appleton, James, 1785-1862.
... The Missouri compromise; or, The extension of
the slave power. By General James Appleton. [Boston,
New England Anti-Slavery Tract Association, 18--?]
4 p.   18 cm.   ([New England Anti-Slavery Tract
Association] Tract no. 3)
Caption title.

23912 Appomattox, pseud.
The letter of Appomatox [!] to the people of Virginia:
exhibiting a connected view of the recent proceedings
in the House of Delegates, on the subject of the
abolition of slavery; and a succinct account of the
doctrines broached by the friends of abolition, in
debate: and the mischievous tendency of those proceedings and doctrines. Richmond, T. W. White,

printer, 1832.
  47 p.   22½ cm.

23913 Apuntes sobre la cuestión de la reforma política y de la
introducción de Africanos en las islas de Cuba y
Puerto Rico. Madrid, Estab. tip. de T. Fortanet, 1866.
  347, [2] p.   23½ cm.

23914 Armas y Céspedes, José de, 1834-1900.
  El trabajo libre. Informe dado al presidente del
Consejo de ministros, d. Antonio Canovas del Castillo,
por José de Armas y Céspedes. Habana, La Propaganda
literaria, 1880.
  xi, 65 p.   19½ cm.

23915 [Armistead, Wilson] 1819?-1868, comp.
  Five hundred thousand strokes for freedom; a series
of anti-slavery tracts, of which half a million are now
first issued by the friends of the Negro. London, W. &
F. Cash, 1853.
  1 v. (various pagings) illus.   17 cm.
  Consists of reprints of no. 1-82 of the Leeds anti-
slavery series.

23916 [Armistead, Wilson] 1819-1868.
  The garland of freedom; a collection of poems, chiefly
anti-slavery... London, 1853.
    v.   18 cm.

23917 Ashley, James Monroe, 1824-1896.
  ... Speech of Hon. J. M. Ashley, of Ohio, in the
House of Representatives, April 11, 1862, on the bill
for the release of certain persons held to service
or labor in the District of Columbia. Washington, D.C.,
Scammell & co., printers, 1862.
  8 p.   24 cm.

23918 Ashmore, John D   1819-
  Speech of Hon. John D. Ashmore, of South Carolina,
on the slavery question. Delivered in the House of
Representatives, March 1, 1860. [Washington, Printed
by L. Towers, 1860]
  16 p.   22 cm.

23919 Ashmun, George, 1804-1870.
  Speech of Mr. G. Ashmun, of Massachusetts, on the
revolution in France, and emancipation in its colonies.
Delivered in the House of Representatives of the
United States... [Washington] J. & G. S. Gideon,

[1848?]
16 p.   24 cm.

23920   Association of Friends for Promoting the Abolition of
        Slavery, and Improving the Condition of the Free People
        of Color.
            An Address to the members of the Society of Friends,
        by the Association of Friends for Promoting the Abolition
        of Slavery, and Improving the Condition of the Free
        People of Color.   Philadelphia, Merrihew and Thompson,
        printers, 1843.
            12 p.   18 cm.
            Signed: John D. Griscom, Rebecca B. Neall, clerks.

23921   Association of Friends for Promoting the Abolition of
        Slavery, and Improving the Condition of the Free People
        of Color.
            An address to the Society of Friends, on the subject
        of American slavery, by "The Association of Friends
        for Promoting the Abolition of Slavery," &c.   Phila-
        delphia, Merrihew and Thompson, printers, 1842.
            8 p.   18½ cm.
            Signed: Caleb Clothier, Sarah M. Palmer, clerks.

23922   Atkins, Smith Dykins, 1836-1913.
            Democracy and Dred Scott.   Speech delivered by Smith
        D. Atkins, before the Freeport Wide Awakes, at Plymouth
        hall, Monday evening, Aug. 14, 1860.   Pub. by order of
        the joint-executive committee of the Freeport Wide
        Awakes, and the Republican Club.   [Freeport, Ill.,
        1860]
            24 p.   21 cm.
            Caption title.

23923   [Atlee, Benjamin Champneys] 1872-
            ... Thaddeus Stevens and slavery...   Lancaster, Pa.,
        1911.
            2 p.l., 167-188 p.   24½ cm.   (Papers read before
        the Lancaster County Historical Society, June 2, 1911,
        vol. 15, no. 6)

23924   Aughey, John Hill, 1828-
            The iron furnace: or, Slavery and secession.   By
        Rev. John H. Aughey, a refugee from Mississippi...
        Philadelphia, J. S. Claxton, 1865.
            296 p.   front. (port.) 2 pl.   18½ cm.

23925   Aunt Sally; or, The cross the way to freedom.   A narrative
        of the slave-life and purchase of the mother of Rev.

14

Isaac Williams, of Detroit, Michigan... Cincinnati,
American Reform Tract and Book Society, 1862.
   vii, 9-216 p.   front. (port.) illus., port. group.
15½ cm.

23926 [Austin, James Trecothick] 1784-1870.
          Remarks on Dr. Channing's "Slavery." By a citizen
       of Massachusetts. Charleston [S.C.] Re-printed by
       A. E. Miller, 1836.
          45 p.   22½ cm.

23927 Autographs of prominent men of the southern confederacy
       and historical documents. E. M. Bruce collection...
       [Houston, Tex., Cumming & sons, printers, 190-]
          32 p.   facsims.   15½ x 25 cm.
          Issued by the Passenger department, Southern Pacific
       railroad.
          "Introductory" signed: S. B. M.
          Introductory note signed: T. J. Anderson. G. P. &
       T. A. [of the Galveston, Harrisburg and San Antonio
       railroad, one of the lines under control of the
       Southern Pacific Company]

23928 Averill, James P   comp.
          Andersonville Prison Park. Report of its purchase
       and improvement. Accompanied by a plat of the
       grounds, made from actual survey. Comp. by James P.
       Averill... Atlanta, Ga. [Byrd printing company, 1899?]
          21, [3] p. incl. illus., plates.   22½ cm.

23929 Awad, Mohamed.
          ... Slavery.   New York 1965.
          27, 8, 224 p.   28 cm.   (United Nations.
       [Document] E/4056)
          Report of the special rapporteur on slavery appointed
       under Council resolution 960 (XXXVI).
          Caption title.
          At head of title: United Nations. Economic and
       Social Council.

                        B

23930 Bacon, Leonard Woolsey, 1830-1907.
          Anti-slavery before Garrison; an address before the
       Connecticut Society of the Order of the Founders and
       Patriots of America, New Haven, September 19, 1902:
       Being a contribution toward the hitherto unwritten life

                        15

of the true William Lloyd Garrison, by Leonard Woolsey
Bacon... New Haven, Press of the Tuttle, Morehouse &
Taylor company, 1903.
    1 p.l., [7]-37 p.   23 cm.

23931   Bacon, Thomas, 1700 (ca.)-1768.
        Four sermons, upon the great and indispensible duty
    of all Christian masters and mistresses to bring up
    their Negro slaves in the knowledge and fear of God.
    Preached at the parish church of St. Peter in Talbot
    county, in the province of Maryland. By the Rev.
    Thomas Bacon, rector of the said parish... London,
    Printed by J. Oliver, 1750.
        xxvi, 27-142 p.   16½ cm.

23932   Bailey, Alexander Hamilton, 1817-1874.
        The President's special message. Speech of Hon. A. H.
    Bailey, in the Senate, upon the Resolution to instruct
    our senators and to request our members to vote for the
    adoption of the recommendation of the President,
    contained in his Special message of March 6th, 1862.
    Albany, Weed, Parsons and company, printers, 1862.
        7 p.   23 cm.

23933   Bailey, Rufus William, 1793-1863.
        The issue, presented in a series of letters on
    slavery. By Rev. Rufus Wm. Bailey, of South Carolina.
    New-York, J. S. Taylor, 1837.
        vi, [7]-110 p.   19 cm.

23934   [Baird, Henry Carey] 1825-1912.
        The South. An attempt to indicate the nature and
    the cause of its diseases and the remedies for them.
    From the New York Tribune, October 22, 1874.
    [Philadelphia? 1874]
        5 p.   21 cm.
        Caption title.

23935   Baird, Thomas H
        Memorial of Hon. Th. H. Baird, praying for the enact-
    ment of measures to preserve the Constitution and union
    of the states. Presented to the House of Representatives,
    February 7, 1863, and referred to the Committee on the
    judiciary. Pittsburgh, A. A. Anderson & sons, printers,
    1864.
        23 p.   22½ cm.

23936   Baldwin, Roger Sherman, 1793-1863.
        Speech of Hon. R. S. Baldwin, of Connecticut, in

favor of the admission of California into the union, and
on the territorial bills, and the bill in relation to
fugitive slaves, in connection with Mr. Bell's compromise
resolutions. Delivered in Senate of the United States,
March 27 and April 3, 1850. Washington, Printed at the
Congressional globe office, 1850.
20 p.   24½ cm.

23937 Ballagh, James Curtis.
A history of slavery in Virginia, by James Curtis
Ballagh... Baltimore, The Johns Hopkins press, 1902.
1 p.l., viii, 160 p.   24 cm.   (Half-title:
Johns Hopkins University studies in historical and
political science. Extra volume, 24)

23938 Ballagh, James Curtis.
... White servitude in the colony of Virginia: a
study of the system of indentured labor in the American
colonies; by James Curtis Ballagh, A. B. Baltimore,
The Johns Hopkins press, 1895.
99 p.   24½ cm.   (Johns Hopkins University studies
in historical and political science... 13th ser.,
VI-VII)

23939 Ballou, Adin, 1803-1890.
Non-resistance in relation to human governments. By
Adin Ballou. Boston, Non-resistance Society, 1839.
24 p.   15½ cm.

23940 Barbados. Legislature. House of Assembly.
The report from a select committee of the House of
Assembly, appointed to inquire into the origin, causes,
and progress, of the late insurrection... Barbados,
Printed (by order of the Legislature) by W. Walker
[1818?]
63 p.   20½ cm.

23941 [Barbosa da Silva, Luiz] 1840-1875.
Elemento servil; estudo por Theodoro Parker [pseud.]
Rio de Janeiro, Typ. da rua da Ajuda n. 20, 1871.
58 p.   17½ cm.

23942 Barbour, James, 1775-1842.
Speech of Mr. J. Barbour, of Virginia, on the
restriction of slavery in Missouri. Delivered in the
Senate... January 31, 1820. [Washington, 1820]
26 p.   18½ cm.

23943 Barksdale, William, 1821-1863.
Speech on [!] Hon. Wm. Barksdale, of Mississippi,

17

on the presidential election. Delivered in the House
of Representatives, July 23, 1856. Washington, 1856.
    24 p.   24 cm.

23944 Barry, Henry W   d. 1875.
       Ku Klux democracy. Speech of Hon. Henry W. Barry, of
       Mississippi, delivered in the House of Representatives,
       April 5, 1871... Washington, F. & J. Rives & G. A.
       Gailey, printers, 1871.
           15 p.   24 cm.

23945 Bartlett, John Russell, 1805-1886.
       The literature of the rebellion. A catalogue of
       books and pamphlets relating to the civil war in the
       United States, and on subjects growing out of that
       event, together with works on American slavery, and
       essays from reviews and magazines on the same subjects.
       Comp. by John Russell Bartlett... Boston, Draper and
       Halliday; Providence, S. S. Rider and bro., 1866.
           iv, [5]-477 p.   25 cm.

23946 [Barton, Seth] 1795-1850.
       The Randolph epistles. [Washington, 1850]
           15 p.   25½ cm.
       Dated Washington city, July 18, 1850, and signed,
       Randolph of Roanoke.

23947 Barton, William Eleazar, 1861-1930.
       The Cumberland Mountains and the struggle for
       freedom... [Boston] 1897.
           25 p.   illus.   19 cm.
       Cover-title. Reprinted from the New England magazine,
       March, 1897.

23948 Baruchelli, Paolo.
       [Carceri e schavitù fino al secolo XIX. Carceri del
       nostro tempo sino al 1869. Dottrine e istituzioni.
       Brescia, Tip. Apollonio, 1871]
           22 p.   22½ cm.

23949 Bassett, John Spencer, 1867-1928.
       ... Slavery and servitude in the colony of North
       Carolina; by John Spencer Bassett... Baltimore, The
       Johns Hopkins press, 1896.
           86 p.   24½ cm.   (Johns Hopkins University
       studies in historical and political science... 14th
       ser., 4-5)

23950 Baudissin, Adelbert Heinrich, graf von, 1820-1871.
       Peter Tütt. Zustände in Amerika illustrirt von

Graf A. Baudissin. 3. Ausg. Altona, A. Mentzel [1866]
vi, 273, [1] p. 22 cm.

23951 [Bausman, Lottie M   ]
The general position of Lancaster County in negro
slavery. [Lancaster, Pa., 1911]
[5]-21 p. 23 cm.
Reprinted from Lancaster County Historical Society,
Historical papers and addresses, v. 15, 1911.

23952 Bay, William Van Ness, 1818-1894.
President's message--slavery--California. Speech
of Hon. W. V. N. Bay, of Missouri, in the House of
Representatives, February 20, 1850, in committee of
the whole on the state of the Union, on the resolution
referring the President's message to the various
standing committees. [Washington, Printed at the
Congressional globe office, 1850]
8 p. 24½ cm.

23953 Beard, Oliver Thomas, 1832-
... Bristling with thorns. By O. T. Beard. Detroit,
The Detroit news company, 1884.
1 p.l., 7-424 p. incl. plates. front. 19 cm.
At head of title: A story of war and reconstruction.

23954 Bearse, Austin.
Reminiscences of fugitive-slave law days in Boston.
By Austin Bearse. Boston, Printed by W. Richardson,
1880.
41 p. front. 23 cm.

23955 Beaumont, Augustus Hardin.
The Jamaica petition for representation in the
British House of Commons, or for independence. By
Augustus H. Beaumont... [London, E. H. Beumont,
printer] 1831
24 p. 18½ cm.

23956 Beaumont de La Bonninière, Gustave Auguste de, 1802-1866.
Maria; ou, A escravidão nos Estados-Unidos, quadro
de costumes americanos. Traduzida do francez.
Lisboa, Typographia Rollandiana, 1847.
2 v. 16 cm. (Peculio de recreto; bibliotheca
de 200 romances originaes e traduzidos)

23957 Beckford, William, d. 1799.
A descriptive account of the island of Jamaica:
with remarks upon the cultivation of the sugar-cane,

throughout the different seasons of the year, and
chiefly considered in a picturesque point of view;
also observations and reflections upon what would
probably be the consequences of an abolition of the
slave-trade, and of the emancipation of the slaves.
By William Beckford... London, Printed for T. and J.
Egerton, 1790.
   2 v.   22½ cm.

23958 Beebe, Gilbert J
      A review and refutation of Helper's "Impending crisis,"
by Gilbert J. Beebe... Middletown, N. Y., 1860.
   64 p.   20 x 15 cm.

23959 Belinfante, George, 1837-
      Het eiland St. Martin, zijn toestand, uitzigten en
goed regt, naar de jongste berigten, door Mr. G. Belinfant
... 's Gravenhage, Gebroeders Belinfante, 1863.
   38 p.   22½ cm.

23960 Bell, Agrippa Nelson, 1820-1911.
      The debt to Africa--the hope of Liberia, by A. N. Bell.
New York, American church review press; London,
Trübner & co., 1881.
   1 p.l., [85]-112 p.   22 cm.
   Reprint from American church review, October, 1881.

23961 Bell, Marcus A
      Message of love. South-side view of Cotton is king;
and the philosophy of African slavery, by Marcus A.
Bell... Atlanta, Printed at the Daily locomotive job
office, 1860.
   47 p.   23 cm.

23962 Benedict, George Wyllys, 1796-1871.
      An oration, delivered at Burlington, Vt., on the
fourth of July, 1826. Being the fiftieth anniversary
of American independence. By George W. Benedict, A.M.
Burlington, Printed by E. & T. Mills, 1826.
   26 p.   20 cm.

23963 [Benezet, Anthony] 1713-1784.
      Serious considerations on several important subjects;
viz., on war and its inconsistency with the gospel:
observations on slavery. And remarks on the nature and
bad effects of spirituous liquors... Philadelphia,
Printed by J. Crukshank, 1778.
   48 p.   16 cm.

23964   [Benezet, Anthony] 1713-1784.
        A short account of that part of Africa, inhabited by
        the Negroes. With respect to the fertility of the
        country; the good disposition of many of the natives,
        and the manner by which the slave trade is carried on.
        Extracted from divers authors, in order to shew the
        iniquity of that trade, and the falsity of the arguments
        usually advanced in its vindication. With quotations
        from the writings of several persons of note, viz.
        George Wallis, Francis Hutcheson, and James Foster,
        and a large extract from a pamphlet, lately published
        in London, on the subject of the slave trade. 2d ed.,
        with large additions and amendments... Philadelphia,
        Printed by W. Dunlap, 1762.
        80 p.   19½ cm.

23965   Benners, Alfred H
        Slavery and its results... by Alfred H. Benners.
        [Macon, Ga., The J. W. Burke company, c1923]
        58 p.   17 cm.

23966   Benton, Thomas Hart, 1782-1858.
        Nebraska and Kansas. Speech of Mr. Benton, of
        Missouri in the House of Representatives, April 25, 1854.
        [Washington, Printed at the Congressional Globe
        office, 1854?]
        8 p.   23 cm.

23967   Benton, Thomas Hart, 1782-1858.
        Speech of the Hon. Thos. H. Benton, delivered at the
        Capitol at Jefferson City, May 26th, 1849... [Saint
        Louis, Union job print, 1849?]
        16 p.   23 cm.
        Caption title.

23968   Bernard, Pierre, 1895-
        ... Étude sur les esclaves et les serfs d'église en
        France du VIe au XIIIe siècle... Paris, Société du
        Recueil Sirey, 1919.
        2 p.l., 315, 1 p.   25 cm.
        Thèse - Univ. de Paris.

23969   Bernhard, Karl, duke of Saxe-Weimar-Eisenach, 1792-1862.
        Travels through North America, during the years 1825
        and 1826. By His Highness, Bernard, Duke of Saxe-
        Weimar Eisenach... Philadelphia, Carey, Lea & Carey;
        sold by G. & C. Carvill. New York, 1828.
        2 v. in 1.   22 cm.

23970   Betker, John P
        The M. E. Church and slavery, as described by Revs.
        H. Mattison, W. Hosmer, E. Bowen, D.D., D. De Vinne,
        and J. D. Long, with a Bible view of the whole subject.
        By Rev. John P. Betker. Syracuse, N. Y., S. Lee, 1859.
        32 p.   18 cm.

23971   Bettle, Edward.
        Notices of Negro slavery, as connected with Pennsylvania
        By Edward Bettle... [Philadelphia, 1826]
        [353]-388 p.   22½ cm.
        Reprinted from Pennsylvania Historical Society,
        Memoirs, v. 1, pt. 2, 1826.

23972   Bevan, William.
        The operation of the apprenticeship system in the
        British colonies. A statement, the substance of which
        was presented and adopted at the meeting of the Liverpool
        Anti-Slavery Society, December 19th, 1837; with references
        to official documents, authentic narratives, and
        additional subsequent information. Liverpool, D. Marples,
        T. Taylor; London, Hamilton, Adams, 1838.
        61 p.   22½ cm.

23973   Bigotry exposed, or A calm discussion of the abolition
        question. By a constitutionalist... New York, Printed
        for the benefit of the public, 1835.
        16 p.   23 cm.

23974   Bijdragen tot de kennis der Nederlandsche en vreemde kolo-
        niën, bijzonder betrekkelijk de vrijlating der slaven.
        [1.]-4. dl.; 1844-47. Utrecht, C. van der Post, jr.,
        1844-47.
        4 v.   fold. map, fold. tab.   22½ cm.

23975   Billinghurst, Charles, 1818-1865.
        A review of the President's message. Speech of Hon.
        Charles Billinghurst, of Wisconsin, delivered in the
        House of Representatives, August 9, 1856. [Washington,
        Printed at the office of the Congressional globe,
        1856]
        8 p.   24½ cm.

23976   Bingham, Kinsley Scott, 1808-1861.
        Speech of Mr. Bingham, of Michigan, on the admission
        of California. Delivered in the House of Representa-
        tives, June 4, 1850. Washington, Printed at the
        Congressional globe office, 1850.
        22 p.   24½ cm.

23977   Birney, William, 1819-1907.
        James G. Birney and his times; the genesis of the
        Republican party with some account of abolition move-
        ments in the South before 1828, by William Birney...
        New York, D. Appleton and company, 1890.
        xii, 443 p.   front. (port.)   19½ cm.

23978   Bishop, Levi, 1815-1881.
        Observations, upon the proposal to amend the federal
        Constitution abolishing slavery throughout the United
        States, and the history of parties and the condition
        and prospects of the country. By Hon. Levi Bishop.
        [Detroit, 1865]
        8 p.   21½ cm.
        Caption title.

23979   Bissette, Cyrille Charles Auguste, 1795-1858.
        Du projet Mackau, tendant à violer la loi du 24 avril
        1833 sur le régime législatif des colonies, par C. A.
        Bissette. Paris, Imprimerie de P. Dupont, 1844.
        23 p.   20½ cm.

23980   [Bissette, Cyrille Charles Auguste] 1795-1858.
        Les esclaves des colonies françaises au clergé
        français. Paris, Imprimerie de Poussielgue, 1844.
        16 p.   20½ cm.

23981   Blair, Francis Preston, 1821-1875.
        The President's policy; speech on the policy of the
        President for the restoration of the Union and esta-
        blishment of peace, delivered in the House of Repre-
        sentatives, April 11, 1862. New York, Baker & Godwin,
        1862.
        8 p.   23 cm.

23982   Blair, Francis Preston, 1821-1875.
        Speech of Hon. Frank P. Blair, jr., of Missouri, on
        the acquisition of territory in Central and South
        America, to be colonized with free blacks, and held
        as a dependency by the United States. Delivered in
        the House of Representatives, on the 14th day of
        January, 1858. With an appendix. Washington, Buell
        & Blanchard, printers, 1858.
        31 p.   24 cm.

23983   Blair, Francis Preston, 1821-1875.
        Speech of Hon. Francis P. Blair, jr., of Missouri,
        on the Kansas question; delivered in the House of
        Representatives, March 23, 1858. Washington, Printed

at the Congressional globe office, 1858.
8 p.   24 cm.

23984   Blanchard, Jonathan, 1811-1892.
Sermon on slave-holding: preached by appointment,
before the Synod of Cincinnati, at their late stated
meeting at Mount Pleasant, Ohio, October 20th, 1841.
By Rev. J. Blanchard. Cincinnati, 1842.
8 p.   21 cm.

23985   Bliss, George, 1813-
Response of Hon. George Bliss, representative of the
fourteenth congressional district of Ohio, to resolutions of the legislature of Ohio, requesting the
senators and representatives of that state in Congress
to vote for a proposed amendment to the Constitution
of the United States to abolish slavery. [Washington,
1865]
7 p.   23 cm.
Caption title.

23986   Bolling, Philip A
... The speches of Philip A. Bolling (of Buckingham,)
in the House of Delegates of Virginia, on the policy
of the state in relation to her colored population:
delivered on the 11th and 25th of January, 1832...
Richmond, Printed by T. W. White, 1832.
16 p. $22\frac{1}{2}$ cm.

23987   Borthwick, Peter, 1804-1852.
Report of a lecture on colonial slavery and gradual
emancipation. Delivered in the assembly rooms on
Friday, March 1, 1833. By P. Borthwick, esq. Taken
in short-hand. Edinburgh, Printed by W. Ritchie and
co., 1833.
30, 4 p. $21\frac{1}{2}$ cm.

23988   Boston.
Bronze group commemorating emancipation. A gift to
the city of Boston from Hon. Moses Kimball. Dedicated
December 6, 1879... [Boston] Printed by order of the
City Council, 1879.
75 p.   front. (phot.)   24 cm.   (City document
no. 26)
"Poem. By John G. Whittier": p. 22.
"Oration, by His Honor Frederick O. Prince": p. [27]-75

23989   Boston. Citizens.
Address of the committee appointed by a public meeting

24

held at Faneuil Hall, September 24, 1846, for the
purpose of considering the recent case of kidnapping
from our soil, and of taking measures to prevent the
recurrence of similar outrages. With an appendix.
Boston, White & Potter, printers, 1846.
    8, 42 p.   22½ cm.
Signed by S. G. Howe and thirty-four others.

23990   Boston. Citizens.
        A memorial to the Congress of the United States, on
the subject of restraining the increase of slavery in
new states to be admitted into the Union. Prepared
in pursuance of a vote of the inhabitants of Boston
and its vicinity, assembled at the State House, on the
third of December, A.D. 1819. Boston, Sewell Phelps,
printer, no. 5, Court street... 1819.
        22 p.   24½ cm.
Submitted Dec. 15, 1819, by a committee consisting
of Daniel Webster, George Blake, Josiah Quincy, James
T. Austin, and John Gallison.

23991   Boston. Constitutional Meeting, 1850.
        Proceedings of the Constitutional Meeting at Faneuil
Hall, November 26th, 1850. Boston, Printed by Beals &
Greene, 1850.
        46 p.   23 cm.
John C. Warren, president.

23992   Boston. Garrison Meeting, 1846.
        Proceedings of a crowded meeting of the colored
population of Boston, assembled the 15th July, 1846,
for the purpose of bidding farewell to William Lloyd
Garrison, on his departure for England: with his
speech on the occasion... Dublin, Printed by Webb and
Chapman, 1846.
        16 p.   18 cm.

23993   Botts, John Minor, 1802-1869.
        Union or disunion. The union cannot and shall not
be dissolved. Mr. Lincoln not an abolitionist.
Speech of the Hon. John M. Botts, at Holcombe hall,
in Lynchburg, Virginia, on Thursday evening, October 18.
[Lynchburg? Va., 1860]
        23 p.   22 cm.
        Caption title.

23994   Boucher, Chauncy Samuel, 1886-
        In re that aggressive slavocracy, by Chauncy Samuel
Boucher... [Cedar Rapids? Ia., 1921]

cover-title, p. [13]-79.   25½ cm.
Reprinted from the Mississippi Valley historical
review, vol. 8, nos. 1-2, 1921.

23995   Bourne, George, 1780-1845.
The Book and slavery irreconcilable. With animadver-
sions upon Dr. Smith's philosophy. By George Bourne...
Philadelphia, Printed by J. M. Sanderson & co., 1816.
2 p.l., [3]-141 p., 1 l., [12] p.   17 cm.

23996   [Bourne, George] 1780-1845.
Slavery illustrated in its effects upon woman and
domestic society... Boston, I. Knapp, 1837.
4 p.l., [v]-viii, [9]-127 p.   18½ cm.

23997   Boutwell, George Sewall, 1818-1905.
Emancipation: its justice, expediency and necessity,
as the means of securing a speedy and permanent peace.
An address delivered by Hon. George S. Boutwell, in
Tremont Temple, Boston, under the auspices of the
Emancipation League, December 16, 1861. [Boston,
Wright & Potter, printers, 1861]
12 p.   23 cm.
Caption title.

23998   Boutwell, George Sewall, 1818-1905.
Speeches and papers relating to the rebellion and the
overthrow of slavery. By George S. Boutwell. Boston,
Little, Brown, and company, 1867.
vii, 628 p.   20 cm.

23999   Bouvé, Mrs. Pauline Carrington (Rust)
Their shadows before; a story of the Southamptom
insurrection, by Pauline Carrington Bouvé. Boston,
Small, Maynard & company, 1899.
3 p.l., [8]-202 p.   19 cm.

24000   Bowditch, William Ingersoll, 1819-1909.
The anti-slavery reform, its principle and method.
By William I. Bowditch. Boston, R. F. Wallcut, 1850.
19 p.   23½ cm.

24001   Bowen, Nathaniel, 1779-1839.
A pastoral letter, on the religious instruction of
the slaves of members of the Protestant Episcopal
Church in the state of South Carolina, prepared at
the request of the convention of the churches of the
diocese. To which is appended a table of Scripture
lessons, prepared in conformity with the resolution

of the convention. By Nathaniel Bowen, D.D., bishop of
the Pro. Epis. church in South Carolina. Charleston,
Printed by A. E. Miller, 1835.
    30 p.   21½ cm.

24002 Boyd, Samuel Stillman, 1807-1867.
        Speech of Hon. Samuel S. Boyd, delivered at the great
    union festival, held at Jackson, Mississippi, on the
    10th day of October, 1851. Reported especially for the
    Natchez courier. Natchez [Miss.] Printed at the office
    of the Natchez courier, 1851.
        19 p.   23 cm.

24003 Boyden, Ebenezer, 1803-1891.
        The epidemic of the nineteenth century. By E. Boyden,
    of Hopedale, Albemarle county, Va. Richmond, C. H.
    Wynne, printer, 1860.
        25 p.   23 cm.

24004 Bradburn, George, 1806-1880.
        A memorial of George Bradburn. By his wife. Boston,
    Cupples, Upham and company, 1883.
        vi p., 1 l., 250 p.   2 port. (incl. front.)   19 cm.

24005 Bradford, Arthur Bullus, 1810-1899.
        Address delivered at the Re-union Convention of the
    Old Abolitionists of Eastern Ohio and Western Pennsyl-
    vania, October 1st, 1879, at Alliance, Ohio, by A. B.
    Bradford... Alliance, O., J. G. Garrison's copperplate
    print [1879]
        18 p.   20 cm.

24006 [Bradford, Gamaliel] 1795-1839.
        A letter to the Hon. Harrison Gray Otis, Peleg Sprague,
    and Richard Fletcher, esq. ... Boston, J. Munroe and
    company, 1836.
        35 p.   20 cm.

24007 ... The branded hand. [Salem, O., The Anti-slavery
    bugle, 184-]
        [33]-36 p.   22½ cm.
        Caption title. At head of title: No. 9.

24008 Brawley, Benjamin Griffith, 1882-1939.
        A social history of the American Negro, being a
    history of the negro problem in the United States,
    including a history and study of the republic of
    Liberia, by Benjamin Brawley. New York, The Macmillan
    company, 1921.
        xv, 420 p.   23 cm.

24009   Brazil. Congresso. Camara dos deputados.
        Elemento servil. Parecer e projecto de lei apresentados
        á Camara dos srs. deputados na sessão de 16 de agosto
        de 1870 pela Commissão especial nomeada pela mesma
        Camara em 24 de maio de 1870. Rio de Janeiro, Typographia
        nacional, 1870.
        172, 2 p.   tables (1 fold.)   22½ cm.
        Signed: Jeronymo José Teixeira Junior [etc.]

24010   Brazil. Directoria geral de estatistica.
        ... Relatorio e trabalhos estatisticos apresentados ao
        Illm. e Exm. Sr. conselheiro dr. Carlos Leoncio de
        Carvalho, ministro e secretario de estado dos negocios
        do imperio, pelo director geral conselheiro Manoel
        Francisco Correia em 20 de novembro de 1878. Rio de
        Janeiro, Typographia nacional, 1878.
        2 p.l., 179, [1] p.   2 tab.   29 cm.
        Cover dated 1879.

24011   Brazil. Laws, statutes, etc., 1879.
        Regulamento para arrecadação da taxa dos escravos a
        que se refere o decreto n. 7536 de 15 de novembro de
        1879. Rio de Janeiro, Typographia nacional, 1879.
        cover-title, 8 p.   21½ cm.
        Signed: Affonso Celso de Assis Figueiredo [ministro
        da fazenda]

24012   Brazil. Ministerio da agricultura, commercio e obras
        publicas.
        ... Homenagem á José Bonifacio no 88º anniversario
        da independencia do Brazil. Inauguração do Serviço
        de protecção aos Indios e localisação de trabalhadores
        nacionaes... [Rio de Janeiro, Typ. da estatistica] 1910.
        19 p.   port.   22 cm.
        Includes "Apontamentos para a civilisação dos Indios
        bravos do Imperio do Brazil" and "Representação a
        Assemblea geral constituinte a legislativa do Imperio
        do Brazil sobre a escravatura," by José Bonifacio de
        Andrada e Silva.

24013   Brazilian slave trade, 1838.   Norwich, Josiah Fletcher
        [1839?]
        3 p.   43 cm.

24014   Breckinridge, John Cabell, 1821-1875.
        ... Speech of Hon. John C. Breckinridge... at
        Ashland, Kentucky, September 5th, 1860, repelling the
        charge of disunion and vindicating the national
        Democracy. Washington, National Democratic executive

committee, 1860.
16 p.   23 cm.   (Breckinridge and Lane campaign
documents, no. 18)

24015 Bridge, Horatio, 1806-1893.
       Journal of an African cruiser; comprising sketches of
the Canaries, the Cape de Verde, Liberia, Madeira,
Sierra Leone, and other places of interest on the west
coast of Africa. By an officer of the U. S. Navy.
Edited by Nathaniel Hawthorne. New York & London,
Wiley and Putnam, 1845.
       179 p.   19 cm.

24016 Bristol and Clifton Ladies' Anti-slavery Society, Bristol,
       Eng.
       Statements respecting the American abolitionists;
by their opponents and their friends: indicating the
present struggle between slavery and freedom in the
United States of America. Comp. by the Bristol and
Clifton Ladies' Anti-slavery Society. Dublin, Webb
and Chapman, printers, 1852.
       24 p.   21 cm.

24017 British and Foreign Anti-slavery Society, London.
       ... The crisis in the United States [address of the
Committee of the British and Foreign Anti-slavery
Society] London, 1862
       4 p.   20½ cm.   (Tracts on slavery in America. no. 2)
       Caption title.

24018 British and Foreign Anti-slavery Society, London.
       Invitation of the London General Conference on
Commerce on June 12, 1840. London [1840?]
       [2] p.   32½ cm.

24019 British and Foreign Anti-slavery Society, London.
       Slavery and the internal slave trade in the United
States of North America; being replies to questions
transmitted by the committee of the British and Foreign
Anti-slavery Society, for the abolition of slavery
and the slave trade throughout the world. Presented
to the general Anti-slavery Convention, held in
London, June, 1840. By the Executive Committee of
the American Anti-slavery Society. London, T. Ward and
co., 1841.
       3 p.l., 4, [v]-viii, 280 p.   22 cm.

24020 British Honduras. Citizens.
       The defence of the settlers of Honduras against the

unjust and unfounded representations of Colonel George
Arthur, late superintendent of that settlement. Principally contained in his Correspondence relative to
the condition and treatment of the slaves of Honduras,
1820-1823, and printed by order of the House of commons,
16th June, 1823. Pub. by order of the inhabitants of
Honduras, and by whose resolution every member of the
imperial Parliament is to be presented with a copy...
To which is added (by the printer) an account of the
descent of the Spaniards on the settlement in the year
1798. Jamaica, Printed by A. Aikman, jun., 1824.
        2 p.l., 101 p.   33 cm.

24021   [Brookes, Iveson L   ]
        A defence of southern slavery. Against the attacks
of Henry Clay and Alex'r. Campbell... By a southern
clergyman. Hamburg, S. C., Printed by Robinson and
Carlisle, 1851.
        46, [2] p.   21 cm.

24022   Brookes, Iveson L
        A defence of the South against the reproaches and
incroachments of the North: in which slavery is shown
to be an institution of God intended to form the
basis of the best social state and the only safeguard
to the permanence of a republican government. By Rev.
Iveson L. Brookes, A.M. Hamburg, S.C., Printed at the
Republican office, 1850.
        2 p.l., 12, 17-48 p.   20½ cm.
        Reply to an article in the Christian review for
January, 1849, on the extension of slavery.

24023   Brooks, Erastus, 1815-1886.
        Speech of Hon. Erastus Brookes, in the Senate,
Feb. 7th, 8th, and 13th, 1855, the Lemmon slave case
and slavery--secret societies and oaths--grounds of
opposition to Mr. Seward--the common schools of New
York--the Bible in our schools--the pure franchise--
a better system of naturalization--American ambassadors
abroad--American rulers at home. [Albany? 1855]
        15 p.   25 cm.
        Caption title.

24024   Brookes, James, 1810-1873.
        ... Speech of Hon. James Brooks, of New York, on the
President's message, in the House of Representatives,
December, 1864. [Washington? 1864]
        24 p.   22½ cm.

24025 Brown, Albert Gallatin, 1813-1880.
       Protection to slave property; speech of Hon. A. G.
       Brown, of Mississippi, in defence of his proposition
       for immediate congressional protection to slave property
       in the territories, with the reply of Senator Fitch.
       Delivered in the Senate of the United States, March 6,
       1860. Washington, 1860.
          30 p.   22 cm.

24026 Brown, Albert Gallatin, 1813-1880.
       The slave question. Speech of Mr. A. G. Brown, of
       Mississippi, in the House of Representatives, January
       30, 1850, on the subject of slavery, and on the action
       of the administration in relation to California and
       New Mexico. [Washington, Printed at the Congressional
       globe office, 1850]
          8 p.   25 cm.
       Caption title.

24027 Brown, Benjamin Gratz, 1826-1885.
       ... An address by Col. B. Gratz Brown. Slavery in
       its national aspects as related to peace and war.
       Delivered before the General emancipation society of
       the state of Missouri, at St. Louis, on Wednesday
       evening, September 17, 1862. [n.p., 1862?]
          8 p. $22\frac{1}{2}$ cm.
       Caption title.
       At head of title: 2d edition.

24028 Brown, Benjamin Gratz, 1826-1885.
       Freedom for Missouri. Letter of B. Gratz Brown, to
       the "Weekly new era," published at St. Joseph, Mo.
       [St. Joseph, 1862]
          8 p.   24 cm.
       Caption title.

24029 Brown, Benjamin Gratz, 1826-1885.
       Immediate abolition of slavery by act of Congress.
       Speech of Hon. B. Gratz Brown, of Missouri, delivered
       in the U. S. Senate, March 8, 1864. Washington,
       H. Polkinhorn, printer, 1864.
          16 p. $25\frac{1}{2}$ cm.

24030 Brown, Charles, 1797-1883.
       Speech of Charles Brown, of Pennsylvania, on abolition
       and slavery: delivered in the House of Representatives,
       February 3 and 7, 1849. Washington, Printed at the
       Congressional globe office, 1849.
          15 p.   24 cm.

24031   Brown, Hugh, 1811?-1888.
        Review of Rev. Dr. Raphael's [!] disco'rse on
        "American slavery as being consistent with the Hebrew
        servitude of the Old Testament," a sermon preached
        (by request) in the Baptist Church, Shushan, on Wednesday,
        March 27th, 1861, by Rev. Hugh Brown... North White
        Creek, N. Y., R. K. Crocker, 1861.
        cover-title, 39 p.   22½ cm.

24032   Brown, Isaac Van Arsdale, 1784-1861.
        White diamonds better than "black diamonds"; slave
        states impoverished by slave labor. Read the appendix,
        and decide from fact. By Isaac V. Brown, D.D.   Trenton,
        N. J., Printed by Murphy & Bechtel, 1860.
        144 p.   22½ cm.

24033   Brown, John, 1771-1850.
        Circular-schreiben an die deutschen Einwohner von
        Rockingam und Augusta, und den benachbarten Caunties [!]
        Erster band. Von Johannes Braun, Prediger des Evangelii
        in den Caunties Rockingham und Augusta, Virginia.
        Harrisonburg, Gedruckt bey Laurentz Wartmann, Rock-
        ingham County, Virginia, 1818.
        x, [4]-400, [2] p.   16½ cm.
        Published under the auspices of the Rockingham Bible
        society.

24034   Brown, John, fl. 1854.
        Slave life in Georgia: a narrative of the life,
        sufferings, and escape of John Brown, a fugitive slave,
        now in England. Ed. by L. A. Chamerovzow... London
        [W. M. Watts] 1855.
        1 p.l., ii, 250 p.   front. (port.)   16½ cm.

24035   Brown, William B
        Religious organizations, and slavery. By Rev. Wm. B.
        Brown... Oberlin, J. M. Fitch, 1850.
        cover-title, 32 p.   22 ᴄm.
        "Extract from a Scriptural argument, in favor of
        withdrawing fellowship from churches... tolerating
        slaveholding... by Rev. Silas M'Keen": p. [30]-32.

24036   Brown, William H   1796-1867.
        An historical sketch of the early movement in
        Illinois for the legalization of slavery, read at the
        annual meeting of the Chicago Historical Society,
        December 5th, 1864: by Hon. William H. Brown...
        Chicago, Steam press of Church, Goodman and Donnelley,
        1865.
        44 p.   22 cm.

24037 Brown, William Wells, b. 1814.
           Clotelle; or, The colored heroine; a tale of the
       southern states... Boston, Lee & Shepard, 1867.
           114 p. incl. plates.   front.   19 cm.

24038 Brown, William Wells, b. 1814.
           A lecture delivered before the Female Anti-slavery
       Society of Salem, at Lyceum hall, Nov. 14, 1847. By
       William W. Brown, a fugitive slave. Reported by Henry
       M. Parkhurst... Boston, Massachusetts Anti-slavery
       Society, 1847.
           22 p.   19 cm.

24039 Brown, William Wells, b. 1814.
           The rising son; or, The antecedents and advancement
       of the colored race. By Wm. Wells Brown... Boston,
       A. G. Brown & co., 1874.
           ix, 9-552 p.   front. (port.)   21 cm.

24040 [Browne, Martha (Griffith)] d. 1906.
           Autobiography of a female slave. New York, Redfield,
       1857.
           401 p.   19 cm.

24041 Browning, Orville Hickman, 1806-1881.
           ... The diary of Orville Hickman Browning... edited
       with introduction and notes by Theodore Calvin Pease...
       and James G. Randall... Springfield, Ill., The Trustees
       of the Illinois State Historical Library, 1925-[33]
           2 v.   22½ cm.   (Collections of the Illinois State
       Historical Library, v. 20, 22, Lincoln series, v. 2-3)

24042 Browning, Orville Hickman, 1806-1881.
           Speech of Hon. O. H. Browning, delivered at the
       Republican mass-meeting, Springfield, Ill., August 8th,
       1860. Quincy, Ill., Whig and Republican steam power
       press print., 1860.
           16 p.   23 cm.

24043 Brownlow, William Gannaway, 1805-1877.
           A sermon on slavery; a vindication of the Methodist
       Church, South: her position stated. Delivered in
       Temperance Hall, in Knoxville, on Sabbath, August 9th,
       1857, to the delegates and others in attendance at the
       Southern Commercial Convention. By William G. Brownlow
       ... Knoxville, Tenn., Printed by Kinsloe & Rice, 1857.
           31 p.   21½ cm.

24044 Bruce, Henry Clay, 1836-1902.
           The new man. Twenty-nine years a slave. Twenty-nine

years a free man. Recollections of H. C. Bruce.
York, Pa., P. Anstadt & sons, 1895.
x, [11]-176 p.   front. (port.)   23½ cm.

24045 Brussels. Conference, 1889-1890.
         ... Accession of the Orange Free State to the general
       act of the Brussels conference of July 2, 1890. August 3,
       1894... London, Printed for H. M. Stationery off. by
       Harrison and sons [1895]
         1 p.l., 2 p.   24½ cm.   ([Gt. Brit. Foreign office]
       Treaty series, no. 1, 1895)
         Gt. Brit. Parliament. Papers by command. C. 7594.

24046 Bryan, Edward B
         The rightful remedy. Addressed to the slaveholders
       of the South. By Edward B. Bryan... Pub. for the
       Southern Rights Association. Charleston, Press of
       Walker & James, 1850.
         1 p.l., 152 p.   23 cm.

24047 Bryan, Wilhelmus Bogart.
         A fire in an old time F street tavern and what it
       revealed. By W. B. Bryan. [Washington, 1906]
         198-215 p.   illus.   23½ cm.
         Reprinted from Columbia Historical Society, Records,
       v. 9, 1906.

24048 Bryant, Joshua.
         Account of an insurrection of the negro slaves in
       the colony of Demerara, which broke out on the 18th of
       August, 1823. By Joshua Bryant. Georgetown, Demerara,
       Printed by A. Stevenson at the Guiana chronicle office,
       1824.
         vii, 125 p.   13 pl. (part fold.; incl. front., plan)
       19 cm.

24049 Buchanan, George, 1763-1808.
         An oration upon the moral and political evil of
       slavery. Delivered at a public meeting of the Maryland
       Society, for promoting the abolition of slavery, and
       the relief of free negroes, and others unlawfully held
       in bondage. Baltimore, July 4th, 1791. By George
       Buchanan... Baltimore, Printed by Philip Edwards, 1793.
         20 p.   20 cm.

24050 Buchanan, James, Pres. U.S., 1791-1868.
         Message of the president of the United States,
       communicating... in relation to the African slave
       trade. Washington, 1858.

85 p.   23½ cm.   (35th Cong., 1st sess. Senate,
Ex. doc. no. 49)

24051 Bücher, Karl, 1847-1930.
Die Aufstände der unfreien Arbeiter 143-129 v. Chr.,
von Karl Bücher... Frankfurt a. M., J. D. Sauerländer,
1874.
132 p.   20½ cm.

24052 Buck, William C
The slavery question. By Wm. C. Buck... Louisville,
Ky., Printed by Harney, Hughes & Hughes, 1849.
29, [1] p.   25 cm.

24053 Buffinton, James, 1817-1875.
Position of Massachusetts on the slavery question.
Speech of Hon. James Buffinton, of Massachusetts, in
the House of Representatives, April 30, 1856.
[Washington, Buell & Blanchard, printers, 1856]
7, [1] p.   24 cm.
Caption title.

24054 Bugbee, Lester G
Slavery in early Texas. I, II. [n.p., 1898]
389-412, 648-668 p.   20 cm.
Reprinted from Political science quarterly, v. 13,
Sept. 1898 and Dec. 1898.

24055 Bullitt, Thomas Walker, 1838-1910.
My life at Oxmoor; life on a farm in Kentucky before
the war, by Thomas W. Bullitt... Louisville, J. P.
Morton & co., 1911.
viii, 132 p.   illus.   25 cm.

24056 [Bunn, Thomas]
An essay on the abolition of slavery throughout the
British dominions, without injury to the master or his
property, with the least possible injury to the slave,
without revolution, and without loss to the revenue.
Frome, Printed by W. P. Penny, 1833.
vii, 97 p.   22½ cm.

24057 Bunsen, Christian Karl Josias, Freiherr von, 1791-1860.
The law of slavery in the United States. By
Christian Charles Josias Bunsen... Boston, Little,
Brown and company, 1863.
12 p.   19 cm.

24058 Burden, Jesse R
Remarks of Dr. J. R. Burden, of Philadelphia Co.,

in the Senate of Pennsylvania, on the abolition
question, February, 1838. Also his valedictory
address as speaker of the Senate, April, 1838.
Philadelphia, Printed by order of the Democratic
Association of Pennsylvania, 1838.
16 p.   21 cm.

24059   Burgess, John William, 1844-1931.
... The middle period, 1817-1858, by John W. Burgess...
New York, C. Scribner's sons, 1904.
xvi, 544 p.   maps.   19 cm.   (The American
history series. [v. 4])

24060   Burke, Edmund, 1809-1882.
An important appeal to the people of the United
States. Slavery and abolitionism. Union and disunion.
By Edmund Burke, of New Hampshire. [n.p., 1856?]
16 p.   23 cm.
Caption title.

24061   Burleigh, Charles Calistus, 1810-1878.
No slave-hunting in the Old Bay State; speech of
Charles C. Burleigh at the annual meeting of the
Massachusetts A. S. Society, Friday, January 28, 1859.
Boston, Mass., A. S. Society, 1859.
32 p.   14 cm.

24062   [Burleigh, Charles Calistus] 1810-1878.
Reception of George Thompson in Great Britain.
Compiled from various British publications. Boston,
I. Knapp, 1836.
xvi, [13]-238 p.   15½ cm.

24063   Burmeister, Hermann, 1807-1892.
The black man. The comparative anatomy and psychology
of the African negro. By Hermann Burmeister... Tr. by
Julius Friedlander... and Robert Tomes... New York,
W. C. Bryant & co., printers, 1853.
29 p.   23½ cm.
Translated from v. 2 of the author's Geologische bilder
zur geschichte der erde, 1851-53.

24064   Burnett, Henry Clay, 1825-1926.
Speech of Hon. H. C. Burnett, of Kentucky, in favor
of the admission of Kansas under the Lecompton constitution; delivered in the House of Representatives,
Tuesday, March 23, 1858. [n.p., n.d.]
16 p.   23 cm.
Caption title.

24065   Burroughs, Wilbur Greeley, 1886-
        Oberlin's part in the slavery conflict.   By Wilbur
        Greeley Burroughs... [Columbus, O., 1911]
            269-334 p.   23 cm.
        Reprinted from Ohio archaeological and historical
        quarterly, v. 20, 1977.

24066   Bush, Isidor, 1822-1898.
        Minority report and motion to adjourn "sine die."
        Speech of Isidor Bush, of Saint Louis, delivered in the
        Missouri State Convention, June 29, 1863.   [St. Louis,
        1863]
            7 p.   23 cm.
        Caption title.

24067   Butler, James, 1755?-1842.
        Fortune's foot-ball, or, The adventures of Mercutio.
        Founded on matters of fact... Harrisburgh, Pennsylvania,
        Printed by John Wyeth, 1797-98.
            2 v. in 1.   17 cm.

24068   Butt, Martha Haines, b. 1834.
        Anti fanaticism: a tale of the South. By Miss Martha
        Haines Butt. Philadelphia, Lippincott, Grambo, and
        co., 1853.
            xii, [13]-268 p.   19½ cm.

24069   Byrne, Lee, 1876-
        Quarry slaves, a drama, by Lee Byrne. Boston, The
        Poetlore company, 1904.
            31 p.   20 cm.

                              C

24070   C   , F
        La guerre civil en Amérique et l'esclavage, par
        F. C. ... Paris, E. Dentu, 1861.
            31 p.   19 cm.

24071   Cadwalader, John, 1805-1879.
        Speech of Hon. John Cadwalader, of Pennsylvania,
        on the legislation of the United States upon the
        subject of slavery in the territories. Delivered in
        the House of Representatives, March 5, 1856. Washington,
        Printed at the Congressional globe office, 1856.
            16 p.   25 cm.

24072　Caffrey, Andrew.
　　　　... An essay on slavery, with a reasonable proposition
　　　　made how to dispense with it. With a brief investiga-
　　　　tion of what is termed civilized life, showing unmasked,
　　　　without colouring, a picture of some of its practices
　　　　and results... By Andrew Caffrey. [Philadelphia?
　　　　1859]
　　　　　4 p.　　22½ cm.
　　　　　Caption title.

24073　Cairnes, John Elliott, 1823-1875.
　　　　Who are the canters? By J. E. Cairnes... London,
　　　　Pub. for the Ladies' London Emancipation Society, by
　　　　E. Faithfull [1863]
　　　　　8 p.　　15 cm.　　(Ladies' London Emancipation
　　　　Society, Tracts, no. 3)

24074　Caius Gracchus, pseud.
　　　　Controversy between Caius Gracchus and Opimius
　　　　[pseud.] in reference to the American Society for
　　　　Colonizing the Free People of Colour of the United
　　　　States... Georgetown, D. C., J. C. Dunn, 1827.
　　　　　118 p.　　22 cm.
　　　　　Article signed Opimius written by William Henry
　　　　Fitzhugh.

24075　Caldwell, John H　　　1820-
　　　　Slavery and southern Methodism: two sermons
　　　　preached in the Methodist Church in Newman, Georgia.
　　　　By... John H. Caldwell... [Newman? Ga.] Printed for
　　　　the author, 1865.
　　　　　xiii, [15]-80 p.　　19½ cm.

24076　Calhoun, John Caldwell, 1782-1850.
　　　　Address of the Hon. John C. Calhoun, in the Senate
　　　　of the United States, on the subject of slavery.
　　　　Read for him by Hon. Mr. Mason, March 4, 1850.
　　　　[Washington, 1850]
　　　　　32 p.　　23 cm.
　　　　　"Speech of the Hon. Daniel Webster, in the Senate
　　　　of the United States, on the subject of slavery...":
　　　　p. [13]-32.

24077　Calhoun, John Caldwell, 1782-1850.
　　　　Speech of Mr. Calhoun, of South Carolina, on the
　　　　Oregon Bill, delivered in the Senate of the United
　　　　States, January 24, 1843. Washington, Printed at
　　　　the Globe Office, 1843.
　　　　　8 p.　　23 cm.

24078   Call, Richard Keith, 1791-1862.
          Union. - Slavery. - Secession. Letter from Governor
        R. K. Call, of Florida, to John S. Littell, of German-
        town, Pennsylvania. Philadelphia, C. Sherman & son,
        printers, 1861.
          31 p.   24 cm.

24079   Una Campaña parlamentaria; colección de proposiciones
        presentadas y discursos pronunciados en las Córtes
        españolas de 1872-73 por la diputación radical de
        Puerto Rico. Madrid, Impr. de M. G. Hernandez, 1873.
          395, [3] p.   20½ cm.

24080   Campbell, John Campbell, 1st baron, 1779-1861.
          Atrocious judges. Lives of judges infamous as tools
        of tyrants and instruments of oppression. Compiled
        from the judicial biographies of John lord Campbell...
        With an appendix, containing the case of Passmore
        Williamson. Edited, with an introduction and notes,
        by Richard Hildreth. New York and Auburn, Miller,
        Orton & Mulligan, 1856.
          432 p.   18½ cm.

24081   Campbell, Lewis Davis, 1811-1882.
          Speech of Hon. Lewis D. Campbell, of Ohio, in reply
        to Mr. Stephens, of Georgia, delivered in the House
        of Representatives, February 28, 1855. Washington,
        Printed at the Congressional globe office, 1855.
          15 p.   24 cm.

24082   Candler, John, 1787-1869.
          West Indies. Extracts from the journal of John
        Candler, whilst travelling in Jamaica. Part I-[11]
        London, Harvey and Darton, 1840-41.
          2 v.   21 cm.

24083   Canning, George, 1770-1827.
          The speech of the Right Hon. George Canning, in the
        House of Commons, March 16th, 1824, on laying before the
        House the "Papers in explanation of the measures
        adopted by His Majesty's government, for the amelioration
        of the condition of the slave population in His Majesty's
        dominions in the West Indies". [London, Maurice and
        co., printers, 1830?]
          16 p.   22 cm.
          Caption title.

24084   Capen, Nahum, 1804-1886.
          Letter to Rev. Nathaniel Hall, of Dorchester, Mass.,

by Nahum Capen, concerning politics and the pulpit.
Boston and Cambridge, J. Munroe & company [1855]
cover-title, 4 p.   23 cm.

24085   Capitan, Louis, 1854-1929.
... Le travail en Amérique avant et après Colomb,
par L. Capital... et Henri Lorin... avec 27 gravures
dans le texte et 6 planches en couleurs hors texte.
Paris, F. Alcan, 1914.
2 p.l., 463, [1] p.   illus., VI pl. (4 col.)   23 cm.
(Histoire universelle du travail)

24086   [Carey, Henry Charles] 1793-1879.
The North and the South. Reprinted from the New York
Tribune. New York, Office of the Tribune, 1854.
48 p.   23½ cm.

24087   Carey, John L
Slavery and the Wilmot Proviso; with some suggestions
for a compromise. By John L. Carey. Baltimore, J. N.
Lewis, 1847.
64 p.   23 cm.

24088   Carlyle, Thomas, 1795-1881.
Occasional discourse on the nigger question.
Communicated by T. Carlyle. London, T. Bosworth,
1853.
2 p.l., 48 p.   18 cm.

24089   Carnes, J   E
Address, on the duty of the slave states in the
present crisis, delivered in Galveston, Dec. 12th, 1860,
by Rev. J. E. Carnes, by special invitation of the
Committee of Safety and Correspondence, and many of
the oldest citizens. Galveston, Printed at the "News"
book and job office, 1860.
16 p.   21 cm.

24090   Carnochan, Janet, 1839-
A slave rescue in Niagara sixty years ago. By
Janet Carnochan. [Niagara, Ont., 1897]
8-18 p.   21 cm.
Reprinted from Niagara Historical Society, [Publica-
tions] no. 2, 1897.

24091   Carreira, António.
O tráfico português de escravos na costa oriental
africana nos começos do século XIX (estudo de um caso)
por António Carreira. Lisboa, Junta de Investigações

Científicas do Ultramar, Centro de Estudos de Antropologia Cultural, 1979.
135 p.   illus., fold. map, tables.   24 cm.
(Estudos de antropologia cultural, no. 12)

24092 Carreira, António.
O trafico de escravos no rios de Guiné e ilhas de
Cabo Verde (1810-1850) (Subsídios para o seu estudo)
Lisboa, Junta de Investigações Científicas do Ultramar,
Centro de Estudos de Antropologia Cultura, 1981.
55 p.   tables.   24 cm.   (Estudos de antropologia
cultural, 14)

24093 Carroll, Joseph Cephas.
Slave insurrections in the United States, 1800-1865,
by Joseph Cephas Carroll, Ph.D. Boston, Chapman &
Grimes, inc. [c1938]
229 p.   20½ cm.

24094 Casas, Bartolomé de las, bp. of Chiapa, 1474-1566.
... Colección de tratados, 1552-1553, con advertencia
de Emilio Ravignani. Buenos Aires, Talleres s.a. Casa
Jacobo Peuser, ltda., 1924.
[vii]-xiii p., 1 l., 648, 15 p.   24½ cm.
(Biblioteca argentina de libros raros americanos, t. 3)

24095 Casas, Bartolomé de las, bp. of Chiapa, 1474-1566.
OEuvres de don Barthélemi de las Casas, évêque de
Chiapa, défenseur de la liberté des naturels de
l'Amérique; précédées de sa vie, et accompagnées de
notes historiques, additions, développemens, etc.,
etc.; avec portrait; par J.-A. Llorente... Paris,
A. Eymery; [etc., etc.] 1822.
2 v.   front. (port.)   20½ cm.
Includes commentaries by Juan Antonio Llorente,
Henri Grégoire, and José Servando Teresa de Mier
Norriega y Guerra.

24096 Case of the slave Isaac Brown. An outrage exposed.
[n.p., 1847?]
8 p.   22½ cm.
Caption title.

24097 The Case of William L. Chaplin; being an appeal to all
respecters of law and justice, against the cruel and
oppressive treatment to which, under color of legal
proceedings, he has been subjected, in the District of
Columbia and the state of Maryland. Boston, Pub. by
the Chaplin Committee, 1851.
54 p.   front. (port.)   23 cm.

24098   Cass, Lewis, 1782-1866.
        The power of Congress over the territories. Speech
of Hon. Lewis Cass, of Michigan, in Senate of the
United States, March 13 and 14, 1850, on the compromise
resolutions of Mr. Bell, of Tennessee, and the proposition to refer them to a select committee. [Washington,
Printed at the Congressional globe office, 1850]
        15 p.   22 cm.
        Caption title.

24099   Castelar y Ripoli, Emilio, 1832-1899.
        Discurso pronunciado en contra de la esclavitud, por
el ciudadano Emilio Castelar, en la Asamblea constitu-
yente el dia 21 de junio de 1870... Madrid, Librería
nueva, 1870.
        31 p.   18 cm.

24100   Castleman, John Breckinridge, 1841-1918.
        Active service. Louisville, Ky., Courier-Journal
Job Print. Co., 1917.
        269 p.   plates, ports, facsims.   27 cm.
        "The Northwestern Conspiracy [of 1864]": p. 129-195.
        Autobiographical.

24101   Castro Paes Barretto, Fernando de.
        ... A abolição e a federação no Brasil. Paris,
V. Giard e E. Brière, 1906.
        2 p.l., 183 p.   25½ cm.

24102   Cathcard, James Leander, 1767-1843.
        The captives, by James Leander Cathcard, eleven years
a prisoner in Algiers. Compiled by his daughter, J. B.
Newkirk. La Porte, Ind., Herald print [1899]
        xvi, 312 p. incl. 2 port.   24 cm.

24103   Cazneau, Jane Maria (McManus) 1807-1878.
        The king of rivers, with a chart of our slave and
free soil territory. By Cora Montgomery. New York,
C. Wood, 1850.
        19 p.   map.   23 cm.

24104   Chace, Elizabeth (Buffum) 1806-1899.
        Anti-slavery reminiscences. Elizabeth Buffum Chace.
Central Falls, R. I., E. E. Freeman & son, state
printers, 1891.
        47 p.   21½ cm.

24105   Chandler, Rev. Joseph.
        The confederacy of Judah with Assyria: a sermon

preached in the Congregational church, West Brattle-
boro, Vt., July 4th, 1852. By Joseph Chandler, pastor
of the church... [West Brattleboro] J. B. Miner,
printer [1852]
    12 p.   21 cm.

24106   Chandler, Joseph Ripley, 1792-1880.
            Speech of Mr. J. R. Chandler, of Penn., on the admission
        of California: delivered in the House of Representatives
        of the United States, March 28, 1850. Washington,
        Gideon & co., printers, 1850.
            15 p. $24\frac{1}{2}$ cm.

24107   Channing, William Ellery, 1780-1842.
            Emancipation: by William E. Channing. Boston,
        E. P. Peabody, 1840.
            iv, [5]-111 p.   19 cm.
            The work was called out by the author's reading
        Gurney's "Familiar letters to Henry Clay."

24108   Chapman, John Jay, 1862-1933.
            William Lloyd Garrison, by John Jay Chapman...
        2d ed., rev. and enl. Boston, The Atlantic monthly
        press [c1921]
            xii, 289 p.   front. (port.) $19\frac{1}{2}$ cm.

24109   Charleston, South Carolina, a satiric poem; shewing that
        slavery still exists in a country, which boasts,
        above all others, of being the seat of liberty.
        By a Westindian. London, S. Y. Collins, 1851.
            12 p.   21 cm.

24110   Charleston, S. C.
             An account of the late intended insurrection among a
        portion of the blacks of this city. Pub. by the
        authority of the corporation of Charleston. Charleston,
        A. E. Miller, 1822.
            48 p.   23 cm.

24111   Charleston, S. C. Citizens.
            Proceedings of the citizens of Charleston, on the
        incendiary machinations, now in progress against the
        peace and welfare of the southern states. Pub. by
        order of Council. Charleston, Printed by A. E. Miller,
        1835.
            12 p. $20\frac{1}{2}$ cm.

24112   Charleston, S. C. Meeting on Religious Instruction of
        Negroes.

Proceedings of the Meeting in Charleston, S. C.,
May 13-15, 1845, on the Religious Instruction of the
Negroes, together with the report of the committee,
and the address to the public. Pub. by order of the
meeting. Charleston, S. C., Printed by B. Jenkins,
1845.
72 p.   21 cm.
Daniel E. Huger, chairman of the meeting and of the
standing committee.

24113   Chase, Salmon Portland, 1808-1873.
Speech of Hon. Salmon P. Chase, delivered at the
Republican mass meeting in Cincinnati, August 21, 1855;
together with extracts from his speeches in the Senate
on kindred subjects. Columbus, Printed by the Ohio
state journal company, 1855.
20 p.   21½ cm.

24114   Chase, Salmon Portland, 1808-1873.
Speech of Salmon P. Chase, in the case of the colored
woman, Matilda, who was brought before the Court of
Common Pleas of Hamilton County, Ohio, by writ of habeas
corpus; March 11, 1837. Cincinnati, Pugh & Dodd,
printers, 1837.
40 p.   18 cm.

24115   Cheek, Thomas A
A sketch of the history of the colored race in the
United States, and a reminiscence of slavery. By Thos. A.
Cheek, the self-educated colored boy of Peoria, Illinois.
Peoria, Ill., Printed at the Transcript book and job
printing office, 1873.
21 p.   22 cm.

24116   Cheever, George Barrell, 1807-1890.
The curse of God against political atheism: with
some of the lessons of the tragedy at Harper's Ferry.
A discourse delivered in the Church of the Puritans,
New York, on Sabbath evening, Nov. 6, 1859. By Rev.
George B. Cheever, D.D. Boston, Walker, Wise & Co.,
1859.
24 p.   22½ cm.

24117   Chevalier, Henri Émile, 1828-1879.
Un drame esclavagiste; prologue de la sécession
américaine; suivi de Notes sur John Brown, son procès
et ses derniers moments, par H. Émile Chevalier et
F. Pharaon. Paris, Charlieu et Huillery [1864]
2 p.l., 60 p.   front., plates.   27½ cm.

24118   Cheves, Langdon, 1776-1857.
        Letter of the Hon. Langdon Cheves, to the editors of
        the Charleston Mercury, Sept. 11, 1844. [Charleston,
        Printed by Walker & Burke, 1844]
            15 p.   24 cm.
            Caption title.

24119   Cheves, Langdon, 1776-1857.
        Speech of Hon. Langdon Cheves, in the Southern Con-
        vention, at Nashville, Tennessee, November 14, 1850.
        [Nashville? Tenn.] Southern Rights Association, 1850.
            30 p.   23½ cm.

24120   [Chickering, Jesse] 1797-1855.
        Letter addressed to the President of the United States
        on slavery, considered in relation to the constitutional
        principles of government in Great Britain and in the
        United States. By an American citizen... Boston,
        Redding and company, 1855.
            1 p.l., 91 p.   22½ cm.

24121   Child, Lydia Maria (Francis) 1802-1880.
        Correspondence between Lydia Maria Child and Gov. Wise
        and Mrs. Mason, of Virginia. Boston, The American anti-
        slavery society, 1860.
            28 p.   19½ cm.

24122   Childs, David Lee.
        An appeal from David L. Childs... to the abolitionists...
        [Albany, 184-]
            24 p.   21½ cm.
            Caption title.

24123   Christian Journal, extra. New York, Wednesday, March 20,
        1839.
            [4] p.   48 cm.
            "To the Abolitionists of Massachusetts."

24124   Christianity versus treason and slavery. Religion re-
        buking sedition. [Philadelphia, H. B. Ashmead, 1864]
            16 p.   20½ cm.

24125   Christie, William Dougal, 1816-1874.
        Notes on Brazilian questions. By W. D. Christie,
        late Her Majesty's envoy extraordinary and minister
        plenipotentiary in Brazil... London and Cambridge,
        Macmillan and co., 1865.
            1 p.l., [v]-lxxi, 236 p.   19 cm.

24126   Christy, David, b. 1802.
        A lecture on African civilization: including a brief
        outline of the social and moral condition of Africa;
        and the relations of American slavery to African

civilization. Delivered in the hall of the House of
Representatives of the state of Ohio, January 19, 1850.
By David Christy, agent of the American Colonization
Society. Columbus, J. H. Riley & co., 1853.
    53 p.   22 cm.   (His Lectures on African coloni-
zation, and kindred subjects. [no. 2])

24127 Christy, David, b. 1802.
        Republic of Liberia. Oxford, O., 1848.
        [1] p.   27½ cm.

24128 [Church Anti-slavery Society]
        Circular. [n.p., 1859]
        8 p.   23 cm.
        Caption title.

24129 Ciccotti, Ettore, 1863-1839.
        ... Le déclin de l'esclavage antique. Éd. française
        rev. et augm. avec préface de l'auteur. Traduit par
        G. Platon. Paris, M. Rivière et c^ie, 1910.
        2 p.l., xix, 451, [1] p.   23 cm.   (Systèmes et
        faits sociaux)

24130 A civil record of Major-General Winfield S. Hancock,
        during his administration in Louisiana and Texas...
        [n.p.] 1880.
        30 p.   23 cm.

24131 The civil war & slavery in the United States. A lecture
        delivered at Arley chapel, Bristol, June 10, 1862...
        3d ed. London, A. W. Bennett; Bristol, R. W. Bingham,
        1862.
        24 p.   20 cm.

24132 Clapp, Theodore, 1792-1866.
        Slavery: a sermon, delivered in the First Congrega-
        tional Church in New Orleans, April 15, 1838. By
        Theodore Clapp. Pub. by request. New Orleans, J. Gibson,
        printer, 1838.
        67 p.   20 cm.

24133 Clark, Daniel, 1809-1891.
        Kansas--the law of slavery. Speech of Hon. Daniel
        Clark, of New Hampshire. Delivered in the Senate
        of the United States, March 15, 1858. [Washington,
        D. C., Buell & Blanchard, printers, 1858]
        23, [1] p.   25 cm.
        Caption title.

24134　Clark, Daniel, 1809-1891.
　　　　　Speech of Hon. Daniel Clark, of New Hampshire, on
　　　　the proposed amendment of the Constitution, forever
　　　　prohibiting slavery in the United States, and all
　　　　places under their jurisdiction.　Delivered in the
　　　　Senate of the United States, March 31, 1864.　[Washington,
　　　　Printed by L. Towers for the Union Congressional Com-
　　　　mittee, 1864]
　　　　　8 p.　　22½ cm.
　　　　Caption title.

24135　[Clark, George Washington] b. 1812.
　　　　　On the Constitution.　[Rochester, N. Y., 1860]
　　　　　4 p.　　22½ cm.
　　　　Caption title.

24136　Clark, Rufus Wheelwright, 1813-1886.
　　　　　Conscience and law.　A discourse preached in the
　　　　North church, Portsmouth, New Hampshire, on fast day,
　　　　April 3, 1851, by Rufus W. Clark, pastor.　Boston,
　　　　Tappan & Whittemore; Portsmouth, S. A. Badger, 1851.
　　　　　25 p.　　22½ cm.

24137　Clark, Thomas Dionysius, 1903-
　　　　　The slave trade between Kentucky and the cotton
　　　　kingdom.　[n.p., 1934]
　　　　　332-342 p.　　24 cm.
　　　　Reprinted from Mississippi valley historical review,
　　　　v. 21, no. 3, Dec. 1934.

24138　Clarke, James Freeman, 1810-1888.
　　　　　Anti-slavery days.　A sketch of the struggle which
　　　　ended in the abolition of slavery in the United States.
　　　　By James Freeman Clarke...　New York, J. W. Lovell
　　　　company [c1883]
　　　　　1 p.l., 6, [5]-223 p.　　18½ cm.　　(Lovell's library,
　　　　v. 4, no. 167)

24139　Clarke, James Freeman, 1810-1888.
　　　　　Causes and consequences of the affair at Harper's
　　　　Ferry.　A sermon preached in the Indiana Place Chapel,
　　　　on Sunday morning, Nov. 6, 1859.　By James Freeman
　　　　Clarke.　Boston, Walker, Wise, & co., 1859.
　　　　　14 p.　　23½ cm.

24140　Clarke, James Freeman, 1810-1888.
　　　　　The rendition of Anthony Burns.　Its causes and
　　　　consequences.　A discourse on Christian politics,
　　　　delivered in Williams Hall, Boston, on Whitsunday,

June 4, 1854. By James Freman Clarke. [... 2d ed. of
two thousand] Boston, Crosby, Nichols, & co. [etc.]
1854.
28 p.   23½ cm.

24141 Clarke, Walter, 1812-1871.
The American Anti-slavery Society at war with the
church. A discourse, delivered before the First Congregational Church and Society, in Canterbury, Conn.,
June 30th, 1844. By Walter Clarke... Hartford, Press
of E. Geer, 1844.
21 p.   22½ cm.

24142 Clarkson, Thomas, 1760-1846.
Not a labourer wanted for Jamaica; to which is added,
an account of the newly erected villages by the peasantry
there, and their beneficial results; and of the consequences of reopening a new slave trade, as it relates
to Africa, and the honour of the British government in
breaking her treaties with foreign powers: in a letter
addressed to a member of Parliament, appointed to sit
on the West India Committee, by Thomas Clarkson.
London, T. Ward & co., 1842.
15 p.   20½ cm.

24143 Clay, Cassius Marcellus, 1810-1903.
Cassius M. Clay, and Gerrit Smith. A letter of
Cassius M. Clay, of Lexington, Ky., to the mayor of
Dayton, O., with a review of it by Gerrit Smith, of
Peterboro, N. Y. [Utica, N. Y.] Jackson & Chaplin
[1844]
12 p.   19 cm.

24144 Clay, Cassius Marcellus, 1810-1903.
Letters of Cassius M. Clay. [New-York, Greeley &
McElrath, 1844?]
8 p.   22½ cm.
Caption title.

24145 Clay, Cassius Marcellus, 1810-1903.
A review of the late canvass, and R. Wickliffe's
speech on the "Negro law". Lexington, Ky., N. L. Finnell,
1840.
22 p.   22 cm.

24146 Clay, Cassius Marcellus, 1810-1903.
Speech of C. M. Clay of Fayette, in the House of
Representatives of Kentucky, upon the bill to repeal
the law of 1832, "prohibiting the importation of slaves

into this state." Delivered in the Committee of the
Whole House, January, 1841. Frankfort, A. G. Hodges,
1841.
16 p.   22 cm.

24147 Clay, Clement Claiborne, 1819-1882.
Speech on slavery issues delivered at Huntsville,
Alabama, September 5th, 1859. [Huntsville, 1859?]
15 p.   26 cm.
Caption title.

24148 Clay, Henry, 1777-1852.
Speech of Mr. Clay, of Kentucky, on the subject of
abolition petitions. Delivered in the Senate of the
United States. February 7, 1839. Boston, James Munroe,
1839.
42 p.   19 cm.

24149 Clemens, Sherrard, 1826-
State of the Union. Speech of Hon. Sherrard Clemens,
of Virginia, in the House of Representatives, January 22,
1861. [Washington, Printed at the office of the
Congressional globe, 1861]
8 p.   24 cm.
Caption title.

24150 Clephane, Walter Collins, 1867-
The local aspect of slavery in the District of
Columbia. By Walter C. Clephane.   Washington, 1900
224-256 p.   23½ cm.
Reprinted from Columbia Historical Society, Records...
v. 3, 1900.

24151 Cleveland, Charles Dexter, 1802-1869.
Anti-slavery addresses of 1844 and 1845. By Salmon
Portland Chase and Charles Dexter Cleveland. London,
S. Low, son, and Marston; Philadelphia, J. A. Bancroft
and co., 1867.
167 p.   18 cm.

24152 Clingman, Thomas Lanier, 1812-1897.
Speech of Hon. Thomas L. Clingman, of North Carolina,
against the revolutionary movement of the Anti-slavery
Party; delivered in the Senate of the United States,
January 16, 1860. Washington, Printed at the Congressional
globe office, 1860.
16 p.   23½ cm.

24153 Clingman, Thomas Lanier, 1812-1897.
Speech of Hon. Thomas L. Clingman, of North Carolina,

on the subject of congressional legislation, as to the
rights of property in the territories, delivered in the
Senate of the United States, May 7 & 8, 1860.
Baltimore, Printed by J. Murphy & co., 1860.
    16 p. $24\frac{1}{2}$ cm.

24154 Clinkscales, John George, 1855-
    On the old plantation; reminiscences of his childhood,
    by J. G. Clinkscales... Spartanburg, S. C., Band &
    White, 1916.
    142 p.   20 cm.

24155 Cobbett, William, 1763-1835.
    Cobbett's exposure of the practices of the pretended
    friends of the blacks... [London, Printed by Mills,
    Jowett, and Mills, 1830?]
    23, [1] p.   22 cm.
    Caption title.

24156 Cochran, William Cox, 1848-
    ... The Western Reserve and the fugitive slave law;
    a prelude to the Civil War [by] William C. Cochran...
    Cleveland, O., 1920.
    235 p.   front. (port.) $24\frac{1}{2}$ cm.   (Publication
    no. 101. Collections, The Western Reserve Historical
    Society)

24157 Cockrum, William Munroe, 1837-
    History of the Underground Railroad as it was
    conducted by the Anti-slavery League; including many
    thrilling encounters between those aiding the slaves
    to escape and those trying to recapture them, by Col.
    William M. Cockrum... Oakland City, Ind., Press of
    J. W. Cockrum printing company [c1915]
    vii, [1], 9-328 p.   front., illus. (map) plates,
    ports. $20\frac{1}{2}$ cm.

24158 Coffin, Levi, 1798-1877.
    Reminiscences of Levi Coffin, the reputed president
    of the Underground Railroad; being a brief history of
    the labors of a lifetime in behalf of the slave, with
    the stories of numerous fugitives, who gained their
    freedom through his instrumentality... 2d ed. -
    with appendix. Cincinnati, R. Clarke & co., 1880.
    1 p.l., viii, 3-732 p.   2 port. (incl. front.)
    $20\frac{1}{2}$ cm.
    Appendix: 1. Memoir of Richard Dillingham. 2. Memoir
    of Calvin Fairbank. 3. Death and funeral of the author.

24159 Coghlan, John M   1835-1879.
       Chinese slave trade--coolyism. Speech of Hon. John M.
       Coghlan, of California, in the House of Representatives,
       March 16, 1872. [Washington, D. C., 1872]
       8 p.   23 cm.
       Caption title.

24160 Cole, Arthur Charles, 1886-
       Lincoln's "House divided" speech; did it reflect a
       doctrine of class struggle? An address delivered before
       the Chicago historical society on March 15, 1923, by
       Arthur Charles Cole... Chicago, Ill., The University
       of Chicago press [c1923]
       36 p.   23½ cm.

24161 Coleman, Amoss Lee, 1913-
       Black farm operators and rural-farm population in
       Kentucky, 1900-1970, by A. Lee Coleman and Dong I. Kim.
       Lexington, University of Kentucky, Agricultural Experiment
       Station [and] College of Agriculture, Department of
       Sociology, 1975.
       11 p.   tables on unnumb. p.   27 cm.   (RS 42)

24162 Coleman, John Winston, 1898-1983.
       Lexington's slave dealers and their southern trade.
       By J. Winston Coleman. Louisville, Kentucky, 1938.
       23 p.   25 cm.
       Reprinted from The Filson Club history quarterly,
       v. 12, no. 1, Jan. 1938.

24163 Coleman, John Winston, 1898-1983.
       Mrs. Stowe, Kentucky and Uncle Tom's cabin, by J.
       Winston Coleman, Jr. Harrogate, Tenn., Department of
       Lincolniana, Lincoln Memorial University, 1946.
       1 p.l., 8, [1] p.   port., plates.   25 cm.
       Reprinted from the Lincoln Herald, v. 48, no. 2,
       June 1946.

24164 Collier, Robert R
       Remarks on the subject of the ownership of slaves,
       delivered by R. R. Collier of Petersburg, in the Senate
       of Virginia, October 12, 1863. Richmond, Printed by
       J. E. Goode, 1863.
       28 p.   22½ cm.

24165 Collin, John Francis, 1802-1889.
       Financial and political affairs of the country...
       Being a series of communications on various topics, to
       the "Hudson gazette," during the years 1876-79.

By John F. Collin. Hudson, N. Y., Printed by M. P.
Williams, 1879-84.
     4 v.   2 port. (incl. front., v. 1)   23 cm.

24166 Collins, John A
          The anti-slavery picknick; a collection of speeches,
     poems, dialogues and songs; intended for use in schools
     and anti-slavery meetings... Boston, H. W. Williams;
     New York [etc.] Amer. A. S. Soc. [etc.] 1842.
          144 p.   music.   17 cm.

24167 Collins, John A
          Right and wrong amongst the abolitionists of the
     United States. With an introductory letter by Harriet
     Martineau... and an appendix. By John A. Collins...
     2d ed. Glasgow, G. Gallie; [etc., etc.] 1841.
          76 p.   22½ cm.

24168 Collyer, Isaac J   P
          Review of Rev. W. W. Eell's thanksgiving sermon, by
     Rev. Isaac J. P. Collyer, delivered in the Methodist
     Episcopal church, Newburyport, Dec. 29, 1850...
     Newburyport, C. Whipple, 1851.
          20 p.   20½ cm.

24169 Colman, Mrs. Lucy Newhall (Danforth) 1817-1906.
          Reminiscences of Lucy N. Colman... Buffalo, N. Y.,
     H. L. Green, 1891.
          86 p. incl. port.   front.   23½ cm.
          "Amy Post. A paper read by Lucy N. Colman before
     the Woman's political club of Rochester, N. Y.":
     p. 83-86.

24170 Colonization Society, Maine.
          Address of the board of managers. [Portland, Me.?]
     1855.
          7 p.   22 cm.

24171 Colton, Calvin, 1789-1857.
          Colonization and abolition contrasted. By Rev. Calvin
     Colton. [Philadelphia? H. Hooker, 1839?]
          16 p.   23 cm.
          Caption title.

24172 Columbus [pseud.]
          The origin and true causes of the Texas Insurrection,
     commenced in the year 1835. Philadelphia, 1836.
          32 p.   22 cm.

24173   Colver, Nathaniel, 1794-1870.
        The Fugutive slave bill; or, God's laws paramount to
    the laws of men. A sermon, preached on Sunday, October
    20, 1850, by Rev. Nathaniel Colver, pastor of the
    Tremonth st. church. Published by request of the
    church. Boston, J. M. Hewes & co., 1850.
        24 p.   22½ cm.

24174   Comments on the Nebraska bill, with views on slavery in
    contrast with freedom; respectfully addressed to the
    free states, by one acquainted with southern institutions.
    Albany, J. Munsell, 1854.
        58 p.   23 cm.
        Attributed to William Bayard.   cf. N. Y. State libr.
    cat., 1861.

24175   Common sense. [New Orleans? c1859]
            cover-title, 8 p.   23 cm.
        Copyright by Dr. John Anderson.
        In verse.

24176   Compagnie des colons de la Guyane française, Paris.
            ... Pièces diverses... [Paris? Impr. de C. H.
    Lambert] 1844-
            v. in   25½ cm.
        Submitted to the Ministry of marine and colonies by
    H. Sauvage, A. de Saint-Quantin (members of the
    Colonial council of French Guiana) and others.

24177   A comparison of slavery with abolitionism; together with
    reflections deduced from the premises, touching the
    several interests of the United States. By Amor
    patriae... New York, Printed for the publisher, 1848.
        16 p.   23 cm.

24178   Confederate States of America. Laws, statutes, etc.
        An act to perpetuate testimony in cases of slaves
    abducted or harbored by the enemy, and of other pro-
    perty seized, wasted, or destroyed by them. No. 270...
    [n.p., 1861?]
        1 l.   27 cm.
        Caption title.

24179   Confederate States of America. Laws, statutes, etc.
        Amendments proposed by Committee on the Judiciary to
    a bill to authorize retaliation on the enemy for vio-
    lations of the usages of civilized warfare. [Richmond,
    1863?]
        1 l.   24 cm.

24180   Confederate States of America. Laws, statutes, etc.
            ... Joint resolutions relative to the plan of retalia-
        tion proposed in the President's message.   [Richmond,
        1863]
            2 p.   24 cm.

24181   Confederate States of America. President (Davis)
            An address to the people of the free states by the
        President of the Southern Confederacy.   [Richmond]
        Richmond enquirer print [1863]
            broadside.   30½ cm.
            Signed: Jefferson Davis; dated: Richmond, January 5,
        1863.

24182   Confederate States of America. War Dept.
            [Communication from the secretary of war, enclosing
        a copy of the orders published by the department in
        pursuance of the act of Congress "to protect the rights
        of owners of slaves taken by or employed in the army".
        Richmond, 1863]
            6 p.   23½ cm.
            James A. Seddon, secretary of war.
            Transmitted with "Message of the President. Richmond,
        Va., March 25, 1863.
            General orders, no. 25, 1863: p. [4]-6.

24183   Confederate States of America. War Dept.
            ... Communication from the secretary of war [relative
        to the steps taken to carry out the provisions of the
        act of Congress "in relation to the arrest and dispo-
        sition of slaves who have been recaptured from the
        enemy". Richmond, 1864]
            3 p.   24 cm.
            James A. Seddon, secretary of war.
            Transmitted with "Message of the President... Feb. 5,
        1864."
            General orders, no. 25, 1863: p. 2-3.

24184   Confederate States of America. War Dept.
            [Communications from the secretary of war and the
        attorney general relative to whether the government
        holds, or has at any time held, itself liable for the
        value of slaves impressed by its authority and
        escaping to the enemy while so impressed and whether
        the owners of such slaves have been paid. Richmond,
        1863]
            14 p.   22½ cm.
            James A. Seddon, secretary of war; T. H. Watts,
        attorney general.
            Transmitted with "Message of the President... April 21,
        1863."

24185   Congregational Churches in Massachusetts. General Asso-
        ciation.
            Report of the committee of correspondence with southern
        ecclesiastical bodies on slavery; to the General Asso-
        ciation of Massachusetts. Pub. by vote of the Association.
        Salem, J. P. Jewett and company, 1844.
        23 p.   21½ cm.

24186   Congrès international antiesclavagiste. 2d, Paris, 1900.
            ... Congrès international antiesclavagiste, tenu à
        Paris du 6 au 8 août 1900.   Procès-verbaux sommaires.
        Paris, Imprimerie nationale, 1901.
        12 p.   25 cm.

24187   Conneau, Theophile.
            Vingt années de la vie d'un négrier [par] Capitaine
        Canot [pseud.]   Paris, Amyot [185-?]
        2 v.   16½ cm.

24188   Connelsville, Pa. Citizens.
            ... Resolutions of a meeting of the citizens of
        Connellsville,Newhaven, &c., Fayette County, Pennsylvania,
        adverse to any interference, by the people of the
        states, with the subject of slavery in the District of
        Columbia... [Washington] Gales & Seaton, print. [1836]
        4 p.   23 cm.   (24th Cong., 1st sess. [Senate.
        Doc.] 81)

24189   Considerations; addressed to professors of Christianity,
        of every denomination, on the impropriety of consuming
        West-India sugar & rum, as produced by the oppressive
        labour of slaves...   The 3d ed., corr.   Manchester,
        Printed by C. Wheeler, 1792.
        8 p.   17½ cm.

24190   Considerations on the present crisis of affairs, as it
        respects the West-India colonies, and the probable
        effects of the French decree for emancipating the
        negroes, pointing out a remedy for preventing the
        calamitous consequences in the British Islands...
        London, Printed by T. Gillet, 1795.
        2 p.l., 76 p.   21½ cm.

24191   Constitution of the Anti-slavery Society.   Boston,
        Printed by J. Knapp, 1838.
        12 p.   15 x 8½ cm.
            Includes Constitution of the Massachusetts Anti-
        slavery Society.

24192   The Constitution of the United States, with the acts of
        Congress, relating to slavery, embracing, the

Constitution, the Fugitive slave act of 1793, the
Missouri Compromise act of 1820, the Fugitive slave
law of 1850, and the Nebraska and Kansas bill, carefully compiled. Rochester, D. M. Dewey [1854]
1 p.l., 43, [1] p., 1 l.   21½ cm.

24193   Convention for the Improvement of the Free People of Color.
Minutes and proceedings of the 1st annual convention.
1831-   Philadelphia.
      v.   18-20 cm.
1831 as Convention of the People of Color. Library
has 1831.

24194   Convention of Abolitionists, West Bloomfield, N. Y., 1847.
An address from the American abolitionists, to the
friends of the slave in Great Britain. [Newcastle-on-
Tyne, Printed at the Guardian office, 1847]
      11 p.   17½ x 10½ cm.
Caption title. Signed: By order and on behalf of a
Convention of Abolitionists held in West Bloomfield,
Ontario County, western New York, on the 4th of March,
1847... Henry E. Peck. Timothy Stow.

24195   Convention of the Friends of Freedom in the Eastern and
Middle States, Boston, 1845.
Proceedings of the great convention of the Friends of
Freedom in the Eastern and Middle States, held in
Boston, Oct. 1, 2, & 3, 1845. Lowell, Pillsbury and
Knapp, printers, 1845.
      34 p.   18½ cm.

24196   Convention on the Abolition of Slavery, the Slave Trade,
and Institutions and Practices Similar to Slavery.
Convention on the abolition of slavery, the slave trade
and institutions and practices similar to slavery,
supplementary to the international convention signed at
Geneva on September 25, 1926; Geneva, September 7, 1956.
London, H. M. Stationery Off., 1957.
      51 p.   25 cm.   ([Great Britain. Foreign Office]
Treaty series, 1957, no. 59) ([Great Britain. Parliamen
Papers by command] cmnd. 257)

24197   Convention relative à l'esclavage, Genève, le 22 septembre
1926... Slavery convention, Geneva, September 25th,
1926.   Geneva, Imp. Kundig, 1926
      1 , 2-4, 2-11 p.   33 cm.   (Publication de la
Société des Nations. VI.B. Esclavage. 1926. VI.B.7)
Official no.: C.586.M.223. 1926. VI.

24198   Convention relative à l'esclavage, Genève, le 25 septembre
1926... Slavery convention, Geneva, September 25th,

1926. [Lausanne, Imp. réunies s.a., 1927]
[1], 2-5, 2-5, 6-10 p.   33 cm.   (C. 210. M. 83.
1927. vi. [C. 586 (1). M. 223 (1). 1926. vi.]

24199 Convention relative à l'esclavage (Genève, le 25 septembre
1926) Le Caire, Imp. nationale, 1940.
1 p.l., 14 p.; 1 p.l., 14 p.   24 cm.

24200 Converse, John Kendrick, 1801-1880.
The history of slavery, and means of elevating the
African race. A discourse delivered before the Vermont
Colonization Society, at Montpelier, Oct. 15, 1840.
By J. K. Converse... Burlington, C. Goodrich, 1840.
24 p.   21½ cm.

24201 Conway, Moncure Daniel, 1832-1907.
Autobiography, memories and experiences of Moncure
Daniel Conway... Boston and New York, Houghton, Mifflin
and company, 1904.
2 v.   fronts., plates, ports., facsims.   22½ cm.

24202 Conway, Moncure Daniel, 1832-1907.
Testimonies concerning slavery. By M. D. Conway,
a native of Virginia. 2d ed. London, Chapman and Hall,
1865.
viii, 140 p.   19 cm.

24203 Cook, Daniel Pope, 1795-1827.
Speech of Mr. Cook, of Illinois, on the restriction
of slavery in Missouri. Delivered in the House of
Representatives... February 4, 1820. [Washington,
1820]
27 p.   19 cm.   [Missouri Compromise. Speeches...
Washington, 1820. no. 10]

24204 Cooley, Henry Scofield.
... A study in slavery in New Jersey; by Henry Scofield
Cooley. Baltimore, The Johns Hopkins press, 1896.
60 p.   24½ cm.   (Johns Hopkins University studies
in historical and political science... 14th ser., 9-10)

24205 [Cooper, David]
A mite cast into the treasury: or, Observations on
slavekeeping... Philadelphia, Printed 1772. To be had
at most of the booksellers in town.
v, 5-24 p.   18 cm.

24206 [Cooper, David]
A serious address to the rulers of America, on the

inconsistency of their conduct respecting slavery: forming a contrast between the encroachments of England on American liberty, and American injustice in tolerating slavery... Trenton, printed; London, Reprinted by J. Phillips, 1783.
    24 p.   21 cm.

24207 Cooper, Joseph, 1800-1881.
    The lost continent; or, Slavery and the slave-trade in Africa, 1875, with observations on the Asiatic slave-trade, carried on under the name of the labour traffic, and some other subjects. London, Longmans, Green, 1875.
    viii, 138 p.   fold. map.   23 cm.

24208 Cooper, Peter, 1791-1883.
    The death of slavery. Letter from Peter Cooper to Governor Seymour. [New York, 1863]
    7 p.   23 cm.   (Loyal Publication Society.
[Pamphlets] no. 28)
    Caption title.

24209 Cooper, Peter, 1791-1883.
    ... A letter from Peter Cooper. To His Excellency Abraham Lincoln, president of the United States.
New York, 1863
    4 p.   22 cm.   (Loyal Publication Society.
[Pamphlets] no. 28, pt. 2)
    Caption title.

24210 Cooper, Peter, 1791-1883.
    ... Letter of Peter Cooper on slave emancipation.
New York, Oct., 1863. New York, W. C. Bryant & co., printers, 1863.
    cover-title, 8 p.   21½ cm.   (Loyal Publication Society. [Pamphlets] no. 23)

24211 Cooper, Thomas, 1791 or 2-1880.
    A letter to Robert Hibbert, jun. esq., in reply to his pamphlet, entitled, "Facts verified upon oath, in contradiction of the report of the Rev. Thomas Cooper, concerning the general condition of the slaves in Jamaica," &c. &c.; to which are added, a letter from Mrs. Cooper to R. Hibbert, jun. esq., and an appendix containing an exposure to the falsehoods and calumnies of that gentlemen's affidavit-men. By Thomas Cooper... London, J. Hatchard and son, 1824.
    iv, 90 p.   22½ cm.

24212 Corley, Daniel B
         A visit to Uncle Tom's cabin by D. B. Corley...
       Chicago, Laird & Lee, 1892.
         78 p.   front. (port.) illus.   20 cm.
         A cabin on the former estate of Robert McAlpin (the
       supposed original of Simon Legree) in Natchitoches parish.

24213 ... Correspondence respecting slavery in Abyssinia...
       London, Printed & pub. by H. M. Stationery off., 1923.
         6 p.   24½ cm.   ([Gt. Brit. Foreign office]
       Abyssinia, no. 1 (1923))
         Gt. Brit. Parliament. Papers by command. Cmd. 1858.

24214 Corte Real, José Alberto Homem da Cunha, 1832-1885.
         ... Resposta á Sociedade anti-esclavista de Londres
       por J. A. Corte Real... Lisboa, Typ. de C. A. Rodrigues,
       1884.
         23 p.   24 cm.
         At head of title: Sociedade de geographia de Lisboa.

24215 Corwin, Gabriel Smith, b. 1802.
         Hebrew and American slavery. A discourse, by Rev. G. S.
       Corwin... Rochester, N. Y., Press of A. Strong & co.,
       1863.
         36 p.   22½ cm.

24216 Corwin, Thomas, 1794-1865.
         Free soil vs. slavery. Speech of Mr. Corwin, of Ohio,
       against the Compromise bill, delivered in the Senate
       of the United States, Monday, July 24, 1848. Washington,
       Printed by Buell & Blanchard, 1848.
         16 p.   23½ cm.

24217 Cory, Charles Eatabrook, 1852-
         Slavery in Kansas. By C. E. Cory... [Topeka, 1902?]
         15 p.   23 cm.
         Reprinted from Collections of the Kansas State
       Historical Society, v. 7.

24218 Cowan, Alexander M
         Liberia, as I found it, in 1858. By Rev. Alexander M.
       Cowan... Frankfort, Ky., A. G. Hodges, printer, 1858.
         184 p.   23 cm.

24219 Cox, Leander M
         Organization of the House. Speech of Hon. L. M. Cox,
       of Kentucky, in the House of Representatives, Dec. 16 &
       17, 1855, on the election of speaker and the organization
       of the House of Representatives, and on the principles

of the National American Party. [Washington, Printed
at the Congressional globe office, 1855]
    23 p.   24 cm.
    Caption title.

24220 Cox, Samuel Sullivan, 1824-1889.
        Emancipation and its results--is Ohio to be Africanized?
    Speech of Hon. S. S. Cox, of Ohio. Delivered in the
    House of Representatives, June 6, 1862. [Washington,
    L. Towers & co., printers, 1862]
        16 p.   23½ cm.
        Caption title.

24221 Coxe, Richard Smith, 1792-1865.
        ... The present state of the African slave-trade: an
    exposition of some of the causes of its continuance and
    prosperity, with suggestions as to the most effectual
    means of repressing and extinguishing it; by Richard S.
    Coxe... Washington [D.C.] Printed by L. Towers, 1858.
        36 p.   23½ cm.
        From De Bow's Review for November, 1858.

24222 Cragin, Aaron Harrison, 1821-1898.
        Jefferson against Douglas. Speech of Hon. A. H.
    Cragin, of New Hampshire, in the House of Representatives
    August 4, 1856. [Washington, D. C., Buell & Blanchard,
    printers, 1856]
        14 p.   23½ cm.
        Caption title.

24223 [Crane, William] 1790-1866.
        ... Anti-slavery in Virginia: extracts from Thos.
    Jefferson, Gen. Washington and others relative to the
    "blighting curse of slavery." Debates on the "Nat Turner
    insurrection," Queries y William Crane, &c. Baltimore,
    J. F. Weishampel, 1865.
        23 p.   22 cm.

24224 Crewdson, John M
        Slavery in Texas: illegal aliens, seafood and coyotes.
    [New York, 1980]
        [1] p.   illus.   25 x 24 cm.
        Reprinted from the New York Times, October 20, 1980.

24225 Crisfield, John Woodland, 1808-1897.
        Speech of Mr. J. W. Crisfield, of Maryland, on the
    power of Congress to pass laws excluding slavery from
    the territories of the United States. Delivered in the
    House of Representatives, June 22, 1848. Washington,

60

Printed by J. T. Towers, 1848.
16 p.   23 cm.

24226   The crisis. New York, D. Appleton and company, 1863.
96 p.   22 cm.
Signed: Cae. S.
p. 31-94 in form of an imaginary dialogue between
George Washington and a Bostonian on the subjects at
issue between North and South.

24227   The crisis, no. 2, or Thoughts on slavery, occasioned by
the Missouri question. New Haven, Printed by A. H.
Maltby & co., 1820.
19 p.   21 cm.

24228   Crittenden, John Jordan, 1786-1863.
Kansas - The Lecompton Constitution. Speech of Hon.
John J. Crittenden, of Kentucky, in the Senate of the
United States, March 17, 1858. Washington, D. C.,
G. W. Fenton, 1858.
16 p.   21½ cm.

24229   Crittenden, John Jordan, 1786-1863.
Speech of Hon. John J. Crittenden, of Kentucky, on
emancipation. Delivered in the House of Representatives,
March 11, 1862.   Washington, Towers, printers, 1862
8 p.   22 cm.
Caption title.

24230   [Croly, David Goodman] 1829-1889.
Miscegenation; the theory of the blending of the races,
applied to the American white man and negro...
New York, H. Dexter, Hamilton & co., 1864.
cover-title, ii, 72 p.   18 cm.
Attributed by Sabin to D. G. Croly, George Wakeman, and
E. C. Howell.

24231   Cromwell, John Wesley, 1846-
The Negro in American history; men and women eminent
in the evolution of the American of African descent, by
John W. Cromwell. Washington, The American Negro
Academy, 1914.
xiii, 284 p.   front., plates, ports.   24 cm.

24232   Cropper, James, 1773-1840.
... A letter to Thomas Clarkson, by James Cropper:
and Prejudice vincible; or, The practicability of
conquering prejudice by better means than by slavery
and exile; in relation to the American Colonization

Society. By C. Stuart... New York, Re-printed from an
English edition, 1833.
15 p.   25½ cm.

24233 Crosby, Alpheus, 1810-1874.
The present position of the seceded states, and the
rights and duties of the general government in respect
to them. An address to the Phi Beta Kappa society of
Dartmouth college, July 19, 1865, by Alpheus Crosby...
Boston, Press of G. C. Rand & Avery, 1865.
16 p.   23 cm.

24234 Cuba. Laws, statutes, etc.
Ley y reglamento de la abolición de la esclavitud de
13 de febrero de 1880. Publicada en la Gaceta de la
Habana en 8 de mayo del mismo año, con las modificaciones
introducidas por el gobierno supremo. Habana, Imprenta
del gobierno y capitanía general por S. M., 1880.
35 p.   21 cm.

24235 Cuba before the United States. Remarks on the Hon. Chas.
Sumner's speech, delivered at the Republican Convention
of Massachusetts, the 22d September, 1869. (Adopted
and approved by the Central Republican Junta of Cuba and
Porto-Rico) New York, Styles & Cash, printers, 1869.
39 p.   21½ cm.

24236 Cuban Anti-slavery Committee, New York.
Slavery in Cuba. A report of the proceedings of the
meeting held at Cooper Institute, New York City,
December 13, 1872. Newspaper extracts, official
correspodence... New York [Powers, MacGowan and Slipper,
printers, 1872]
42 p.   20 cm.

24237 Curd, William H
... An apology for the American people. A reason and
an apology for American slavery. A duty. By William H.
Curd. Chicago, Ill., B. Hand & co., printers, 1879.
60 p. incl. front. (port.)   19½ cm.

24238 Curiosity visits to southern plantations. By a northern
man. London, H. F. Mackintosh, 1863.
31 p.   22 cm.
Reprinted from Fraser's magazine, February 1863, where
it appeared under title "Negroes and slavery in the
United States. By a white Republican".

24239 Curry, Jabez Lamar Monroe, 1825-1903.
The constitutional rights of the states. Speech of

62

J. L. M. Curry, of Alabama, in the House of Representatives, March 14, 1860. [Washington] T. McGill, print.
[1860]
    8 p.   21½ cm.

24240 Curry, Jabez Lamar Monroe, 1825-1903.
       Speech of J. L. M. Curry, of Alabama, on the election
of speaker, and the progress of anti-slaveryism.
Delivered in the House of Representatives, December 10,
1859. Washington, Printed by L. Towers, 1859.
    15 p.   21 cm.

24241 Cushing, Caleb, 1800-1879.
       Speech delivered in Faneuil Hall--Boston, October 27,
1857. Also, speech delivered in city hall--Newburyport,
October 31, 1857. By Caleb Cushing. [Boston] Printed
at the office of the Boston post, 1857.
    48 p.   24½ cm.

24242 Cushing, Caleb, 1800-1879.
       Speech of Hon. Caleb Cushing, in Norombega Hall,
Bangor, October 2, 1860, before the democracy of Maine...
[Bangor? 1860]
    12 p.   23½ cm.
    Caption title.
    A discussion of the constitutional principles of the
Democratic party.

24243 Cushing, Caleb, 1800-1879.
       Speech of Mr. Cushing, of Massachusetts, on the right
of petition, as connected with petitions for the
abolition of slavery and the slave trade in the District
of Columbia: in the House of Representatives, January 25,
1836. Washington, Printed by Gales and Seaton, 1836.
    15 p.   24 cm.

24244 Cuthbert, Alfred, 1785-1856.
       Speech of Mr. Cuthbert, of Georgia, on the position
of the Society of Friends of Lancaster County, Pennsylvania, praying for the abolition of slavery in the
District of Columbia, in Senate, March 7, 1836.
Washington, Blair & Rives, 1836.
    8 p.   23 cm.

24245 Cutler, William Parker, 1812-1889.
       Slavery--a public enemy, and ought therefore to be
destroyed; a nuisance that must be abated. Speech of
Hon. W. P. Cutler, of Ohio, in the House of Representatives, April 23, 1862. Washington, D. C., Scammell &

co., printers, 1862.
12 p.   24½ cm.

24246   Cutting, Sewall Sylvester, 1813-1882.
Influence of Christianity on government and slavery:
a discourse, delivered in the Baptist Church, in West
Boylington, Mass., January 15, 1837. By Sewall S.
Cutting, pastor. Worcester, Printed by H. J. Howland,
1837.
14 p.   23½ cm.

D

24247   Daggs, Ruel, plaintiff.
Fugitive slave case. District Court of the United
States for the Southern Division of Iowa, Burlington,
June term, 1850. Ruel Daggs, vs. Elihu Frazier, et als.,
trespass on the case. Reported by Geo. Frazee.
Burlington, Printed by Morgan & M'Kenny, 1850.
40 p.   22 cm.

24248   Daiches, Samuel, 1878-
Altbabylonische Rechtsurkunden aus der Zeit der
Hammurabi-dynastie; von Samuel Daiches... Leipzig,
J. C. Hinrichs'sche buchhandlung, 1903.
iv, 100 p.   22½ cm.   (On cover: Leipziger semi-
tistische studien, I, 2)

24249   Dalhoff, N
Her er ikke trael og fri; en fortaelling om Abraham
Lincoln og negerslavernes frigørelse. [n.p., 1902?]
1 v. (unpaged) illus., ports.   19 cm.
Caption title.

24250   Dana, Richard Henry, 1815-1882.
Remarks of Richard H. Dana, jr., esq. before the
Committee on federal regulations, on the proposed
removal of Edward G. Loring, esq. from the office of
judge of probate. March 5, 1855. Boston, Printed by
A. Mudge & son, 1855.
28 p.   21 cm.
The removal of Loring was sought because of his
decision returning Anthony Burns to slavery.

24251   Dana, Richard Henry, 1815-1882.
Richard Henry Dana, jr. ... speeches in stirring times
and letters to a son, ed., with introductory sketch and

64

notes by Richard H. Dana [3d]   Boston and New York,
Houghton Mifflin company, 1910.
   vi p., 1 l., 520 p., 1 l.   illus. (map) 5 port.
(incl. front.)   22½ cm.

24252 [Daniel, Thomas, and company]
       A letter to His Grace the Duke of Newcastle, on West
India affairs, called forth by the misrepresentations
of the Anti-slavery Society. London, Printed by C.
Skipper & East, 1854.
       36 p.   20 cm.

24253 Danvers Historical Society. Danvers, Mass.
       Old anti-slavery days. Proceedings of the commemorative
meeting, held by the Danvers Historical Society, at the
Town hall, Danvers, April 26, 1893, with introduction,
letters and sketches. Danvers, Danvers mirror print,
1893.
       xxvii p., 1 l., 151 p.   port. group.   23½ cm.
       Edited by A. P. Putnam.

24254 [Darlington, William] 1782-1863.
       Desultory remarks on the question of extending slavery
into Missouri: as enunciated during the first session
of the Sixteenth Congress, by the representative from
Chester county, state of Pennsylvania... Extracted from
the American republican newspaper of 1819-20. West
Chester, Pa., L. Marshall, printer, 1856.
       37 p.   22 cm.

24255 [D'Arusmont, William E   Guthrie]
       The betrothed. A nation's vow. By Dr. W. E. Guthrie...
Edinburgh, W. P. Nemmo, 1867.
       3 p.l., [3]-64 p.   front. (port.)   17½ cm.
       In verse.

24256 Datt, Johann Philipp, 1654-1722.
       Joh. Philippi Dattii... De venditione liberorum
diatriba occasione legis 2. Cod de patrib. qui fil.
distrax. ex germanicis, & aliarum gentium legibus;
jure romano, secundum diversas... periodos; juris-
prudentiae universalis fontibus & principiis; patribus
latinis & graecis; historia denique byzantina & syn-
chronis scriptoribus deducta. Vlmae, impensis
Georgii Wilhelmi Kühnii, 1700.
       4 p.l., 162, [12] p., 1 l.   18 cm.

24257 Davidson, John Nelson.
       ... Negro slavery in Wisconsin [by] John Nelson David-

son. [Milwaukee, Wis., 1896]
    cover-title, [103]-131 p.   24 cm.   (Parkman Club
publications, no. 6...)

24258 Davis, Jefferson, pres., Confederate States of America,
    1808-1889.
      Reply of Hon. Jefferson Davis, of Mississippi, to the
    speech of Senator Douglas, in the U. S. Senate, May 16
    and 17, 1860. [Baltimore, Murphy & co., 1860]
      16 p.   24 cm.
    Caption title.

24259 Davis, Jefferson, pres., Confederate States of America,
    1808-1889.
      Speech of Hon. Jefferson Davis, of Mississippi, on his
    resolutions relative to the rights of property in the
    territories, etc. Delivered in the Senate of the United
    States, May 7, 1860. [Washington] Printed by L. Towers
    [1860]
      16 p.   22 cm.
    Caption title.

24260 Davis, Jefferson, pres., Confederate States of America,
    1808-1889.
      Speech of Mr. Davis, of Mississippi, on the subject
    of slavery in the territories. Delivered in the Senate
    of the United States, February 13 & 14, 1850.
    [Washington, Towers, print., 1850]
      32 p. $23\frac{1}{2}$ cm.
    Caption title.

24261 [Davis, Nicholas Darnell] 1846-1915, comp.
      Pages from the early history of Barbados. [n.p.,
    19-?]
      6 l. $31\frac{1}{2}$ cm.

24262 Davis, Owen.
      Sketches of sermons, delivered by Rev. Owen Davis, in
    the First Free Bethel church, in West Centre street,
    Boston. Boston, Printed for the author, 1837.
      12 p.   21 cm.

24263 Dawes, Henry Laurens, 1816-1903.
      The new dogma of the South--"Slavery a blessing."
    Speech of Hon. Henry L. Dawes, of Mass. Delivered in
    the House of Representatives, April 12, 1860.
    [Washington, 1860]
      7, [1] p. $23\frac{1}{2}$ cm.
    Caption title.

24264   Day, Thomas, 1748-1789.
        The dying Negro, a poem. By the late Thomas Day and
        John Bicknell, esquires. To which is added, a Fragment
        of a letter on the slavery of the Negroes. By Thomas
        Day... London, J. Stockdale, 1793.
        2 p.l., xi, 82, [2] p.   front.   22 cm.

24265   Day, Thomas, 1748-1789.
        Fragment of an original letter on the slavery of the
        negroes. Written in the year 1776. By Thomas Day...
        London, Printed for John Stockdale, opposite Burlington
        House, 1784.
        vi, [11]-40 p.   23½ cm.

24266   Dean, Paul, 1789-1860.
        A discourse delivered before the African Society, at
        their meeting-house, in Boston, Mass. on the abolition
        of the slave trade by the government of the United
        States of America, July 14, 1819. By Paul Dean, pastor
        of the First Universal Church in Boston... Boston,
        Printed for Nathaniel Coverly, 1819.
        16 p.   21½ cm.

24267   Deane, Charles, 1813-1889.
        The connection of Massachusetts with slavery and the
        slave-trade. Read at the annual meeting of the American
        Antiquarian Society at Worcester, Mass., October 21,
        1886. By Charles Deane. Worcester, Mass., Printed by
        C. Hamilton, 1886.
        34 p.   24 cm.

24268   Deane, Charles, ed., 1813-1889.
        Letters and documents relating to slavery in Massa-
        chusetts. [Boston, 1877]
        373-342 p.   22 cm.
        Reprinted from Collections of the Massachusetts
        Historical Society, ser. 5, v. 3, 1877.

24269   De Charms, Richard, 1796-1864.
        A discourse on the true nature of freedom and slavery.
        Delivered before the Washington Society of the New
        Jerusalem, in view of the one hundred and eighteenth
        anniversary of Washington's birth. By Richard De
        Charms... Philadelphia, J. H. Jones, printer, 1850.
        iv, [5]-63 p.   24½ cm.

24270   Declaration of the Anti-slavery Convention, assembled in
        Philadelphia, December 4, 1833. [Philadelphia] Merrihew
        & Gunn, printers [1834?]
        [1] p.   47 cm.

24271 Degenkolb, Heinrich, 1832-1909.
         Die Befreiung durch Census, von Heinrich Degenkolb.
      [Tübingen, Druck von H. Laupp jr., 1892]
         3 p.l., 32 p.   24½ cm.
         "Sonderabzug aus der Festschrift der Tübinger Juris-
      tenfakultät für Rudolph von Jhering."

24272 De Jarnette, Daniel C   1822-1881.
         Secession of South Carolina. Speech of Hon. D. C.
      De Jarnette, of Virginia, in the House of Representatives,
      January 10, 1861. [Washington, Printed at the office
      of the Congressional globe, 1861]
         7 p.   23 cm.
         Caption title.

24273 De Jarnette, Daniel C   1822-1881.
         State of the Union. Speech of the Hon. D. C. De
      Jarnette, of Virginia, in the House of Representatives,
      February 14, 1861. [Washington, Printed by F. H. Sage,
      1861]
         8 p.   22½ cm.
         Caption title.

24274 Delaware. Governor, 1863-1865 (Cannon)
         Inaugural address of William Cannon, delivered at Dover,
      upon taking the oath of office as governor of the state
      of Delaware, January 20, 1863. Wilmington, Printed by
      H. Eckel, 1863.
         29, [1] p.   22 cm.

24275 De Leon, Thomas Cooper, 1839-1914.
         John Holden, unionist, a romance of the days of
      destruction and reconstruction, by T. C. De Leon...
      in collaboration with Erwin Ledyard... St. Paul, The
      Price-McGill company [c1893]
         ix, [11]-338 p.   front., plates.   20 cm.

24276 Democratic Party. National Committee, 1848-1852.
         ..."It is a right inherent in every freeman to
      possess himself of the political principles and opinions
      of those into whose hands the administration of the
      government may be placed."--Gen. Taylor to Mr. Deloney.
      [Washington, D. C., Pub. under authority of the National
      and Jackson Democratic Association Committee, 1848]
         8 p.   23½ cm.
         Caption title.

24277 Democratic Party. New Jersey.
         Address of the New Jersey Democratic State Central

Committee to the voters of the state. [Trenton, 1862]
    16 p.   22½ cm.
    Caption title.

24278 [Democratic party. Pennsylvania. Philadelphia]
    Letters addressed to John Sergeant, Manuel Eyre,
    Lawrence Lewis, Clement C. Biddle, and Joseph P. Norris,
    esqs. authors of An address to the people of Pennsylvania,
    adopted at a meeting of the friends to the election of
    John Quincy Adams, held in Philadelphia, July 7, 1828:
    containing strictures on their address. By the committee
    of correspondence, of Philadelphia, appointed by a
    Republican convention, held at Harrisburg, January 8,
    1828. Philadelphia, Printed bv W. Stavely, 1828.
    88 p.   21½ cm.
    Pages 39-40 omitted.

24279 Democratus, pseud.
    An appeal for the Constitution. Theory and practice
    of the government. By Democratus. Baltimore, Printed
    by W. M. Innes, 1862.
    44 p.   21½ cm.

24280 Demund, Isaac S   1803-1888.
    Liberty defended. Fourth of July. To the patriotic
    citizens of Pompton Plains, the oration... is most
    respectfully dedicated by the speaker, Isaac S. Demund...
    New-York, Printed by J. A. Gray, 1851.
    20 p.   23 cm.

24281 A description of the nature of slavery among the Moors.
    And the cruel sufferings of those that fall into it...
    to which is added, an account of Capt. Stuart's nego-
    ciations for the redemption of the English captives...
    Written by one of the said redeem'd captives.
    Lonon [!] Printed by J. Peele, 1721.
    1 p.l., 38 p.   19½ cm.

24282 Dessaulles, Louis Antoine, 1819-1895.
    La guerre américaine; son origine et ses vraies
    causes. Lecture publique faite à l'Institut-Canadien,
    le 14 décembre 1864. Par l'Hon. L. A. Dessaulles.
    Montréal, Typ. du journal "Le Pays" 1865.
    1 p.l., [5]-75 p.   15 cm.

24283 De Vinné, Daniel, 1793-1883.
    The Methodist Episcopal Church and slavery. A
    historical survey of the relation of the early Methodists
    to slavery. By Daniel De Vinné... New York, F. Hart,

1857.
2 p.l., [vii]-viii, [9]-95, [1] p.   23 cm.

24284   Dewey, Loring Daniel, 1791-1867.
Correspondence relative to the emigration to Hayti,
of the free people of colour, in the United States.
Together with the instructions to the agent sent out
by President Boyer. New York, Printed by M. Day, 1824.
32 p.   20 cm.

24285   Dickinson, Daniel Stevens, 1800-1866.
Sectional agitation. Remarks of Hon. D. S. Dickinson,
of New York, in the Senate of the United States, Jan. 17,
1850, upon Mr. Clemens's resolutions calling for the
instructions of the President concerning California;
with a sketch of the debate on that day.   [Washington,
Printed at the Congressional globe office, 1850]
8 p.   25 cm.
Caption title.

24286   Dickinson, Noadiah Smith, 1815-1876.
Slavery: the nation's crime and danger. A sermon,
preached in the Congregational church, Foxborough, Mass.
Sept. 30, 1960. By Rev. N. S. Dickinson. Boston,
Press of G. Noyes, 1860.
40 p.   23 cm.

24287   Dickson, John, 1783-1852.
Remarks of Mr. Dickson, of New York, on the presen-
tation of several petitions for the abolition of
slavery and the slave trade in the District of Columbia.
Delivered in the House of Representatives of the United
States, February 2, 1835. Washington, Printed by Gales
and Seaton, 1835.
7 p. $24\frac{1}{2}$ x $17\frac{1}{2}$ cm.

24288   Dickson, Moses.
A manual of the Knights of Tabor, and Daughters of
the Tabernacle, including the ceremonies of the order,
constitutions, installations, dedications, and funerals,
with forms, and the Taborian drill and tactics. St.
Louis, Mo. [G. I. Jones] 1879.
255 p. $20\frac{1}{2}$ cm.

24289   Dickson, Samuel Henry, 1798-1872.
Remarks on certain topics connected with the general
subject of slavery: by S. Henry Dickson... Re-printed
at the request of several friends. Charleston,
Observer office press, 1845.
35 p. $21\frac{1}{2}$ cm.

24290 [Dillwyn, William] 1743-1824.
        Brief considerations on slavery, and the expediency
    of its abolition. With some hints on the means whereby
    it may be gradually effected. Recommended to the
    serious attention of all, and especially of those
    entrusted with the powers of legislation... Burlington,
    Printed and sold by Isaac Collins, 1773.
        16 p.   18½ cm.

24291 Los Diputados americanos en las Córtes españolas. Los
    diputados de Puerto-Rico. 1872-1873. Madrid, Impr. de
    A. J. Alaria, 1880.
        vii, 395, [3] p.   19½ cm.
        Contents. - Al lector. - Córtes de 1872... - Asamblea
    nacional, 1873... - Córtes constituyentes de 1873... -
    A los electores de Puerto-Rico. (Memorandum) por R. M.
    de Labra. - Discursos: Las elecciones de Puerto-Rico...
    por J. M. Sanromá. La casación criminal en ultramar...
    por J. F. Cintron y R. M. de Labra. El código penal
    en ultramar... por R. M. de Labra. La diputación de
    Puerto-Rico ante las reformas ultramarinas... por R. M.
    Labra. La abolición de la esclavitud en Puerto Rico...
    por J. M. Sanromá, J. F. Cintron, R. M. de Labra y J.
    Alvarez Peralta. Los sucesos de Camery... por R. M. de
    Labra. La reforma electoral... por L. Padial y R. M.
    de Labra. Publicación de leyes y reglamentos... por
    R. M. de Labra. - Proposiciones de ley y dictamenes. -
    Apéndice.

24292 Discipline of earth and time for freedom and immortality.
    Four books of an unpublished poem. Boston, 1854.
        vi, [7]-147 p.   17½ cm.
        Copyrighted by John Smith.

24293 District of Columbia. Citizens.
        ... Memorial of inhabitants of the District of
    Columbia, praying for the gradual abolition of slavery
    in the District of Columbia. March 24, 1828. Referred
    to the Committee for the District of Columbia.
    Washington, Printed by Gales & Seaton, 1828.
        5 p.   22 cm.   ([U. S.] 20th Cong., 1st sess.
    House. Doc. 215)

24294 Dix, John Adams, 1798-1879.
        Speech of Hon. John A. Dix, of New York, on the
    three million bill. Delivered in the Senate of the
    United States, March 1, 1847. Washington, Printed at
    the office of Blair and Rives, 1847.
        15 p.   23½ cm.

24295 Dixon, Thomas, 1864-1946.
      The black hood, by Thomas Dixon... New York, London,
D. Appleton and company, 1924.
      viii p., 1 l., 336 p.   front.   19½ cm.

24296 Dixon, Thomas, 1864-1946.
      The clansman; an historical romance of the Ku Klux
Klan, by Thomas Dixon, jr.; illustrated by Arthur I.
Keller. New York, Doubleday, Page & company, 1906.
      8 p.l., 3-374 p.   front., plates.   20½ cm.

24297 Dixon, Thomas, 1864-1946.
      The foolish virgin; a romance of today, by Thomas
Dixon... illustrated by Walter Tittle. New York and
London, D. Appleton and company, 1915.
      vii, [3], 362 1 p.   front., plates.   19½ cm.

24298 Dixon, Thomas, 1861-1946.
      ... The leopard's spots; a romance of the white man's
burden--1865-1900, by Thomas Dixon, jr.; illustrated by
C. D. Williams. New York, Doubleday, Page & co., 1903.
      xiii, 465 p.   front., 6 pl., port.   20 cm.

24299 Dixon, Thomas, 1864-1946.
      The southerner; a romance of the real Lincoln, by
Thomas Dixon... illustrated by J. N. Marchand. New
York and London, D. Appleton and company, 1913.
      7 p.l., 3-543, [1] p.   front., plates.   19½ cm.

24300 Dixon, Thomas, 1864-1946.
      The traitor; a story of the fall of the invisible
empire, by Thomas Dixon, jr., illustrated by C. D.
Williams. New York, Doubleday, Page & company, 1907.
      8 p.l., 3-331 p.   col. front., 3 col. pl.   20½ cm.
      "This volume closes... 'The trilogy of reconstruction'!"

24301 Dobbins, J   B
      The Bible against slavery; a vindication of the sacred
Scriptures against the charge of authorizing slavery.
A reply to Bishop Hopkins. By Rev. J. B. Dobbins...
Philadelphia, King & Baird, printers, 1864.
      24 p.   21 cm.
      Criticism of a pamphlet by John H. Hopkins, bishop
of Vermont, entitled "Bible view of slavery."

24302 Documentary history of slavery in the United States. By
a native of Maryland. Washington, Printed by J. T.
Towers, 1851.
      64 p.   22½ cm.
      Attributed to John L. Dorsey.

24303 Donavin, Simpson K   1831-1902.
       John Brown at Harper's Ferry and Charlestown; a
       lecture. By S. K. Donovan [!] Columbus, 0., 1921.
       300-336 p.   illus.   23 cm.
       Reprinted from Ohio archaeological and historical
       quarterly, v. 30, p. 300-336.

24304 Doolittle, James Rood, 1815-1897.
       Speech of the Hon. James R. Doolittle, of Wisconsin,
       on the bill to organize the territory of Arizuma.
       Delivered in the Senate of the United States, December
       27, 1860. [Washington, W. H. Moore, printer, 1861?]
       16 p.   24½ cm.
       Caption title.

24305 Dorr, James Augustus.
       Objections to the act of Congress, commonly called the
       Fugitive slave law answered, in a letter to Hon.
       Washington Hunt... By James A. Dorr... New York, 1850.
       15 p.   23 cm.

24306 [Dorsey, John Larkin]
       Documentary history of slavery in the United States.
       By a native of Maryland. Washington, Printed by J. T.
       Towers, 1851.
       64 p.   22½ cm.

24307 Douglas, Stephen Arnold, 1813-1861.
       Report of Senator Douglas, of Illinois, on the Kansas-
       Lecompton Constitution, February 18, 1858. [Washington,
       D. C.] Lemuel Towers [1858]
       16 p.   24 cm.

24308 Douglas, Stephen Arnold, 1813-1861.
       Speech of Hon. Stephen A. Douglas on the "Measures
       of adjustment," delivered in the City Hall, Chicago,
       October 23, 1850. Washington, Gideon & co., printers,
       1851.
       32 p.   22½ cm.

24309 Douglas, Stephen Arnold, 1813-1861.
       Speech of Senator S. A. Douglas, on the invasion of
       states; and his reply to Mr. Fessenden. Delivered in
       the Senate of the United States, January 23, 1860.
       Baltimore, Printed by J. Murphy & co., 1860.
       16 p.   23 cm.

24310 Douglass, Frederick, 1817-1895.
       Abolition fanaticism in New York. Speech of a runaway

slave from Baltimore, at an abolition meeting in New
York, held May 11, 1847. [Baltimore] 1847.
   8 p.   24 cm.

24311 Douglass, Frederick, 1817-1895.
      Anti-Fugitive slave law meeting. [New York, 1851]
    [4] p.   32 cm.

24312 Douglass, Frederick, 1817-1895.
      The anti-slavery movement. A lecture by Frederick
Douglass, before the Rochester Ladies' Anti-Slavery
Society. Rochester [N. Y.] Press of Lee, Mann & co.,
1855.
    44 p.   21½ cm.

24313 Downs, Solomon Weathersbee, 1801-1854.
      Speech of the Hon. Solomon W. Downs, of Louisiana,
on the resolution submitted by Mr. Foote, of Mississippi,
declaring the compromise measures a definitive adjustment of the agitating questions growing out of the
institution of domestic slavery. Delivered in the
Senate of the United States, January 10, 1852.
Washington, Printed by Donelson & Armstrong, 1852.
    24 p.   25 cm.

24314 Drake, Charles Daniel, 1811-1892.
      The war of slavery upon the Constitution. Address
of Charles D. Drake, on the anniversary of the Constitution. Delivered in the city of Saint Louis, Sept. 17,
1862. [St. Louis? 1862]
    7 p.   23 cm.
    Caption title.

24315 Dreveton, Théodore.
      Choses coloniales. Guadeloupe. Août 1845...
Paris, Ledoyen, 1846.
    4 p.l., 80 p.   19 cm.

24316 Drewry, William Sidney, 1870-
      The Southampton insurrection, by William Sidney Drewry
... Washington [D. C.] The Neale company, 1960
    201 p.   front., plates, ports., fold. map.   22½ cm.
    Another edition issued at Washington the same year,
with title: Slave insurrections in Virginia (1830-1865)

24317 Drisler, Henry, 1818-1897.
      ... Bible view of slavery, by John H. Hopkins. D.D.,
bishop of the diocese of Vermont, examined by Henry
Drisler... Bible view of slavery, reconsidered. Letter

to Rt. Rev. Bishop Hopkins, by Louis C. Newman.
New York, C. S. Westcott & co., printers, 1863.
    2 pt. in 1 v.   22 cm.   (Loyal Publication Society...
[Pamphlets] no. 39, pt. 1-2)
    Cover-title.

24318   Du Bois, William Edward Burghardt, 1868-1963.
    The enforcement of the slave-trade laws, by W. E. B.
Du Bois. [Washington, 1892]
    161-174 p.   24½ cm.
    Reprinted from American Historical Association,
Annual report... for the year 1891, 1892.

24319   Dunbar, Paul Laurence, 1872-1906.
    Folks from Dixie. By Paul Laurence Dunbar... with
illustrations by E. W. Kemble. New York, Dodd, Mead
and company, 1898.
    6 p.l., 3-263 p.   col. front., 7 pl. (1 col.)
19 cm.
    Contents. - Anner' Lizer's stumblin' block. - The
ordeal at Mt. Hope. - The colonel's awakening. - The
trial sermons on Bull-Skin. - Jimsella. - Mt. Pisgah's
Christmas 'possum. - A family feud. - Aunt Mandy's
investment. - The intervention of Peter. - Neise
Hatton's vengeance. - At Shaft 11. - The deliberation
of Mr. Dunkin.

24320   Duncan, James.
    A treatise on slavery; in which is shewn forth the
evil of slave holding, both from the light of nature
and divine revelation... By James Duncan... Vevay,
Printed at the Indiana register' office, 1824.
    88 p.   20½ cm.

24321   Duniway, Clyde Augustus, 1866-
    Slavery in California after 1848, by Clyde A. Dunaway...
[Washington, 1906]
    241-248 p.   24½ cm.
    Reprinted from American Historical Association,
Annual report for the year 1905, 1906.

24322   Dunn, Jacob Piatt, 1855-1924.
    ... Indiana; a redemption from slavery, by J. P. Dunn,
jr. ... Boston and New York, Houghton, Mifflin and
company, 1888.
    2 p.l., [iii]-viii, 453 p.   front. (fold. map)
18½ cm.   (Half-title: American commonwealths, ed.
by H. E. Scudder, v. 12)

24323　Dunn, Jacob Piatt, 1855-1924, ed.
　　　　... Slavery petitions and papers, by Jacob Piatt Dunn.
　　　　Indianapolis, The Bowen-Merrill company, 1894.
　　　　[443]-529 p.　24½ cm.　(Indiana Historical Society,
　　　　Publications, v. 2, no. 12)

24324　Dunne, Henry C
　　　　... Democracy versus Know-Nothingism and Republicanism.
　　　　Letter from Dunne, to Jones & Given.　Philadelphia,
　　　　1858.
　　　　　cover-title, 12 p.　　21 cm.
　　　　At head of title:　2d ed.

24325　[Dupierris, Martial]
　　　　... Cuba y Puerto-Rico.　Medios de conservar estas dos
　　　　Antillas en su estado de esplendor.　Por un negrófilo
　　　　concienzudo.　Madrid, Impr. de J. Cruzado, 1866.
　　　　2 p.l., [3]-157 p.　　19 cm.

24326　[Dupuy, Eliza Ann] 1814?-1881.
　　　　The planter's daughter; A tale of Louisiana...
　　　　Halifax, Milner and Sowerby, 1862.
　　　　5-351 p.　　front. (port.)　　13 cm.

24327　Du Puynode, Michel Gustave Partounau, b. 1817.
　　　　De l'esclavage et des colonies, par Gustave du
　　　　Puynode...　Paris, Joubert, 1847.
　　　　2 p.l., xv, 223, [1] p.　　22 cm.

24328　Duque-Estrada, Osorio, 1870-1927.
　　　　... A aboliçao (esboção historico) 1831-1888, com um
　　　　prefacio do conselheiro Ruy Barbosa.　Rio [de Janeiro]
　　　　Leite Ribeiro & Maurillo, 1918.
　　　　2 p.l., xii, [5]-328 p., 2 l.　　19½ cm.

24329　Dwight, Henry O
　　　　Uncle Sam's legacy of slaves.　[n.p., 1900]
　　　　273-279 p.　　20½ cm.
　　　　Reprinted from Forum, v. 29, May 1900.

E

24330　Early, Jubal Anderson, 1816-1894.
　　　　The heritage of the South; a history of the intro-
　　　　duction of slavery; its establishment from colonial
　　　　times and final effect upon the politics of the United
　　　　States, by Jubal A. Early...　[Lynchburg, Va., Press

of Brown-Morrison co., c1915]
119 p.   20 cm.

24331 Eaton, Clement, 1898-1980.
Slave-hiring in the upper south: a step toward
freedom. [n.p., 1960]
662-678 p.   24 cm.
Reprinted from Mississippi valley historical review,
v. 46, no. 4, Mar. 1960.

24332 Eaves, Lucile, 1869-
... A history of California labor legislation, with an
introductory sketch of the San Francisco labor movement,
by Lucile Eaves... Berkeley, The University press [1910]
xiv, 461 p.   27 cm.   (University of California
publications in economics, v. 2)

24333 Edgar, Cornelius Henry, 1811-1884.
The curse of Canaan rightly interpreted, and kindred
topics. Three lectures, delivered in the Reformed
Dutch Church, Easton, Pa. January and February, 1862.
New York, Baker and Godwin, 1862.
48 p.   23 cm.

24334 Edge, Frederick Milnes.
America yesterday and to-day. The United States prior
to the rebellion; and the prospects of reconstruction
of the South... London, F. Farrah [1869?]
viii p., 1 l., [ix]-xv, 224, iii p.   19 cm.

24335 Edge, Frederick Milnes.
Slavery doomed; or, The contest between free and slave
labour in the United States. By Frederick Milnes Edge.
London, Smith, Elder and co., 1860.
xv, 224 p. $19\frac{1}{2}$ cm.

24336 Edgerton, Joseph Ketchum, 1818-1893.
The relations of the federal government to slavery.
Speech of Joseph K. Edgerton. Delivered at Fort Wayne,
Ind., October 30th, 1860... Fort Wayne, Dawson's
daily and weekly times print, 1861.
64 p.   22 cm.

24337 Edgerton, Walter, b. 1806.
A history of the separation in Indiana Yearly Meeting
of Friends; which took place in the winter of 1842 and
1843, on the anti-slavery question; containing a brief
account of the rise, spread, and final adoption by the
Society, of its testimony against slavery; together

77

with a record of some of the principal facts and circumstances relating to that separation; embracing the documents issued by both parties relative thereto; and some account of the action of other Yearly Meetings of Friends, touching the controversy, especially that of London, etc. By Walter Edgerton. Cincinnati, A. Pugh, printer, 1856.
viii, [9]-352 p.   20 cm.

24338   [Edinburgh Emancipation Society]
A voice to the United States of America, from the metropolis of Scotland; being an account of various meetings held in Edinburgh on the subject of American slavery, upon the return of Mr. George Thompson, from his mission to that country... Edinburgh, W. Oliphant and son, 1836.
51 p.   21½ cm.

24339   Edwards, Bryan, 1743-1800.
The history, civil and commercial, of the British West Indies. By Bryan Edwards... With a continuation to the present time. 5th ed. With maps and plates... London, G. and W. B. Whittaker; [etc., etc.] 1818-19.
5 v.   front. (port.) tables (part fold.)   22 cm. and atlas of 22 pl. (incl. maps, part fold.)
28 x 22½ cm.

24340   Edwards, Harry Stillwell, 1855-1938.
How Sal came through, by Harry Stillwell Edwards... Macon, Ga., The J. W. Burke company [1920]
31 p.   17 cm.

24341   Eggleston, George Cary, 1839-1911.
Dorothy South; a love story of Virginia just before the war, by George Cary Eggleston... illustrated by C. D. Williams. Boston, Lothrop pub. co.   [1902]
453 p.   front., pl.   19½ cm.

24342   Einhorn, David, 1809-1879.
The Rev. Dr. M. J. Raphall's Bible view of slavery reviewed by the Rev. D. Einhorn, D. D. Tr. from the February number of the "Sinai," a Jewish monthly periodical, published in Baltimore. New York, Thalmessinger, Cahn & Benedicks, printers, 1861.
1 p.l., [5]-22 p.   18½ cm.

24343   Eisele, Fridolin, 1837-1920.
Studien zur römischen Rechtsgeschichte. Von dr. Fridolin Eisele... Tübingen, Mohr, 1912.

iii, 106 p.   23 cm.
Contents. - Zum Streit um das Nexum. - Nochmals zur
Zivilität der Cognitur.

24344   Eitrem, Samson, 1872-
Ein Sklavenkauf aus der Zeit des Antonius Pius, von
S. Eitrem; mit 1 Tafel... Kristiana, Im kommission bei
J. Dybwad, 1916.
24 p.   facsim. $23\frac{1}{2}$ cm.   (Videnskapeselskapets
Forhandlinger for 1916. no. 2)

24345   Eliot, Thomas, Dawes, 1808-1870.
The territorial slave policy; the Republican Party;
what the North has to do with slavery. Speech of Hon.
Thomas D. Eliot, of Mass. Delivered in the House of
Representatives, Apr. 25, 1860. [Washington, 1960]
8 p.   23 cm.
Caption title.

24346   Ellis, Alexander.
A sermon on the operations of Divine Providence: as
seen in the abolition of slavery, and in the enactment
and ratification of the fifteenth amendment to the
federal Constitution. Preached at Joy street church,
April 10, 1870, by Rev. Alexander Ellis. Boston, Printed
by D. Clapp & son, 1870.
20 p.   24 cm.

24347   Ellison, Thomas, 1833-1904.
Slavery and secession in America, historical and
economical. By Thomas Ellison... With map and appendices.
London, S. Low, son & co. [pref. 1861]
1 p.l., xvi, 371, [1] p.   front. (fold. map)   19 cm.

24348   Emancipatie door centralisatie. Schetz van een ontwerp
tot behoud van Suriname... 's Gravenhage, P. H. Noorden-
dorp, 1847.
iv, 157 p., 1 l.   6 plans.   23 cm.

24349   Emancipation in disguise, or The true crisis of the
colonies. To which are added, considerations upon
measures proposed for their temporary relief and
observations upon colonial monopoly. Shewing, the
different effects of its enforcement and relaxation,
exposing the advantages derived by America from Louisiana;
and lastly, suggestions for a permanent plan to supply
our colonies with provisions and our navy with certain
naval stores independent of foreign supplies. London,
Printed for J. Ridgway [etc.] 1807.
2 p.l., iv, 220 p.   22 cm.
A reply to James Stephen's War in disguise.

24350   Emancipation of the Negro slaves in the West India colonies
        considered, with reference to its impolicy and injustice;
        in answer to Mr. Wilberforce's Appeal. By the author
        of 'A statement of the claims of the West India colonies
        to a protecting duty against East India sugar.'...
        London, Whitmore and Fenn, 1824-
            v.   20½ cm.

24351   Emerson, Frederick Valentine, 1871-
            Geographic influences in American slavery. [New York,
        1911]
            13-26, 106-118, 170-181 p.   illus., maps (1 fold.)
        23 cm.
            Reprinted from American Geographical Society, Bulletin,
        v. 43, 1911.

24352   [Emerson, William H   ] 1833-
            Tha ole watah mill deserted by man and doomed to silence
        and decay. And Mellissy and tha chillens. As told by
        Josiah. The black woman's burden, 1840-1865. A story of
        human slavery in Kentucky. A veneere of fiction, a
        density of fact... Astoria, Ill., Search light printing
        house, 1903.
            2 p.l., 426 p.   20 cm.

24353   Encroachments of the slave power, upon the rights of the
        North. By a northern man. Boston, For sale by B. Marsh,
        1848.
            36 p.   18½ cm.

24354   The end of the irrepressible conflict. By a merchant of
        Philadelphia. Printed for the author. Philadelphia,
        King & Baird, printers, 1860.
            47 p.   23 cm.
            A criticism of Mr. Seward's speeches in the campaign.

24355   Endemann, Wilhelm, 1825-1899.
            Die Behandlung der Arbeit im Privatrecht. Von dr. W.
        Endemann... Jena, G. Fischer, 1896.
            1 p.l., 92 p.   24½ cm.
            "Abdruck aus den Jahrbüchern für Nationalökonomie und
        Statistik. Dritte Folge, Bd. XII (LXVII)."

24356   England, John, bp., 1786-1842.
            Letters of the late Bishop England to the Hon. John
        Forsyth, on the subject of domestic slavery: to which
        are prefixed copies, in Latin and English, of the pope's
        apostolic letter, concerning the African slave trade,
        with some introductory remarks, etc. Baltimore, J.

Murphy, 1844.
    xi, [13]-156 p.   21 cm.
    Introductory notice signed: Wm. Geo. Read.

24357 [Erwin, Andrew]
        Gen. Jackson's negro speculations, and his traffic in
        human flesh, examined and established by positive proof.
        [n.p., 1828]
        16 p.   23 cm.

24358 L'esclavage dans les États Confédérés, par un missionnaire.
        2. éd. ... Paris, E. Dentu, 1865.
        ix, 147 p.   22 cm.

24359 La esclavitud de los negros y la prensa madrileña. Madrid,
        Est. tip. de T. Fortanet, 1870.
        40, [1] p.   21 cm.

24360 Essex County Anti-slavery Convention, Danvers, Mass., 1838.
        Proceedings of the Essex County Anti-slavery Convention,
        held at Danvers, October 24, 1838, with an address to
        the voters, on their duties to the enslaved. Salem,
        Printed at the Gazette office, 1838.
        12 p.   19½ cm.

24361 Estimates of the value of slaves, 1815. [New York, 1914]
        cover-title, p. 813-838.   27 cm.
        Reprinted from the American historical review, vol. XIX,
        no. 4, July 1944.

24362 Evangelical Union Anti-slavery Society of the City of
        New York.
        Address to the churches of Jesus Christ, by the
        Evangelical union anti-slavery society, of the city of
        New York, auxiliary to the Am. A. S. Society. With the
        constitution, names of officers, board of managers, and
        executive committee. April, 1839. New York, Printed
        by S. W. Benedict, 1839.
        51, [2] p.   23 cm.

24363 Evangelicus, pseud.
        Onesimus: or, The apostolic directions to Christian
        masters, in reference to their slaves, considered. By
        Evangelicus. Boston, Gould, Kendall & Lincoln, 1842.
        54 p.   15½ cm.

24364 Evans, Josiah James, 1786-1858.
        South Carolina and Massachusetts. Speech of Hon. J. J.
        Evans, of South Carolina, in reply to Mr. Sumner of

Massachusetts, Delivered in the Senate of the United
States, June 23, 1856. Washington, Printed at the
Congressional globe office, 1856.
        16 p.   24 cm.

24365   Evans, Lemuel Dale, 1810-1877.
        Speech of Hon. Lemuel D. Evans, of Texas, on the stabi-
        lity of American institutions; delivered in the House of
        Representatives, February 4, 1857. Washington, Printed
        at the Congressional globe office, 1857.
        38 p.   24 cm.

24366   Ewing, Elbert William Robinson, 1867-
        Legal and historical status of the Dred Scott decision;
        a history of the case and an examination of the opinion
        delivered by the Supreme Court of the United States,
        March 6, 1857. By Elbert William R. Ewing... Washington,
        D. C., Cobden publishing company, 1909.
        228 p.   2 port. (incl. front.) $23\frac{1}{2}$ cm.

24367   Ewing, Elbert William Robinson, 1867-
        Northern rebellion and southern secession. By E. W. R.
        Ewing, LL.B. Richmond, Va., J. L. Hill company, 1904.
        1 p.l., 383 p.   23 cm.

24368   Ewing, Thomas, 1789-1871.
        Speech of the Hon. Thomas Ewing, of Chillicothe, Ohio,
        before a Republican mass meeting, September 29th, 1860.
        Cincinnati, Rickey, Mallory & co., 1860.
        24 p.   22 cm.

24369   Extracts from a few scattered leaves of the panorama of
        liberty, democracy and slavery; their champions and
        attendants. An allegory, by a "small-fisted farmer"...
        Utica, N. Y., The author, 1861.
        76 p. $19\frac{1}{2}$ cm.
        Prose and verse.

24370   Extracts from writings of Friends, on the subject of slavery.
        Pub. by direction of the "Association of Friends for
        Advocating the Cause of the Slave, and Improving the
        condition of the Free People of Color." Philadelphia,
        Merrihew and Thompson, printers, 1839.
        24 p. $18\frac{1}{2}$ cm.

24371   Facts for the people.   v. 1, June 1853-May 1854; new ser.,
        v. 1, May 1855-Apr. 1856. Washington, G. Bailey,
        1853-56.
            2 v.   23½ cm.   (v. 1: 30 cm.)   monthly.
            Gamaliel Bailey, editor.   Publication suspended June?
        1854-Apr. 1855, inclusive.   Composed chiefly of papers
        from the National era.   No more published?

24372   Facts proving the good conduct and prosperity of emanci-
        pated negroes, and remarks on melioration.   [n.p., 183-?]
            35 p.   19 cm.
            Caption title.

24373   Fairchild, James Harris, 1817-1902.
            ... The Underground Railroad.   By James H. Fairchild...
        An address delivered for the society in Association hall,
        Cleveland, January 24, 1895.   [Cleveland?] 1895.
            [89]-121 p.   23 cm.   (Western Reserve Historical
        Society, Tracts, v. 4, no. 87)

24374   Falck, George Karel.
            ... De servo, libertate donato, si Europae solum
        attigit...   Amstelodami, ex officina typographica C. A.
        Spin, 1834.
            viii, 66 p.   21½ cm.
            Diss. - Utrecht.

24375   Farnsworth, John Franklin, 1820-1897.
            Speech of Hon. J. F. Farnsworth, of Illinois, delivered
        in the House of Representatives, December 23, 1859.
        [Washington, Buell & Blanchard, printers, 1859]
            16 p.   24½ cm.
            Caption title.

24376   Farrar, Nathan.
            Dissolution of the union, and its inevitable results,
        unless national prayers are offered up to the Supreme
        Ruler of the universe, and eminent divines again invoke
        the aid of Heaven to preserve the union unimpaired to
        the latest posterity.   By Nathan Farrar...   Louisville,
        Ky., The author, 1860.
            29, ii p.   21 cm.

24377   Fast day sermons: or, The pulpit on the state of the
        country.   New York, Rudd and Carleton, 1861.
            viii, [9]-336 p.   19½ cm.
            Contents. - Thornwell, J. H.   Our national sins. -

Palmer, B. M.   Slavery a divine trust. - Dabney, R. L.
The Christian's best motive for patriotism. - Breckinridge, R. J.   The union to be preserved. - Van Dyke,
H. J.   The character and influence of abolitionism. -
Lewis, T.   Patriarchal and Jewish servitude no argument
for American slavery. - Raphall, M. J.   Bible view of
slavery. - Vinton, F.   Fanaticism rebuked. - Beecher,
H. W.   Peace, be still. - Bellows, H. W.   The crisis of
our national disease. - Adams, W.   Prayers for rulers;
or duty of Christian patriots.

24378   Fawcett, Benjamin, 1715-1780.
        A compassionate address to the Christian negroes in
Virginia, and other British colonies in North America.
With an appendix, containing some account of the rise
and progress of Christianity among that poor people.   By
Benjamin Fawcett...   The 2d ed.   Salop, Printed by
F. Eddowes and F. Cotton, 1756.
        40 p.   15 cm.

24379   Fearon, Henry Bradshaw, b. ca. 1770.
        Sketches of America.   A narrative of a journey of
five thousand miles through the eastern and western
states of America; contained in eight reports addressed
to the thirty-nine English families by whom the author
was deputed, in June 1817, to ascertain whether any, and
what part of the United States would be suitable for
their residence.   With remarks on Mr. Birkbeck's "Notes"
and "Letters."   By Henry Bradshaw Fearon.   3d ed.
London, Longman, Hurst, Rees, Orme, and Brown, 1819.
        xv, 454 p., 1 l.   22 cm.

24380   Félice, Guillaume de, 1803-1871.
        Appel en faveur des noirs émancipés dans les États-
Unis.   Discours prononcé le 25 juin 1865, dans le Temple
de Toulouse, par G. de Félice...   Paris, C. Meyrueis
[etc.] 1865.
        32 p.   21 cm.

24381   Feliú Cruz, Guillermo, 1901-
        ... La abolición de la esclavitud en Chile; estudio
histórico y social.   [Santiago] Universidad de Chile,
1942.
        7 p.l., [3]-368 p., 1 l.   XLVII pl. (incl. ports.,
facsims.) on 27 l.   19½ cm.

24382   The fellowship of slaveholders incompatible with a Christian
        profession.   New York, American Anti-Slavery Society,
1859.
        20 p.   14 cm.

24383 Fenton, Reuben Eaton, 1819-1885.
       Designs of the slave power. Speech of Hon. Reuben E.
Fenton, of New York. Delivered in the U. S. House of
Representatives, February 24, 1858. Washington, D. C.,
Buell & Blanchard, printers, 1858.
       15 p.   25 cm.

24384 Ferguson, Jesse Babcock, 1819-1870.
       Address on the history, authority and influence of
slavery delivered in the 1st Presbyterian Church,
Nashville, Tenn., 21st of November 1830. Nashville,
J. T. S. Fall, printer, 1850.
       32 p.   22 cm.

24385 Fermin, Philippe, 1720-1790.
       D. Philipp Fermins Reise durch Surinam. Aus dem
französischen übersetzt... Potsdam, C. C. Horvath, 1782.
       2 v. in 1. 2 fold. pl., fold. map. $20\frac{1}{2}$ cm.

24386 Fernández Golfín y Ferrer, Luis, 1825-1889.
       Breves apuntes sobre las cuestiones mas importantes de
la isla de Cuba, por... D. Luis Fernández Golfín.
Barcelona, Estab. tip. del Lloyd español, 1866.
       4 p.l., 159 p.   21 cm.

24387 Ferrer de Couto, José, b. 1820.
       Enough of war! The question of slavery conclusively
and satisfactorily solved, as regards humanity at large
and the permanent interests of present owners, by D.
José Ferrer De Couto... New York, S. Hallet, printer,
1864.
       312 p. $23\frac{1}{2}$ cm.
Translation of Los negros en sus diversos estados.

24388 Ferrer de Couto, José, b. 1820.
       Los negros en sus diversos estados y condiciones;
tales como son, como se supone que son, y como deben ser,
por Don José Ferrer de Couto... Nueva York, Impr. de
Hallet, 1864.
       310 p., 1 l.   23 cm.

24389 Fielder, Herbert.
       The disunionist: a brief treatise upon the evils of
the union between the North and the South, and the
propriety of separation and the formation of a southern
United States. By Herbert Fielder, esq. of Georgia.
[n.p.] Printed for the author, 1858.
       iv p., 1 l., 7-72 p.   22 cm.

24390 Fillmore, Millard, pres. U. S., 1800-1874.
       Mr. Fillmore's views relating to slavery. The
       suppressed portion of the third annual message to
       Congress, December 6, 1852. [Buffalo, 1907]
          311-324 p.   24½ cm.
       Reprinted from Buffalo Historical Society, Publications,
       v. 10, 1907.

24391 Fisher, Elwood, 1808-1862.
          ... Lecture on the north and the south, delivered
       before the Young Men's Mercantile Library Association
       of Cincinnati, Ohio, January 16, 1849. By Elwood
       Fisher. Cincinnati, Chronicle book and job rooms, 1849.
          64 p.   21 cm.

24392 Fisher, George Purnell, 1817-1899.
          The olive branch. Remarks of Hon. George P. Fisher,
       of Delaware. Delivered in the House of Representatives,
       March 11, 1862. [Washington, L. Towers & co., printers,
       1862]
          7 p.   24½ cm.
       Caption title.

24393 [Fisher, Joshua Francis] 1807-1873.
          ... Concessions and compromises. Philadelphia,
       C. Sherman & son, printers [1860]
          cover-title, 14 p.   23½ cm.

24394 [Fisher, Sidney George] 1809-1871.
          The laws of race, as connected with slavery. By the
       author of "The law of the territories", "Rustic rhymes",
       etc. ... Philadelphia, W. P. Hazard, 1860.
          70 p.   21 cm.

24395 Fisher, Sidney George, 1809-1871.
          The trial of the Constitution. By Sidney George
       Fisher... Philadelphia, J. B. Lippincott & co.; [etc.,
       etc.] 1862.
          xv, [17]-391 p.   24 cm.

24396 [Fisher, Thomas] 1781?-1836.
          The Negro's memorial; or, Abolitionist's catechism,
       by an Abolitionist. London, Printed for the author and
       sold by Hatchard, 1825.
          iv, 127 p.   23 cm.

24397 Fisk, Theophilus.
          The bulwark of freedom. An oration delivered at the
       Universalist Church, in the city of Charleston, S. C.,

June 28, 1836, on the anniversary of the glorious
victory at Fort Moultrie, June 28, 1776. By Theophilus
Fisk. Charleston, S. C., Printed for the publishers at
the office of the Southern evangelist, 1836.
20 p.   20 cm.

24398   Fitch, Charles, 1803-1843.
Slaveholding weighed in the balance of truth, and its
comparative guilt illustrated. By Charles Fitch...
Boston, I. Knapp, 1837.
36 p. $18\frac{1}{2}$ cm.

24399   [Fitch, John] of Alton, Ill.
Chickamauga, the price of Chattanooga. A description
of the strategic plans, marches, and battles of the
campaign of Chattanooga... By the author of the "Annals
of the Army of the Cumberland". Philadelphia, J. B.
Lippincott & co., 1864.
2 p.l., 451-482, [703]-716 p.   front. (map) $22\frac{1}{2}$ cm.
"This pamphlet is issued as an addition to the first
editions of the 'Annals of the Army of the Cumberland'."
"Gen. Rosecrans' report of the Chickamauga campaign":
p. [703]-716.

24400   Fitzgerald, W   P   N
A scriptural view of slavery and abolition. By W. P. N.
Fitzgerald... New Haven, 1839.
24 p.   23 cm.

24401   [Fitzhugh, George] 1806-1881.
Slavery justified; by a southerner... Fredericksburg,
Va., Recorder printing office, 1850.
14 p.   22 cm.

24402   Fleming, William Henry, 1856-
Treaty-making power; Slavery and the race problem
in the South, by William H. Fleming. Boston, Mass.,
The Stratford company, 1920.
2 p.l., 100 p. $19\frac{1}{2}$ cm.

24403   Fletcher, John.
Studies on slavery, in easy lessons. Compiled into
eight studies, and subdivided into short lessons for
the convenience of readers. Natchez, Published by
Jackson Warner, 1852.
637 p. $22\frac{1}{2}$ cm.

24404   [Fletcher, Thomas]
The question, "How far is slavery prohibited by the

Christian religion and the Holy Scriptures?" impartially
examined. [London, Robson, Blades & co., printers] 1828.
14 p.   22 cm.

24405   Fletcher, Thomas Clement, 1827-1899.
        Missouri's jubilee. Speech of Thomas C. Fletcher,
        governor of Missouri, delivered in the State capitol,
        on the occasion of the reception by the legislature of
        the news of the passage of the convention ordinance
        abolishing slavery in Missouri. Jefferson City, W. A.
        Curry, public printer, 1865.
        6, [2] p.   22 cm.

24406   Flinter, George Dawson, d. 1838.
        A view of the present condition of the slave population
        in the island of Puerto Rico under the Spanish government.
        Showing the impolicy and danger of prematurely emanci-
        pating the West India slaves. With observations on
        the destructive tendency of injudicious reform and
        revolutionary principles on the prosperity of nations
        and colonies... By George Dawson Flinter... Philadelphia
        Printed by A. Waldie, 1832.
        1 p.l., 117 p.   21½ cm.

24407   Flournoy, John Jacobus.
        A reply, to a pamphlet, entitled "Bondage, a moral
        institution, sanctioned by the Scriptures and the Saviour,
        &c. &c." so far as it attacks the principles of
        expulsion. With no defence, however, of abolitionism.
        By J. J. Flournoy... Athens, Ga., 1838.
        67 p., 1 l.   22 cm.

24408   Follie,   b. 1761
        Voyage dans les déserts du Sahara, par M. Follie...
        Contenant, 1°. La relation de son naufrage et de ses
        aventures pendant son esclavage; 2°. Un précis exact
        des moeurs, des usages et des opinions des habitans du
        Sahara. Paris, Impr. du Cercle social (1792) l'an
        premier de la République française.
        171 p.   19½ cm.

24409   Fonseca, Luiz Anselmo da, 1853-
        A escravidão, o clero e o abolicionismo, por L. Anselmo
        da Fonseca... Bahia, Imprensa economica, 1887.
        3 p.l., [v]-vii, 686 (i.e. 742) p.   23 cm.
        Errors in paging: no. 73-112, 417-432 repeated.

24410   Foote, Henry Stuart, 1804-1880.
        California, territorial governments, &c. Remarks of

88

Hon. Mr. Foote, of Mississippi, on the plan of
adjusting the questions growing out of slavery,
reported from the special committee of the Senate.
Delivered in the Senate, May 15, 16, and 20, 1850.
[Washington, 1850]
    16 p.   23 cm.
    Caption title.

24411 Foote, Henry Stuart, 1804-1880.
    Rev. Theobald Mathew. Remarks of Hon. H. S. Foote,
of Mississippi in the Senate, December 10, 1849, on the
resolution to permit the Rev. Theobald Mathew to sit
within the bar of the Senate. [Washington, Printed at
the Congressional globe office, 1849]
    8 p.   24½ cm.
    Caption title.

24412 Forbes, Alexander C   defendant.
    The state of Ohio vs. Forbes and Armitage, arrested
upon the requisition of the government of Ohio, on
charge of kidnapping Jerry Phinney, and tried before
the Franklin Circuit Court of Kentucky, April 10, 1846.
[n.p., 1846]
    cover-title, 41 p.   23½ cm.
    Preface signed: William Johnston.

24413 Ford, Lewis, b. 1812.
    The variety book containing life sketches and reminis-
cences, by Lewis Ford. Boston, "Washington press":
G. E. Crosby & co., printers, 1892.
    243, [1] p.   23½ cm.

24414 Forman, Jacob Gilbert.
    The Christian martyrs; or, The conditions of obedience
to the civil government: a discourse by J. G. Forman,
minister of the Second Congregational Church in Nantucket;
until recently minister of the First Church and
congregation in West Bridgewater, Mass. To which is
added, a friendly letter to said church and congregation
on the pro-slavery influences that occasioned his
removal. Boston, W. Crosby and H. P. Nichols, 1851.
    51 p.   23½ cm.

24415 Forslag til ordning af vestindiske fortfatningsforhold
angaaende negerne med mere. Anon. 1826. (A proposal
for regulating the situation of negroes in the West
Indies, etc.) Translated with an introduction and
notes by N. A. T. Hall. [Charlotte Amalie, V. I.]
Bureau of Libraries, Museums & Archaeological Services,

1979.
    23 (i.e., 25) p.   illus., facsims.   27½ cm.
(Occasional papers, no. 5)

24416   [Forsyth, John] 1780-1841.
        Address to the people of Georgia. [n.p., 1840]
        8 p.   23½ cm.
        Caption title. Dated Fredericksburg, Va., August 29,
        1840.
        "Apostolical letter of our most holy lord, Gregory XVI,
        by divine providence, pope, against traffic in Negroes":
        p. 6-8.

24417   Forsyth, John, 1812-1877.
        Letters of Hon. John Forsyth... to Wm. F. Samford,
        esq., in defence of Stephen A. Douglas. [Washington,
        Printed by L. Towers] 1859.
        16 p.   22½ cm.
        Caption title.

24418   Forsyth, John, 1812-1877.
        Speech of Hon. John Forsyth... on the Senatorial
        question, in the House of Representatives of the Alabama
        legislature, November 29, 1859. [Washington] Printed
        by L. Towers [1859]
        16 p.   22½ cm.
        Caption title.

24419   Foss, John.
        A journal of the captivity and sufferings of John Foss;
        several years a prisoner at Algiers: together with
        some account of the treatment of Christian slaves when
        sick:-- and observations on the manners and customs of
        the Algerines... 2d ed. Pub. according to act of
        Congress. Newburyport, Printed by A. March [1798?]
        189 p.   18½ cm.

24420   Foster, Stephen Symonds, 1809-1881.
        The brotherhood of thieves; or, A true picture of the
        American church and clergy: a letter to Nathaniel
        Barney, of Nantucket. By Stephen S. Foster. Boston,
        Anti-slavery office, 1844.
        72 p.   17½ cm.

24421   Fourcroy, Bonaventure de, 1610(ca.)-1691.
        Les sentimens dv ievne Pline svr la poesie. Tirez de
        quelquesvnes de ses lettres. Par m^r de Fovrcroy aduocat
        en Parlement. A Paris, Chez Lovis Billaine, 1661.
        2 p.l., 207, [1] p.   15½ cm.

24422 Fox, Early Lee, 1890-
        ... The American Colonization Society, 1817-1840, by
        Early Lee Fox... Baltimore, The Johns Hopkins press,
        1919.
        vii, 9-231 p.   25 cm.   (Johns Hopkins University
        studies in historical and political science, ser. 37,
        no. 3)
        Published also as thesis (Ph.D.) by Johns Hopkins
        University, 1917.

24423 France. Chambre des députés, 1814-1848. Commission chargée
        d'examiner la proposition de m. de Tracy, relative aux
        esclaves de colonies.
        Report made to the Chamber of deputies on the abolition
        of slavery in the French colonies, by Alexis de Tocque-
        ville, July 28, 1839. Tr. from the French. Boston,
        J. Munroe and co., 1840.
        54 p.   24 cm.

24424 France. Commission des affaires coloniales.
        ... Rapport fait au ministre secrétaire d'état de la
        marine et des colonies. Paris, Imprimerie royale, 1843.
        xvi, 438 p.   28½ cm.

24425 France. Conseil d'état.
        Arrest du Conseil d'estat du roy, qui subroge la
        Compagnie des Indes aux droits & pretentions appartenant
        à la Compagnie de Saint Domingue, tant en France qu'à
        l'Amérique & autres lieux, avec le privilege exclusif
        de fournir à l'isle de Saint Domingue trente mille negres
        tirez de l'estranger. Du 10. septembre 1720...
        [A Paris, Imprimerie royale, 1720]
        4 p.   26 cm.
        Caption title.

24426 France. Laws, statutes, etc., 1643-1715 (Louis XIV)
        Code noir; ou, Edit servant de réglement pour le
        gouvernement et l'administration de la justice et de la
        police des isles françoises de l'Amérique, et pour la
        discipline et le commerce des negres et esclaves dans
        ledit pays. Du mois de mars 1685.
        414-424 p.   26½ cm.
        Reprinted from Moreau de Saint-Méry, M. L. É., ed.
        Loix et constitutions des colonies françoises de
        l'Amérique sous le vent. Paris [1784-90] v. 1,
        p. 414-424)

24427 France. Laws, statutes, etc., 1715-1774 (Louis XV)
        Ordonnace du roy, concernant les esclaves des isles

91

françoises de l'Amérique. Du 15. juin 1736... [Paris,
Imprimerie royale, 1736]
   3 p.   27 cm.
   Caption title.

24428 France. Ministère de la marine.
       ... Compte rendu au roi de l'emploi des fonds alloués,
       depuis 1839, pour l'enseignement religieux et élémentaire
       des noirs, et de l'exécution des lois dans 18 et 19
       juillet 1845, relatives au régime des esclaves, à
       l'introduction des travailleurs libres aux colonies,
       etc. Paris, Imprimerie royale, 1846.
          2 p.l., 119 p.   26 x 20½ cm.
       Signed: Bon de Mackau.

24429 Free and friendly remarks on a speech lately delivered
       to the Senate of the United States, by Henry Clay, of
       Kentucky, on the subject of the abolition of North
       American slavery... New-York, M. Day & co., 1839.
          24 p.   22½ cm.

24430 Free Church of Scotland. General Assembly.
       ... Report of the proceedings of the General Assembly
       on Saturday, May 30, and Monday, June 1, 1846. Re-
       garding the relations of the Free Church of Scotland,
       and the Presbyterian churches of America. Rev.
       Edinburgh, J. Johnstone [etc.] 1846.
          52 p.   21 cm.

24431 ... Free negroism: or, Results of emancipation in the
       North and the West India islands; with statistics of
       the decay of commerce, idleness of the Negro, his
       return to savageism, and the effect of emancipation
       upon the farming, mechanical and laboring classes.
       New York, Van Evrie, Horton & co., 1862.
          cover-title, 32 p.   21 cm.   (Anti-abolition
       tracts, no. 2)

24432 Free Produce Association of Friends, of New-York Yearly
       meeting.
          Report of the Board of managers. New-York, 18
          v.   13½-17 cm.   annual.

24433 Free Will Baptists (Founded in N. H.) Anti-slavery
       Society.
          Report. Dover [N. H.]
          v.   19 cm.   annual.

24434 Freeman, Frederick, 1799-1883.
          Yaradee; a plea for Africa, in familiar conversations

on the subject of slavery and colonization. By F.
Freeman... Philadelphia, J. Whetham, 1836.
    360 p.   17½ cm.
Also published under titles: "A plea for Africa,"
and "Africa's redemption."

24435 Freeman, George Washington, bp. 1789-1858.
       The rights and duties of slave-holders. Two dis-
       courses, delivered on Sunday, November 27, 1836. In
       Christ Church, Raleigh, North-Carolina. By George W.
       Freeman... Re-published by permission of the author,
       for "The Protestant Episcopal Society for the Advancement
       of Christianity in South-Carolina." Charleston, A. E.
       Miller, printer to the Society, 1837.
           40 p.   20 cm.

24436 Freemen awake! Would you sustain the Union; preserve
       order, tranquility and Christian feeling in your
       respective churches and congregations; and secure peace
       and happiness around your domestic firesides? Then "to
       the rescue!" (and defeat the revolutionary scheme of a
       deceitful gang of hypocritical... brawling traitors and
       dark hearted, aspiring, amalgamation demagogues.) And
       maintain your position! "and indignantly frown upon
       the first dawning of every attempt to alienate any
       portion of our country from the rest; or to enfeeble
       the sacred ties which now link together the various
       parts." Philadelphia, 1839.
           23, [1] p.   17 cm.
       Signed: Frank.

24437 Freemen's ticket. For Congress, Henry Fitzhugh, Benjamin
       P. Johnson. For Assembly, Hamilton Littlefield,
       Edward B. Judson. Address, To the Democratic electors
       of Oswego County. [n.p.] 1838.
           [1] p.   45 cm.

24438 Freire de Andrade, Alfredo Augusto.
       Rapport présenté au ministre des colonies, à propos du
       livre Portuguese slavery du missionnaire John Harris,
       par le directeur géneral des colonies A. Freire de
       Andrade. Traduction imprimée à Lisbonne le 25 janvier
       1913. Lisbonne, Imprimerie nationale, 1914.
           116 p.   22½ cm.

24439 ... A fresh catalogue of southern outrages upon northern
       citizens. New York, American Anti-slavery Society,
       1860
           iv, [5]-72 p.   19 cm.   (Anti-slavery tracts, New
       ser., no. 14)

93

24440   Freyreiss, Georg Wilhelm, 1789-1825.
        Beiträge zur näheren Kenntniss des Kaiserthums
        Brasilien nebst einer Schilderung der neuen Colonie
        Leopoldina, und der wichtigsten Erwerbzweige für euro-
        päische Ansiedler, so wie auch einer Darstellung der
        Ursachen, wodurch mehrere Ansiedelungen missglückten,
        von Georg Wilhelm Freyreiss... Erster Theil. Frankfurt
        am Main, J. D. Sauerländer, 1824.
        xii, 170 p., 1 l.   19 cm.

24441   [Frías y Jacott, Francisco de, conde de Pozos Dulces]
        1809-1877.
        Isla de Cuba. Refutación de various artículos concer-
        nientes a ese país publicados en el Diario de Barcelona
        en los meses de junio y julio 1859, por un cubano.
        Paris, Imprenta de d'Aubusson y Kugelmann, 1859.
        2 p.l., 56 p.   21 cm.

24442   Friends, Society of. London Yearly Meeting. Meeting for
        Sufferings.
        The case of our fellow creatures, the oppressed
        Africans, respectfully recommended to the serious
        consideration of the legislature of Great Britain by the
        people called Quakers. London, printed, Philadelphia,
        reprinted by Joseph Crukshank, 1784.
        13 p.   20 cm.

24443   Friends, Society of. New York Yearly Meeting.
        An address of Friends of the Yearly Meeting of New-
        York, to the citizens of the United States, especially
        to those of the Southern states, upon the subject of
        slavery. New-York, Press of M. Day & co., 1844.
        16 p.   21½ cm.

24444   Friends, Society of. New England Yearly Meeting.
        Address of the Yearly Meeting of Friends for New-
        England, held on Rhode-Island, in the sixth month,
        1837, to its own members, and those of other Christian
        communities. Pub. by direction of said meeting. New
        Bedford, J. C. Parmenter, printer, 1837.
        7 p.   23 cm.

24445   Friends, Society of. New York Yearly Meeting.
        Report of a committee of representatives of New York
        Yearly Meeting of Friends upon the condition and wants
        of the colored refugees. [New York, 1862]
        30 p.   22 cm.

24446   Friends, Society of. Philadelphia Yearly Meeting.
        An address to the quarterly, monthly and preparative

meetings and the members thereof, composing the Yearly
Meeting of Friends, held in Philadelphia, by the
committee appointed at the late Yearly Meeting to have
charge of the subject of slavery. Philadelphia,
Printed by J. Richards, 1839.
12 p.   19 cm.

24447 Friends, Society of. Philadelphia Yearly Meeting.
        Minute on slavery. [Philadelphia, 1839]
        1 l.   33 cm.

24448 Friends, Society of. Philadelphia Yearly Meeting.
        To our fellow citizens of the United States of North
America and others to whom it may concern. [Philadelphia,
1799]
        3 p.   22 cm.

24449 Friends, Society of. Philadelphia Yearly Meeting.
        Meeting for Sufferings.
        Address of the representatives of the religious
Society of Friends, commonly called Quakers, in Pennsylvania, New Jersey, Delaware, &c. to the citizens of the
United States. Philadelphia, J. & W. Kite, printers,
1837.
        15 p.   23 cm.

24450 Friends of liberty! Read this before you vote!! [n.p.,
        1838?]
        [2] p.   47 cm.

24451 [Frost, Mrs. Josephine C   ]
        Quaker marriages, births, deaths, slaves, Nine
Partners M. M., Dutchess Co., N. Y. [Brooklyn, 191-]
        1 p.l., 110, 6 numb. l.   27 cm.

24452 Frothingham, Octavius Brooks, 1822-1895.
        The last signs; a sermon preached at the Unitarian
Church in Jersey City, on Sunday morning, June 1,
1856. New York, John A. Gray's Fire-proof printing
office, 1856.
        22 p.   23 cm.

24453 Froude, James Anthony, 1818-1894.
        English seamen in the sixteenth century. Lectures
delivered at Oxford, Easter terms, 1893-4, by James
Anthony Froude... New York, C. Scribner's sons, 1895.
        3 p.l., 228 p.   21 cm.

24454 Fugette, James Preston, 1825-1899.
        ... Our country and slavery. A friendly word to the

Rev. Francis L. Hawks... and other northern clergymen.
By the Rev. James Preston Fugitt. Baltimore, Printed
by J. Robinson, 1861.
   cover-title, 86 p.   18½ cm.

24455 Fuller, Richard, 1804-1876.
       Address before the American Colonization Society.
       Delivered at Washington, D. C., January 21, 1851. By
       Richard Fuller. Baltimore, Printed at the office of
       the True union, 1851.
       17 p.   23½ cm.

24456 Fuller, Richard, 1804-1876.
       Domestic slavery considered as a Scriptural institu-
       tion: in a correspondence between the Rev. Richard
       Fuller... and the Rev. Francis Wayland... Rev. and corr.
       by the authors. New York, L. Colby; Boston, Gould,
       Kendall and Lincoln, 1845.
       viii, 254 p.   15½ cm.

24457 Fuller, Richard, 1804-1876.
       Our duty to the African race. An address delivered at
       Washington, D. C., January 21, 1851, by Richard Fuller.
       Baltimore, Printed by W. M. Innes, 1851.
       17 p.   22 cm.

24458 [Fulton, John] 1834-1907.
       The dual revolutions. Anti-slavery and pro-slavery.
       By S. M. Johnson [pseud.]   Baltimore, Printed by W. M.
       Innes, 1862.
       52 p.   22 cm.

24459 Furman, Richard, 1755-1825.
       Rev. Dr. Richard Furman's exposition of the views
       of the Baptists, relative to the coloured population
       of the United States, in a communication to the governor
       of South Carolina. Charleston, Printed by A. E. Miller,
       1823.
          p.   21 cm.

24460 Furness, William Henry, 1802-1896.
       An address delivered before a meeting of the
       members and friends of the Pennsylvania Anti-slavery
       society during the annual fair December 19, 1849. By
       W. B. Furness. Philadelphia, Merrihew & Thompson,
       printers, 1850.
       16 p.   22 cm.

24461 Furness, William Henry, 1802-1896.
       The moving power. A discourse delivered in the First

Congregational Unitarian Church in Philadelphia,
Sunday morning, Feb. 9, 1851, after the occurrence of
a fugitive slave case. By W. H. Furness. Philadelphia,
Merrihew and Thompson, printers, 1851.
16 p.   22 cm.

24462 Furness, William Henry, 1802-1896.
Put up thy sword. A discourse delivered before
Theodore Parker's society, at the Music Hall, Boston,
Sunday, March 11, 1860. By W. H. Furness... Boston,
R. F. Wallcut, 1860.
23 p.   18½ cm.

G

24463 Gaines, Thomas S
Buried alive (behind prison walls) for a quarter of a
century. Life of William Walker by Thomas S. Gaines.
Saginaw, Mich., Friedman & Hynan, 1892.
1 p.l., [5]-208 p.   20 cm.

24464 Galbreath, Charles Burleigh, 1858-1934.
Anti-slavery movement in Columbiana County. By C. B.
Galbreath. [Columbus, O., 1921]
355-395 p.   illus.   23 cm.
Reprinted from Ohio archaeological and historical
quarterly, v. 30, 1921.

24465 Galbreath, Charles Burleigh, 1858-
Ohio's fugitive slaw law, by C. B. Galbreath.
[Columbus, O., 1925]
216-240 p.   23 cm.
Reprinted from Ohio archaeological and historical
quarterly, v. 34, 1925.

24466 Galbreath, Charles Burleigh, 1858-
Thomas Jefferson's views on slavery, by C. B.
Galbreath. [Columbus, O., 1925]
184-202 p.   23 cm.
Reprinted from Ohio archaeological and historical
quarterly, v. 34, 1925.

24467 Gallatin, Albert, 1761-1849.
Peace with Mexico. By Albert Gallatin. New York,
Bartlett & Welford, 1847.
cover-title, 16 p., 1 l.   22½ cm.

24468 Garfield, James Abram, pres. U. S., 1831-1881.
Speech of Hon. James A. Garfield, of Ohio, on the

constitutional amendment to abolish slavery, delivered
in the House of Representatives, January 13, 1865.
[Washington, McGill & Witherow, printers, 1865]
   8 p.   22 cm.
   Caption title.

24469 Garnet, Henry Highland, 1815-1882.
   A memorial discourse; by Rev. Henry Highland Garnet,
delivered in the hall of the House of Representatives,
Washington city, D. C., on Sabbath, February 12, 1865.
With an introduction by James McCune Smith, M.D.
Philadelphia, J. M. Wilson, 1865.
   1 p.l., [15]-91 p.   front. (port.)   23 cm.

24470 Garnett, Muscoe Russell Hunter, 1821-1864.
   An address delivered before the Society of Alumni
of the University of Virginia, at its annual meeting.
Held in the rotunda, on the 29th of June, 1850. By
M. R. H. Garnett. Pub. by order of the Society.
Charlottesville, Printed by O. S. Allen & co., 1850.
   36 p.   22 cm.

24471 Garrettson, Freeborn, 1752-1827.
   A dialogue between Do-Justice and Professing-Christian.
Dedicated to the respective and collective abolition
societies, and to all other benevolent, humane philanthropists, in America. By Freeborn Garretson [!]...
Wilmington, Printed by P. Brynberg [1820?]
   58 p.   20 cm.

24472 Gasparin, Agénor Étienne, comte de, 1810-1871.
      Esclavage et traite, par Agénor de Gasparin...
   Paris, Joubert, 1838.
      xvi, 261 p., 1 l.   21 cm.

24473 Gasparin, Agénor Étienne, comte de, 1810-1871.
   Un grand peuple qui se relève, par le c^{te} Agénor de
Gasparin. 5. éd., rev. et cor. Paris, Calmann Lévy,
1877.
   2 p.l., viii, 414 p., 1 l.   18 cm.

24474 Gates, Seth M
   Answer of the Hon. Seth M. Gates, to the letter of
Gerrit Smith. Le Roy, N. Y., October 29, 1839.
   [1] p.   53 cm.
   Le Roy Gazette - Extra.

24475 Gaylord, N   M
   Letter to Rev. Edwin H. Chapin, Lucius R. Paige et

et al., containing reasons for refusing to sign a
protest against American slavery, by N. M. Gaylord...
Memphis, Enquirer office, 1846.
vi, [7]-31 p.   20½ cm.

24476   Gee, Joshua, 1654(ca.)-1723?
Narrative of Joshua Gee of Boston, Mass., while he
was captive in Algeria of the Barbary pirates, 1680-
1687. Hartford, 1943.
30 p.   22½ cm.   (On cover: Wadsworth Atheneum,
Publication no. 1)
Foreword, signed: Charles A. Goodwin.

24477   Geiger, Joseph H.
Remarks of Joseph H. Geiger, esq., senator from the
district of Ross and Pickaway, in the Senate of Ohio,
on Friday, January 17, 1851: to which are affixed,
a sketch of a reply by Mr. Walker, senator from
Montgomery, with Mr. Geiger's rejoinder. Chillicothe,
O., Press of the Daily Scioto gazette, 1851.
16 p.   23½ cm.

24478   George, James Zachariah, 1826-1897.
The political history of slavery in the United States...
by James Z. George... with a foreword and with a
sketch of the author's life by William Hayne Leavell...
and with a preface, somewhat in the nature of a personal
tribute, by John Bassett Moore... read carefully in
proof by Dr. Austin Baxter Keep... New York, The Neale
publishing company, 1915.
xxiv, 342 p.   front. (port.) plates.   22½ cm.

24479   Georgia. Convention, 1850.
Journal of the State convention, held in Milledgeville, in December, 1850. Milledgeville, R. M. Orme,
state printer, 1850.
34 p.   23 cm.

24480   Gibbs, Jesse Thomas, 1865-
Slavery, by J. T. Gibbs. Okawville, Ill., J. T.
Gibbs, 1913.
18 p.   16 cm.

24481   [Gilbert, Olive]
Narrative of Sojourner Truth; a bonds-woman of olden
time, emancipated by the New York Legislature in the
early part of the present century; with a history of
her labors and correspondence drawn from her "Book of
Life." Battle Creek, Mich., For the author, 1881.
xii, 13-320 p.   front. (port.) illus.   20 cm.

Narrative of Sojourner Truth, by Olive Gilbert.
Book of life, by Frances W. Titus.

24482   Gilbert, William A
        Slavery--Kansas.   Speech of Hon. William A. Gilbert,
of New York, delivered in the House of Representatives,
August 6, 1856.   [Washington, Printed at the Office
of the Congressional globe, 1856]
        8 p.   24½ cm.
        Caption title.

24483   Giles, William Branch, 1762-1830.
        Political miscellanies, comp. by William B. Giles.
[Richmond, 1829]
        569 p.   21½ cm.

24484   Gillmer, D   R
        The problem solved, or the slaveholder tested, by a
series of letters, written by D. R. Gillmer, Gerrit
Smith and Carter Braxton.   Cazenovia, Printed at the
office of the "Union Herald", 1838.
        23 p.   10½ cm.

24485   Gladstone, Sir John, bart., 1764-1851.
        A statement of facts connected with the present state
of slavery in the British sugar and coffee colonies
and in the United States of America together with a
view of the present situation of the lower classes in
the United Kingdom, contained in a letter addressed
to the Right Hon. Sir Robert Peel, bart.   London,
Baldwin and Cradock, 1830.
        30 p.   22 cm.

24486   Glasgow Emancipation Society.
        The American Board of Commissioners for Foreign
Missions, and the Rev. Dr. Chalmers, on Christian
fellowship with slaveholders: an address, by the
Glasgow Emancipation Society, to Christians of all
denominations, but especially to members of the Free
Church of Scotland.   Glasgow, Printed by D. Russell,
sold by G. Gallie [etc.] 1845.
        11 p.   18½ cm.

24487   Glasgow Female Anti-slavery Society.
        An appeal to the ladies of Great Britain, in behalf
of the American slave, by the committee of the Glasgow
Female Anti-slavery Society.   With the constitution
of the Society.   Glasgow, J. M'Leod; [etc., etc.] 1841.
        16, 2 p.   18½ cm.

24488   Glave, E   J
            Glave in Nyassaland; British raids on the slave-traders.
        Glimpses of life in Africa, from the journals of the
        late E. J. Glave. [n.p., 1896]
            589-696 p.   illus., map.   25 cm.
            Reprinted from Century, v. 62 (n.s., v. 30), Aug. 1896.

24489   Gleanings in Africa; exhibiting a faithful and correct
        view of the manners and customs of the inhabitants of
        the Cape of Good Hope and surrounding country... Inter-
        spersed with observations and reflections on the state
        of slavery in the southern extremity of the African
        continent. In a series of letters from an English
        officer during the period in which that colony was under
        the protection of the British government. Illus. with
        engravings. London, J. Cundee, 1806.
            xxi, 320 p.   fold. front., plates.   21½ cm.

24490   Glotz, Gustave, 1862-1935.
            ... Le travail dans la Grèce ancienne; histoire
        écononomique de la Grèce depuis la période homérique
        jusqu'à la conquête romaine, par Gustave Glotz...
        avec 49 gravures. Paris, F. Alcan, 1920.
            2 p.l., 468 p.   illus.   23 cm.   (Histoire
        universelle du travail)

24491   God bless Abraham Lincoln! A solemn discourse by a
        local preacher. Dedicated to the faithful. [n.p.,
        186-?]
            cover-title, 16 p.   22½ cm.

24492   [Goepp, Charles] 1827-1907.
            E pluribus unum. A political tract on Kossuth and
        America... Philadelphia, F. W. Thomas, 1852.
            cover-title, 36 p.   18½ cm.

24493   Goeschen, Otto, 1808-1865.
            Per eum hominem, qui serviat, quemadmodum nobis acquira-
        tur. Dissertatio inauguralis quam... publice defendet
        Otto Goeschen... Gottingae, ex officina Friderici
        Ernesti Huth [1832]
            62 p., 1 l.   19½ cm.
            Inaug.-diss. - Göttingen.

24494   [Goldie, William Ferguson]
            Sunshine and shadow of slave life. Reminiscences
        as told by Isaac D. Williams to "Tege" [pseud.]
        East Saginaw, Mich., Evening news printing and
        binding house, 1885.
            91 p.   22 cm.
            Title vignette (portrait)

24495   Goldschmidt, Levin, 1829-1897.
         Studien zum Besitzrecht. Sklavenbesitz. Insbesondere:
Tradition durch Urkunden. Possessio absentis. Verlust
des sklavenbesitzes. Von dr. L. Goldschmidt...
Berlin, J. Springer, 1888.
         1 p.l., 35 p.   24½ cm.
         "Sonderabdruck aus Festgabe für Rudolf von Gneist",
Jena, 1888.

24496   Gongora, Joannes de, fl. 1636.
         Don Ioannis de Gongora... Disceptatio perpolita, et
singvlaris, licêt impraemeditate apud Salmanticense
theatrum in ore magistrorum habita. Ad Salvivm Ivlianvm
lib. 3. Ad Vrseium Ferocem in 1. quidam 19. D. De
manumissis testamento. Pro obtinenda caesarea vesperorum
cathedra, & eisdem verbis, quibus tunc auditoribus
dicta, nunc typographo dictata... Salmanticae, apud
Didacum a Cossio [1636?]
         4 p.l., 28 p., 1 l.   coat of arms.   19 cm.

24497   Gooch, Daniel Wheelwright, 1820-1891.
         Organization of the territories. Speech of Hon.
Daniel W. Gooch, of Mass. Delivered in the House of
Representatives, May 11, 1860. [Washington, Buell &
Blanchard, printers, 1860]
         7, [1] p.   24½ cm.
         Caption title.

24498   Goode, William O   1798-1859.
         Admission of new states. Speech of Hon. William O.
Goode, of Virginia, in the House of Representatives,
June 9, 1858, on the policy of admitting new states
into the union, and in defense of the South against
the charge of perfidy in the repeal of the Missouri
Compromise. [Washington, Printed at the Congressional
globe office, 1858]
         8 p.   24 cm.

24499   Goodloe, Daniel Reaves, b. 1814.
         Emancipation and the war. Compensation essential to
peace and civilization... [Washington? D.C., 1861]
         12 p.   23 cm.
         Caption title.

24500   Goodloe, Daniel Reaves b. 1814.
         Inquiry into the causes which have retarded the
accumulation of wealth and increase of population in
the southern states: in which the question of slavery
is considered in a politico-economical point of view.
By a Carolinian. Washington, D. C., W. Blanchard,

printer, 1846.
    27 p.   22½ cm.

24501 Goodrich, John Z   1801-
    Non-extension of slavery the policy of "the fathers
of the Republic."--Slavery allowed, though disapproved,
in the old states, but absolutely prohibited in the
territories and new states.--Effect of this policy, and
its bearing upon the modern doctrine of state rights
and state equality, stated and considered. Speech of
Hon. J. Z. Goodrich, of Mass., delivered in the Peace
Convention in Washington, February, 1861. Boston, J. E.
Farwell and company, printers, 1864.
    31 p.   21½ cm.

24502 Goodwin, Thomas Shepard.
    The natural history of secession; or, Despotism and
democracy at necessary, eternal, exterminating war.
By Thomas Shepard Goodwin... New York, Derby & Miller,
1865.
    xvii, 19-328 p.   19½ cm.

24503 Gorman, Willis Arnold, 1816-1876.
    Boundary of Texas. Speech of Hon. W. A. Gorman of
Indiana, in the House of Representatives, Friday,
August 30, 1850, on the Texas boundary bill and slavery
agitation. [Washington, Printed at the Congressional
globe office, 1850]
    8 p.   22 cm.
    Caption title.

24504 The governing race: a book for the time, and for all
    times. By H. O. R. ... Washington, T. McGill, printer,
1860.
    102 p.   23 cm.

24505 Grady, Benjamin Franklin, 1831-
    The case of the South against the North; or, Historical
evidence justifying the southern states of the American
Union in their long controversy with the northern states.
By Benjamin Franklin Grady... Raleigh, N. C., Edwards &
Broughton, 1899.
    xxix, 345 p.   23 cm.

24506 Graffenried, Edward de.
    The effect of slavery upon the constitutions and laws
of the United States and of the state of Alabama. By
Edward de Graffenried... Read before the Alabama state
bar association, at Montgomery, Alabama, June 20th,
1903. Greensboro, Ala., The Greensboro record press

[1903]
cover-title, [11] p.   20½ cm.

24507 Granger, Amos Phelps, 1789-1866.
State sovereignty--The Constitution--slavery. Remarks
of Hon. A. P. Granger, of New York, in the House of
Representatives, February 17, 1859. [Washington? 1859]
8 p.   22½ cm.
Caption title.

24508 Granier de Cassagnac, Bernard Adolphe, 1806-1880.
... Histoire des classes ouvrières et des classes
bourgeoises, par M. Adolphe Granier de Cassagnac.
Paris, A. Desrez [etc.] 1838.
xxxii, 574 p.   20 cm.

24509 Granier de Cassagnac, Bernard Adolphe, 1806-1880.
Voyage aux Antilles, françaises, anglaises, danoises,
espagnoles; à Saint-Domingue et aux États-Unis
d'Amérique... Par A. Granier de Cassagnac. Paris,
Dauvin et Fontaine, 1842-44.
2 v.   21½ cm.
Imprint of v. 2, Au comptoir des imprimeurs-unis.

24510 Grattan, Peachy R   1801-1881.
Speech of Peachy R. Grattan, esq., in the General
Assembly at Cleveland, June 2, 1857. Richmond, H. K.
Ellyson's steam power presses, 1857.
22 p.   23 cm.

24511 [Grayson, William John] 1788-1863.
Reply to Dr. Dewey's address, delivered at the elm
tree, Sheffield, Mass. With extracts from the same.
Charleston, S. C., Published by request, 1856.
32 p.   23½ cm.

24512 Gt. Brit. Colonial Office.
Sierra Leone. Correspondence relating to domestic
slavery in the Sierra Leone Protectorate. Presented
by the secretary of state for the colonies to Parliament
by command of His Majesty, January, 1928. London,
H. M. Stationery off., 1928.
78 p. incl. form.   24½ cm.   ([Parliament.
Papers by command] Cmd. 8020)

24513 Gt. Brit. Foreign Office.
... Papers relating to slavery in the Sudan. Presented
by the secretary of state for foreign affairs to
Parliament by command of His Majesty. London, H. M.
Stationery off. [1926]

18 p.   24½ cm.   (Sudan, no. 1 (1926))
Parliament. Papers by command. Cmd. 2650.

24514   Gt. Brit. Foreign Office.
... The question of slavery. Letters from the British
government, transmitting despatches showing the situation
with respect to slavery in the British colonies and
protectorates and territories under British mandate.
Geneva, 1924.
12 p.   33 cm.
Caption title. At head of title: ... League of nations.
Official no.: A.25(a)1924.VI.

24515   Gt. Brit. India Office.
... Memorandum regarding slavery in the Kukawng Valley
in upper Burma. Geneva, 1925.
2 p.   33 cm.
Caption title. At head of title: ... League of nations.
Official no.: A.50.1925.VI (C.T.E.53)

24516   Gt. Brit. Parliament.
Substance of the debates on a resolution for abolishing
the slave trade, which was moved in the House of Commons
on the 10th June, 1806, and in the House of Lords on the
24th June, 1806. With an appendix, containing notes and
illustrations. London, Phillips and Fardon [etc.] 1806.
xi, [1], 216 p.   fold. pl.   19½ cm.

24517   Gt. Brit. Parliament, 1819.
Papers relating to the slave trade. Presented to
both Houses of Parliament by command of the Prince
Regent. [London] 1819.
23-92 p.   23½ cm.

24518   Gt. Brit. Parliament, 1839. House of Commons.
Extracts from papers, printed by order of the House
of Commons, 1839, relative to the West Indies... By
authority. London, Printed by W. Clowes & sons, for
H. M. Stationery off., 1840.
xxiii, 678 p., 1 l. incl. tables.   25 cm.

24519   Gt. Brit. Treaties, etc., 1837-1901 (Victoria)
Additional article to the treaty concluded at Lisbon,
July 3, 1842, between Her Majesty and the Queen of
Portugal, for the suppression of the traffick in slaves,
signed at Lisbon, October 22, 1842... London, Printed
by T. R. Harrison [1843]
1 p.l., 2 p.   35 cm.

24520   Gt. Brit. Treaties, etc., 1837-1901 (Victoria)
        ... Convention between Great Britain and Egypt for the
        suppression of slavery and the slave trade. Signed at
        Cairo, November 21, 1895. London, Printed for H. M.
        Stationery off. by Harrison and sons [1896]
            1 p.l., 8 p.   24 cm.   ([Gt. Brit. Foreign office]
        Treaty series, no. 16. 1895)
            Gt. Brit. Parliament. Papers by command. C.7929.

24521   Great orations by Clay, Fox, Gladstone, Lincoln, O'Connell,
        Phillips, Pitt, Webster, and others; with a critical
        introduction by Thomas B. Reed... New York, D. Appleton
        and company, 1899.
            1 p.l., xiii, 451 p.   front., 8 port., facsim. in
        colors. $23\frac{1}{2}$ cm.   (Half-title: The World's great
        books... Aldine ed.)
            Contents. - Lord Chatham on the American stamp act. -
        Henry Grattan on the Declaration of Irish rights. -
        William Pitt on the slave-trade. - John Philpot Curran
        on the trial of Archibald Hamilton Rowan. - Charles
        James Fox on the French overtures for peace. - Daniel
        O'Connell on the recovery of Catholic rights. - Daniel
        Webster. The Bunker Hill monument. - Henry Clay in
        defence of the American system. - Richard Lalor Sheil
        on the Irish municipal bill. - John Bright on the
        foreign policy of England. - Wendell Phillips. Toussaint
        L'Ouverture. - Henry Ward Beecher. Union and emancipa-
        tion. - Abraham Lincoln. The Gettysburg address.
        Second inaugural address. - Lord Beaconsfield on the
        principles of the conservative party. - William Ewart
        Gladstone. Domestic and foreign affairs. - James
        Gillespie Blaine. James Abram Garfield.

24522   Greeley, Horace, 1811-1872.
            The American conflict: a history of the great rebellion
        in the United States of America, 1860-'65: its causes,
        incidents, and results: intended to exhibit especially
        its moral and political phases, with the draft and
        progress of American opinion respecting human slavery,
        from 1776 to the close of the war for the Union. By
        Horace Greeley... Hartford, O. D. Case & company,
        1879, '77.
            2 v.   fronts., illus., plates, ports., maps. $24\frac{1}{2}$ cm.

24523   Greene, Beriah, 1795-1874.
            The counsel of Caiaphas: a sermon. [n.p., 18--?]
            8 p.   26 cm.

24524   Green, Elisha Winfield.
            Life of Rev. Elisha W. Green, one of the founders of

the Kentucky Normal and Theological Institute...
and over thirty years a pastor of the colored Baptist
churches of Maysville and Paris. Written by himself.
Maysville, Ky., The Republican printing office, 1888.
3 p.l., 60 p.   front. (port.)   32 cm.

24525 Green, James Stephen, 1817-1870.
California and New Mexico. Speech of Hon. James S.
Green, of Missouri, in the House of Representatives,
April 4, 1850, in Committee of the Whole on the State
of the Union, on the President's message transmitting
the constitution of California. [Washington, Printed
at the Congressional globe office, 1850]
8 p.   23 cm.
Caption title.

24526 Green, James Stephen, 1817-1870.
Territorial policy. Speech of Hon. James S. Green, of
Missouri, in the Senate of the United States, January 10
and 11, 1860. [Washington, Printed at the office of the
Congressional globe, 1860]
24 p.   22 cm.
Caption title.

24527 Green, William, Slave.
Narrative of events in the life of William Green,
(formerly a slave) Written by himself. Springfield
[Mass.] L. M. Guernsey, printer, 1853.
23 p.   19 cm.

24528 Greville, Robert Kaye, 1794-1866.
Slavery and the slave trade in the United States of
America; and the extent to which the American churches
are involved in their support. Drawn up at the request
of the committee of the Edinburgh Emancipation Society,
by Robert Kaye Greville, LL.D. Edinburgh, W. Oliphant
and sons, and W. P. Kennedy; [etc., etc.] 1845.
24 p.   17½ cm.

24529 Grimes, James Wilson, 1816-1872.
Speech of Hon. James W. Grimes, of Iowa, on the
surrender of slaves by the army; delivered in the Senate
of the United States, April 14, 1862. Washington,
Printed at the Congressional globe office, 1862.
7 p.   23 cm.

24530 Grimes, William, b. 1784.
Life of William Grimes, the runaway slave. Written
by himself. New-York, 1825.
iv, [5]-68 p.   23½ cm.

24531   Grimke, Angelina Emily, 1805-1879.
         Slavery and the Boston riot. Philadelphia, 1835.
         Philadelphia, 1835.
         [1] p.   32 cm.
         Printed copy of the letter written to William Lloyd
         Garrison.

24532   Gross, Ezra Carter, d. 1829.
         Speech of Mr. Gross, of New York, on the restriction
         of slavery in Missouri. Delivered in the House of
         Representatives of the United States, February 1, 1820.
         [Washington, 1820]
         14 p.   19 cm.
         Caption title.

24533   Grow, Galusha Aaron, 1822-1907.
         Remarks of Messrs. Grow, Quitman, and T. L. Harris,
         on the Missouri compromise, and the responsibility for
         the organization of the House. Delivered January 18
         and 19, 1856. Washington, Printed at the Congressional
         globe office, 1856.
         8 p. $24\frac{1}{2}$ cm.

24534   Grunebaum-Ballin, Paul Frédéric Jean, 1871-
         Henri Grégoire, l'ami des hommes de toutes les couleurs;
         la lutte pour la suppression de la traite et l'abolition
         de l'esclavage, 1789-1831. [Paris, Société d'éditions
         françaises et internationales, 1948]
         278 p.   20 cm.   (Collection de la Société des amis
         de l'abbé Grégoire, 1)

24535   Gupte, Pranay B
         City of Moors and blacks fights old evil: slavery.
         [New York, 1980]
         [1] p.   map.   37 cm.
         Reprinted from The New York Times, September 10, 1980.

24536   Gurley, Ralph Randolph, 1797-1872.
         Letter on the American Colonization Society, and
         remarks on South Carolina opinions on that subject.   By
         R. R. Gurley. [Washington? 1832]
         16 p.   24 cm.
         Caption title.

24537   Gurley, Ralph Randolph, 1797-1872.
         Letter to the Hon. Henry Clay, president of the
         American Colonization Society, and Sir Thomas Powell
         Buxton, chairman of the general committee of the African
         Colonization Society, on the colonization and civilizatior

of Africa. With other documents on the same subject.
By R. R. Gurley. London, Wiley and Putnam, 1841.
x, 66 p.   21½ cm.

24538 Guseo, Marco.
... Le riforme cinesi; costituzione cinese, assemblea
nazionale, abolizione della schiavitu. Agosto del 1910.
Torino [etc.] Fratelli Bocca, 1911.
2 p.l., [7]-89 p., 3 l., 71 p.   24 cm.

24539 Gutiérrez y Salazar, Pedro.
Reformas de Cuba. Cuestión social. Abolición de la
esclavitud, indemnización á los perjudicados con la
abolición por medio de la organización del trabajo, de la
inmigración y de las reformas económicas y administra-
tivas que deben plantearse immediatamente, con dos
apéndices de interés para los generales y permanentes
de la isla de Cuba, por el doctor Don Pedro Gutiérrez
y Salazar... Madrid, Impr. de M. G. Hernandez, 1879.
85 p., 1 l.   22½ cm.

H

24540 Haerne, Désiré Pierre Antoine de, 1804-1890.
The American question, by Canon de Haerne... translated
by Thomas Ray. London, W. Ridgeway, 1863.
1 p.l., iii, [5]-114 p.   23 cm.

24541 Haiser, Franz, 1871-
Die Sklaverei, ihre biologische Begründung und sittliche
Rechfertigung. Zwei Vorlesungen. München, J. F. Lehmann,
1923.
71 p.   23 cm.

24542 Hale, John Parker, 1806-1873.
Speech of John P. Hale, of New Hampshire, on the
abolition of slavery in the District of Columbia.
Delivered in the Senate of the United States, March 18,
1862. [Washington, L. Towers & co., printers, 1862]
8 p.   22½ cm.
Caption title.

24543 Halkin, Léon, 1872-
Les esclaves publics chez les Romains. Bruxelles,
Société belge de librairie, 1897.
254 p.   23 cm.   (Bibliothèque de la Faculté de
philosophie & lettres de l'Université de Liége, fasc. 1)

24544 Hall, James.
          An address to the free people of color of the state of
       Maryland, by James Hall, general agent of the Maryland
       State Colonization Society. Baltimore, Printed by J. D.
       Troy, 1859.
          cover-title, 15, [1] p. incl. ports.   22½ cm.

24545 Hallett, Benjamin Franklin, 1797-1862.
          Speech of the Hon. B. F. Hallett at the Democratic
       ratification meeting [i]n Waltham, Mass., Friday evening,
       November 2, 1855. Published at the request of the
       Democratic town committee. [Boston] Printed at the
       office of the Boston post [1855]
          12 p.   22 cm.

24546 Hamilton, James Cleland, 1836-
          The Panis; an historical outline of Canadian Indian
       slavery in the eighteenth century, by James Cleland
       Hamilton... Toronto, Arbuthnot brothers & co., printers
       [1897]
          1 p.l., 19-27 p.   26 cm.
          "From Proceedings of the Canadian institute, n.s. -
       vol. I, part I, no. 1, 1897."

24547 Hamilton, John Church, 1792-1882.
          ... The slave power: its heresies and injuries to the
       American people. A speech, by John C. Hamilton.
       November, 1864. [New York, 1864?]
          23 p.   22 cm.   (Loyal Publication Society...
       [Pamphlets, no. 74])

24548 [Hamilton, Joseph Grégoire de Roulhac] 1878-
          ... Benjamin Sherwood Hedrick. Chapel Hill, N. C.,
       The University, 1910.
          42 p.   22½ cm.   (University of North Carolina,
       James Sprunt Historical Publications, v. 10, no. 1)

24549 Hamilton, Robert S
          Discourse on the scheme of African colonization,
       delivered before the colonization society, of Greene
       County, O. at Xenia, July 4, 1849. By Robert S.
       Hamilton... Cincnnati, Chronicle book and job rooms,
       1849.
          32 p.   22 cm.

24450 Hamilton, William.
          An oration delivered in the African Zion Church, on
       the fourth of July, 1827, in commemoration of the
       abolition of domestic slavery in this state. By

William Hamilton. New-York, Printed by Gray & Bunce, 1827.
16 p. 20½ cm.

24551 Hamilton, William Thomas, 1796-1884.
The duties of masters and slaves respectively: or, Domestic servitude as sanctioned by the Bible: a discourse, delivered in the Government-street church, Mobile, Ala., by Rev. W. T. Hamilton... on Sunday night, December 15, 1844. Mobile, F. H. Brooks, 1845.
24 p. 23 cm.
Caption title.

24552 Hamlin, Hannibal, 1809-1891.
Speech of Hon. Hannibal Hamlin, of Maine, in the United States Senate, March 9 and 10, 1858, in reply to Governor Hammond, and in defence of the North and northern laborers. [Washington, 1858]
16 p. 23 cm.
Caption title.

24553 [Hammond, James Henry] 1807-1864, supposed author.
The North and the South; a review of the lecture on the same subject, delivered by Mr. Elwood Fisher, before the Young men's mercantile association of Cincinnati, Ohio... Charleston, Printed by J. S. Burges, 1849.
2 p.l., 39 p. 21 x 12 cm.
From the Southern quarterly review for July, 1849.

24554 Hammond, James Henry, 1807-1864.
Selections from the letters and speeches of the Hon. James H. Hammond, of South Carolina. New York, J. F. Trow & co., printers, 1866.
iv, [5]-368 p. 24 cm.

24555 Hammond, James Henry, 1807-1864.
Two letters on slavery in the United States, addressed to Thomas Clarkson, esq., by J. H. Hammond. Columbia, Allen, McCarter & co., 1845.
51, [1] p. 23½ cm.

24556 Hardin, Benjamin, 1784-1852.
Speech of Mr. Hardin, of Kentucky... delivered in the House of Representatives of the United States, February 4, 1820. [Washington? 1820]
27 p. 18½ cm.
Caption title.

24557 Harding, Aaron.
Emancipation of slaves in rebel states. Speech of

Hon. A. Harding, of Kentucky, in the House of Representatives, December 17, 1861, on the joint resolution relative to the right and duty of the President in regard to persons held as slaves in any military district in a state of insurrection. [Washington, Scammell & co., printers, 1861]
    16 p.   22 cm.
    Caption title.

24558 Hardwick, Mrs. J   P
    ... Liberty or death! or, The mother's sacrifice. By Mrs. J. P. Hardwick. Harrisburg, Printed for the authoress, 1862.
    cover-title, 9-104 p. $19\frac{1}{2}$ x $11\frac{1}{2}$ cm.

24559 Harper, Francis P
    ... A catalogue of a very complete collection of books and pamphlets relating to the American Civil War 1861-5 and slavery. Including many rare regimental histories, prison narratives, Confederate reports, privately printed biographies, poetry, etc. ... For sale by Francis P. Harper. New York [1898]
    cover-title, 63 p.   23 cm.
    At head of title: No. 79, February, 1898.

24560 Harper, Robert G
    An argument against the policy of re-opening the African slave trade, by Robert G. Harper, esq. Atlanta, Ga., Printed by C. R. Hanleiter, 1858.
    78 p.   21 cm.

24561 Harper, William, 1790-1847.
    Memoir on slavery, read before the Society for the Advancement of Learning, of South Carolina, at its annual meeting at Columbia, 1837. By Chancellor Harper. Charleston, J. S. Burges, 1838.
    61 p.   24 cm.

24562 Harris, Joel Chandler, 1848-1908.
    Uncle Remus, his songs and his sayings: the folk-lore of the old plantation, by Joel Chandler Harris: with illustrations by Federick S. Church and James H. Moser. New York, D. Appleton and company, 1881 [i.e. 1880]
    231 p.   front., illus., plates. $19\frac{1}{2}$ cm.

24563 Harris, Sir John Hobbis, 1874-
    Africa: slave or free? By John H. Harris... with preface by Sir Sydney Oliver... London, Student Christian Movement [c1919]
    [4], v-xix, [3], 3-244 p. $21\frac{1}{2}$ cm.

24564   Harris, Sir John Hobbis, 1874-
         The chartered millions; Rhodesia and the challenge
         to the British commonwealth, by John H. Harris...
         London, The Swarthmore press ltd. [1920]
             320 p.   22½ cm.
             Map on lining-papers.

24565   Harris, Sir John Hobbis, 1874-
         Dawn in darkest Africa, by John H. Harris; with an
         introduction by the Right Hon. the Earl of Cromer...
         New York, E. P. Dutton & company, 1912.
             xxxvi, 308 p.   front., plates, ports., fold. map.
         24½ cm.

24566   Harris, Sir John Hobbis, 1874-
             Portuguese slavery: Britain's dilemma. London,
         Methuen [1913]
             127 p.   19 cm.

24567   Harris, Sir John Hobbis, 1874-
             Slavery or "sacred trust"? By John H. Harris...
         preface by Prof. Gilbert Murray... with an appendix
         giving the complete text of the mandates (with the
         exception of repetition clauses) conferred upon the
         mandatory power by the League of Nations. London,
         Williams and Norgate ltd., 1926.
             xii, 195 p.   20 cm.

24568   Harris, Norman Dwight, 1870-
             The history of Negro servitude in Illinois, and of
         the slavery agitation in that state, 1719-1864, by
         N. Dwight Harris... Chicago, A. C. McClurg & co., 1904.
             x p., 1 l., 276 p.   front., ports., facsims.   20½ cm.

24569   Harris, Thaddeus Mason, 1768-1842.
             A discourse delivered before the African Society in
         Boston, 15th of July, 1822, on the anniversary cele-
         bration of the abolition of the slave trade. By Rev.
         Thaddeus Mason Harris, D.D. Boston, Printed by
         Phelps and Farnham, 1822.
             27 p.   20 cm.

24570   Harris, Thomas L   1816-1858.
             Letter of Hon. Thos. L. Harris, of Illinois, upon
         the repeal of the fugitive slave law. Washington,
         Printed by J. T. Towers, 1851.
             12 p.   23½ cm.

24571   Harris, Thomas L   1816-1858.
             Speech of Hon. T. L. Harris, of Illinois, upon the

Kansas and other political questions, and in reply to
Messrs. Foster, of Georgia, and Norton, of Illinois.
Delivered in the House of Representatives, August 9,
1856. Washington, Printed by J. T. & L. Towers, 1856.
16 p.   22½ cm.

24572   [Harrison, Jesse Burton] 1805-1841.
        Review of the slave question, extracted from the
American quarterly review, Dec. 1832; based on the speech
of Th. Marshall, of Fauquier: showing that slavery is the
essential hindrance to the prosperity of the slave-
holding states; with particular reference to Virginia.
Though applicable to other states where slavery exists.
By a Virginian. Richmond, Printed by T. W. White, 1833.
        48 p.   23 cm.

24573   Harrison, Richard Almgill, 1824-1904.
        The suppression of the rebellion. Speech of Hon.
Richard A. Harrison, of Ohio. Delivered in the House of
Representatives, January 23, 1862. [Washington, L. Tower
& co., printers, 1862]
        8 p.   24½ cm.
        Caption title.

24574   Harrison's national debt. Assumption of the state debts.
        [n.p., 1840?]
        4 p.   22½ cm.
        Caption title.
        Contains also "British and American abolitionists."

24575   Hart, Albert Bushnell, 1854-1943, ed.
        ... The romance of the Civil war; selected and
annotated by Albert Bushnell Hart... with the collabora-
tion of Elizabeth Stevens... New York, The Macmillan
company; London, Macmillan & co., ltd., 1903.
        xiv p., 1 l., 418 p.   front., illus. (incl. ports.)
        19½ cm.   (Source-readers in American history, no. 4)

24576   Hart, Albert Bushnell, 1854-1943.
        Slavery and abolition, 1831-1841, by Albert Bushnell
Hart. New York, London, Harper & brothers, 1906.
        xv, 360 p.   front. (port.) maps.   22 cm.
        (The American nation: a history, v. 16)

24577   Hatfield, Edwin Francis, 1807-1883, comp.
        Freedom's lyre; or, Psalms, hymns, and sacred songs,
for the slave and his friends. Comp. by Edwin F.
Hatfield. New-York, S. W. Benedict, 1840.
        vi, 265 p.   11½ cm.

24578 Havana. Ordinances, etc.
       [Reglas que deban seguirse en el recibo, entrega,
       destino y cuenta y razon de cimarrones. Habana? 1856?]
       7 p., 2 l. incl. forms.   20½ cm.

24579 Hawkins, William George, 1823-1909.
       Lunsford Lane; or, Another helper from North Carolina.
       By the Rev. William G. Hawkins... Boston, Crosby &
       Nichols, 1863.
       xii, 13-305 p.   front. (port.)   19 cm.

24580 Hazard, Caroline, 1856-
       Thomas Hazard, son of Robt, call'd College Tom. A study
       of life in Narragansett in the XVIIIth century, by his
       grandson's granddaughter, Caroline Hazard. Boston and
       New York, Houghton, Mifflin and company, 1893.
       viii p., 1 l., 324 p.   front. (map)   facsims. 22½ cm.

24581 Heathcote, Charles William, 1882-
       The Lutheran Church and the civil war, by Charles William
       Heathcote... New York, Chicago [etc.] Fleming H. Revell
       company [c1919]
       160 p.   19½ cm.

24582 Hebbard, William Wallace.
       The night of freedom: an appeal, in verse, against the
       great crime of our country, human bondage! By William
       Wallace Hebbard... Boston, S. Chism, 1857.
       42 p.   23½ cm.

24583 [Heeckeren, Godard Philip Cornelis van]? 1791-1833.
       Aanteekeningen, betrekkelyk de kolonie Suriname...
       Arnhem, C. A. Thieme, 1826.
       1 p.l., iv p., 1 l., 131 p.   2 maps.   22 cm.

24584 Helper, Hinton Rowan, 1829-1909.
       Nojoque; a question for a continent. By Hinton Rowan
       Helper... New York, G. W. Carleton & co.; [etc., etc.]
       1857.
       x, [11]-479 p.   18½ cm.

24585 [Helps, Sir Arthur] 1813-1875.
       The conquerors of the New World and their bondsmen;
       being a narrative of the principal events which led to
       Negro slavery in the West Indies and America...
       London, W. Pickering, 1848-52.
       2 v.   19 cm.

24586 [Helps, Sir Arthur] 1813-1875.
       Friends in council: a series of readings and discourse

　　　　thereon.　London, W. Pickering, 1851.
　　　　2 v.　　18 cm.

24587　Hendrick, John Thilman, b. 1811.
　　　　Union and slavery. A Thanksgiving sermon, delivered in
　　　　the Presbyterian Church, Clarksville, Tennessee, November
　　　　28th, 1850. By J. T. Hendrick, pastor. Clarksville,
　　　　Tenn., Printed by C. O. Faxon, 1851.
　　　　28 p.　　18 cm.

24588　Henry, Howell Meadoes, 1879-
　　　　The police control of the slave in South Carolina...
　　　　by H. M. Henry... Emory, Va., 1914.
　　　　x, 216 p.　　23½ cm.
　　　　Thesis (Ph.D.) - Vanderbilt university, 1913.

24589　Henry, Jabez, d. 1835.
　　　　Points in manumission and cases of contested freedom.
　　　　By J. Henry... London, W. Reed, 1817.
　　　　1 p.l., [v]-xxii p., 1 l., 164 p.　　21½ cm.

24590　Henry, Joseph.
　　　　A statement of facts respecting the condition & treatme
　　　　of slaves, in the city of Vicksburgh and its vicinity,
　　　　in the state of Mississippi, in 1838 & '39. By Joseph
　　　　Henry. Medina, O., Printed, 1839.
　　　　24 p.　　18½ cm.

24591　Henson, Josiah, 1789-1883.
　　　　Father Henson's story of his own life. With an intro-
　　　　duction by Mrs. H. B. Stowe. Boston, J. P. Jewett and
　　　　company; Cleveland, O., H. P. B. Jewett, 1858.
　　　　xii, 212 p.　　front. (port.)　　19 cm.

24592　Hernández Arvizu, Juan A
　　　　Proyecto de ley sobre abolición de la esclavitud en la
　　　　isla de Puerto Rico. Redactado por D. Juan A. Hernández
　　　　Arvizu... Madrid, Impr. á cargo de T. Alonso, 1869.
　　　　30 p.　　23½ cm.

24593　Hernández Iglesias, Fermín, 1833-
　　　　La esclavitud y el Señor Ferrer de Couto, por don Fermí
　　　　Hernández Iglesias, con un prólogo de don Julián Sánchez
　　　　Ruano. Madrid, Imprenta universal, á cargo de L. Polo,
　　　　1866.
　　　　52 p., 1 l.　　23 cm.

24594　Heston, Alfred Miller, 1854-
　　　　Story of the slave: paper read before the Monmouth

County Historical Association on October 30th, 1902,
wherein is given some account of slavery and servitude
in New Jersey, with notes concerning slaves and redemp-
tioners in other states, by Alfred M. Heston... Camden,
N. J., S. Chew & sons company, 1903.
40 p.   22 cm.

24595   Heward, Robert.
Slavery in the West Indies. Re-published from the West-
minster review, no. XXII [Oct. 1829] on the 1st Jan. 1830;
by Robert Heward... London, Cowie and Strange [etc., 1830]
8 p.   1 illus.   22 cm.
Caption title.
Illustration by George Cruikshank.

24596   Heyburn, Henry R[ueter] 1957-
Looking backward in the New South: the rise of agra-
rianism. Submitted in partial requirements [!] for the
degree of bachelor of arts with honors in the Department
of History, Middlebury College, April 16, 1979.
[Middlebury, Vt., 1979?]
83 p.   28 cm.

24597   [Heyrick, Elizabeth (Coltman)]   1769-1831.
No British slavery; or, An invitation to the people
to put a speedy end to it. Abridged. Birmingham,
Printed by B. Hudson, 1829.
8 p.   20 cm.

24598   [Higginson, Francis John] 1806-1872.
Remarks on slavery and emancipation... Boston, Hilliard,
Gray, and company, 1834.
2 p.l., 105 p.   19 cm.

24599   Higginson, Thomas Wentworth, 1823-1911.
Cheerful yesterdays, by Thomas Wentworth Higginson...
Boston and New York, Houghton, Mifflin and company, 1898.
5 p.l., 374 p., 1 l.   19½ cm.

24600   Higginson, Thomas Wentworth, 1823-1911.
Massachusetts in mourning. A sermon, preached in
Worcester, on Sunday, June 4, 1854. By Thomas Wentworth
Higginson... Boston, J. Munroe and company, 1854.
15 p.   24 cm.

24601   Higginson, Thomas Wentworth, 1823-1911.
Travellers and outlaws; episodes in American history,
by Thomas Wentworth Higginson... Boston, Lee and Shepard;
New York, C. T. Dillingham, 1889.
5, 11-340 p.   18 cm.

24602   Hildreth, Richard, 1807-1865.
        ... L'esclave blanc, par Hildreth; traduction de La
Bédollière. Paris, G. Barba, 1853.
       2 p.l., 332 p.   18½ cm.
       At head of title: Le compagnon du père Tom.
       Cover dated: 1856.
       The first edition of the English original was published
in Boston, 1836, under title: The slave; or, Memoirs of
Archy Moore.

24603   Hill, Isaac, 1788-1851.
        Speech of Mr. Hill, of New Hampshire, on the motion of
Mr. Calhoun that the Senate refuse to receive a petition
from the Society of Friends, in the state of Pennsylvania
to abolish slavery in the District of Columbia. In
Senate, February 12, 1836. [Washington, 1836]
       8 p.   26 cm.
       Caption title.

24604   Hill, Pascoe Grenfell, 1804-1882.
        Fifty days on board a slave-vessel in the Mozambique
Channel, in April and May, 1843. New York, J. Winchester
[1844]
       29 p.   map, music.   22 cm.

24605   [Hillard, Isaac] b. 1737.
        To the Honorable the General Assembly of the state of
Connecticut, to be holden at Hartford, on the second
Thursday of May next. The memorial of Harry, Cuff, and
Cato, black men, now in slavery in Connecticut, in behalf
of ourselves and the poor black people of our nation in
like circumstances... [n.p., 1797?]
       12 p.   21 cm.
       Caption title.

24606   [Hillhouse, William] 1757-1833.
        The crisis, no. 1-2. Or Thoughts on slavery, occasione
by the Missouri question... New-Haven, Printed by A. H.
Maltby & co., no. 4, Globe-building, Chapel-street,
1820.
       2 nos.   21½ cm.

24607   [Hillhouse, William] 1757-1833.
        Pocahontas; a proclamation: with plates. [New Haven,
J. Clyme, 1820]
       16 p.   2 pl.   23 cm.

24608   Hilliard, Henry Washington, 1808-1892.
        De Vane: a story of plebeians and patricians. By Hon.

Henry W. Hilliard... New York, Blelock & company, 1865.
2 v. in 1.   19 cm.
Paged continuously.
Announced by West and Johnston, Richmond, Va., under
title "De Vere" as in press January 1862, to be published
in February. Probably never issued, however, with
Confederate States imprint.

24609 Hillis, Newell Dwight, 1858-1929.
The battle of principles; a study of the heroism and
eloquence of the anti-slavery conflict, by Newell Dwight
Hillis, D.D. New York, Chicago [etc.] Fleming H. Revell
company [c1912]
334 p.   18½ cm.

24610 Hints on a cheap mode of purchasing the liberty of a slave
population... New York, G. A. Newmann, 1838.
21 p.   17 cm.

24611 Historia de la revolución de México contra la dictadura de
general Santa-Ana, 1853-1855... Reimpreso en San Diego,
Tex., Impr. del Sun [1901]
1 p.l., ii, 300, [iii]-lxi p.   20½ cm.
First pub. in Mexico, 1855.

24612 Historical notes on slavery and colonization; with particular
reference to the efforts which have been made in favor of
African colonization in New Jersey. Elizabeth-Town [N. J.]
Printed by E. Sanderson, 1842.
53 p.   2 pl. (incl. front.)   23 cm.

24613 A history of the trial of Castner Hanway and others, for
treason, at Philadelphia in November, 1851. With an
introduction upon the history of the slave question. By
a member of the Philadelphia bar. Philadelphia, U. Hunt
& sons, 1852.
86 p.   22 cm.

24614 Hodges, William R
... "Lest we forget," by Companion William R. Hodges.
Saint Louis, Woodward & Tiernan printing company [1912]
14 p.   23 cm.
At head of title: Commandery of the state of Missouri,
Military Order of the Loyal Legion, April 6, 1912.

24615 [Hodgman, Stephen Alexander]
The nation's sin and punishment; or, The hand of God
visible in the overthrow of slavery. By a chaplain of
the U. S. Army, who has been, thirty years, a resident

of the slave states. New York, American news company, 1864.
274 p.   19 cm.

24616   Hodgson, Studholme John, 1805-1890.
Truths from the West Indies. Including a sketch of Madeira in 1833. By Captain Studholme Hodgson... London W. Ball, 1838.
xv, 372 p.   front.   20 cm.

24617   Holcombe, James Philemon, 1820-1873.
An address delivered before the seventh annual meeting of the Virginia State Agricultural Society, November 4th, 1858, by J. P. Holcombe, esq. Pub. by unanimous request of the Society. Richmond, Macfarlane & Fergusson, 1858.
21 p.   23 cm.

24618   [Holland, Edwin Clifford] 1794-1824.
A refutation of the calumnies circulated against the southern and western states, respecting the institution and existence of slavery among them. To which is added, a minute and particular account of the actual state and condition of their negro population. Together with historical notices of all the insurrections that have taken place since the settlement of the country... By a South-Carolinian. Charleston, Printed by A. E. Miller, 1822.
vi, [7]-86 p., 1 l.   23½ cm.

24619   Holley, Myron, 1779-1841.
Address delivered before the Rochester Anti-slavery Society, on the 19th January, and again, by request of several citizens, at the court house, in Rochester, on the 5th February, 1837. Rochester, Printed by Hoyt and Porter, 1837.
22 p.   21 cm.

24620   Holley, Sallie, 1818-1893.
A life for liberty; anti-slavery and other letters of Sallie Holley; edited with introductory chapters by John White Chadwick... New York & London, G. P. Putnam's sons, 1899.
ix, 292 p.   front., plates, ports.   20 cm.

24621   Hollick, Frederick, b. 1818.
An inquiry into the rights, duties, and destinies, of the different varieties of the human race, with a view to a proper consideration of the subjects of slavery, abolition, amalgamation, and aboriginal rights; by

Dr. F. Hollick. New York, Printed by W. B. & T. Smith, 1843.
    33 p.   19 cm.

24622 Honey, William.
    Narrative on the captivity and sufferings of William Honey and two other British merchant-seamen on the Island of Arguin on the West Coast of Africa in the years 1844-5. London, Smith, Elder, 1845.
    31 p.   20 cm.

24623 Hopkins, John Henry, bp., 1792-1868.
    Slavery; its religious sanction, its political dangers, and the best mode of doing it away. A lecture delivered before the Young Mens' [!] Associations of the City of Buffalo, and Lockport, on Friday, January 10, and Monday, January 13, 1851. By John H. Hopkins... Pub. by request. Buffalo, Phinney & co., 1851.
    32 p. $22\frac{1}{2}$ cm.

24624 [Hopkins, Samuel] 1721-1803.
    A dialogue concerning the slavery of the Africans; shewing it to be the duty and interest of the American states to emancipate all their African slaves. With an address to the owners of such slaves. Dedicated to the honourable the Continental Congress. To which is prefixed, the institution of the Society, in New-York, for Promoting the Manumission of Slaves, and Protecting Such of Them As have Been, or May Be Liberated... Norwich [Conn.] Printed by Judah P. Spooner, 1776. New-York, Reprinted for Robert Hodge, 1785.
    72 p. $18\frac{1}{2}$ cm.

24625 Horner, Joseph Andrew, ed.
    ... The American Board of Missions and Slavery. A reprint of the correspondence in the "Nonconformist" newspaper; to which is added, an article on the fall of Dr. Pomroy [!] and his consequent dismissal from office, by Charles K. Whipple... Ed. by Joseph A. Horner, hon. sec. to the Wakefield Anti-slavery Association... Leeds, J. B. Barry & co., 1860.
    20 p. $19\frac{1}{2}$ cm.   (Anti-slavery tracts for the times, no. 1)

24626 Hourani, F   ed.
    Manchester and Abraham Lincoln; a side-light on an earlier fight for freedom, by F. Hourani, B.A. [Manchester, R. Aikman & son, printers, 19--]
    11, [1] p.   illus. (port.)   22 cm.

24627   How, Henry K
        Slaveholding not sinful: an answer by Henry K. How,
        to John Van Kyke, esq.'s reply to the argument of Rev.
        Dr. How. New-Brunswick, N. J., Printed at the Fredonian
        and Daily New-Brunswicker office, 1856.
        34 p.   21 cm.

24628   Howe, Daniel Wait, 1839-1920.
        Political history of secession, to the beginning of the
        American civil war, by Daniel Wait Howe... New York and
        London, G. P. Putnam's sons, 1914.
        xxx p., 1 l., 649 p.   22 cm.

24629   Howe, Samuel Gridley, 1801-1876.
        The refugees from slavery in Canada West. Report to
        the Freedmen's Inquiry Commission, by S. G. Howe. Boston,
        Wright & Potter, printers, 1864.
        iv, 110 p.   23½ cm.

24630   Hubbard, Henry, 1784-1857.
        Speech of Mr. Hubbard, of New Hampshire, on the motion
        not to receive a memorial praying the abolition of slavery
        in the District of Columbia. In Senate, March 7, 1836.
        Washington, Blair & Rives, printers, 1836.
        9 p.   24½ cm.

24631   Huber, Victor Aimé, 1800-1867.
        ... Die nordamerikanische Sclaverei. Von V. A. Huber.
        Nordhausen, F. Förstemann, 1864.
        74 p.   19½ cm.   (In his Sociale Fragen, 2)

24632   Huelsen, Christian Carl Friedrich, 1858-1935.
        Il sito e le iscrizioni della Schola Xantha sul Foro
        romano. [Rome, 1888]
        [208]-232, [312]-313 p.   plan.   24½ cm.
        Reprinted from Archäologisches Institut des Deutschen
        Reichs, Römische Zweiganstalt, Mitteilungen, v. 3, 1888.
        Supplementary article, "Miscellanea epigrafica (da
        lettera di T. Mommsen a C. Hülsen; cf. Bull. p. 222)":
        p. [312]-313.

24633   Hughes, John Starrett.
        Lafayette County and the aftermath of slavery, 1861-
        1870. [Columbia, Mo., State Historical Society of
        Missouri, 1980]
        51-63 p.   illus.   24 cm.
        Reprinted from Missouri historical review, v. 75, no. 1
        October, 1980.

24634   Hughes, Louis, 1832-
            Thirty years a slave. From bondage to freedom. The
         institution of slavery as seen on the plantation and in
         the home of the planter. Autobiography of Louis Hughes.
         Milwaukee, South Side Printing Company, 1897.
            210 p.   front. (port.) plans (facsims.)   21½ cm.

24635   Hughston, Jonas A   d. 1862.
            Speech of Hon. J. A. Hughston, of New York, on the
         slavery question, delivered in the House of Representatives,
         April 8, 1856. Washington, Printed at the Congressional
         globe office, 1856.
            7 p.   24 cm.

24636   Humanitas, pseud.
            Reflections on slavery; with recent evidence of its
         inhumanity. Occasioned by the melancholy death of Romain,
         a French negro. By Humanitas. Philadelphia, Printed for
         the author, 1803.
            vi, [7]-40 p. incl. front.   22½ cm.

24637   Hume, John Ferguson, 1830-
            The abolitionists; together with personal memories of
         the struggle for human rights, 1830-1864, by John F. Hume.
         New York and London, G. P. Putnam's sons, 1905.
            vi p., 1 l., 224 p.   19½ cm.

24638   Hunter, Robert Mercer Taliaferro, 1809-1887.
            Speech of Hon. R. M. T. Hunter, of Virginia, on
         invasion of states. Delivered in the Senate of the
         United States, January 30, 1860. [Washington] Printed
         by L. Towers [1860]
            16 p.   24 cm.
         Caption title.

24639   Hunter, Robert Mercer Taliaferro, 1809-1887.
            Speech of Hon. R. M. T. Hunter, of Virginia, on the
         admission of the state of Kansas. Delivered in the
         Senate of the United States, March 12, 1856.
            16 p.   23½ cm.

24640   Hunter, Robert Mercer Taliaferro, 1809-1887.
            The territorial question. Speech of Hon. R. M. T.
         Hunter, of Virginia, in the Senate of the United States,
         March 25, 1850. [Washington, Printed at the Congressional
         globe office, 1850]
            15 p.   23 cm.
         Caption title.

24641   Hurd, John Codman, 1816-1892.
        The question: Is slavery a condition supported by law,
    in the territories of the United States? in an extract
    from the second volume of "The law of freedom and bondage
    in the United States". In press, March, 1861. By John C.
    Hurd. [Boston, Little, Brown & company; New York, D. Var
    Nostrand, 1861]
        cover-title, p. [177]-224.   23 cm.

24642   Hutchins, John, 1812-1891.
        Speech of Hon. John Hutchins, of Ohio, on the bill for
    the release of certain persons held to service or labor ir
    the District of Columbia; delivered in the House of
    Representatives, April 11, 1862. Washington, Printed at
    the Congressional globe office, 1862.
        7 p.   24½ cm.

                                I

24643   Illinois. Negro Emancipation Celebration Commission.
        Annual report. 1st-   1913/14- [Chicago? 1914-
            v.   ports.   25½ cm.

24644   Indiana (Terr.) Governor, 1801-1812 (Harrison)
        Letter from William Henry Harrison, governor of the
    Indiana Territory, inclosing certain resolutions passed
    by the Legislative Council and House of Representatives
    of the said territory, relative to a suspension, for a
    certain period, of the sixth article of compact between
    the United States and the territories and states, north-
    west of the river Ohio, made 13 July, 1787... City of
    Washington, A. & G. Way, printers, 1807.
        7 p.   20½ cm.

24645   Infidelity unmasked. Edited and published by Dyer Burgess.
        v. 1; June 5, 1831-Apr. 22, 1832. Cincinnati [1831-32]
            384, iv p.   illus.   24 cm.

24646   Information concerning the present state of the slave trade
        [n.p.] 1824
            26 p.   18½ cm.

24747   Ingersoll, Charles Jared, 1782-1862.
        African slavery in America. By C. J. Ingersoll.
        Philadelphia, T. K. and P. G. Collins, printers, 1856.
            62 p.   23 cm.

24648   Ingram, John Kells, 1823-1907.
        A history of slavery and serfdom, by John Kells Ingram...
        London, A. and C. Black, 1895.
        xiv, 285 p.   19 cm.

24649   An inquiry into the nature and results of the anti-slavery
        agitation, with a view at the prospect before us. By a
        citizen of Alabama. Part I. Mobile [Ala.] Dade,
        Thompson & co., printers, 1851.
        cover-title, 50 p.   22 cm.

24650   Institut d'Afrique, Paris.
        Annales...   1. -   année. jan. 1841-   [Paris,
        1841]
            v.   28 cm.   monthly.
        Caption title.

24651   Interesting memoirs and documents relating to American
        slavery, and the glorious struggle now making for complete
        emancipation. London, Chapman brothers, 1846.
        1 p.l., 7-286 p., 1 l.   17 cm.
        Contents. - Narrative of Lewis Clarke. -- Narrative of
        Milton Clarke. -- American slavery as it is: testimony
        of a thousand witnesses [extracts from a work of that
        title published by the American anti-slavery society] --
        The way in which Americans use the friends of the slave,
        as shown in the trial and imprisonment of Jonathan Walker
        [written by himself] -- Extracts from a work entitled
        "Facts and arguments on American slavery," by the Rev.
        La Roy Sunderland.

24652   International Convention with the Object of Securing the
        Abolition of Slavery and the Slave Trade.
        International convention with the object of securing
        the abolition of slavery and the slave trade. Signed
        at Geneva, September 25, 1926. [British ratification
        deposited, June 18, 1927]... London, H. M. Stationery
        Off., 1927.
            12 p.   25 cm.   ([Gt. Brit. Foreign Office] Treaty
        series, 1927, no. 16) (Gt. Brit. Parliament. Papers
        by command, cmd. 2910)

24653   International Convention with the Object of Securing the
        Abolition of Slavery and the Slave Trade.
        International convention with the object of securing
        the abolition of slavery and the slave trade, September
        25, 1926. Accession of the Irish Free State notified on
        July 18, 1830... Dublin, Stationery Office [1931]
            12 p.   25 cm.   ([Irish Free State. Treaties, etc.]
        Treaty series, 1930, no. 2)

24654 International Convention with the Object of Securing the
           Abolition of Slavery and the Slave Trade.
              International Slavery Convention. Signed at Geneva,
           the 25th September, 1926. Canadian ratification deposited
           the 6th August, 1928. Ottawa, F. A. Acland, printer, 1929.
              10 p.   25 cm.   (Canada. Treaties, etc. Treaty
           series, 1928, no. 5)

24655 International Convention with the Object of Securing the
           Abolition of Slavery and the Slave Trade. French & English.
              Convention between the United States and other powers.
           Slavery. Signed at Geneva, September 25, 1926...
           Washington, U. S. Govt. Print. Off., 1929.
              1 p.l., 17 p.   23 cm.   ([United States. Treaties, etc
           Treaty series, no. 778)

24656 Irish Unitarian Christian Society.
              Address of the Irish Unitarian Christian Society to their
           brethren in America. Boston, Office of the Christian
           World, 1846.
              7 p.   15 cm.

24656a Is Millard Fillmore an abolitionist? Boston, American
           patriot office, 1856.
              29 p.   23 cm.   (Added t.-p.: The agitation of
           slavery. Who commenced and who can end it? ... Washington,
           1856)

24657 Isla de Cuba. Refutación de various articulos concernientes
           á ese pais publicados en el Diario de Barcelona en los
           meses de junio y julio 1859 por un Cubano. Paris,
           D'Aubusson y Kugelmann, 1859.
              2 p.l., 56 p.   21 cm.

24658 Ist der Süden zur Restoration bereit? [n.p., 1866?]
              20 p.   23 cm.
              Caption title.

                                    J

24659 Jack, Isaac Allen.
              The loyalists and slavery in New Brunswick. [n.p., 1898]
              137-185 p.   illus.   22 cm.
              Reprinted from Royal Society of Canada, Transactions,
           ser. 2, v. 4, sect. 2, 1898.

24660 Jackson, James C[aleb] 1811-1895.
              ... The duties and dignities of American freemen. By

James C. Jackson.   [Boston, New England Anti-slavery
Tract Association, 1843?]
    12 p.   19 cm.   (Tract no. 6)
    Caption title.

24661   [Jackson, John] d. 1855.
    Considerations on the impropriety of Friends participating
    in the administration of political governments.   Phila-
    delphia, 1840.
        12 p.   19 cm.

24662   Jackson, William, 1789-1864.
    Views on slavery, in its effects on the wealth, popula-
    tion, and character of nations.   By William Jackson, of
    Chester Co., Pennsylvania.   Philadelphia, Junior Anti-
    slavery Society, 1838.
        12 p.   23½ cm.

24663   Jacobs, Ferdinand.
    The committing of our cause to God: a sermon preached
    in the Second Presbyterian Church, Charleston, S. C. on
    Friday, the 6th of December; a day of fasting, humiliation,
    and prayer, appointed by the legislature of South Carolina,
    in view of the state of our federal relations.   By Rev.
    Ferdinand Jacobs.   Charleston, S. C., Printed by A. J.
    Burke, 1850.
        24 p.   22½ cm.

24664   Jacobs, Harriet Brent, 1817-1896.
    The grandmother of slaves, by her granddaughter [i.e.,
    H. B. Jacobs]   Boston, Ticknor and Fields, 1865.
        [346]-361 p.   20 cm.
    In Child, Lydia Maria Frances, 1802-1880.   Looking
    toward sunset.   2nd ed.   Boston, Ticknor and Fields, 1865.

24665   Jagger, William.
    To the people of Suffolk Co.   Information, acquired
    from the best authority, with respect to the institution
    of slavery.   By William Jagger.   New York, R. Craighead,
    printer, 1856.
        28 p.   22 cm.

24666   James, Alexander MacGregor.
    Virginie: a tale of the slave-trade: and other poems.
    By Alexander MacGregor James.   Kingston [Jamaica] M. C.
    Desouza, printer, 1895.
        53 p.   22½ cm.

24667   James, Horace, 1818-1875.
    Our duties to the slave.   A sermon, preached before the

original Congregational Church and Society, in Wrentham, Mass., on Thanksgiving Day, November 28, 1846. By Horace James, junior pastor. Boston, Printed by Richardson & Filmer, 1847.
23 p.   22 cm.

24668   Jameson, John Franklin, 1859-1937, ed.
Essays in the constitutional history of the United State in the formative period, 1775-1789, by graduates and former members of the Johns Hopkins university; ed. by J. Franklin Jameson.·. Boston and New York, Houghton, Mifflin and company, 1889.
2 p.l., [vii]-xiii p., 1 l., 321, [1] p.   21½ cm.
Contents. - The predecessor of the Supreme court, by the editor. - The movement towards a second constitutional convention in 1788, by E. P. Smith. - The development of the executive departments, by J. C. Guggenheimer. - The period of constitution-making in the American churches, by W. P. Trent. - The status of the slave, 1775-1789, by J. R. Brackett.

24669   Jameson, Russell Parsons, 1878-
Montesquieu et l'eslavage; étude sur les origines de l'opinion antiesclavagiste en France au XVIIIe siècle, par Russell Parsons Jameson... Paris, Hachette et c^{ie}, 1911.
3 p.l., 371 p.   25 cm.

24670   Japheth, pseud.
Cause and cure. By Japheth. Charleston, S. C., 1868.
cover-title, 27 p.   19½ cm.

24671   Jastrow, Ignaz, 1856-1937.
Zur strafrechlichen Stellung der Sklaven bei Deutschen und Angelsachsen, von dr. Ignaz Jastrow. Breslau, W. Koebner, 1878.
4 p.l., [3]-83, 1 p.   22 cm.   (Untersuchungen zur deutschen Staats und Rechtsgeschichte, hrsg. von dr. Otto Gierke... 2)

24672   Jay, John, 1817-1894.
Correspondence between John Jay, esq., and the Vestry of St. Matthew's Church, Bedford, N. Y. [Bedford? N. Y.] 1862.
16 p.   21½ cm.

24673   [Jay, John] 1817-1894.
Voting by proxy in charitable societies. Speech of the Hon. Mr. Noodle against the Assembly bill empowering members of benevolent and other societies to vote by proxy

With an introduction, containing the bill, the New York remonstrance, opinions of the press, and notice of Mr. Noodle. New York, R. Lockwood & son, 1859.
19 p.   23½ cm.
Relates to the remonstrance of the American tract society and its attitude on the slavery question.

24674 [Jay, William] 1789-1858.
The Creole case, and Mr. Webster's despatch; with the comments of the N. Y. American. New York, Pub. at the office of the "New-York American", 1842.
iv, [5]-39 p.   22½ cm.

24675 Jay, William, 1789-1858.
A reply to Webster, in a letter from Hon. William Jay to Hon. Wm. Nelson, M. C. Boston, W. Crosby and H. P. Nichols, 1850.
12 p.   20 cm.

24676 Jernegan, Marcus Wilson.
Slavery and conversion in the American colonies, by Marcus W. Jernegan... [New York, The Macmillan company, 1916]
cover-title, [1], [504]-527 p.   27 cm.
Reprinted from the American historical review, vol. 21, no. 3, April 1916.

24677 Johnson, Homer Uri.
From Dixie to Canada; romances and realities of the underground railroad, by H. U. Johnson... Vol. I, 1st thousand. Orwell, O., H. U. Johnson; Buffalo, C. W. Moulton, 1894.
vi p., 1 l., [9]-194 p.   front. (port.) plates. 18 cm.

24678 Johnson, James Weldon, 1871-1938, ed.
The book of American Negro spirituals, edited with an introduction of James Weldon Johnson; musical arrangements by J. Rosamond Johnson, additional numbers by Lawrence Brown. New York, The Viking press, 1925.
187 p.   26 cm.

24679 Johnson, John.
A defence of Republicanism by John Johnson, esq. (ex-mayor of Kansas City) An address delivered before the Kansas City Republican Club, on the 15th day of September 1860.   Published at their request. [Kansas City, Mo., Printed at the Free state Republican office, 1860]
15 p.   24 cm.
Caption title.

24680   Johnson, Oliver, 1809-1889.
        The abolitionists vindicated in a review of Eli Thayer's
paper on the New England Emigrant Aid Company. By Oliver
Johnson... Worcester, Mass., The Worcester society of
antiquity, 1887.
        29 p.   25½ cm.   (Worcester Society of Antiquity.
[Collections. vol. 7, no. 25])

24681   Johnson, Oliver, 1809-1889.
        William Lloyd Garrison and his times; or, Sketches of
the anti-slavery movement in America, and of the man who
was its founder and moral leader. By Oliver Johnson.
With an introduction by John G. Whittier... Boston, B. B
Russell & co.; New York, C. Drew; [etc., etc.] 1880.
        xviii, [19]-432 p.   plates.   19 cm.

24682   Johnston, David Claypoole, 1797-1865.
        Slavery: (voluntary) as it exists north, west, east
and south [by] D. C. Johnston. [n.p., c1871]
        14 phot. incl. title. 37 x 30 cm.

24683   Johnston, Elizabeth Bryant, 1833-1907.
        Christmas in Kentucky, 1862. By Elizabeth Bryant
Johnston. Washington, D. C., Gibson bros., printers, 189
        24 p.   illus., 4 pl. (incl. front.)   23½ x 18½ cm.

24684   Johnston, Josiah Stoddard, 1833-1913, ed.
        Memorial history of Louisville from its first settlemen
to the year 1896; ed. by J. Stoddard Johnston... Chicago
and New York, American biographical publishing co. [pref.
1896]
        2 v.   front. (map) illus., ports.   30½ cm.

24685   Johnston, William Dawson, 1871-1928.
        Slavery in Rhode Island, 1755-1776, by William D.
Johnston, A. B. Providence, Printed for the Society,
1894.
        2 p.l., [52] p.   24½ cm.   (Rhode Island historical
society, Publications, 1894-95, new series, v. 2, p. [113
164)

24686   [Johnstone, Elizabeth]
        The British mission of the Church of the Puritans. It
true origin and prosecution under the policy of Dr. H. A.
Hartt. Published by the author. New-York, J. A. Gray,
printer, 1861.
        36 p.   23 cm.

24687   Jones, Charles Colcock, 1831-1893.
        A roster of general officers, heads of departments,

senators, representatives, military organizations, &c.,
&c., in Confederate service during the War between the
States. By Charles C. Jones, jr. ... Richmond, Southern
Historical Society, 1876.
135 p.   23½ cm.
Issued as supplement to Southern historical society
papers. v. 1-3, 1876-77. Detached from first set of that
publication for separate binding.

4688   Jones, Charles Edgeworth, 1867-1931.
Georgia in the war, 1861-1865, by Chas. Edgeworth Jones...
[Atlanta, Ga., Printed by Foote & Davies, co., c1909]
167, [1] p.   17½ cm.

4689   Jouet, Alphonse, 1867-
... Droit romain: De la condition juridique des
affranchis. Droit français: Des clubs... Paris, A.
Giard [etc.] 1891.
343 p.   24½ cm.
Thèse - Faculté de droit de Paris.

4690   Journaal wegens de rampspoedige reys-tocht, van de ed:
gestrengen heer capiteyn Hendrik Cornelis Steenis...
Met her oorlogschip genaamt het Hvys in 't Bosch, gestrand
op es, op ... devi 20 December 1751. Als meede een korte
beschryvinge van de steeden Tetuan en Fez, de handeling
met den keiser van Marokko... Nevens een lyst der genoomene
scheepen door de Saleesche der geloste Holandsche gevangenen.
Door kunstige plaaten verbeeld. 5. druk. Te Amsteldam.
By B. Mourik [n.d.]
4 p.l., 35 p.   4 pl.   21 cm.
Preface by B. M. i.e. Bernardus Mourik.

4691   Journal du rachat des captifs d'Alger et de Tunis en 1779.
[Bastia, Ollagnier, 1886]
1 p.l., [165]-218 p.   25 cm.

4692   [Judson, Elisha] 1796-1871.
Epistles from the Old Man of the Hills to the people
of the valley... Kingsboro [N.Y.] The author, 1859.
46 p.   22½ cm.
Sketches of places and people in Fulton and Montgomery
counties, New York, with chapters on slavery, temperance,
etc.

4693   Jugler, Johann Friedrich, 1714-1791.
Ioh. Frid. Ivgleri... 'Ανδραποδοκαπηλειον.
Sive De nvndinatione servorvm apvd veteres liber singvlaris
historico-ivridicvs. Ex qvo lvcem capere possvnt

131

avctorvm loca complvra. Accedit Medicvs romanvs servvs
sexaginta solidis aestimatvs: rarissimvm nostris in oris
opvscvlvm. Lipsiae, apvd I. G. Loewivm, CIƆIƆCCXXXXII.
    4 p.l., 166, [8] p., 1 l.   18 cm.
    Head and tail pieces.
    "Medicus romanvs servvs... Primvm ipsis nonis julii
CI I CLXXI. Secvndvm editvs XII. kal. febr. CIƆ IƆCLXXXI
Lvgdvni Batavorvm. Tertivm nvnc editvs..." with special
t.-p.: p. [129]-166.

24694 Julian, George Washington, 1817-1899.
    ... The rank of Charles Osborn as an anti-slavery pionee
By George W. Julian. Indianapolis, The Bowen-Merrill
company, 1891.
    37 p.   25 cm.   (Indiana Historical Society, Publica
tions, v. 2, no. 6)

24695 Junkin, George, 1790-1868.
    An address delivered before the literary societies of
Rutgers College, by Rev. George Junkin... July 1st, 1856
New York, Pruden & Martin, printers, 1856.
    34 p.   22 cm.

K

24696 The Kansas war; or, The conquests of chivalry in the
    crusades of the nineteenth century. A heroic poem. New
    York, Mason brothers, 1856.
    vi, [7]-164 p.   19 cm.

24697 Kapp, Friedrich, 1824-1884.
    Geschichte der Sklaverei in den Vereinigten Staaten
von Amerika. Von Friedrich Kapp. Hamburg, O. Meissner,
1861.
    x, 516 p.   map.   19½ cm.

24698 Kaufman, David Spangler, 1813-1851.
    Speech of Hon. David S. Kaufman, of Texas, on the
slavery question. Delivered in the House of Representatives, February 10, 1847. Washington, Printed at the
office of Blair and Rives, 1847.
    14 p.   22½ cm.

24699 Keifer, Joseph Warren, 1836-1932.
    Slavery and four years of war; a political history of
slavery in the United States, together with a narrative
of the campaigns and battles of the Civil War in which

the author took part: 1861-1865, by Joseph Warren Keifer...
New York and London, G. P. Putnam's sons, 1900.
2 v.   front., pl., ports., maps.   23½ cm.

24700 Keitt, Laurence Massillon, 1824-1864.
       Speech of Hon. Lawrence M. Keitt, of South Carolina,
       on the origin of slavery; delivered in the House of Repre-
       sentatives, May 24, 1858. Washington, Printed at the office
       of the Congressional globe, 1858.
       13 p.   24½ cm.

24701 Kelley, William Darrah, 1814-1890.
       Address delivered at the Colored Department of the
       House of Refuge. By the Hon. William D. Kelley. On
       December 31st, 1849. This department of the institution
       having been opened for the reception of inmates on
       December 29th, 1849. Philadelphia, T. K. and P. G. Collins,
       printers, 1850.
       24 p.   22½ cm.

24702 Kelley, William Darrah, 1814-1890.
       The practice of justice our only security for the future.
       Remarks of Hon. William D. Kelley, of Pennsylvania, in
       support of his proposed amendment to the bill "To guaranty
       to certain states whose governments have been usurped or
       overthrown a republican form of government"; delivered in
       the House of Representatives, January 16, 1865.
       Washington, 1865.
       23 p.   22 cm.

24703 Kelley, William Darrah, 1814-1890.
       The recognition of Hayti and Liberia; speech of Hon.
       William D. Kelley, of Pennsylvania, delivered in the ·
       House of Representatives, June 3, 1862...   Washington,
       D. C., Scammel & co., printers, 1862.
       8 p.   23 cm.

24704 Kelley, William Darrah, 1814-1890.
       The South--its resources and wants. By Hon. Wm. D.
       Kelley, embracing his address to the citizens of New
       Orleans... address at Montgomery, Ala. ... and his
       address to his constituents... Washington, Union
       Republican Congressional Executive Committee [1866]
       30 p.   22½ cm.

24705 Kelley, William D[arrah] 1814-1890.
       Speech of Hon. William D. Kelley, of Pennsylvania, on
       protection to American labor; delivered in the House of
       Representatives, January 31, 1866. Washington, Printed

at the Congressional globe office, 1866.
31 p.   24 cm.

24706 Kelly, Mrs. Florence (Finch) 1858-
       Rhoda of the Underground, by Florence Finch Kelly...
       with illustrations by the Kinneys. New York, Sturgis &
       Walton company, 1909.
       v, 376 p.   front., 3 pl.   19½ cm.

24707 Kelsey, William H   1812-1879.
       Speech of Hon. W. H. Kelsey, of New York, on the slavery
       question; delivered in the House of Representatives,
       July 29, 1856. Washington, Printed at the Congressional
       globe office, 1856.
       8 p.   24 cm.

24708 Kennedy, Anthony, 1811-1892.
       Speech of Hon. A. Kennedy, of Md., on the abolition of
       slavery in the District of Columbia. Delivered in the
       Senate of the United States, March 25, 1862. [Washington,
       L. Towers & co., printers, 1862]
       8 p.   24 cm.
       Caption title.

24709 Kennedy, John, 1813-1900.
       Hebrew servitude and American slavery: an attempt to
       prove that the Mosaic law furnishes neither a basis nor
       an apology for American slavery. By the Rev. John Kennedy..
       London, Jackson, Walford, & Hodder, 1863.
       2 p.l., 60 p.   17½ cm.

24710 [Kennedy, John Pendleton] 1795-1870.
       Slavery the mere pretext for the rebellion; not its
       cause. Andrew Jackson's prophecy in 1833. His last will
       and testament in 1843. Bequests of his three swords...
       Picture of the conspiracy. Drawn in 1863, by a southern
       man. Philadelphia, C. Sherman, son & co., printers, 1863.
       cover-title, 16 p.   23½ cm.
       Signed: Paul Ambrose [pseud.]
       From the National intelligencer, Washington, March 1863.

24711 [Kenney, Lucy]
       A death blow to the principles of abolition. By a lady
       of Fredericksburg, Va. [Washington? 183-?]
       12 p.   20 cm.
       Caption title. Signed (in ms.): Lucy Kenney.

24712 Kenrick, John, 1755-1833.
       Horrors of slavery. In two parts. Part I. Containing

observations, facts, and arguments, extracted from the speeches of Wilberforce, Grenville, Pitt, Burke, Fox, Martin, Whitehead, and other distinguished members of the British Parliament. Part II. Containing extracts, chiefly American, comp. from authentic sources: demonstrating that slavery is impolitic, antirepublican, unchristian, and highly criminal: and proposing measures for its complete abolition through the United States. By John Kenrick. Cambridge Mass. Printed by Hilliard and Metcalf, 1817. Sold by Cummings & Hilliard, no. 1, and Lincoln & Edmonds, no. 53, Cornhill, Boston.
    59 p. $17\frac{1}{2}$ cm.

24713 Kentucky. Commission on Human Rights.
    Kentucky's black heritage. The role of the black people in the history of Kentucky from pioneer days to the present. A supplement to current texts on Kentucky history. Frankfort, 1971.
    iv, 162 p.   illus.   29 cm.

24714 Kentucky. Constitutional Convention, 1849-1850.
    Report of the debates and proceedings of the Convention for the revision of the constitution of the state of Kentucky. 1849. R. Sutton, official reporter to the Convention... Frankfort, Ky., Printed at the office of A. G. Hodges & co., 1849.
    1129 p.   24 cm.

24715 Kentucky. Laws, statutes, etc.
    The statute law of Kentucky; with notes, praelections, and observations on the public acts. Comprehending also, the laws of Virginia and acts of Parliament in force in this commonwealth; the charter of Virginia, the federal and state constitutions, and so much of the King of England's proclamation in 1763, as relates to the titles to land in Kentucky. Together with a table of references to the cases adjudicated in the Court of appeals... By William Littell... Frankfort (Ken.) Printed by and for William Hunter, 1809-1819.
    5 v. $21\frac{1}{2}$ cm.

24716 [Ker, John]
    A brief history of an attempt during the last session of the Legislature, in 1841, to interfere with the judgments of the courts, in relation to the wills of the late Captain Ross and Mrs. Reed. Natchez [Miss.] Printed by Baldwin & Risk, 1842.
    13 p. $20\frac{1}{2}$ cm.

24717 Ker, Leander.
       Slavery consistent with Christianity. By the Rev.
Leander Kerr [!] Baltimore, Printed by Sherwood & co.,
1840.
       31 p.   22 cm.

24718 Kettell, George F
       A sermon on the duty of citizens, with respect to the
fugitive slave law, by Rev. G. F. Kettell, of the
Methodist Episcopal Society, Poughkeepsie, N. Y. White
Plains, N. Y., Eastern state journal print, 1851.
       20 p.   21 cm.

24719 Key, Francis Scott, 1779-1843.
       A part of a speech pronounced by Francis S. Key, esq.,
on the trial of Reuben Crandall, M.D., before the Circuit
Court of the District of Columbia, at the March term
thereof, 1836, on an indictment for publishing libels
with intent to excite sedition and insurrection among the
slaves and free coloured people of said district...
Washington, 1836.
       15 p.   26 cm.
       From the African repository for November 1836.

24720 Kiefl, Franz Xaver, 1869-
       Die Theorien des modernen Sozialismus über den Ursprung
des Christentums. Zugleich ein Kommentar zu 1 Kor. 7,
21, von F. X. Kiefl. Kempten und München, J. Kosel, 1915.
       xxxii, 222 p., 1 l.   23½ cm.

24721 King, Daniel Putnam, 1801-1850.
       The California question and the ordinance of '87.
Speech of Hon. D. P. King, of Massachusetts, in the House
of Representatives, May 21, 1850, in Committee of the
Whole on the state of the Union, on the President's
message transmitting the Constitution of California.
[Washington, Printed at the Congressional globe office,
1850]
       8 p.   23 cm.

24722 King, Martin Luther, 1929-1968.
       Letter from Birmingham City Jail. [Birmingham, Ala.
(?), 1963 (?)]
       15 p.   22 cm.
       Introductory statement by Colin W. Bell, Executive
Secretary, American Friends Service Committee.

24723 King, Preston, 1806-1865.
       The rights of the people of Kansas. Speech of Preston
King, of New York, in the Senate of the United States,

March 16th, 1858, on the frauds, usurpation, and purpose, in which the slave constitution of the Lecompton convention had its origin. Washington, D.C., Buell & Blanchard, printers, 1858
7, [1] p. 23 cm.

24724 Kingsbury, Harmon, d. 1868.
Thoughts on the Fugitive slave law and Nebraska bill. New York, 1855.
26 p. 19½ cm.

24725 Kingsford, Edward.
The claims of abolitionism upon the church of Christ, candidly examined. A sermon, delivered at the Baptist church, Harrisburg, on the morning of Sabbath, February 18th, 1838, by Edward Kingsford. Pub. by request of several members of the Senate and House of Representatives of the legislature of Pennsylvania. Harrisburg, Printed by E. Guyer, 1838.
2 p.l., [3]-46 p. 22 cm.

24726 Kingsley, Henry, 1830-1876.
Tales of old travel. Re-narrated by Henry Kingsley... London, Macmillan & co., 1869.
4 p.l., 368 p. front., plates. 19 cm.
Title vignette.
Contents. - Marco Polo. - The shipwreck of Pelsart. - The wonderful adventures of Andrew Battel. - The wanderings of Capuchin. - Peter Carder. - The preservation of the "Terra nova". - Spitzbergen. - D'Ermenonville's acclimatization adventure. - The old slave trade. - Miles Philips. - The sufferings of Robert Everard. - John Fox. - Alvaro Nunez [!] - The foundation of an empire.

24727 [Kingsley, Vine Wright]
Reconstruction in America. By a member of the New York bar. New York, W. I. Pooley, 1865.
1 p.l., 153, [1] p. 23½ cm.

24728 Kingsley, Zaphaniah.
A treatise on the patriarchal, or co-operative, system of society as it exists in some governments, and colonies in America, and in the United States, under the name of slavery, with its necessity and advantages. By an inhabitant of Florida. 2d ed. [n.p.] 1829.
16 p. 23 cm.

24729 Kirkland, Charles Pinckney, 1820-1904.
A letter to Peter Cooper on "The treatment to be extended to the rebels individually," and "The mode of

restoring the rebel states to the union." With an appendi
containing a reprint of a review of Judge Curtis' paper on
the Emancipation proclamation, with a letter from Presiden
Lincoln. By Charles P. Kirkland. New York, A. D. F.
Randolph, 1865.
    46 p., 2 l., [3]-20 p.   23½ cm.

24730 Kitchel, Harvey Denison, 1812-1895.
    An appeal for discussion and action on the slavery
question. By H. D. Kitchel... Hartford, Printed by
L. Skinner, 1840.
    28 p.   22 cm.

24731 Kittle, William.
    Freedom and slavery. Madison, Wis., State journal
printing co., 1900.
    108 p.   22 cm.

24732 Kittredge, Frank Edward.
    The man with the branded hand. An authentic sketch
of the life and services of Capt. Jonathan Walker; with...
a brief history of the Douglas Monument. [Douglas
souvenir ed. Rochester, N. Y., H. L. Wilson pr. co.]
1899.
    46 p.   illus., port.   19 cm.

24733 Knapp, Georg Friedrich, 1842-1926.
    Die Landarbeiter in Knechtschaft und Freiheit. Vier
Vorträge von Georg Friedrich Knapp. Leipzig, Duncker &
Humblot, 1891.
    2 p.l., 92 p., 1 l.   21½ cm.

24734 Knibb, William.
    Rev. William Knibb's speech. Proceedings of the public
meeting held in Exeter-Hall, May 22, 1840, on occasion
of the public reception of the Rev. William Knibb,
H. Beckford, and E. Barrett. [London, George Wightman,
1840?]
    24 p.   18 cm.

24735 Kortbondige beschryvinqe van de colonie de Berbice...
    Vervolgens een beschryving van de negers of slaven;
mitsgaders de staat der Européanen, die zich aldaar
voorheen bevonden; en verder een beschryving van de
voornaamste producten, welke deeze colonie voortbrengt.
Verrykt met merkwaardige berichten wegens de onlangs
onstaane en noch aanhoudende opstand door de negers, en
de gesteldheid aldaar... Uit de aanteekeningen van een
voornaam heer opgemaakt, die eenige jaaren op de colonie
zyn verblyf gehouden heeft... 2. druk. Amsteldam,

S. J. Baalde, 1763.
   3 p.l., 34 p.   pl., map.   21 cm.

24736   Koster, Henry.
   On the amelioration of slavery.   By Henry Koster...
   [London, 1816]
   305-336 p.   22½ cm.
   Reprinted from The Pamphleteer, v. 8, 1896.

24737   Koster, Henry.
   Travels in Brazil.   By Henry Koster.   London, Longman,
   Hurst, Rees, Orme, and Brown, 1816.
   ix, [1] p., 1 l., 501, 1 p.   col. pl., maps.   28½ cm.

24738   Koster, Henry.
   Voyage dans la partie septentrionale du Brésil, depuis
   1809 jusqu'en 1815, comprenant les provinces de Pernambuco
   (Fernambouc), Seara, Paraĭba, Maragnan, etc.; par Henri
   Koster: tr. de l'anglais par M. A. Jay...   Paris,
   Delaunay, 1818.
   2 v.   front., plates, 2 fold. maps.   23 cm.

24739   Kramer, John Theophilus.
   The slave-auction.   By Dr. John Theophilus Kramer,
   late of New Orleans, La. ...   Boston, R. F. Wallcut, 1859.
   48 p.   14½ cm.

24740   Krebs, John Michael, 1804-1867.
   The American citizen.   A discourse on the nature and
   extent of our religious subjection to the government
   under which we live: including an inquiry into the
   Scriptural authority of that provision of the Constitution
   of the United States, which requires the surrender of
   fugitive slaves.   Delivered in the Rutgers Street Presbyterian Church, in the city of New York...   December 12,
   1850...   By John M. Krebs, D.D.   New York, C. Scribner,
   1851.
   40 p.   23 cm.

24741   Kuhn, F   A
   Beschouwing van den toestand der surinaamsche plantagie-
   slaven.   Eene oeconomisch-geneeskundige bijdrage tot
   verbetering deszelven.   Door F. A. Kuhn...   Amsterdam,
   C. G. Sulpke, 1828.
   2 p.l., [iii]-vii, 138 p., 1 l.   III pl. (2 fold.
   plans, diagrs.)   fold. tab.   22½ cm.

24742   Kuo, Mo-jo, 1892-
   奴隷制時代 郭沫若著 北京 人民
   出版社 1954.

181 p.   illus.   20 cm.
Title romanized: Nu li chih shih tai.

L

24743   Laboria.
        De la Guyane française et de ses colonisations, par
        Laboria... Paris, J. Corréard, 1843.
        2 p.l., [ix]-x, [2], [v]-viii, 164, 124 p.   22 cm.

24744   Laboulaye, Édouard René Lefebvre de, 1811-1883.
        The United States and France. By Edward Laboulaye...
        Translated for the Boston daily advertiser. Boston,
        The Boston daily advertiser, 1862.
        14 p.   26 cm.

24745   Laboulaye, Édouard René Lefebvre de, 1811-1883.
        Upon whom rests the guilt of the war? Separation:
        war without end. By M. Édouard Laboulaye... New-York,
        W. C. Bryant & co., printers, 1863.
        19 p.   22½ cm.

24746   Laboulaye, Édouard René Lefebvre de, 1811-1883.
        Why the north cannot consent to disunion. By Édouard
        Laboulaye... New York, C. B. Richardson, 1863.
        14 p.   17 cm.

24747   Labra y Cadrana, Rafael María de, 1841-1918.
        La abolición de la esclavitud en las Antillas españolas,
        por Rafael M. de Labra. Madrid, Impr. á cargo de J. E.
        Morete, 1869.
        viii, [9]-118 p.   21½ cm.

24748   Lacascade, Pierre.
        Esclavage et immigration, la question de la main-d'oeuvr
        aux Antilles, le décret du 13 février 1852, et la
        Convention franco-anglaise du 1er juillet 1861, par
        Pierre Lacascade, docteur en droit (thèse de doctorat)
        Paris, A. Michalon, 1907.
        2 p.l., [7]-136 p.   25 cm.

24749   [Lacerda, Pedro Maria de, bp.] 1830-1890.
        Carta pastoral do bispo de S. Sebastião do Rio de
        Janeiro annunciando a Lei n. 2040 de 28 de setembro de
        1871 sobre libertação de filhos de escravas e sua
        criação, etc. a recommendando a todos sua execução.
        Rio de Janeiro, Typographia nacional, 1871.
        13 p.   22 cm.

24750   Lacon, pseud.
        The devil in America: a dramatic satire. Spirit-
rapping - Mormonism; woman's rights conventions and
speeches; abolitionism; Harper's Ferry raid and black
republicanism; defeat of Satan, and final triumph of the
gospel. By Lacon. Philadelphia, J. B. Lippincott & co.,
1860.
        1 p.l., 225 p.   19 cm.
        In verse.
        Advertisement on last page "Aberdeen (Miss.) female
college" signed: Rev. R. S. Gladney, M.A.

24751   Lacroix, François Joseph Pamphile, vicomte de, 1774-1842.
        Mémoires pour servir à l'histoire de la révolution de
Saint-Domingue. Par le lieutenant-général baron Pamphile
de Lacroix. Avec une carte nouvelle de l'Île et un plan
topographique de la Crête-à-Pierrot... Paris, Phillet
aîné, 1819.
        2 v.   fold. map, fold. plan. $20\frac{1}{2}$ cm.

24752   La Faye, Jean Baptiste de.
        Relation en forme de journal, du voiage pour la
redemption des captifs, aux roiaumes de Maroc & d'Alger.
Pendant les années 1723, 1724, & 1725. Par Jean de
La Faye [et al.] Paris, L. Sevestre, 1726.
        x, 364, xii p.   front.   18 cm.

24753   [La Faye, Jean Baptiste de]
        Several voyages to Barbary. Containing an historical
and geographical account of the country. With the
hardships, sufferings, and manner of redeeming Christian
slaves. Together with a curious description of Mequinez,
Oran, and Alcazar. With a journal of the late siege and
surrender of Oran. To which are added. The maps of
Barbary, and the sea-coasts; the prospects of Mequinez
and Alcazar; an exact plan of Oran, and a view of the
ancient Roman ruins near Mequinez. All design'd by
Captain Henry Boyde. The whole illustrated with notes,
historical and critical. The 2d ed., cor. London,
O. Payne [etc.] 1736.
        4 p.l., 3-146, 158 p.   2 fold. pl., 2 fold. maps
(incl. front.) fold. plan.   20 cm.
        Tr. by John Morgan.

24754   Lamar, Mirabeau Bonaparte, 1798-1859.
        Gen. Mirabeau B. Lamar's letter to the people of
Georgia. [n.p., 1850?]
        8 p.   24 cm.
        Caption title.

24755   The Land we love, a monthly magazine devoted to literature,
        military history, and agriculture. v. 1-6; May 1866-Mar.
        1869. Charlotte, N. C., J. P. Irwin & D. H. Hill [etc.]
        1866-69.
            6 v.   pl., ports., maps.   23 cm.
            Gen. D. H. Hill, editor.

24756   Landon, Fred, 1880-
            Anthony Burns in Canada, by Fred Landon... [Toronto,
        1925]
            7 p.   25 cm.
            Reprinted from the Ontario Historical Society, Papers
        and records, v. 22, 1925.

24757   Landon, Fred, 1880-
            The relation of Canada to the anti-slavery and abolition
        movements in the United States. By Fred Landon...
        [London? Ont., 1919?]
            4 p.l., 105 numb. l. $28\frac{1}{2}$ cm.
            Thesis (M. A.) - University of Western Ontario, 1919.

24758   Landon, Fred, 1880-
            Social conditions among the negroes in Upper Canada,
        by Fred Landon... [Toronto, 1925]
            20 p.   25 cm.

24759   Landrum, John Morgan, 1815-1861.
            The slavery question. Speech of Hon. John M. Landrum
        of La., delivered in the House of Representatives,
        April 27, 1860. [Washington, 1860]
            8 p. $24\frac{1}{2}$ cm.
            Caption title.

24760   Lane, James Henry, 1814-1866.
            Speech of General J. H. Lane at Waterbury, Conn.,
        Dec. 28, 1863. [Washington, Gibson Bros., printers,
        1864]
            8 p.   24 cm.

24761   Lane, James Henry, 1814-1866.
            Vindication of the policy of the administration.
        Speech of Hon. J. H. Lane, of Kansas, in the Senate of
        the United States, February 16, 1864, on the special
        order, being Senate bill no. 45, to set apart a portion
        of the state of Texas for the use of persons of African
        descent. Washington, D. C., Gibson brothers, printers,
        1864.
            16 p.   22 cm.

24762   Lane, Joseph, 1801-1881.
        The states of the Union - Equality of rights, and frater-
        nity of sentiment. Remarks of Hon. Joseph Lane, of Oregon,
        in the Senate of the United States, December 19, 1859.
        [Washington] Printed by L. Towers [1859]
        8 p.   21½ cm.
        Caption title.

24763   Lane, Henry Smith, 1811-1881.
        Reconstruction and amendments of the Constitution.
        Speech of Hon. Henry S. Lane, of Indiana, in the Senate
        of the United States, Thursday, February 8, 1866...
        [Washington, D. C., H. Polkinhorn & sons, printers, 1866]
        16 p.   23½ cm.
        Caption title.

24764   Lane Theological Seminary, Cincinnati.
        Debate at the Lane Seminary, Cincinnati. Speech of
        James A. Thome, of Kentucky, delivered at the annual
        meeting of the American anti-slavery society, May 6, 1834.
        Letter of the Rev. Dr. Samuel H. Cox, against the American
        Colonization Society. [Letter of Mr. Henry B. Stanton]
        Boston, Published by Garrison & Knapp, 1834.
        16 p.   23 cm.

24765   Langdon, Timothy, 1758-1801.
        A sermon, preached at Danbury, November 8th, A.D. 1798,
        being the day of the execution of Anthony, a free Negro,
        pursuant to sentence of death passed upon him by the hon.
        superior court, for the crime of a rape. By Timothy
        Langdon... Danbury [Conn.], Printed and sold by Douglas
        & Nichols, 1798.
        23 p.   21½ cm.
        "An address made by the Rev. Mr. S. Blatchford, at the
        gallows, immediately preceding the execution of Anthony":
        p. 20-23.

24766   Langer, Carl Rudolf, 1893-
        De servi persona apvd Menandrvm... scripsit Carolvs
        Langer... Bonnae, typis Caroli Georgi, 1919.
        129, [1] p.   22 cm.
        Inaug.-diss. - Bonn.

24767   Lans, W   H
        Bijdrage tot de kennis der kolonie Suriname, door W. H.
        Lans. 's Gravenhage, Nederlandsche maatschappij van
        schoone kunsten, 1842.
        2 p.l., iv, 195 p., 5 l.   illus.   23½ cm.

24768   Laranda, Viletta.
        Neapolitan captive, interesting narrative of the captivit
        and sufferings of Miss Viletta Laranda, a native of Naples,
        who, with a brother, was a passenger on board a Neapolitan
        vessel wrecked near Oran, on the Barbary coast, September
        1829, and who soon after was unfortunately made a captive
        of by a wandering clan of Bedowen Arabs, on their return
        from Algiers to the deserts, and eleven months after provi-
        dentially rescued from barbarian bondage by the commander
        of a detached regiment of the victorious French Army. Com-
        municated by an officer of respectable rank in the army,
        to his friend in Paris. 3d ed. New-York, C. C. Henderson,
        1830.
        36 p.   front.   20 cm.

24769   Larned, Edwin Channing, 1820-1884.
        The new fugitive slave law. Speech of Edwin C. Larned,
        esq. at the City hall in the city of Chicago, on the
        evening of Oct. 25th, 1850, in reply to Hon. S. A. Douglas.
        Chicago, Printed at the Democrat office, 1850.
        16 p.   21½ cm.

24770   Laroche, Benjamin, 1797-1852.
        Histoire de l'abolition de l'esclavage dans les colonies
        françaises. I. ptie. Ile de la Réunion. Administration
        du commissaire général de la république. M. Sarda Garriga,
        du 13 octobre 1848 au 8 mars 1850. Par Benjamin Laroche.
        Paris, Typ. de F. Didot frères, 1851.
        95, [1] p.   23½ cm.

24771   Latham, Milton Slocumb, 1827-1882.
        Remarks of Hon. Milton S. Latham, of California, upon
        slavery in the states and territories, and the doctrine of
        an "irrepressible conflict" between "labor states" and
        "capital states." Delivered in the Senate of the United
        States, April 16, 1860. [Washington, Printed by L. Towers,
        1860]
        16 p.   22 cm.
        Caption title.

24772   Latrobe, John Hazlehurst Boneval, 1803-1891.
        Colonization. A notice of Victor Hugo's views of slavery
        in the United States, in a letter from John H. B. Latrobe,
        of Baltimore, to Thomas Suffern, of New York. Baltimore,
        Printed by J. D. Toy, 1851.
        48 p.   23 cm.
        Contents. - Letter to Thomas Suffern. - Victor Hugo to
        Mrs. Chapman. - John H. B. Latrobe to Victor Hugo.

24773   Latrobe, John Hazlehurst Boneval, 1803-1891.
        The Regina coeli. Correspondence between the Hon.
        James H. Hammond and John H. B. Latrobe, esq., president
        of the American Colonization Society. Baltimore, Printed
        by J. D. Toy, 1858.
            47 p.   21½ cm.
            Reprinted from the Baltimore American, December 20, 1858.
            Appended (p. 39-47) is a letter by J. J. Roberts,
        ex-president of Liberia, to Benjamin Coates, upon the
        sentiment of the Liberians with reference to the slave
        trade and the case of the Regina coeli.

24774   Lauber, Almon Wheeler, 1880-
            Indian slavery in colonial times within the present
        limits of the United States, by Almon Wheeler Lauber...
        New York, 1913.
            2 p.l., 7-352 p., 1 l.   24½ cm.
            Thesis (Ph.D.) - Columbia university, 1913.

24775   Laugel, Auguste, 1830-1914.
            The United States during the war. By Auguste Laugel.
        London, H. Baillière; New York, Baillière brothers [etc.]
        1866.
            xiii p., 1 l., 313 p.   23 cm.

24776   Laurens, Edward R
            A letter to the Hon. Whitemarsh B. Seabrook, of St.
        John's, Colleton; in explanation and defence of "An act
        to amend the law in relation to slaves and free persons
        of color." By Edward R. Laurens... Charleston, Observer
        office press, 1835.
            24 p.   23½ cm.

24777   Laurens, Henry, 1724-1792.
            A South Carolina protest against slavery: being a letter
        from Henry Laurens, second president of the Continental
        Congress, to his son, Colonel John Laurens, dated
        Charleston, S. C., August 14th, 1776. Now first published
        from the original. New York, G. P. Putnam, 1861.
            1 p.l., [5]-6, [17]-34 p.   20½ cm.

24778   [Lavallée, Joseph, marquis de Bois-Robert] 1747-1816.
            The negro as there are few white men. Translated from
        the French, by J. Trapp... London, The author, 1790.
            3 v.   17½ cm.

24779   [Lavallée, Joseph, marquis de Bois-Robert] 1747-1816.
            The negro equalled by few Europeans. Translated from
        the French. To which are added, Poems on various subjects,

moral and entertaining; by Phillis Wheatley, Negro
servant to Mr. John Wheatley, of Boston, in New-England...
Philadelphia, Printed by and for William W. Woodward,
no. 17, Chestnut street, 1801.
　　2 v.　　17 cm.
　　A story.

24780　... The law and the testimony concerning slavery.　[Cincinnati
O., American reform tract and book society, 185-?]
　　24 p.　　18 cm.
　　Caption title. At head of title: No. 1. Ms. note on
page [1]: By A. Rand.

24781　Lawrence, Catherine S
　　Autobiography. Sketch of life and labors of Miss Catherin
S. Lawrence, who in early life distinguished herself as a
bitter opponent of slavery and intemperance... Rev. ed.
Albany, N. Y., J. B. Lyon, printer, 1896.
　　238 p.　　front., ports.　　20 cm.

24782　Lawrence, Sidney.
　　Slavery in the territories. Speech... on the power and
duty of Congress to prohibit slavery in the territories.
Delivered in the House of Representatives June 12, 1848.
Washington, 1848.
　　16 p.　　25 cm.

24783　Lawrence, William, 1819-1899.
　　Reconstruction - organisation of civil state government
in the rebel states. Speech in the House of Representatives. Feb. 17, 1866. [Washington] Congressional globe
office [1866]
　　12 p.　　20 cm.

24784　Lawrence, William Beach, 1800-1881.
　　French commerce and manufactures and negro slavery in
the United States. Letter to the editor of the "Journal
des débats," by William Beach Lawrence... Paris, E.
Dentu, 1860.
　　16 p.　　22½ cm.

24785　Laws of the United States, the State of New York, and New
Jersey, relative to slaves and the slave trade. New York,
Collins, 1811.
　　72 p.　　19 cm.

24786　Lay, Benjamin, 1677-1759.
　　All slave-keepers that keep the innocent in bondage,
apostates pretending to lay claim to the pure & holy
Christian religion, of what congregation so ever, but

especially in their ministers, by whose example the
filthy leprosy and apostacy is spread far and near; it is
a notorious sin which many of the true Friends of Christ
and his pure truth, called Quakers, has been for many years
and still are concern'd to write and bear testimony
against as a practice so gross and hurtful to religion,
and destructive to government beyond what words can set
forth, or can be declared of by men or angels, and yet
lived in by ministers and magistrates in America. Written
for a general service. Philadelphia, 1737.
271 p. 16 cm.

24787 Layres, Augustus.
A defense of the reconstruction acts of Congress, and
critical review of the inaugural of H. H. Haight, governor
of California, comprising important points at issue in the
present campaign; respectfully dedicated to the Union-
Republican congressmen from the Pacific states, and to
the Order of freedom's defenders, by Professor Augustus
Layres. San Francisco, J. Stratman, 1868.
cover-title, 16 p. 23 cm.

24788 Lea, Henry Charles, 1825-1909.
Studies in church history. The rise of the temporal
power.--Benefit of clergy.--Excommunication.--The early
church and slavery. By Henry C. Lea... Philadelphia,
H. C. Lea's son & co., 1869.
xvi, [13]-515, [1] p. 21 cm.

24789 Leach, De Witt Clinton, 1822-
The Amistad case. Men not recognised as property by
the Constitution. Speech of Hon. De Witt C. Leach, of
Michigan. Delivered in the House of Representatives,
January 27, 1858. [Washington, Buell & Blanchard,
printers, 1858]
8 p. 24 cm.
Caption title.

24790 League of Nations. Assembly. Sixth Committee.
Question of slavery. Report presented to the Sixth
Assembly by the Sixth Committee. Rapporteur: Viscount
Cecil of Chelwood, delegate of the British Empire.
Geneva, 1925.
6 p. 33 cm.
Caption title.

24791 League of Nations. Assembly. Sixth Committee.
... Slavery convention. Report presented to the Assembly
by the Sixth committee. Rapporteur: Viscount Cecil of
Chelwood. [Geneva] Imp. Kundig [1926]

6 p.   33 cm.   (A. 104. 1926. VI)
Publications of the League of Nations. VI. B. Slavery.
1926. VI. B. 5.

24792 League of Nations. Assembly. Sixth Committee.
... Slavery convention. Annual report by the Council.
Report of the Sixth committee to the Assembly. Rapporteur:
Sir E. Hilton Young (British Empire) [Geneva, Imp. Kundig,
1927]
[2] p.   33 cm.   (A. 74. 1927. VI)
Publications de la Société des nations. VI. B. Esclavage
1927. VI. B. 5.

24793 League of Nations. Assembly. Sixth Committee.
... Slavery convention. Annual report by the Council.
Report of the Sixth committee to the Assembly. Rapporteur:
The Rt. Hon. G. Locker-Lampson, M. P. (British Empire)
[Geneva, Imp. Jent, s.a., 1928]
[2] p.   33 cm.   (A. 62. 1928. VI)
At head of title: ... Geneva, September 17th, 1928.
Ninth ordinary session of the Assembly of the League of
Nations.

24794 League of Nations. Assembly. Sixth Committee.
... Slavery convention. Annual report of the Council.
Report of the Sixth committee to the Assembly. Rapporteur:
M. Leopoldo Palacios (Spain) [Geneva] Imp. de la Tribune,
1929.
2 p.   33 cm.   (A. 71. 1929. VI)
Series of League of Nations publications. VI. B.
Slavery. 1929. VI. B. 3.

24795 League of Nations. Assembly. Sixth Committee.
... Slavery. Report submitted by the Sixth Committee to
the Assembly. Rapporteur: Jonkheer J. Loudon (Netherlands)
[Geneva] 1930.
3 p.   33 cm.   (A. 77. 1930. VI)

24796 League of Nations. Assembly. Sixth Committee.
... Slavery. Report submitted by the Sixth Committee
to the Assembly. Rapporteur: H. E. Jonkheer J. Loudon
(Netherlands) [Geneva, 1931]
[2] p.   33 cm.   (A. 83. 1931. VI)

24797 League of Nations. Assembly. Sixth Committee.
... Slavery. Report submitted by the Sixth Committee
to the Assembly. Rapporteur: H. E. Jonkheer J. Loudon
(Netherlands) [Geneva] 1932.
2 p.   33 cm.   (A. 57. 1932. VI)

24798 League of Nations. Assembly. Sixth Committee.
... Slavery. Report by the Sixth Committee to the
Assembly. Rapporteur: M. López Oliván (Spain)
[Geneva, 1933]
[2] p.   33 cm.   (A. 51. 1933. VI)

24799 League of Nations. Assembly. Sixth Committee.
... Slavery. Report submitted by the Sixth Committee to
the Assembly. Rapporteur: Mr. A. Noel Skelton (United
Kingdom) [Geneva, 1934]
[2] p.   33 cm.   (A. 43. 1934. VI)

24800 League of Nations. Assembly. Sixth Committee.
... Slavery. Report submitted by the Sixth Committee to
the Assembly. Rapporteur: H. E. M. R. J. Sandler (Sweden)
[Geneva, 1935]
[2] p.   33 cm.   (A. 58. 1935. VI)

24801 Learned, Joseph D
A view of the policy of permitting slaves in the states
west of the Mississippi: being a letter to a member of
Congress. By Joseph D. Learned... Baltimore, Printed
by J. Robinson, 1820.
47 p.   21 cm.

24802 Le Blond, Francis Celeste, 1821-1902.
Reconstruction. Speech of Hon. Frank C. Le Blond, of
Ohio, delivered in the House of Representatives, April 7,
1866. Washington, Printed at the "Constitutional Union"
office, 1866.
8 p.   24½ cm.

24803 Lechevalier, Jules, 1800-1850.
Rapport sur les questions coloniales, adressé à M. le
duc de Broglie, président de la Commission coloniale à la
suite d'un voyage fait aux Antilles et aux Guyanes,
pendant les années 1838 et 1839, par M. Jules Lechevalier;
pub. par ordre de S. Exc. l'amiral baron de Mackau ministre
secrétaire d'état de la marine et des colonies...
Documents et pièces justificatives... Paris, Imprimerie
royale, 1844, '43.
2 v.   tables (partly fold.)   36 cm.
Contents. - t. I, 1. ptie. Pièces écrites et recueillies
pendant le voyage. Enquêtes. - t. 2. 2. ptie. Étude
de l'emancipation dans les colonies anglaises depuis
l'année 1833 jusqu'au 3 décembre 1842.

24804 Leclère, Adhémard, 1853-1917.
Recherches sur la législation cambodgienne (droit privé)

par Adhémard Leclère.   Paris, A. Challamel, 1890.
xiv, 291, [1] p.   23 cm.

24805   Lecomte, Ferdinand, 1826-1899.
Guerre de la sécession, esquisse des événements militaire
et politiques des États-Unis de 1861 à 1865, par Ferdinand
Lecomte... Paris, C. Tanera, 1866-67.
3 v.   fold. maps, diagr.   24 cm.

24806   Lecomte, Ferdinand, 1826-1899.
The war in the United States.   Report to the Swiss
Military Department; preceded by a discourse to the Federal
Military Society assembled at Berne, August 18, 1862.
By Ferdinand Lecomte...   Tr. from the French.   New York,
D. Van Nostrand, 1863.
148 p.   19 cm.

24807   [Lee,   ]
Extract from an address, in the Virginia gazette, of
March 19, 1767.   [Williamsburg? Va., 1767?]
4 p.   17 cm.

24808   [Lee, Arthur] 1740-1792.
An essay in vindication of the continental colonies of
America, from a censure of Mr. Adam Smith, in his Theory
of moral sentiments.   With some reflections on slavery
in general.   By an American...   London, Printed for the
author, 1764.
1 p.l., viii, [9]-46 p. $18\frac{1}{2}$ cm.

24809   Lee, Charles Henry, 1818-1900.
The judge advocate's vade mecum: embracing a general
view of military law, and the practice before courts-
martial of the army and navy, with an epitome of the law
of evidence, as applicable to military and naval trials.
By C. H. Lee.   2d ed., rev. and enl.   Richmond, West and
Johnston, 1864.
308 p.   diagr.   22 cm.

24810   Lee, F   D
Historical record of the city of Savannah.   By F. D. Lee
and J. L. Agnew.   Savannah, J. H. Estill, 1869.
xii, 200 p.   fold. front., illus., fold. maps, plans.
19 cm.

24811   [Leeds, Eli R   ]
The origin and equal rights of all men, and their power
to protect & govern themselves.   Also, the formation of
the original government, and the origin of the Constitution

150

of the United States. Batavia, O., Townsley & Orebaugh, 1867.
 23 p. 22 cm.

24812 Leffingwell, Albert, 1845-
 The lesson of reform; an address before the American Humane Association, Pittsburg, Pa., October 12, 1900, by Albert Leffingwell, M.D. [Pittsburgh] The American Humane Association, 1901.
 32 p. 23 cm.

24813 Legion, pseud.
 A second letter from Legion to His Grace the Duke of Richmond, &c. &c. &c. chairman of the Slavery Committee of the House of Lords: containing an analysis of the antislavery evidence produced before the committee... London, S. Bagster, 1833.
 iv, 152 p. 22 cm.

24814 Legoyt, Alfred, 1815-1885.
 L'émigration européenne, son importance, ses causes, ses effets. Avec un appendice sur l'émigration africaine, hindoue et chinoise... Par A. Legoyt... Paris, Guillaumin & c^{ie}, 1861.
 3 p.l., lv, 333 p. 24 cm.

24815 [Legrand, John Carroll] 1814-1861.
 Letter to Hon. Reverdy Johnson, on the proceedings at the meeting held at Maryland Institute, January 10th, 1861. Baltimore, Murphy & co., printers [1861]
 8 p. 23½ cm.
 Caption title.

24816 Leigh, Benjamin Watkins, 1781-1849.
 Speech of Mr. Leigh, on the question of the reception of certain memorials from citizens of Ohio, praying Congress to abolish slavery within the District of Columbia. Delivered in the Senate of the United States, on the 19th of January, 1836. [Washington, 1836]
 8 p. 25½ cm.
 Caption title.

24817 Leigh, Edwin.
 Bird's eye views of slavery in Missouri. By E. Leigh, M.D. Saint Louis, 1862.
 cover-title, 3 p. 6 double maps. 24 cm.

24818 Leiter, Benjamin Franklin, 1813-1866.
 National politics. Speech of Hon. Benjamin F. Leiter,

of Ohio, delivered in the House of Representatives, August
12, 1856. [Washington, Printed at the office of the
Congressional globe, 1856]
7 p.   23 cm.
Caption title.

24819   [Leland, Charles Godfrey] 1824-1903.
Ye book of copperheads. Philadelphia, F. Leypoldt,
1863.
1 p.l., 24, [6] p.   illus.   13 x 23 cm.
By C. G. Leland and H. P. Leland. cf. Elizabeth R.
Pennell, Charles Godfrey Leland (1906, v. 1, p. 254)

24820   Leland, John, 1754-1841.
The Virginia chronicle; with judicious and critical
remarks, under XXIV heads. By John Leland... Fredericksburg, Printed by T. Green, 1790.
46, [2] p.   22 cm.

24821   Leng, Sir William Christopher.
... The American war: the aims, antecedents, and
principles of the belligerents. A lecture, delivered on
the 10th December, 1862, in Castle street church, by
William C. Leng... Dundee, Printed at the Advertiser
office, 1863.
38 p.   21 cm.

24822   [Lester, Charles Edwards] 1815-1890.
Chains and freedom; or, The life and adventures of
Peter Wheeler, a colored man yet living... By the
author of the 'Mountain wild flower'... New York, E. S.
Arnold & co., 1839.
vii, [1], [9]-260 p.   port.   15 cm.

24823   Lester, Charles Edwards, 1815-1890, ed.
The history of twelve thousand fugitive slaves, who
have emancipated themselves by flight. [London, Manning
and Mason, 1840]
2 p.   29½ cm.

24824   Lester, John C
Ku Klux Klan. Its origin, growth and disbandment. By
J. C. Lester and D. L. Wilson... Nashville, Tenn.,
Wheeler, Osborn & Duckworth manufacturing co., 1884.
117 p.   16 cm.

24825   Letcher, John, 1813-1884.
Speech of Hon. John Letcher, of Virginia, in the House
of Representatives, February 27, 1855, on territorial

policy.   Washington, Printed at the Congressional globe
office, 1855
8 p.   22½ cm.
Caption title.

24826   Letourneau, Charles Jean Marie, 1831-1902.
... L'évolution de l'esclavage dans les diverses races
humaines, par Ch. Letourneau... Paris, Vigot frères, 1897.
xxi, 538 p.   22 cm.   (Bibliothèque anthropologique,
t. 17)

24827   Letter addressed to the Hon. John C. Calhoun, on the law
relating to slaves, free negroes, and mulattoes, by a
Virginian. Published by request. Washington, J. & G. S.
Gideon, printers, 1845.
13 p.   22½ cm.

24828   A letter from an elder in an Old School Presbyterian Church
to his son at college... New York, 1863.
24 p.   23 cm.
A defense of slavery on Scriptural grounds.

24829   A letter from a merchant at Jamaica to a member of Parliament
in London, touching the African trade. To which is added,
A speech made by a black of Gardaloupe [!] at the funeral
of a fellow-negro. London, Printed for A. Baldwin, 1709.
31 p.   19 cm.

24830   A letter from a merchant of the city of London, to the
R---t H----ble W---- P---- esq.; upon the affairs and
commerce of North America, and the West-Indies; our
African trade; the destination of our squadrons and
convoys; new taxes, and the schemes proposed for raising
the extraordinary supplies for the current year...
London, Printed for J. Scott, 1757.
98 p.   20 cm.
Signed: A merchant of London.

24831   Letter to a member of the Congress of the United States of
America, from an English clergyman; including a republica-
tion, with considerable additions, of the tract entitled
"Every man his own property". London, Whittaker, Treacher
and Arnot, 1835.
30 p.   21½ cm.

24832   Letter to a member of the General Assembly of Virginia, on
the subject of the late conspiracy of the slaves; with a
proposal for their colonization. Baltimore, Printed by
Bonsal & Niles, 1801.
23 p.   22 cm.

24833　A letter to Philo Africanus, upon slavery; in answer to his
　　　　of the 22d of November, in the General evening post;
　　　　together with the opinions of Sir John Strange, and
　　　　other eminent lawyers upon this subject, with the sentence
　　　　of Lord Mansfield, in the case of Somerset and Knowles,
　　　　1772, with his Lordship's explanation of that opinion in
　　　　1786. London, Printed for W. Brown, 1788.
　　　　　2 p.l., 40 p.　　22½ cm.
　　　　　Letter signed:　Candidus.　December 10, 1787.

24834　Letter to the Edinburgh reviewers:　by "An American."　First
　　　　published in the National intelligencer of November 16,
　　　　1819. [n.p., 1819?]
　　　　　65 p.　　17½ cm.
　　　　　Caption title.

24835　A letter to Wm. E. Channing, D.D., in reply to one addressed
　　　　to him by R. R. Madden on the abuse of the flag of the
　　　　United States in the island of Cuba, for promoting the
　　　　slave trade.　By a calm observer.　Boston, W. D. Ticknor,
　　　　1840.
　　　　　36 p.　　24 cm.

24836　Letters on American slavery from Victor Hugo, de Tocqueville
　　　　Emile de Girardin, Carnot, Passy, Mazzini, Humboldt,
　　　　O. Lafayette--&c.　Boston, American Anti-slavery Society,
　　　　1860.
　　　　　24 p.　　19 cm.

24837　Letters on the necessity of a prompt extinction of British
　　　　colonial slavery; chiefly addressed to the more influentia
　　　　classes... to which are added, Thoughts on compensation.
　　　　London, Sold by Hatchard and son and by T. Combe and son,
　　　　Leicester, 1826.
　　　　　2 p.l., 219 p.　　22 cm.

24838　Levasnier, Francis E
　　　　　John Brown.　Réflexions sur l'esclavage.　Par Francis E.
　　　　Levasnier...　New York, S. Hallet, imprimeur, 1860.
　　　　　iv, [5]-32 p.　　22½ cm.

24839　[Lewis, Evan]
　　　　　An address to Christians of all denominations, on the
　　　　inconsistency of admitting slave-holders to communion and
　　　　church membership...　Philadelphia, S. C. Atkinson,
　　　　printer, 1831.
　　　　　19 p.　　17 cm.

24840　Lewis, Evan.
　　　　　Address to the coloured people of Philadelphia delivered

at Bethel Church on the evening of the 12th of the 3rd
mo. 1833.   Philadelphia, Printed by J. Richards, 1833.
22 p.   18 cm.
"The farewell address of Elisha Tyson":   p. 18-22.

24841   Lewis, Matthew Gregory, 1775-1818.
Journal of a residence among the Negroes in the West
Indies.   By Matthew Gregory Lewis...   New ed.   London,
J. Murray, 1861.
viii, 184 p.   18½ cm.

24842   Lewis, Robert Benjamin.
Light and truth; collected from the Bible and ancient
and modern history, containing a universal history of the
colored and the Indian race, from the creation of the
world to the present time.   By R. B. Lewis...   Boston,
Pub. by a committee of colored gentlemen, B. F. Roberts,
printer, 1844.
viii, [9]-400 p.   18½ cm.

24843   Lewis, Tayler, 1802-1877.
The heroic periods in a nation's history.   An appeal to
the soldiers of the American armies.   By Tayler Lewis...
New York, Baker & Godwin, printers, 1866.
58 p.   18½ cm.

24844   Lexington, Mo.   Pro-slavery Convention, 1855.
Address to the people of the United States, together
with the proceedings and resolutions of the Pro-slavery
Convention of Missouri, held at Lexington, July, 1855.
St. Louis, Mo., Printed at the Republican office, 1855.
30 p.   22½ cm.

24845   Liberator-extra!   Middlesex awake!!   "Liberty for all, or
chains for all"!!   [n.p., 1838]
[2] p.   51 cm.

24846   Liberia unmasked; or, The incompatibility of the views and
schemes of the American Colonization Society, with those
of the real friends of the immediate abolition of slavery,
proved by facts...   Edinburgh, W. Oliphant; [etc., etc.]
1833.
19 p.   21½ cm.

24847   "Libertomania"; ó, Resultado de la emancipacion en el norte
de los Estados Unidos y en las islas occidentales, con
la estadística de la decadencia del comercio, inclinacion
del negro al ocio, su degeneracion al estado primitivo
salvaje, y el efecto que producirá la emancipacion en las

155

clases agrícolas, mecánicas y jornaleras. Nueva York,
Impr. de Holman, 1862.
iv, [5]-60 p.   22½ cm.

24848   The liberty almanac for 1845. Syracuse, N. Y., Tucker &
Kinney, Publishers, 1845.
35, [1] p.   16½ cm.

24849   The Liberty almanac for 1847-1852. New York, Am. and For.
Anti-Slavery Society [etc., 1847?-52?]
6 v.   illus.   18½-21½ cm.
1847-48 published by W. Harned.
No more published?

24850   The Liberty almanac for 1850. Published by the American &
Foreign Anti-slavery Society. [n.p.] William Harned,
Agent, No. 61 John Street [1850?]
47, [1] p.   16 cm.

24851   The Liberty almanac for 1852. [n.p.] Published by the
American and Foreign Anti-slavery Society: William Harned
Agent, No. 48 Beekman Street [1852?]
39, [1] p.   16½ cm.

24852   The Liberty and property of British subjects asserted: in a
letter from an assembly-man in Carolina, to his friend
in London... London, Printed for J. Roberts, 1726.
xx, [21]-39 p.   19½ cm.
Signed: J---- N----. Dated: Carolina, Charles-Town,
Jan. 15, 1725-6.
The preface, p. [iii]-xx, gives an account of the
discovery, early history, and government of the province o
Carolina. The letter was written to justify the people
of Carolina in their complaints against the proprietary
government.

24853   The liberty bell, Society Sons of the Revolution in the
State of California. v. 1-5; March 1915-October 1919.
5 v.   illus.   25½ cm.   irregular, 17½-20 cm.

24854   Liberty chimes. Providence, Ladies Anti-slavery Society,
1845.
148 p.   17 cm.

24855   Liberty leaguer. v. 1-   1849-   Honeoye, Ontario
county, N. Y.
v.   30 cm.
1849 - editor, William Goodell.

24856   Liberty or slavery; the great national question. Three
            prize essays on American slavery... Boston, Congregational
            Board of Publication, 1857.
                vii (i.e. vi), 138 p.   17 cm.
                Contents. - The error and the duty in regard to slavery,
            by Rev. R. B. Thurston. - Rev. Timothy Williston. Is
            American slavery an institution which Christianity sanc-
            tions, and will perpetuate? and a view of this subject,
            what ought American Christians to do, and refrain from
            doing?

24857   Lieber, Francis, 1800-1872.
                ... A letter to Hon. E. D. Morgan... on the amendment of
            the Constitution abolishing slavery. Resolutions, passed
            by the New York Union League Club, concerning conditions
            of peace with the insurgents. By Francis Lieber... New
            York, 1865.
                4 p.   22½ cm.   (Loyal Publication Society. [Pamphlets]
            no. 79)

24858   Lieber, Francis, 1800-1872.
            Plantations for slave labor the death of the yeomanry.
            By Francis Lieber, LL.D. [Philadelphia, C. Sherman, son
            & co., 1863]
                cover-title, 8 p.   21½ cm.

24859   Lieber, Francis, 1800-1872.
                ... Slavery, plantations and the yeomanry. By Francis
            Lieber. New-York, Oct. 1863. New York, C. S. Westcott &
            co., printers, 1863.
                cover-title, 8 p.   23 cm.   (Loyal Publication
            Society. [Pamphlets] no. 29)

24860   Liggins, Joseph.
            A refutation of the calumnies circulated by the Anti-
            slavery Agency Committee, against the West Indian planters.
            London, E. Wilson, 1833.
                47 p.   21 cm.

24861   The light and truth of slavery. Aaron's history. [Worcester,
            Mass., 184-?]
                48 p.   illus.   23 cm.
                Caption title.

24862   [Linck, F   W   G   ]
            De nopal-gouverneur der kolonie Suriname. [Naarden, 1848]
                16 p.   17½ cm.

24863   Lincoln, Abraham, Pres. U. S., 1809-1865.
            Address in Cincinnati, Ohio, September 17, 1859.

Cincinnati, C. F. Lotz Print. & Stationery Co., 1910.
60 p.   illus.   17 cm.

24864   Lincoln, Abraham, pres. U. S., 1809-1865.
        Letter of President Lincoln to the Missouri radicals,
        and Speech of S. T. Glover at the Court House in Jefferson
        City, Mo., Saturday, October 17th, 1863. [n.p., 1863]
        18 p.   22 cm.
        Caption title.

24865   Lincoln, Abraham, pres. U. S., 1809-1865.
        The President's letter to the Hon. James C. Conkling...
        Aug. 26, 1863. [Washington? D.C., 1863?]
        4 p.   22½ cm.

24866   Lincoln, Abraham, pres. U. S., 1809-1865.
        The Republican-party vindicated - the demands of the
        South explained. Speech of Hon. Abraham Lincoln, of
        Illinois, at the Cooper Institute, New York City, February
        27, 1860. [Washington? 1860]
        8 p.   22 cm.

24867   Lincoln, Jairus.
        Anti-slavery melodies: for the friends of freedom.
        Prepared for the Hingham Anti-slavery Society, by Jairus
        Lincoln. Hingham [Mass.] E. B. Gill [1843]
        96 p.   19½ cm.

24868   Lindley, Harlow, 1875.
        The Quakers in the old Northwest, by Harlow Lindley...
        [Cedar Rapids, Ia., The Torch press, 1912]
        15 p.   25 cm.
        Reprinted from the Proceedings of the Mississippi Valley
        Historical Association, v. 5, 1912.

24869   Linstant, Pradine, S   baron, d. 1884.
        De l'émigration européenne dans ses rapports avec la
        prospérité future des colonies, par S. Linstant...
        Paris, 1850.
        2 p.l., 212 p.   22 cm.

24870   Linstant Pradine, S   baron, d. 1884.
        Essai sur les moyens d'extirper les préjugés des blancs
        contre la couleur des Africains et des sang-mêlés.
        Ouvrage couronné par la Société française pour l'abolition
        de l'esclavage, dans sa séance du 1er juillet 1840, sous
        la présidence de m. Laisné de Villêveque; par S. Linstat.
        [Paris] Pagnerre, 1841.
        3 p.l., xiv, [4], 170 p.   22½ cm.

24871 [Lintz, Frederick Gustav]
Letters from an adopted citizen of the republic to his
mother in Germany. [Hopedale, Mass., Prog. age office,
1864]
24 p. 18 cm.
Caption title.
Signed: Treviranus.

24872 Little, Mrs. Laura Jane (Roys)
A mother's peace offering to American houses; or, The
martyr of the nineteenth century. By Mrs. L. J. Little.
New-York, J. A. Gray, printer, 1861.
109 p. 23½ cm.

24873 Little, Lucius P
Ben Hardin: his times and contemporaries, with selections
from his speeches. By Lucius P. Little. Louisville [Ky.]
Printed by the Courier-journal job printing company, 1887.
xi, 6-10, xiii-xxii p. front., illus. (incl. ports.,
facsims.) 24 cm.

24874 Livermore, George, 1809-1865.
An historical research respecting the opinions of the
founders of the republic on negroes as slaves, as citizens
and as soldiers. Read before the Massachusetts Historical
Society, August 14, 1862. By George Livermore. Boston,
Printed by J. Wilson and son, 1862.
xiv, [2], 215, [1] p. 23½ cm.

24875 [Livermore, George] 1809-1865.
A merchant of the old school. A tribute to the memory
of James Johnson. Boston, Printed for private distribution,
1855.
19 p. 22½ cm.

24876 Liverpool Society for Promoting the Abolition of Slavery.
Declaration of the objects of the Liverpool Society for
promoting the Abolition of Slavery, 25th March, 1823.
London, Hatchard & son; [etc., etc., 1823]
14 p. 20½ cm.

24877 Loehnis, H
Die Vereinigten Staaten von Amerika. Deren Vergangenheit
und Gegenwart in socialer, politischer und finanzieller
Beziehung. Von H. Loehnis. Leipzig, E. H. Mayer [etc.]
1864.
x p., 1 l., xxxi, 352 p. tables (part fold.) 22 cm.

24878 Logan, John Alexander, 1826-1886.
Reconstruction. Speech of Hon. J. A. Logan, of Illinois,

in the House of Representatives, July 11, 1867, on the
supplementary reconstruction bill, and in reply to Hon.
William E. Robinson, of New York... [Washington, Printed
at the Great republic office, 1867]
7 p.   24 cm.
Caption title.
Published by the Union Republican congressional committee.
Washington, D. C.

24879   Lomax, John Tayloe, 1781-1862.
Digest of the laws respecting real property, generally
adopted and in use in the United States; embracing, more
especially, the law of real property in Virginia. By John
Tayloe Lomax... Philadelphia, J. S. Littell, 1839.
3 v.   24 cm.

24880   London. Citizens.
American slavery; report of a public meeting held at
Finsbury Chapel, Moorfields, to receive Frederick Douglass,
the American slave, on Friday, May 22, 1846. Joseph Sturge,
Esq., in the chair. London, 1846.
24 p.   22 cm.

24881   London Missionary Society.
The London Missionary Society's report of the proceedings
against the late Rev. J. Smith, of Demerara... who was
tried under martial law, and condemned to death, on a
charge of aiding and assisting in a rebellion of the negro
slaves; from a full and correct copy... and including the
documentary evidence omitted in the Parliamentary copy;
with an appendix; containing the letters and statements of
Mr. & Mrs. Smith... The whole pub. under the authority
of the directors of the said society. London, F. Westley
[etc.] 1824.
vii, 204 p.   23 cm.

24882   Long, Alexander, 1816-1886.
The present condition and future prospects of the
country. Speech delivered in the House of Representatives,
April 8, 1864. [Washington? D.C.] 1864.
19 p.   23 cm.
Caption title.

24883   Long, Daniel Albright, 1844-
Jefferson Davis: an address delivered at Concord, North
Carolina, June 3, 1921, by Daniel Albright Long. Raleigh,
N. C., Edwards & Broughton printing company, 1923.
20 p.   front. (port.)   23½ cm.

24884 [Long, Edward] 1734-1813.
The history of Jamaica: or, General survey of the ancient
and modern state of that island: with reflections on its
situation, settlements, inhabitants, climate, products,
commerce, laws, and government... Illustrated with copper
plates... London, T. Lowndes, 1774.
3 v. fold. fronts. (v. 1-2) plates (1 fold.) fold.
maps, plan. 28 x 22 cm.

24885 Longfellow, Henry Wadsworth, 1807-1882.
Poems on slavery. By Henry Wadsworth Longfellow.
Cambridge, J. Owen, 1842.
31 p. 18½ cm.

24886 Longstreet, Augustus Baldwin, 1790-1870.
Letters on the Epistle of Paul to Philemon, or The
connection of apostolical Christianity with slavery. By
Augustus B. Longstreet, L.L.D. Charleston, S. C., Printed
by B. Jenkins, 1845.
47 p. 22½ cm.

24887 Lord, Charles Eliphalet, 1817-1902.
Slavery, secession and the Constitution. An appeal to
our country's loyalty, by Rev. Charles E. Lord... Boston,
1864.
58 p. 22½ cm.

24888 [Lord, Daniel] 1795-1868.
The effect of secession upon the commercial relations
between the North and South, and upon each section.
London, H. Stevens, 1861.
78 p. fold. map. 21½ cm.

24889 Lord, John Chase, 1805-1877.
Causes and remedies of the present convulsions: a
discourse by Rev. John C. Lord, D.D. Buffalo, J. Warren
& co., printers, 1861.
25 p. 22 cm.

24890 Lord, John Chase, 1805-1877.
"The higher law," in its application to the Fugitive
slave bill. A sermon on the duties men owe to God and
to governments. Delivered at the Central Presbyterian
church, Buffalo, on Thanksgiving-day, by John C. Lord...
New-York, Pub. by order of the "Union safety committee,"
1851.
16 p. 22½ cm.

24891 [Lord, Nathan] 1793-1870
A letter of inquiry to ministers of the gospel of all

denominations, on slavery. By a northern presbyter.
Boston, Little, Brown, and company, 1854.
32 p.   27½ cm.

24892   Lord, Nathan, 1793-1870.
A northern presbyter's second letter to ministers of
the gospel of all denominations on slavery. By Nathan
Lord... Boston, Little, Brown and company; New York,
D. Appleton and company, 1855.
99 p.   22½ cm.
The writer replies here to critics of the first letter
(1850), and especially to the New Englander and Yale
review.

24893   Loria, A
The historical origin of slavery. [n.p., 1900]
466-477 p.   21 cm.
Reprinted from Sewanee review, v. 8, Oct. 1900.

24894   Louis, Paul, 1872-
Le travail dans le monde romain, par Paul-Louis; avec
41 gravures dans le texte. Paris, F. Alcan, 1912.
2 p.l., 416 p.   illus.   22½ cm.   (Histoire universelle du travail)

24895   Louisville. Free Public Library.
Some books and pamphlets, music, magazines and newspaper
by negro writers, composers and editors, in the Colored
Department of the Louisville Free Public Library. Louisville, Ky., 1921.
11, [1] p.   20 cm.

24896   Lounsbury, Thomas.
Pro-slavery overthrown; and the true principles of
abolitionism declared. Or a series of lectures in answer
to the question "What do the Scriptures teach on the
subject of slavery". By Rev. Thomas Lounsbury... 2d ed.
Geneva, N. Y., G. H. Derby & co.; [etc., etc.] 1847.
1 p.l., iii, 153 p.   16 cm.

24897   [Love, Horace Thomas] 1807-1895.
Slavery in its relation to God. A review of Rev. Dr.
Lord's Thanksgiving sermon, in favor of domestic slavery,
entitled The higher law, in its application of the
fugitive slave bill. By a minister of the gospel, in
Massachusetts. Written by special request. Buffalo, A. M
Clapp & co., printers, 1851.
56 p.   22 cm.

24898   Lovejoy, Joseph Cammet, 1805-1871.
         ... The alliance of Johashaphat and Ahab. A sermon
         preached on the annual fast April 4, 1844, at Cambridge-
         port. By Rev. J. C. Lovejoy.   Boston, Printed by Leavitt
         & Alden, 1844
         7, [1] p.   23 cm.
         Caption title.
         A sermon against slavery and dueling.

24899   Lovejoy, Joseph Cammett, 1805-1871.
         The North and the South! Letter from J. C. Lovejoy, esq.,
         to his brother, Hon. Owen Lovejoy, M. C., with remarks by
         the editor of the Washington union. [n.p., 1859]
         8 p.   21½ cm.
         Caption title.

24900   Lovejoy, Joseph Cammet, 1805-1871.
         The robbers of Adullam; or, A glance at "organic sins."
         A sermon, preached at Cambridgeport, November 27, 1845.
         By J. C. Lovejoy... Boston, D. H. Ela, printer, 1845.
         22 p.   18½ cm.

24901   Lowell, James Russell, 1819-1891.
         The anti-slavery papers of James Russell Lowell.   Boston
         and New York, Houghton, Mifflin and company, 1902.
         2 v.   24 cm.
         Edited from the manuscripts of W. B. Parker.

24902   Lowell, James Russell   1819-1891.
         ... The Biglow papers, edited, with an introduction,
         notes, glossary, and copious index, by Homer Wilbur, A.M.,
         pastor of the First Church in Jaalam, and (prospective)
         member of many literary, learned and scientific societies
         (for which we see page 13)... Boston, New York, Houghton,
         Mifflin and company, 1865.
         vi, [9]-198 p.   18 cm.   (The Riverside Aldine series.
         [no. 8])
         First series.

24903   Loyal meeting of the people of New-York, to support the
         government, prosecute the war, and maintain the union,
         held at the Cooper Institute, Friday evening, March 6,
         1863. Reported by A. F. Warburton. New York, G. F.
         Nesbitt & co., 1863.
         80 p.   23½ cm.
         Appendix: Inauguration of the Loyal League of Union
         Citizens at the Academy of Music, Saturday, 14th March,
         1863.

24904 Loyal National League of the State of New York.
            Address of the Loyal National League of the State of
       New York. [New York, 1861]
            cover-title, 8 p.   25½ cm.

24905 Loyal National League of the State of New York.
            Dialogue between an old-fashioned Jackson Democrat and
       a Copperhead. [New York? 186-?]
            4 p.   22½ cm.

24906 Loyal National League of the State of New York.
            ... Opinions of prominent men concerning the great
       questions of the times expressed in their letters to the
       Loyal National League, on occasion of the great mass
       meeting of the League and other loyalists at Union Square,
       New York, on the anniversary of Sumter... New York, C. S.
       Westcott & co., printers, 1863.
            72 p.   23½ cm.

24907 Loyal National League of the State of New York.
            Proceedings at the organization of the Loyal National
       League at the Cooper Institute, Friday evening, March 20th
       1863. Speeches of Gen. Cochrane and Gen. Hamilton;
       Hon. Roscoe Conkling, and Senator Foster of Conn. New
       York, C. S. Westcott & co., printers, 1863.
            47, [1] p.   23 cm.

24908 Loyal National League of the State of New York.
            The Sumter anniversary, 1863. Opinions of loyalists
       concerning the great questions of the times; expressed in
       the speeches and letters from prominent citizens of all
       sections and parties, on occasion of the inauguration of
       the Loyal National League, in mass meeting on Union Square
       New York, on the 11th of April, 1863, the anniversary of
       the attack on fort Sumter. Published by order of the
       council and executive committee of the Loyal National
       League. New York, C. S. Westcott & con., printers, 1863.
            144 p.   23½ cm.

24909 Loyal National Repeal Association of Ireland.
            Daniel O'Connell and the committee of the Irish Repeal
       Association of Cincinnati. (From the Catholic telegraph
       of Wednesday August 5th, 1863) Stereotype ed. Cincinnati
       O., Printed at the Catholic telegraph office, 1863.
            cover-title, 8 p.   23 cm.

24910 The Loyalist's ammunition. Philadelphia, Printed [by H. B.
       Ashmead] for gratuitous distribution, 1863.
            16 p.   22 cm.
            Cover title.

24911 Loyalty. What is it? To whom or what due? [n.p., 1863]
          12 p.   22½ cm.

24912 The loyalty for the times [A voice from Kentucky. April,
          1864. Philadelphia, Printed by H. B. Ashmead, 1864]
          24 p.   23 cm.
          Cover-title.

24913 Lugenbeel, James Washington, 1819?-1857.
          Sketches of Liberia: comprising a brief account of the
          geography, climate, productions, and diseases, of the
          republic of Liberia. 2d ed. - rev. To which is added
          a brief sketch of the history of Liberia, and a succinct
          account of the customs and superstitions of the contiguous
          native tribes. By J. W. Lugenbeel... Washington,
          C. Alexander, printer, 1853.
          48 p.   22 cm.

24914 Lunan, John.
          An abstract of the laws of Jamaica relating to slaves.
          (From 33 Charles II. [1681] to 59 George III inclusive
          [1818] With the slave law at length, also, an appendix,
          containing an abstract of the acts of Parliament relating
          to the abolition of the slave-trade. By John Lunan.
          Jamaica, Printed at the office of the Saint Jago de la
          Vega gazette, 1819.
          2 p.l., xv, 192, [8] p.   28½ x 22 cm.

24915 [Lundy, Benjamin] 1789-1839.
          The war in Texas; a review of facts and circumstances,
          showing that this contest is a crusade against Mexico,
          set on foot and supported by slaveholders, land-speculators,
          &c. in order to re-establish, extend, and perpetuate the
          system of slavery and the slave trade. 2d ed., rev. and
          enl. By a citizen of the United States. Philadelphia,
          Printed for the publishers by Merrihew and Gunn, 1837.
          64 p.   illus. (map)   23½ cm.

24916 [Lundy, John Patterson] 1823-1892.
          Review of Bishop Hopkins' Bible view of slavery, by a
          presbyter of the church in Philadelphia. [Philadelphia,
          1863]
          15 p.   23 cm.

24917 Lunt, George, 1803-1885.
          The origin of the late war: traced from the beginning
          of the Constitution to the revolt of the Southern States.
          New York, Appleton, 1866.
          xiv, 491 p.   20 cm.

24918   Luther, jr. [pseud.]
        Right and wrong of the Boston reformers showing them
        to be a bad remedy for a bad disease. New England, 1841.
        42 p.   18 cm.

24919   [Lyman, Darius] 1821?-1892.
        Leaven for doughfaces; or, Threescore and ten parables
        touching slavery. By a former resident of the South...
        Cincinnati, Bangs and company [etc.]; Cleveland, L. E.
        Barnard & co., 1856.
        332 p. incl. plates.   front.   18 cm.

24920   Lyon, James Adair, 1814-1882.
        A lecture on Christianity and the civil laws, by Rev.
        James A. Lyon... Columbus, "Mississippi Democrat" print,
        1859.
        32 p.   20½ cm.

24921   Lyrics of the war. Philadelphia, D. Scattergood [18--]
        cover-title, 3-14 p.   col. illus. (incl. music)
        27½ x 21½ cm.

                                M

24922   Macaulay, Zachary, 1768-1838.
        Faits et renseignemens, prouvant les avantages du
        travail libre sur le travail forcé, et indiquent les
        moyens le plus propres à hâter l'abolition de l'esclavage
        dans les colonies européennes; par Zachary Macaulay...
        Paris, Hachette, 1835.
        vii, 128 p.   21 cm.

24923   [Macaulay, Zachary] 1768-1838.
        Haïti, ou, Renseignemens authentiques sur l'abolition
        de l'esclavage et ses résultats à Saint-Domingue et à la
        Guadeloupe, avec des détails sur l'état actuel d'Haïti
        et des noirs émancipés qui forment sa population. Traduit
        de l'anglais. Paris, L. Hachette, 1835.
        2 p.l., iv, 207 p.   21 cm.
        Contents. - Lettre de l'éditeur à m. le duc de Broglie...
        [signed Z. Macaulay] - Mémoire sur l'abolition de l'escla-
        vage à Haïti. - Extraits des lettres d'un voyageur
        [Richard Hill, of Jamaica] à Haïti, pendant les années
        1830 et 1831. - Examen du rapport de m. Charles Mackenzie,
        consul général d'Angleterre à Haïti... - Mémoire sur la
        abolition de l'esclavage à la Guadeloupe.

                               166

24924 Macbeth, James.
         The church and the slaveholder; or, Light and darkness:
       an attempt to prove, from the word of God and from reason,
       that to hold property in man is wholly destitute of divine
       warrant, is a flagrant crime, and demands excommunication.
       Earnestly and respectfully addressed to the members of
       the approaching assembly of the Free Church of Scotland,
       and to the churches generally. By the Rev. James Macbeth...
       Edinburgh, J. Johnstone; [etc., etc., 1850]
         36 p.   23 cm.

24925 [McCall, Eli Robinson]
         No-history versus no-war; or, The great tootle rebellion
       exposed... By Michael Magaul [pseud.] New York, E. R.
       McCall, 1886.
         vii p., 1 l., 402 p.   19 cm.

24926 M'Carter, J   Mayland.
         Border Methodism and border slavery. Being a state-
       ment and review of the action of the Philadelphia Annual
       Conference Concerning Slavery, at its late session at
       Easton, Pa., including the case of Rev. J. D. Long: the
       shaveholding among members of the body: the extent and
       character of slaveholding in our territory: and "the
       crushing out" of Rev. J. S. Lame since the late session
       of the Conference. By Rev. J. Mayland M'Carter, of the
       Philadelphia Annual Conference. [2d ed.] Philadelphia,
       Collins, printer; for sale by Higgins & Perkinpine, 1858.
         88 p.   23 cm.

24927 M'Clintock, Thomas.
         Letter from T. M'Clintock to the Association of Friends
       for Promoting the Abolition of Slavery, &c. Philadelphia,
       Printed by Merrihew and Thompson, 1840.
         8 p.   16 cm.

24928 McCoy, A   D   b. 1813.
         Thoughts on labor in the South, past, present and
       future, by A. D. McCoy... New Orleans, Blelock & co.,
       1865.
         viii, 2 l., [13]-35 p.   19½ cm.

24929 McCrady, Edward, 1833-
         Slavery in the province of South Carolina, 1670-1770.
       [Washington, 1896]
         631-673 p.   22 cm.
         Reprinted from American Historical Association, Annual
       report for 1895.

24930 MacDonald, James Madison, 1812-1876.
The perfect law of liberty. An address, delivered in Rehoboth Church, Iowa, July 4th, 1860. By J. M. M'Donald. Pub. by request of the audience. Philadelphia, W. S. Young, printer, 1861.
24 p.   23½ cm.

24931 M'Donnell, Alexander.
An address to the members of both houses of Parliament on the West India question. By Alexander M'Donnell, esq. 2d ed. London, J. Ridgway, 1830.
vii, 112 p.   20½ cm.

24932 [McDougall, Mrs. Frances Harriet (Whipple) Greene] 1805-1878, ed.
The envoy. From free hearts to the free... Pawtucket, R. I., Juvenile eman. society, 1840.
vi, [7]-112 p.   front.   16 cm.
Poems and anecdotes on slavery.

24933 McDougall, Marion Gleason.
... Fugitive slaves (1619-1865) by Marion Gleason McDougall; prepared under the direction of Albert Bushnell Hart... Boston, Ginn & company, 1891.
viii, 150 p.   23½ cm.   (Publications of the Society for the Collegiate Instruction of Women. Fay House Monographs, no. 3)

24934 McDougle, Ivan Eugene.
Slavery in Kentucky, 1792-1865, by Ivan E. McDougle... [Lancaster, Pa., Press of the New era printing company, 1918]
2 p.l., 125 p.   25 cm.
Thesis (Ph.D.) - Clark university, 1918.
Reprinted from the Journal of negro history, vol. III, no. 3, July, 1918.

24935 McDowell, James, 1796-1851.
A lecture... by the late Hon. James M'Dowell, of Lexington, Va., and an address. by the late Rev. A. Alexander, D.D. Philadelphia, For sale by J. M. Wilson, 1851.
48 p.   23 cm.

24936 McDowell, James, 1796-1851.
Speech of James M'Dowell, jr. (of Rockbridge) in the House of Delegates of Virginia, on the slave question: delivered Saturday January 21, 1832. 2d ed. ...
Richmond, Printed by T. W. White, 1832.
33 p.   20½ cm.

24937   McDowell, Joseph Nashe, 1805-1868.
        A letter to the Rev. Henry Ward Beecher, and an address
        to the legislature of the state of Missouri, by Joseph N.
        McDowell... Saint Louis, Mo., Office of the Morning
        herald, 1860.
        cover-title, 12 p.   23½ cm.

24938   McElroy, John, 1846-1929.
        ... History of slavery in the U. S., by John McElroy...
        Washington, D. C., The National tribune, 1896.
        32 p.   illus.   23 cm.   (The National tribune
        library, v. 1, no. 5)

24939   McGill, Alexander Taggart, 1807-1889.
        The hand of God with the black race. A discourse
        delivered before the Pennsylvania Colonization Society,
        by Rev. Alexander T. McGill... Philadelphia, W. F.
        Geddes, printer, 1862.
        19 p.   22½ cm.

24940   [Macías, Juan Manuel] ed.
        The Cuban question in the Spanish parliament. (Debate
        in the Cortes) Extracts from speeches made by Señores
        Díaz Quintero, Benot, Salmeron... and others. London,
        "Anglo-American times" press, 1872.
        1 p.l., 32 p.   21 cm.

24941   McIntosh, Maria Jane, 1803-1878.
        Letter on the Address of the women of England to their
        sisters of America, in relation to slavery. By Miss
        M. J. M'Intosh... New York, T. J. Crowen, 1853.
        3 p.l., [5]-32 p.   15 cm.

24942   Mack, Alonzo W   1822-1871.
        Speech of Hon. A. W. Mack, on the slavery question in the
        state Senate, January 20, 1865. Springfield [Ill.] Baker &
        Phillips, printers, 1865.
        20 p.   21½ cm.

24943   McKee, Samuel, 1833-1898.
        Speech of Hon. Samuel McKee, of Kentucky, on recons-
        truction. Delivered in the House of Representatives,
        March 3, 1866. [Washington, D.C., Printed by L. Towers,
        1866]
        8 p.   24 cm.
        Caption title.

24944   [McKenney, Samuel]
        Slavery indispensable to the civilization of Africa.

3d ed. Baltimore, Printed by J. D. Toy, 1855.
51 p.   23 cm.

24945   McLane, Louis, 1786-1857.
Speech of Mr. M'Lane, of Delaware, on the following
amendment proposed by Mr. Taylor, of N. Y. to the bill
authorising the people of Missouri to form a constitution.
Delivered in the House of Representatives of the United
States, February 7, 1820. [Washington, 1820]
44 p.   19 cm.

24946   McLaughlin, Andrew Cunningham, 1861-1947.
... Lewis Cass, by Andrew C. McLaughlin... Boston
and New York, Houghton, Mifflin and company, 1899.
3 p.l., [v]-ix p., 2 l., 390 p., 1 l.   front., ports.,
fold. facsim.   22½ cm.   (Half-title: American statesmen... vol. XXIV)

24947   McLaughlin, John.
... A word with Bishop Hopkins. By John M'Laughlin.
[Philadelphia, 1864]
cover-title, 17 p.   21½ cm.

24948   M'Mahon, Benjamin.
Jamaica plantership, by Benjamin M'Mahon... London,
E. Wilson, 1839.
2 p.l., viii, [9]-304 p.   19½ cm.

24949   McMurray, William, 1783-1835.
A sermon, preached in behalf of the American colonization society, in the Reformed Dutch church, in Market-
street, New-York, July 10, 1825. By William M'Murray...
New York, Printed by J. Seymour, 1825.
28 p.   21 cm.

24950   MacNaul, Willard Carey, 1864-
The Jefferson-Lemen compact; the relations of Thomas
Jefferson and James Lemen in the exclusion of slavery
from Illinois and the Northwest Territory, with related
documents, 1781-1818; a paper read before the Chicago
historical society, February 16, 1915, by Willard C.
MacNaul. [Chicago] The University of Chicago press, 1915.
58 p., 1 l.   21½ cm.

24951   [Macon, Nathaniel]
Letters to Chas. O'Conor. The destruction of the union
is emancipation. Philadelphia, J. Campbell, 1862.
cover-title, 38 p.   22 cm.

24952   Macon, Nathaniel, 1757-1837.
            Speech of Mr. Macon, on the restriction of slavery in
        Missouri. Delivered in the Senate... January 20, 1820.
        [Washington, 1820]
            17 p.   18½ cm.

24953   Macpherson, Charles, fl. 1773-1790.
            Memoirs of the life and travels of the late Charles
        Macpherson, esq. in Asia, Africa, and America. Illus-
        trative of manners, customs, and character; with a
        particular investigation of the nature, treatment, and
        possible improvement, of the negro in the British and
        French West India Islands. Written by himself chiefly
        between the years 1773 and 1790... Edinburgh, A.
        Constable, 1800.
            2 p.l., [vii]-xv, 258 p.   17 cm.

24954   McTyeire, Holland Nimmons, bp., 1824-1889.
            Duties of masters to servants: three premium essays.
        I. By the Rev. H. N. McTyeire. II. By the Rev. C. F.
        Sturgis. III. By the Rev. A. T. Holmes. Charleston,
        S. C., Southern Baptist publication society, 1851.
            151 p.   16½ cm.
            Contents. - I. Master and servant, by H. N. McTyeire. -
        II. Melville letters; or, The duties of masters to their
        servants, by C. F. Sturgis. - III. The duties of Christian
        masters, by A. T. Holmes.

24955   Macy, Jesse, 1842-1919.
            The anti-slavery crusade; a chronicle of the gathering
        storm, by Jesse Macy. New Haven, Yale university press;
        [etc., etc.] 1921.
            ix, 245 p.   col. front.   18 cm.   (Half-title:
        The Chronicles of America series, Allen Johnson, editor...
        v. 28)

24956   Madden, Richard Robert, 1798-1886.
            The island of Cuba: its resources, progress, and
        prospects, considered in relation especially to the
        influence of its prosperity on the interests of the
        British West India colonies. By R. R. Madden...
        London, Partridge & Oakey, 1853.
            xxiv, 252 p.   18½ cm.

24957   Madden, Richard Robert, 1798-1886.
            A twelvemonth's residence in the West Indies, during
        the transition from slavery to apprenticeship; with inci-
        dental notices of the state of society, prospects, and
        natural resources of Jamaica and other islands. By R. R.

Madden... Philadelphia, Carey, Lea and Blanchard, 1835.
2 v.   16 cm.

24958 Mahan, Milo, 1819-1870.
Dr. Mahan's speech. [n.p., 1862]
16 p.   21½ cm.
Caption title.
On slavery; apparently spoken in the General convention
of the Protestant Episcopal church, 1862.

24959 Maine historical memorials... [Augusta?] Printed for the
state, 1922.
xi, 199 p.   plates, ports.   23½ cm.
Contents. - A fugitive slave case in Maine, 1837-1841.
[By H. S. Burrage] - James Russell Lowell's two visits
to Portland in 1857. [By H. S. Burrage] - James Phinney
Baxter. [By H. S. Burrage] - Franklin Simmonds, sculptor.
[By H. S. Burrage] - The Maine Historical Society in
Brunswick, 1822-1880. By K. C. M. Sills. - The Maine
Historical Society at Portland, by Hon. A. F. Moulton.

24960 Maine Union in Behalf of the Colored Race.
Proceedings of the convention which formed the Maine
Union in Behalf of the Colored Race. With the address
of the executive committee to the public. Portland,
Merrill and Byram, 1835.
16 p.   20½ cm.

24961 Mallard, Robert Q
Plantation life before emancipation. By R. Q. Mallard..
Richmond, Va., Whittet & Shepperson, 1892.
xi, 3-237 p.   16½ cm.

24962 Mandry, Gustav von, 1832-1902.
Über Begriff und Wesen des peculium. Festschrift zu
Carl Georg von Wächter's fünfzigjährigem Professor-
jubiläum von Gustav Mandry... Tübingen, Gedruckt bei
H. Laupp, 1869.
2 p.l., [3]-92 p.   26½ x 20 cm.

24963 Manigault, Gabriel, 1809-1888.
The United States unmasked. A search into the causes
of the rise and progress of these states, and an
exposure of their present material and moral condition.
With additions and corrections by the author. By G.
Manigault. London, E. Stanford, 1879.
4 p.l., 168 p.   19 cm.

24964 Mann, Charles Wesley, 1862-1909.
The Chicago Common Council and the Fugitive slave law

of 1850. An address read before the Chicago Historical
Society at a special meeting held January 29, 1903. By
Charles W. Mann.   Chicago, 1903.
    32 p.   20½ cm.   (In Chicago Historical Society,
[Proceedings] 1903-1905, [v. 2], p. [55]-86)

24965   Mansfeldt, Junlius.
        Meine Reise nach Brasilien im Jahre 1826. Hrsg. von
    Julius Mansfeldt... Magdeburg, Gedruckt bei Bansch,
    jun., 1828.
        2 v. in 1.   1 pl., fold. map, 2 fold. tab.   19 cm.

24966   Mantero, Francisco.
        ... La main-d'oeuvre à S. Thomé et à l'Île du Prince;
    extrait de la conférence de M. Francisco Mantero, membre
    de la société, faite dans la soirée du 13 février 1911...
    Lisboa, Typ. do Annuario commercial, 1911.
        144 p.   20½ cm.
    At head of title: Association centrale de l'agriculture
    portugaise (syndicate agricole central)

24967   Mantero, Francisco.
        Manual labour in S. Thomé and Principe. By Francis
    Mantero. Translated from the Portuguese. Lisbon, Printing
    office of the Annuario commercial, 1910.
        183 p., 4 l.   plates, ports., fold. maps, fold. tables,
    fold. diagrs.   29 cm.
        "Some of the articles published by Lieut.-Colonel Wyllie
    in the English press": p. [175]-183.

24968   Mantero, Francisco.
        Portuguese planters and British humanitarians; the case
    for S. Thomé. Notes of an address by Francisco Mantero,
    delivered on the 13th February, 1911... Tr. by Lieut.-
    Colonel J. A. Wyllie, F.R.G.S. Lisbon, Redacção da
    Reforma, 1911.
        xvii p., 1 l., 203, [1] p.   21½ cm.

24969   [Manzano, Juan Francisco] 1797-1854.
        Poems by a slave in the island of Cuba, recently
    liberated; translated from the Spanish, by R. R. Madden,
    M.D., with the history of the early life of the negro
    poet, written by himself; to which are prefixed two
    pieces descriptive of Cuban slavery and the slave-traffic,
    by R. R. M. London, T. Ward & co., 1840.
        4 p.l., v p., 1 l., [9]-188 p.   22½ cm.

24970   Manumission Society of North Carolina.
        An address to the people of North Carolina, on the

evils of slavery. By the friends of liberty and equality..
William Swain, printer. Greensborough, N. C. 1830.
[New York, N. Muller, printer, 1860]
1 p.l., 68 p., 1 l.   14½ cm.

24971   Marly; or, The life of a planter in Jamaica; comprehending
characteristic sketches of the present state of society
and manners in the British West Indies. And an impartial
review of the leading questions relative to colonial
policy. 2d ed. Glasgow, Printed for Griffin & co.;
[etc., etc.] 1828.
2 p.l., ii, 363, [1] p.   21½ cm.

24972   Marquand, Henri E
Souvenirs des Indes Occidentales, et impressions intimes;
suivis de Eliza et Maria. Par Henri E. Marquand. Londres,
Simpkin, Marshall & cie.; Guernesey, E. Barbet, 1853.
xiv, [2], 336 p.   23 cm.

24973   [Marsh, Leonard] 1800-1870.
A bake-pan for the dough-faces. By one of them...
Try it. Burlington, Vt., C. Goodrich, 1854.
64 p.   23½ cm.

24974   Marshall, Humphrey, 1812-1872.
California and New Mexico. Speech of Hon. H. Marshall,
of Kentucky, in the House of Representatives, April 3,
1850, in Committee of the Whole on the State of the
Union, on the President's message transmitting the
constitution of California. [Washington, Printed at the
Congressional globe office, 1850]
8 p.   23 cm.
Caption title.

24975   Marshall, Thomas, of Fauquier Co., Va.
The speech of Thomas Marshall, in the House of Delegates
of Virginia, on the abolition of slavery. Delivered
Friday, January 20, 1832. Richmond, Printed by T. W.
White, 1832.
12 p.   21 cm.

24976   [Martineau, Harriet] 1802-1876.
The 'manifest destiny' of the American union... New
York, American Anti-slavery Society, 1857.
72 p.   18 cm.

24977   Marvin, Abijah Perkins.
Fugitive slaves: a sermon, preached in the North Congregational Church, Winchendon, on the day of the annual

fast, April 11, 1850. By A. P. Marvin... Published
by request. Boston, J. P. Jewett & co., 1850.
   24 p.   22 cm.

24978 Maryland. General Assembly. House of Delegates. Committee
on Grievances and Courts of Justice.
   Report of the Committee on Grievances and Courts of
Justice, relative to the surrender of fugitives from
justice, made to the House of Delegates of Maryland,
December session, 1841. [Annapolis?] 1841.
   15 p.   24 cm.

24979 Maryland Society for Promoting the Abolition of Slavery.
   Constitution of the Maryland Society for Promoting the
Abolition of Slavery, and the relief of free negroes,
and others, unlawfully held in bondage. Baltimore,
Printed by William Goddard and James Angell, 1789.
   8 p.   19½ cm.

24980 Maryland State Colonization Society.
   Communication from the Board of managers of the Maryland
State Colonization Society, to the president and members
of the convention now assembled in Baltimore, in
reference to the subject of colonization. Baltimore,
Printed by J. D. Toy, 1841.
   13, [3] p.   24½ cm.

24981 Maschke, Richard, 1862-1926.
   Der Freiheitsprozess im klassischen Altertum, insbe-
sondere der Prozess um Virginia, von Richard Maschke...
Berlin, R. Gaertner, 1888.
   xii, 191, [1] p.   23½ cm.   (Added t.-p.: Historische
Untersuchungen. Bft. VIII)

24982 Mason, James Murray, 1798-1871.
   Property in territories. Speech of Hon. J. M. Mason,
of Virginia, delivered in the Senate of the United States,
May 18, 1860. [Washington] Printed by L. Towers [1860]
   16 p.   23 cm.
   Caption title.

24983 Mason, Richard R
   Slavery in America. An essay for the times. By Richard
R. Mason. Boston, Press of Crocker and Brewster, 1853.
   34 p.   24 cm.

24984 Mason, Vroman.
   The fugitive slave law in Wisconsin, with reference
to nullification sentiment, by Vroman Mason... Madison,

175

State Historical Society of Wisconsin, 1895.
1 p.l., p. 117-144.   24½ cm.
Reprinted from Proceedings of the State Historical
Society of Wisconsin, 1895.

24985   Mason, William, 1725-1797.
An occasional discourse, preached in the Cathedral of
St. Peter in York, January 27, 1788, on the subject of
the African slave-trade. York, Printed by A. Ward for the
author, 1788.
27 p.   25 cm.

24986   Massachusetts, pseud.
The new states; or, A comparison of the wealth,
strength, and population of the northern and southern
states; as also of their respective powers in Congress;
with a view to expose the injustice of erecting new
states at the South. By Massachusetts. Boston, J.
Belcher, printer, 1813.
36 p.   22½ cm.

24987   Massachusetts. General Court. Committee to Prepare a
Memorial to Congress on the Subject of the Prohibition
of Slavery in the United States.
Memorial to the Congress to the United States, on the
subject of restraining the increase of slavery in new
states to be admitted into the Union... Boston, Sewell,
Phelps, 1819.
22 p.   21 cm.
Committee consisted of Daniel Webster and others.

24988   Massachusetts. General Court. House of Representatives.
Committee on Admission into the State of Free Negroes
and Mulattoes.
Free negroes and mulattoes... Report... [Boston,
1822]
16 p.   22 cm.
Caption title.
Report dated: January 16, 1822; signed: For the
Committee, Theodore Lyman, jr.

24989   Massachusetts. General Court. Joint Committee on
Deliverance of Citizens Liable to be Sold as Slaves.
... Report on the deliverance of citizens, liable to be
sold as slaves. [Boston, 1839]
36 p.   25 cm.   ([General court, 1839] House.
[Doc.] 38)
Thomas Kinnicutt, chairman.
Minority report, submitted by Geo. Bradburn: p. 5-36.

176

24990 Massachusetts. General Court. Joint Special Committee
on Memorial of Oliver B. Morris and Others.
... Report and resolves on the right of petition.
Boston, 1838.
20 p.   24½ cm.   [General Court, 1838]   Senate.
[Doc.] 86)
J. C. Alvord, chairman.

24991 Massachusetts. General Court. Joint Special Committee
on Petition of Asa Stoughton and Others.
... Report on the powers and duties of Congress upon
the subject of slavery and the slave trade. [Boston,
1838]
36 p.   25 cm.   ([General Court, 1838] Senate.
[Doc.] 87)
J. C. Alvord, chairman.

24992 Massachusetts. General Court. Joint Special Committee on
Slavery.
... Report and resolves on the subject of slavery.
[Boston, 1836]
59 p.   25 cm.   (Senate [doc.] no. 56)

24993 Massachusetts. General Court. Joint Special Committee on
Slavery.
... Report of the committee to whom was referred the
memorial of the Anti-slavery Society. [Boston, 1836]
10 p.   25 cm.   (Senate [doc.] no. 57)

24994 Massachusetts. General Court. Joint Special Committee on
So Much of the Governor's Address as Relates to Slavery.
[Report of the Joint Special Committee on So Much of
the Governor's Address as Relates to Slavery and on
petitions praying the legislature to instruct their
senators and to request representatives in Congress to
endeavor to procure a repeal of the Fugitive slave law.
Boston, 1851]
19 p.   25 cm.   ([General court, 1851] Senate.
[Doc.] 51)   J. T. Buckingham, chairman.

24995 Massachusetts. General Court. Joint Special Committee on
the Treatment of Samuel Hoar by the State of South
Carolina.
... Resolve and declaration. [Boston] 1845.
54 p.   24½ cm.   (Senate. no. 31)

24996 Massachusetts. General Court, 1836. Senate.
Report and resolves on the subject of slavery. [n.p.,
1836]
59 p.   21 cm.

24997   Massachusetts Abolition Society.
        Formation of the Massachusetts Abolition Society.
        [Boston? 1839?]
        36 p.   21 cm.
        Caption title.

24998   Massachusetts Abolition Society.
        The second annual report of the Massachusetts Abolition
        Society: together with the proceedings of the second
        annual meeting, held at Tremont chapel, May 25, 1841.
        Boston, D. H. Ela, printer, 1841.
        58 p.   24 cm.

24999   Massachusetts Abolition Society.
        The true history of the late division in the anti-slaver
        societies, being part of the second annual report of the
        executive committee of the Massachusetts Abolition Society
        Boston, D. H. Ela, printer, 1841.
        45 p.   21½ cm.

25000   Massachusetts Anti-slavery society.
        An account of the interviews which took place on the
        fourth and eighth of March, between a committee of the
        Massachusetts Anti-slavery Society, and the committee of
        the legislature. Boston, Massachusetts Anti-slavery
        Society, 1836.
        26 p.   26 cm.

25001   Massachusetts Anti-slavery Society.
        An address to the abolitionists of Massachusetts, on
        the subject of political action. By the board of managers
        of the Mass. A. s. Society. [Boston? 1838]
        20 p.   16½ cm.
        Caption title.

25002   Massachusetts Anti-slavery Society.
        Constitution of the New-England Anti-slavery Society:
        with an address to the public. Boston, Printed by
        Garrison and Knapp, 1832.
        16 p.   22 cm.
        The name of the society was changed in 1835 to
        Massachusetts Anti-slavery Society.

25003   Massachusetts Anti-slavery Society.
        ... Proceedings of the Massachusetts Anti-slavery
        society at the annual meetings held in 1854, 1855 &
        1856; with the treasurer's reports and general agent's
        annual statements. Boston, Office of Massachusetts
        Anti-slavery Society, 1856.
        67, [1] p.   23½ cm.

25004   Massachusetts Junior, pseud.
        A plea for the South. By Massachusetts Junior...
        Boston, S. P. Seaman, 1847.
        42 p.   20½ cm.

25005   Massachusetts State Disunion Convention, Worcester, 1857.
        Proceedings of the State Disunion Convention, held at
        Worcester, Massachusetts, January 15, 1857... Boston,
        Printed for the Committee, 1857.
        60, 19 p.   23 cm.

25006   [Massachusetts State Texas Committee]
        How to settle the Texas question. [Boston? E. Wright,
        jr.? 1845]
        11, [1] p.   18 cm.
        Caption title.

25007   Massie, James William, 1799-1869.
        The case stated: the friends and enemies of the
        American slave, by James W. Massie... Manchester, Union
        and emancipation society, 1863.
        8 p.   21½ cm.

25008   Massie, James William, 1799-1869.
        International sympathies. Report of the farewell
        meeting for Rev. J. W. Massie, D. D., of London, at the
        Broadway Tabernacle church, New York, September 27, 1863.
        New York, A. D. F. Randolph, 1863.
        31 p.   23 cm.

25009   Massie, Joseph, d. 1784.
        A state of the British sugar-colony trade; shewing that
        an additional duty of twelve shillings per 112 pounds
        weight may be laid upon brown or muscovado sugar (and
        proportionably higher duties upon sugar refined before
        imported) without making sugar dearer in this kingdom
        than it hath been of late years, and without distressing
        the British sugar planters... Submitted to the consider-
        ation of the honourable House of Commons. By J. Massie.
        London, T. Payne, 1759.
        1 p.l., 40 p.   23½ cm.

25010   Mather, Otis May, 1868-
        Six generations of La Rues and allied families; con-
        taining sketch of Isaac La Rue, senior, who died in
        Frederick county, Virginia, in 1795, and some account
        of his American ancestors and three generations of his
        descendants and families who were connected by inter-
        marriage, among others, Carman, Hodgen, Helm, Buzan, Rust,

McDonald, Castleman, Walters, Alexander, Medley, McMahon, Vertrees, Keith, Wintersmith, Clay, Neill, Grantham, Vanmeter and Enlow; copies of six old wills and other old documents; various incidents connected with the settlement of the Nolynn valley in Kentucky; also a chapter on the La Rue family and the child Abraham Lincoln By Otis M. Mather... Hodgenville, Ky., 1921.
 xiii, 198 p. front., illus. (incl. ports., facsim., geneal. tab.) 21 cm.

25011 Mathews, Samuel Augustus.
 The lying hero; or, An answer to J. B. Moreton's Manners and customs in the West Indies, by Samuel Augustus Mathews St. Eustatius, E. L. Low & co. for the author, 1793.
 2 p.l., 160 p. 19 x 15 cm.

25012 Matlack, Lucius C
 The antislavery struggle and triumph in the Methodist Episcopal Church. By Rev. L. C. Matlack... With an introduction by Rev. D. D. Whedon... New York, Phillips & Hunt: Cincinnati, Walden & Stowe, 1881.
 379 p. 19 cm.

25013 Matthews, Albert, 1860-
 Notes on the proposed abolition of slavery in Virginia in 1785. By Albert Matthews... Cambridge [Mass.] J. Wilson and son, 1903.
 13 p. 24½ cm.
 Reprinted from the Publications of the Colonial society of Massachusetts, vol. 6.

25014 Matthews, Mrs. Essie (Collins)
 Aunt Phebe, Uncle Tom and others; character studies among the old slaves of the South, fifty years after, by Essie Collins Matthews; illustrated from photographs made by the author in the cabins and on the plantations. Columbus, O., The Champlin press, 1915.
 140 p. incl. front., illus. 23½ cm.

25015 [Maupertuis, Pierre Louis Moreau de] 1698-1759.
 Dissertation physique à l'occasion du nègre blanc... Leyde, 1744.
 6 p.l., 132 p. 18 cm.

25016 Maxwell, Augustus Emmett, 1820-1903.
 The President's message - Party-unity - The South on the defensive. Speech of Hon. Augustus E. Maxwell, of Florida, delivered in the House of Representatives, January 27, 1857. Washington, Printed at the office of

the Congressional globe, 1857]
7 p.   23 cm.
Caption title.

25017 Maxwell, Augustus Emmett, 1820-1903.
Slavery - Kansas - Parties thereon. Speech of Hon.
A. E. Maxwell, of Florida, delivered in the House of
Representatives, May 1, 1856. Washington, Printed at the
Congressional globe office, 1856.
12 p.   24 cm.

25018 May, Henry, 1816-1863.
Speech of Hon. Henry May, of Maryland, against the war
and arming negroes, and for peace and recognition; in the
House of Representatives, February 2, 1863. [Washington,
1863]
7 p.   24½ cm.
Caption title.

25019 [May, James] 1805-1863.
Remarks on Bishop Hopkins' letter on the Bible view of
slavery. [n.p., 1863]
20 p.   22½ cm.

25020 [May, Samuel] 1810-1899.
Catalogue of anti-slavery publications in America.
[New York, American Anti-slavery Society, 1864]
[157]-175 p.   23½ cm.
Reprinted from the Proceedings of the American Anti-
slavery Society at its 3d decade, Philadelphia, 1863.
Caption title.

25021 May, Samuel Joseph, 1797-1871.
A discourse on slavery in the United States, delivered
in Brooklyn, July 3, 1831. By Samuel J. May... Boston,
Garrison and Knapp, 1832.
29 p., 1 l.   24½ cm.

25022 May, Samuel Joseph, 1797-1871.
Some recollections of our antislavery conflict. By
Samuel J. May. Boston, Fields, Osgood, & co., 1869.
viii, 408 p.   18½ cm.

25023 Means, Eldred Kurtz, 1878-1957.
Further E. K. Means. Is this a title? It is not.
It is the name of a writer of negro stories, who has
made himself so completely the writer of negro stories
that this third book, like the first and second, needs
no title. Illustrated by kemble. New York and London,

181

G. P. Putnam's sons [c1921]
     iii, 346 p.   front.   19 cm.
     Contents. - The left hind foot. - The 'fraid cat. -
The consolation prize. - The first high janitor. -
Family ties. - The ten-share horse. - A chariot of fire.

25024 Medico, pseud.
     A review of Garrisonian fanaticism and its influence.
By Medico... Boston, Sold by Ticknor, Reed & Fields,
1852.
     24 p.   23 cm.
     Largely an attack on certain anti-slavery writings of
Rev. J. G. Forman.

25025 Meigs, Henry, 1782-1861.
     Speech of Mr. Meigs, of New York, on the restriction of
slavery in Missouri. Delivered in the House of Representatives... January 25, 1820. [Washington, 1820]
     8 p.   18½ cm.

25026 Melbourn, Julius, b. 1790.
     Life and opinions of Julius Melbourn; with sketches of
the lives and characters of Thomas Jefferson, John Quincy
Adams, John Randolph, and several other eminent American
statesmen. Ed. by a late member of Congress. Syracuse,
Hall & Dickson; [etc., etc.] 1847.
     239 p.   front. (port.)   20 cm.

25027 Melville, Herman, 1819-1891.
     Battle-pieces and aspects of the war, by Herman Melvill
New York, Harper & brothers, 1866.
     x, [11]-272 p.
     Poems.
     Supplement, in prose, on the political situation:
p. [257]-272.

25028 [Memminger, Christopher Gustavus] 1803-1888.
     The mission of South Carolina to Virginia. [Baltimore,
From the press of J. Lucas & son, 1860?]
     34 p.   22 cm.

25029 Memorial on the personal liberty law. Boston, 1861
     cover-title, 36 p.   23½ cm.   ([Massachusetts.
General court, 1861] House [doc.] no. 121)
     Signed by David Lee Child, L. Maria Child, Alpheus
Bigelow, and others.

25030 [Memorial reported to have been laid before the "General
Council" of the bishops, clergy and laity, of the

Protestant Episcopal Church in the Confederate States of
America, held in St. Paul's Church, Augusta, Georgia,
November 22, 1862] [n.p., 1862?]
8 p. 22 cm.
Title from J. R. Bartlett's The literature of the
rebellion, Providence, 1866. no. 3170.

25031 Mendoça Corte-Real, Diogo de.
Traduction de la demonstration de la Compagnie des Indes
Occidentales, contenant les raisons pourquoi les Portugais
ne sont point en droit de naviguer vers les côtes de la
Haute & Basse-Guinée, &c. et examen et refutation de toutes
ces raisons; par Diogo de Mendoça Corte-Real...
[Amsterdam?] 1727.
34 p. 24 x 20 cm.

25032 Merle d'Aubigné, Jean Henry, 1794-1872.
Letter of Merle d'Aubigné, D.D. [n.p., 185-?]
8 p. 18½ cm.
Caption title.
Signed by Merle d'Aubigné, L. Gaussen, and others.
On slavery.

25033 Merriam, George Spring, 1843-1914.
The Negro and the nation; a history of American slavery
and enfranchisement, by George S. Merriam. New York,
H. Holt and company, 1906.
iv, 436 p. 21 cm.

25034 Methodist Episcopal Church. General Conferences, Cincinnati.
Debate on "Modern Abolitionism," in the General Conference... Cincinnati, Ohio Anti-slavery Society, 1836.
91 p. 21 cm.

25035 Métral, Antoine Marie Thérèse, 1778-1839.
Histoire de l'insurrection des esclaves dans le nord
de Saint-Domingue. Par Antoine Métral... Paris,
F. Scherff; [etc., etc.] 1818.
2 p.l., viii, [9]-100 p. 21 cm.

25036 Meyer, Eduard, 1855-1930.
Die sklaverei im Altertum. Vortrag, gehalten in der
Gehestiftung zu Dresden am 15. januar 1898, von dr.
Eduard Meyer... Dresden, v. Zahn & Jaensch, 1898.
49 p. 23½ cm.

25037 Meyer, Eduard, 1855-1930.
       Рабство въ древности;〔докладъ,читанный въ
       Дрезденѣ I5 января I898 года〕 Переводъ съ
       нѣмецкаго Е.Н.Каменецкой, подъ ред. В.Э.Дена.
       С.-Петербургъ, Изд.М.И.Водовозовой, I899.
       47 p.   22 cm.
       Title transliterated: Rabstvo v drevnosti.

25038 Meyer, Hugo Christoph Heinrich.
       Der Jude und sein Sklaventum; eine Studie zur Geschichte
       des Gaunertums. München, Deutscher Volksverlag, 1921.
       48 p.   24 cm.

25039 Meynardie, Elias James.
       The siege of Charleston; its history and progress. A
       discourse delivered in Bethel church, Charleston, S. C.,
       November 19, 1863, (Thanksgiving Day) By Rev. E. J.
       Meynardie... Columbia, Steam-power press of Evans &
       Cogswell, 1864.
       15 p.   22½ cm.

25040 Miall, Charles S
       The proposed slave empire: its antecedents, constitution
       and policy... By Charles S. Miall. London, E. Stock,
       1863.
       32 p.   21½ cm.

25041 Michelbacher, Maximilian J   1811?-1879.
       A sermon delivered on the day of prayer, recommended
       by the president of the C. S. of A., the 27th of March,
       1863, at the German Hebrew Synagogue, "Bayth Ahabah,"
       by the Rev. M. J. Michelbacher. Richmond, Macfarlane &
       Fergusson, 1863.
       16 p.   23 cm.

25042 Mifflin, Warner, 1745-1798.
       The defence of Warner Mifflin against aspersions cast
       on him on account of his endeavors to promote righteous-
       ness, mercy and peacy, among mankind... Philadelphia,
       Printed by Samuel Sansom, jun. No. 27, Mulberry-street,
       1796.
       30 p.   21 cm.

25043 [Mifflin, Warner] 1745-1798.
       A serious expostulation with the members of the House
       of Representatives of the United States. Philadelphia,
       Printed by D. Lawrence, 1793.
       16 p.   16½ cm.

25044   Milburn, Page.
        The emancipation of the slaves in the District of
        Columbia. By Rev. Page Milburn...   Washington, 1918
        96-119 p.   23½ cm.
        Reprinted from Columbia Historical Society, Records,
        v. 16, 1913.

25045   [Miles, James Warley] 1818-1875.
        The relation between the races at the South.   Charleston,
        Presses of Evans & Cogswell, 1861.
        20 p.   23½ cm.

25046   ... Military despotism.   Arbitrary arrest of a judge!
        New York, 1863
        16 p.   22½ cm.   (Loyal Publication Society.
        Pamphlets no. 20)
        Caption title.

25047   ... Military despotism! Suspension of the habeas corpus!
        Curses coming home to roost! New York, Oct., 1863.
        New York, W. C. Bryant & co., printers, 1863.
        cover-title, 16 p.   22 cm.   (Loyal Publication
        Society.   [Pamphlets] no. 20)

25048   Mill, John Stuart, 1806-1873.
        The contest in America, by John Stuart Mill...   Boston,
        Little, Brown and company, 1862.
        32 p.   18 cm.
        Reprinted from Fraser's magazine for February, 1862.

25049   Miller, George Funston, 1809-1888.
        Reconstruction. Speech of Hon. George F. Miller, of
        Pennsylvania, in the House of representatives, January 19,
        1867. [Washington, Printed at the Congressional globe
        office, 1867]
        7 p.   24 cm.
        Caption title.

25050   Miller, Marion Mills, 1864-
        American debate; a history of political and economic
        controversy in the United States, with critical digests
        of leading debates, by Marion Mills Miller...   New York
        and London, G. P. Putnam's sons, 1916.
        2 v.   22 cm.

25051   Miller, Samuel, 1769-1850.
        A discourse, delivered April 12, 1797, at the request
        of and before the New York Society for Promoting the
        Manumission of Slaves, and protecting such of them as

have been or may be liberated. By Samuel Miller...
New York, Printed by T. and J. Swords, no. 99 Pearl-
street, 1797.
   36 p.   21½ cm.

25052 Mills, Robert Curtis, 1819-1896.
     The southern states hardened until ruined. A sermon
preached in Salem on Fast day, April 13th, 1865. By
Robert C. Mills, pastor of the First Baptist church...
Boston, J. M. Hewes, printer, 1865.
   21 p.   23½ cm.

25053 Milnor, James, 1773-1845.
     Plea for the American Colonization Society: a sermon,
preached in St. George's church, New-York, on Sunday,
July 9, 1826. By the Rev. James Milnor... New York,
J. P. Haven, 1826.
   31 p.   21 cm.

25054 Miner, Charles, 1780-1865.
     The olive branch; or, The evil and the remedy. By
Charles Miner. Philadelphia [Printed by T. K. & P. G.
Collins] 1856.
   35 p.   23 cm.

25055 Minogue, Anna Catherine, 1874-
     Cardome; a romance of Kentucky, by Anna C. Minogue.
New York, P. F. Collier & son [c1904]
   1 p.l., 5-306 p.   20½ cm.

25056 Mississippi. Constitution.
     Constitution and ordinances of the state of Mississippi,
adopted in convention assembled in pursuance of the
reconstruction acts of Congress, and held, by order of
General E. O. C. Ord, in the city of Jackson, in 1868.
Jackson, Miss., Mississippi state journal office, 1868.
   48 p.   23 cm.

25057 Mississippi. Constitution.
     The constitution of the state of Mississippi. As
revised in convention, on the twenty-sixth day of October
1832. Jackson, P. Isler, 1832.
   27 p.   19½ cm.

25058 Mississippi. Convention, 1849.
     Address of the Committee of the Mississippi Convention
to the southern states. [Jackson? 1850?]
   20 p.   22 cm.
   Caption title.

25059 Mississippi. Legislature. Committee on State and Federal
       Relations.
           Majority and minority reports of the Committee on State
       and Federal Relations, to the Legislature of the state of
       Mississippi... Jackson, Miss., J. J. Shannon & co., state
       printers, 1867.
           7, [1] p.   20½ cm.

25060 Missouri. General Assembly.
           Missouri Compromise act. Resolutions of the General
       Assembly of Missouri, relative to the subject of slavery
       in the organization of new territories or states out of
       territory now belonging to, or hereafter to be acquired
       by the United States. [Washington?] Tippin & Streeter,
       1847.
           [1] p.   19½ cm.

25061 Mitchell, Anne Mary, 1847-
           The freed boy in Alabama. Philadelphia, Presbyterian
       Publication Committee [c1869]
           152 p.   22 cm.

25062 Mitchell, George Washington, 1865-
           The question before Congress, a consideration of the
       debates and final action by Congress upon various phases
       of the race question in the United States, by Geo. W.
       Mitchell. Philadelphia, Pa., The A. M. E. book concern
       [c1918]
           247 p.   23½ cm.

25063 The mongrelites: or, The radicals - so-called. A satiric
       poem. By ----- ... New York, Van Evrie, Horton, & co.,
       1866.
           v, [7]-59 p.   19 cm.

25064 Monod, Guillaume.
           L'émancipation des esclaves des États-Unis d'Amérique;
       discours prononcé à l'Oratoire, le 28 mai 1865, par
       Guillaume Monod. Paris, C. Meyrueis [1865]
           24 p.   22½ cm.

25065 Montagu, Lord Robert, 1825-1902.
           A mirror in America. By Lord Robert Montagu... London,
       Saunders, Otley, & co., 1861.
           108 p.   21½ cm.

25066 Monteiro, Tobias do Rego, 1866-
           ... Pesquisas e depoimentos para a historia. 2. milheiro.
       Rio de Janeiro, F. Alves & c^ia; [etc., etc.] 1913.
           366 p., 1 l.   19 cm.

25067   [Montgomery, John Teackle] b. 1817.
          The writ of habeas corpus, and Mr. Binney.   [Philadelphia
        J. Campbell, bookseller, 1862]
          35 p.   22½ cm.

25068   The Monthly offering. By John A. Collins. v. 1-2; July
          1840-Nov./Dec. 1842. Boston, Anti-slavery office, 1841-42.
          2 v.   17½ cm.
        Includes songs with music.

25069   Montrol, François Mongin de, 1799-1862.
          ... Analyse de la discussion de la Chambre des députés
        et de la Chambre des pairs, relative à l'emancipation des
        esclaves. Par M. F. de Montrol. 3. publication. Paris,
        Impr. de P. Dupont et c^ie, 1835.
          35, 1 p.   20½ cm.   (Société française pour
        l'abolition de l'esclavage... 3. publication)

25070   Montvéran, Tournachon de.
          Essai de statistique raisonnée sur les colonies euro-
        péennes des tropiques, et sur les questions coloniales,
        par M. de Montvéran, avec un appendix des pieces justifi-
        catives, et dix tableaux ou états de population, de com-
        merce... Paris, Delaunay, 1833.
          xv, 127, lxx p.   tables (partly fold.)   23½ cm.

25071   Moody, Vernie Alton, 1888-
          Slavery on Louisiana sugar plantations, by V. Alton
        Moody... [Cabildo, New Orleans, La., 1924]
          112 p.   26½ cm.
        Thesis (Ph.D.) - University of Michigan, 1923.
        Reprinted from the Louisiana historical quarterly,
        April, 1924.

25072   Moore, Ely, 1798-1861.
          Remarks of Mr. Ely Moore, of New York, in the House
        of Representatives, February 4, 1839, on presenting a
        remonstrance from citizens of the District of Columbia
        against the reception of abolition petitions, &c.
        [Washington? 1839]
          16 p.   24 cm.

25073   Moore, George Henry, 1823-1892.
          Notes on the history of slavery in Massachusetts.
        New York, D. Appleton, 1866.
          256 p.   23 cm.

25074   Moore, Henry D
          Our country - its sin and its duty. A discourse: on th

occasion of the national fast, September 26th, 1861. By
Rev. Henry D. Moore... Portland [Me.] H. Packard, 1861.
21 p.   23 cm.

25075   Moore, John Trotwood, 1858-1929.
Ole Mistis, and other songs and stories from Tennessee,
by John Trotwood Moore... illustrated by Howard Weeden
and Robert Dickey. Philadelphia, Chicago, The J. C. Winston
co. [c1909]
vii, 358 p.   front. (port.)   19 cm.

25076   Moraes, Evaristo de.
... A campanha abolicionista (1879-1888) Rio de Janeiro,
Leite Ribeiro, Freitas Bastos, Spicer & cia., 1924.
3 p.l., ii, 446 p., 1 l.   24½ cm.

25077   More, Gerard.
Informe en derecho, sobre que la Compañía de el real
assiento de la Gran Bretaña, establecida para la intro-
duccion de esclavos negros, en estas Indias, debe declararse libre, y exempta de la paga de los reales derechos,
comprehendidos en el nombre de alcavala, en todos los
puertos, y demàs lugares de la tierra adentro de esta
América, por lo que toca á las ropas, y mercaderías de
sus navios annuales, igualmente, como de sus negros. Y
sobre que aunque esto no procediera assi, deben declararse
libres de su contribución los efectos de represalia, sin
que ni en el vno, ni en el otro caso deba Su Magestad
hazer rebaja, ni descuento à los asientistas indianos,
de la renta annual. Escribe lo Don Gerardo Moro...
Mexico, J. F. de Ortega Bonilla, 1724.
1 p.l., 127 numb. l.   28 cm.

25078   More, Hannah, 1745-1833.
The feast of freedom, or, The abolition of domestic
slavery in Ceylon; the vocal parts adapted to music by
Charles Wesley, esq. ... To which are added, several
unpublished little pieces. By Hannah More... London,
T. Cadell, 1827.
39, [1] p.   plates.   22 cm.

25079   More, Hannah, 1745-1833.
Slavery, a poem. London, T. Cadell, 1788.
20 p.   20 cm.

25080   Moreau-Christophe, Louis Mathurin, 1799-1881.
Du droit à l'oisiveté et de l'organisation du travail
servile dans les républiques grecques et romaine, par
L.-M. Moreau-Christophe. Paris, Guillaumin et cᵉ, 1849.
2 p.l., v, 336 p.   21½ cm.

25081   Moreau de Saint-Méry, Médéric Louis Élie, 1750-1819.
        Considérations présentées aux vrais amis du repos et
        du bonheur de la France; a l'occasion des nouveaux mouve-
        mens de quelques soi-disant amis-des-noirs. Par M. L. E.
        Moreau de Saint-Méry, député de la Martinique à l'Assemblée
        nationale. Premier mars mil sept cent quatre-vingt-onze.
        Paris, Imprimerie nationale, 1791.
          1 p.l., 74 p.   19½ cm.

25082   Moreton, J   B
        Manners and customs in the West India Islands. Containing
        various particulars respecting the soil, cultivation,
        produce, trade, officers, inhabitants, &c., &c. With the
        method of establishing and conducting a sugar-plantation;
        in which the ill-practices of superintendants are pointed
        out. Also the treatment of slaves; and the slave-trade.
        By J. B. Moreton. London, Printed for W. Richardson [etc.]
        1790.
          vii, [9]-192 p.   21 cm.

25083   Morgan, Edwin Vernon.
        Slavery in New York; the status of the slave under the
        English colonial government. [New York, 1891]
          337-350 p.   22 cm.

25084   Morrill, Justin Smith, 1810-1898.
        Modern democracy; the extension of slavery in our own
        territory or by the acquisition of foreign territory,
        wrong morally, politically, and economically. Speech
        delivered in the U. S. House of Representatives, June 6,
        1860. [n.p.] Republican Congressional Committee [1860?]
          8 p.   24 cm.
        Caption title.

25085   Morrill, Lot Myrick, 1813-1883.
        Speech of Hon. L. M. Morrill, of Maine, on the confisca-
        tion of property. Delivered in the Senate of the United
        States, March 5, 1862. Washington, L. Towers & co.,
        printers, 1862
          16 p.   23 cm.
        Caption title.

25086   Morris, Benjamin Franklin, 1810-1867, ed.
        The life of Thomas Morris: pioneer and long a legislator
        of Ohio, and U. S. senator from 1833 to 1839. Ed. by his
        son, B. F. Morris... Cincinnati, Printed by Moore,
        Wilstach, Keys & Overend, 1856.
          xii, 13-408 p.   19 cm.

25087   Morris, Daniel, 1812-1889.
        Speech of Hon. Daniel Morris, of N. Y., on the confisca-
tion bill. Delivered in the House of Representatives,
Jan. 21, 1864. [Washington, L. Towers & co., printers,
1864]
        8 p.   24 cm.
        Caption title.

25088   Morris, Edward Joy, 1815-1881.
        Speech of Hon. E. Joy Morris, of Pennsylvania, on the
election of speaker, and in defense of the North; delivered
in the House of Representatives, December 8, 1859.
Washington, Printed at the Congressional globe office,
1859.
        6 p.   24 cm.

25089   Morris, Robert Desha, 1814-1882.
        Slavery, its nature, evils, and remedy. A sermon
preached to the congregation of the Presbyterian Church,
Newtown, Pennsylvania. On... July 27, 1845. By Rev.
Robert D. Morris... Philadelphia, Printed by W. S. Martien,
1845.
        31 p.   22½ cm.

25090   Morse, Isaac Edwards, 1809-1866.
        Speech of Isaac E. Morse, of Louisiana, on the Presi-
dent's message in relation to California. Delivered in
the House of Representatives, March 14, 1850. Washington,
Printed at the Congressional globe office, 1850.
        8 p.   23 cm.

25091   Morse, Samuel Finley Breese, 1791-1872.
        ... An argument on the ethical position of slavery in the
social system, and its relation to the politics of the
day. By Samuel F. B. Morse... [New York, 1863]
        20 p.   23 cm.   (Papers from the Society for the
Diffusion of Political Knowledge, no. 12)

25092   Morse, Sidney Edwards, 1794-1871.
        The Bible and slavery. By Sidney E. Morse, A. M. From
the New York observer of October 4th, 1855.   New York,
1855
        8 p.   25½ cm.
        Caption title.

25093   Morse, Sidney Edwards, 1794-1871.
        Premium questions on slavery, each admitting of a yes
or no answer; addressed to the editors of the New York
independent and New York evangelist, by Sidney E. Morse,

lately editor of the New York observer. New York, Harper & brothers, 1860.
30 p.   23 cm.

25094   Morson, Henry.
The present condition of the British West Indies; their wants, and the remedy for these: with some practical hints shewing the policy of a new system, as a means to their future regeneration. By Henry Morson... London, Smith, Elder and co., 1841.
1 p.l., 63 p.   21½ cm.

25095   Morton, Jeremiah.
The slave question. Speech of Hon. J. Morton, of Virginia, in the House of Representatives, February 6, 1850, on the questions in dispute between the North and the South. [Washington, Printed at the Congressional globe office, 1850]
8 p.   24½ cm.
Caption title.

25096   Munford, Beverley Bland, 1856-
Virginia's attitude toward slavery and secession, by Beverly B. Munford... New York [etc.] Longmans, Green, and co., 1909.
xiii p., 1 l., 329 p.   22 cm.

25097   Murat, Achille, prince, 1801-1847.
A moral and political sketch of the United States of North America. By Achille Murat... With a Note on Negro slavery, by Junius redivivus [pseud. of W. B. Adams] London, E. Wilson [etc.] 1833.
iii -xxxix, [1], 402 p.   front. (fold. map)   19 cm.

25098   Murdock, William David Clark.
Address on the free-soil question. By William D. C. Murdock. "Qu'y-a-t-il?" Georgetown [D. C.] Printed by J. F. & J. A. Crow, 1848.
cover-title, 43 p.   18 cm.

25099   Murphy, Henry Cruse, 1810-1882.
Speech of Hon. H. C. Murphy, of New York, on slavery in the territories. Delivered in the House of Representatives, May 17, 1848. Washington, Printed at the Congressional globe office, 1848.
8 p.   24 cm.

25100   Murray, Orson S
The struggle of the hour; a discourse delivered at the Paine celebration in Cincinnati, January 29, 1861.

Foster's Crossings, O., 1861.
68 p.   23 cm.

25101 Mussey, Osgood.
Review of Ellwood Fisher's lecture, on the North and the
South. By Osgood Mussey. Cincinnati, Wright, Fisher & co.,
printers, 1849.
98 p., 1 l.   22½ cm.
On cover: Cincinnati, H. W. Derby & co., publishers.

25102 [Musson, Eugène]
Lettre à Napoléon III sur l'esclavage aux états du Sud,
par un créole de la Louisiane. Paris, Dentu, 1862.
vii, 160 p.   24 cm.

                                    N

25103 Narrative of facts in the case of Passmore Williamson.
Philadelphia, Pub. by the Pennsylvania Anti-slavery Society,
1855.
24 p.   17½ cm.
The escape of Jane Johnson and two children, slaves of
John H. Wheeler, the trial of Williamson and others
concerned, and refusal of state Supreme court to issue
writ of habeas corpus.

25104 National Anti-slavery Bazaar, Boston.
Report of the... National Anti-slavery Bazaar...
Boston, 1857.
v.   15 cm.

25105 The national crisis; an antidote to abolition of fanaticism,
treason and sham philanthropy. v. 1, no. 1-2, May 15-
June 9, 1860. New York.
1 v.   2 issues.   22 cm.
Ed. by Theophilus Fiske.

25106 The negro labor question. By a New-York merchant. New-York,
J. A. Gray, printer, 1858.
55 p.   19 cm.

25107 The "negro pew": being an inquiry concerning the propriety
of distinctions in the house of God, on account of color.
Boston, I. Knapp, 1837.
v, [7]-108 p.   16½ cm.

25108 Negroes and religion. The Episcopal church at the South
Memorial to the general convention of the Protestant

Episcopal church in the United States of America.
[Charleston? S.C., 1863?]
4 p.   18½ cm.
Caption title.

25109   ... The Negro's place in nature: a paper read before the
London Anthropological Society, by Dr. James Hunt. New
York, Van Evrie, Horton & co., 1866.
27 p.   19 cm.   (Anti-abolition tracts, no. 4)

25110   Neill, Edward D[uffield] 1823-1893.
... Address before Minnesota Commandery of the Loyal
legion. By Chaplain Edward D. Neill... St. Paul, 1892.
[293]-307 p.   24 cm.
Reprinted from Macalester College, Dept. of History,
Literature, and Political Science, Contributions, 2d ser.,
no. 12, 1890-92.

25111   Neilson, Peter, 1795-1861.
The life and adventure of Zamba, an African negro king;
and his experience of slavery in South Carolina. Written
by himself. Corrected and arranged by Peter Neilson.
London, Smith, Elder and co., 1847.
xx, 258 p.   front.   20½ cm.

25112   Nelson, John, 1786-1871.
A discourse on the proposed repeal of the Missouri Compromise; delivered on Fast day, April 6, 1854, in the
First Congregational Church, in Leicester, Mass., by
J. Nelson... Worcester, Mass., Printed by E. R. Fiske
[1854]
14 p.   23 cm.

25113   Nevinson, Henry Woodd, 1856-
A modern slavery, by Henry W. Nevinson... London and
New York, Harper & brothers, 1906.
ix, [1] p., 1 l., 215, [1] p.   front. (port.)
22 pl., map.   21½ cm.

25114   The New England anti-slavery almanac, for 1841. Being the
65th year of American independence. Calculated for
Boston and the eastern states. Boston, J. A. Collins,
1841.
36 p.   illus.   18 cm.

25115   New England Anti-slavery Convention, Boston, 1834.
Address to the people of the United States on the subjec
of slavery. Boston, Garrison & Knapp, 1834.
16 p.   24 cm.

25116   New England Anti-slavery Convention. Boston, 1834.
        Proceedings of the New-England Anti-slavery Convention,
        held in Boston on the 27th, 28th and 29th of May, 1834.
        Boston, Garrison & Knapp, 1834.
        72 p.   22 cm.

25117   New England Anti-slavery Convention. 3d, Boston, 1836.
        Proceedings of the New England Anti-slavery Convention:
        held in Boston, May 24, 25, 26, 1836. Boston, Printed by
        I. Knapp, 1836.
        76 p.   22 cm.

25118   New England Anti-slavery Convention. 4th, Boston, 1837.
        Proceedings of the fourth New-England Anti-slavery
        Convention, held in Boston, May 30, 31, and June 1 and 2,
        1837. Boston, Printed by I. Knapp, 1837.
        124 p.   22 cm.

25119   New England Emigrant Aid Company, Boston.
        Two tracts for the times. The one entitled "Negro-
        slavery, no evil": by B. F. Stringfellow, of Missouri.
        The other, an answer to the inquiry "Is it expedient to
        introduce slavery into Kansas?" by D. R. Goodloe of
        North Carolina. Republished by the N. E. Emigrant Aid
        Co. Boston, A. Mudge and son, printers, 1855.
        56 p.   22½ cm.

25120   New-Hampshire Anti-slavery Society.
        Annual report of the New Hampshire Anti-slavery Society
        ... 1st-   ; 1835-   Concord, 1835-
            v.   20 cm.

25121   New Hampshire Anti-slavery Convention, Concord, 1834.
        Proceedings of the N. H. Anti-slavery Convention, held
        in Concord, on the 11th & 12th of November, 1834.
        Concord, N. H., Eastman, Webster & co., printers, 1834.
        36 p., 1 l.   22 cm.

25122   New-Jersey Society for Promoting the Abolition of Slavery.
        Address of the president of the New-Jersey Society
        for Promoting the Abolition of Slavery, to the general
        meeting at Trenton, on Wednesday the 26th of September,
        1804... Trenton, Printed by Sherman and Mershon, 1804.
        12 p.   22 cm.
        Signed: William Griffith.

25123   New-Jersey Society for Promoting the Abolition of Slavery.
        The constitution of the New-Jersey Society for Promoting
        the Abolition of Slavery; to which is annexed, Extracts

from a law of New-Jersey passed the 2d March, 1786, and
supplement to the same, passed the 26th November, 1788...
Burlington, Printed for the Society, by Isaac Neale, 1793.
16 p.   23½ cm.

25124 A new negro for the new century; an accurate and up-to-date
record of the upward struggles of the negro race. The
Spanish-American war, causes of it; vivid descriptions of
fierce battles; superb heroism and daring deeds of the
negro soldier... Education, industrial schools, colleges,
universities and their relationship to the race problem,
by Prof. Booker T. Washington. Reconstruction and industrial advancement by N. B. Wood... The colored woman and
her part in race regeneration... by... Fannie Barrier
Williams... Chicago, Ill., American publishing house
[1900]
428 p.   front., illus. (ports.)   20 cm.

25125 ... New Orleans as it is. Its manners and customs - morals
fashionable life - profanation of the Sabbath - prostitu-
tion - licentiousness - slave markets and slavery, &c.,
&c., &c. By a resident... [New Orleans?] Printed for
the publisher, 1850.
79 p.   22 cm.

25126 The new pantheon; or, The age of black. New York, Rollo,
1860.
iv, [5]-47 p.   17½ cm.
In verse.

25127 New York. Eighteenth Ward Republican Association.
Liberty and union! Speeches delivered at the Eighteenth
Ward Republican festival, in commemoration of the birth
of Washington, held at the Gramercy Park House, New York,
February 22, 1860. Reported phonographically by William
Anderson. New York, Baker & Godwin, printers, 1860.
40 p.   23 cm.

25128 New York. Union Meeting, Dec. 19, 1859.
Report of proceedings connected with the great Union
meeting, held at the Academy of music, New York, December
19th, 1859. New York, Davies & Roberts, printers, 1859.
92 p.   22½ cm.

25129 New York (State) Court of appeals.
... Report of the Lemmon slave case: containing points
and arguments of counsel on both sides, and opinions of
all the judges. New York, H. Greeley & co., 1860.
146 p.   22 cm.

25130   New York (Sjate) Laws, statutes, etc.
              Laws relative to slaves and the slave-trade. New-York,
          Printed for Samuel Stansbury, no. 111, Water-street, 1806.
              29 p.   18 cm.

25131   New York City Anti-slavery Society.
              Address of the New-York City Anti-slavery Society to the
          people of the city of New-York. New-York, Printed by West
          & Trow, 1833.
              46 p.   21½ cm.

25132   New York Society for Promoting the Manumission of Slaves.
              The act of incorporation and constitution of the New-York
          Society for Promoting the Manumission of Slaves, and
          protecting such of them as have been, or may be liberated.
          Revised and adopted, 31st January, 1809. With the bye-laws
          of the Society annexed. New-York, Printed by S. Wood, 1810.
              23 p.   19½ cm.

25133   New York Society for Promoting the Manumission of Slaves.
              Constitution. New York, Printed by Hopkins, Webb, 1796.
              19 p.   19 cm.

25134   New-York Young Men's Anti-slavery Society.
              Address of the New-York Young Men's Anti-slavery Society,
          to their fellow-citizens. New-York, W. T. Coolidge & co.,
          1834.
              38, [2] p.   22 cm.

25135   Newhall, Fales Henry, 1827-1883.
              The conflict in America. A funeral discourse occasioned
          by the death of John Brown of Ossawattomie, who entered
          into rest, from the gallows, at Charlestown, Virginia,
          Dec. 2, 1859. Preached at the Warren St. M. E. church,
          Roxbury, Dec. 4, by Rev. Fales Henry Newhall, pastor.
          Boston, J. M. Hewes, 1859.
              22 p.   23 cm.

25136   Newman, Francis William, 1805-1897.
              Anglo-Saxon abolition of Negro slavery. By F. W.
          Newman... London, K. Paul, Trench & co., 1889.
              2 p.l., 136 p.   22 cm.

25137   Newman, Henry Stanley.
              Banani: the transition from slavery to freedom in
          Zanzibar and Pemba. By Henry Stanley Newman... London
              etc. Headley brothers 1898
              vii, [3], 216 p.   illus., map.   22 cm.

197

25138   [Newman, Louis C   ]
        The Bible view of slavery reconsidered. A letter to the
        Right Rev. Bishop Hopkins. 2d ed., rev. and somewhat enl.
        Philadelphia, H. B. Ashmead, printer, 1863.
        15 p.   22 cm.
        Signed: Biblicus.

25139   Niblack, William Ellis, 1822-1893.
        Speech of the Hon. William E. Niblack, of Indiana, on
        the admission of Kansas, delivered in the House of Repre-
        sentatives, April 11, 1860. [Washington] Lemuel Towers,
        1860.
        4 p.   21 cm.

25140   Nicholas, Samuel Smith, 1796-1869.
        Emancipation - white and black. By S. S. Nicholas.
        [Louisville?] 1864?
        13 p.   22 cm.
        Caption title.

25141   Nieboer, H   J
        ... Slavery as an industrial system; ethnological re-
        searches. The Hague, M. Nijhoff, 1900.
        xxvii, 474 p.   22 cm.

25142   Niles, John Milton, 1787-1856.
        Speech of Mr. Niles, of Connecticut, on the petition of
        a society of Friends in Pennsylvania, praying for the
        abolition of slavery in the District of Columbia. In
        Senate, February 15, 1836. Washington, Blair and Rives,
        printers, 1836.
        14 p.   22½ cm.

25143   Nixon, Barnaby, 1752?-1807.
        A serious address, to the rulers of America in general,
        and the state of Virginia in particular. By Barnaby
        Nixon... Richmond, Printed by Seaton Grantland, opposite
        the Bell tavern, 1806.
        12 p.   17 cm.

25144   [Nisbet, Richard]
        Slavery not forbidden by Scripture. Or, A defence of
        the West-India planters, from the aspersions thrown out
        against them, by the author of a pamphlet, entitled, "An
        address to the inhabitants of the British settlements in
        America, upon slave-keeping." By a West-Indian...
        Philadelphia printed, 1773.
        1 p.l., iii, 30 p.   21 cm.

25145 Nixon, John Thompson, 1820-1889.
        The rebellion: its origin, and the means of suppressing
        it. Speech of Hon. Jno. T. Nixon, of New Jersey, in the
        House of Representatives, Friday, April 11, 1862. Wash-
        ington, Scammell & co., printers, 1862.
        8 p.   23 cm.

25146 Noel, Baptist Wriothesley, 1798-1873.
        Freedom and slavery in the United States of America. By
        Baptist Wriothesley Noel... London, J. Nisbet & co., 1863.
        vi, 242 p.   18½ cm.

25147 The Non-slaveholder... v. -5,   - Dec. 1850; new ser.,
        vol. 1-2; Jan. 1853- Dec. 1854. Philadelphia,
        Merrihew & Thompson [etc.] 18   -54.
        7 v.   25½ cm.
        Publication suspended, 1851-52.
        Editors: A. L. Pennock, Samuel Rhoads, G. W. Taylor. -
        1848, Samuel Rhoads, G. W. Taylor. - 1849-50, Samuel Rhoads.
        - 1853,54, W. J. Allinson.
        Supersedes by the Citizen of the world.

25148 Nordhoff, Charles, 1830-1901.
        America for free working men! Mechanics, farmers and
        laborers read! How slavery injures the free working man.
        The slave-labor system the free working-man's worst enemy.
        By Charles Nordhoff. New York, Harper & brothers, 1865.
        39 p.   22½ cm.

25149 Norfolk, Va. Citizens.
        Proceedings of the citizens of the borough of Norfolk,
        on the Boston outrage, in the case of the runaway slave
        George Latimer. Norfolk, T. G. Broughton & son, printers,
        1843.
        20 p.   21½ cm.

25150 Nørlund, Poul, 1888-
        ... Det romerske slavesamfund under afvikling, en
        analyse af underklassens retskaar i oldtidens slutning.
        [København] I kommission hos V. Thaning & Appel, 1920.
        4 p.l., 327 p.   25½ cm.
        Thesis - Copenhagen.

25151 North and South... From the New York courier and enquirer.
        [n.p., 1845?]
        24 p.   24 cm.
        Letters addressed to George P. Marsh, signed: A northern
        man with southern citizenship.

25152   Northrup, A[nsel] Judd, 1833-
        ... Slavery in New York, a historical sketch; by ex-
        Judge A. Judd Northrup... Albany, University of the state
        of New York, 1900.
        1 p.l., [243]-313 p.   25 cm.   (State Library Bulletin,
        History, no. 4, May, 1900)

25153   (Number omitted)

25154   Norwood, John Nelson, 1879-
        The schism in the.Methodist Episcopal Church, 1844:
        a study of slavery and ecclesiastical politics, by John
        Nelson Norwood... Alfred, N. Y., Alfred university, 1923.
        6 p.l., [9]-225 p.   fold. map.   21½ cm.   (Alfred
        university studies, vol. I)

25155   Norwood, Thomas Manson, 1830-1913.
        A true vindication of the South, in a review of American
        political history, by Thomas Manson Norwood... [Savannah,
        Ga., Braid & Hutton, Inc., printers, c1917]
        5 p.l., xvi, 450, [1] p.   23½ cm.

25156   Nossiter, Bernard D
        U. N. group gets report on slaves in Mauritania.
        [New York, 1981]
        [1] p.   11 x 26 cm.
        Reprinted from The New York Times, August, 1981.

25157   Notes in defence of the colonies. On the increase and
        decrease of the slave population of the British West
        Indies. By a West Indian. Jamaica, 1826.
        98 p.   19 cm.

25158   Notice of Com. Stockton's letter on the slavery question;
        or, A plea for toleration. Philadelphia [T. K. and P. G.
        Collins, printers] 1850.
        36 p.   22 cm.
        Signed (p. 26): Philadelphian. May, 1850.

25159   Nott, Benjamin.
        Constitutional ethics. Number one. By Benjamin Nott...
        Albany, J. Munsell, 1857.
        20 p.   22½ cm.

25160   Nott, Benjamin.
        A remedy for the "irrepressible conflict"; or,
        Constitutional ethics. By Benjamin Nott... Albany, N. Y.,
        E. J. Clark, general agent; [etc., etc.] 1860.
        96 p.   20 cm.

25161 Nott, Samuel, 1788-1869.
       The necessities and wisdom of 1861. A supplement to
       the 6th ed. of Slavery and the remedy. By Samuel Nott.
       Boston, Crocker and Brewster, 1861.
       12 p.   23 cm.

25162 Nott, Samuel, 1788-1869.
       The present crisis: with a reply and appeal to European
       advisers, from the sixth edition of Slavery and the remedy.
       By Samuel Nott. Boston, Crocker & Brewster, 1860.
       vi, iii-xliii p.   23 cm.

25163 ... The Nutshell. The system of American slavery "tested
       by Scripture," being "a short method" with pro-slavery
       D. D.'s, whether doctors of divinity, or of democracy,
       embracing axioms of social, civil, and political economy,
       as divinely impressed, upon the human conscience and set
       forth in divine revelation. In two lectures. By a layman
       of the Protestant Episcopal Church in the Diocese of
       Connecticut. [2d ed.]... New York, Pub. for the author,
       1862.
       72 p.   19 cm.

                              O

25164 Ober, Benjamin.
       Slavery: a lecture delivered before the Lyceum in
       Attleborough, Jan. 4th, 1838. By Rev. Benjamin Ober.
       Published by request. Pawtucket, Mass., R. Sherman,
       printer, 1838.
       28 p.   23 cm.

25165 Oberbauer, Julius C
       Amerika und die Sklaverei. Von Julius C. Oberbauer.
       (Mit Benützung eines schon im "Janns" abgedruckten
       Aufsatzes) New-York, Helmich & Stark, 1854.
       32 p.   23 cm.

25166 ... Objects of the rebellion, and effects of its success
       upon free laborers and civilization. By a member of
       the Cincinnati bar. Cincinnati, Wrightson & co., printers,
       1863.
       32 p.   23 cm.   (Loyal publications of National
       Union Association of Ohio, no. 7, 1863)

25167 [O'Callaghan, Edmund Bailey] 1797-1880, comp.
       ... Census of slaves, 1755... [Albany, N. Y., 1850]

[843]-868 p.   22½ cm.
Reprinted from the documentary history of the state of
New York. Albany, 1850.

25168 O'Callaghan, Edmund Bailey, 1797-1880, comp.
Voyages of the slavers St. John and Arms of Amsterdam,
1659, 1663; together with additional papers illustrative
of the slave trade under the Dutch. Tr. from the original
manuscripts, with an introduction and index, by E. B.
O'Callaghan. Albany, N. Y., J. Munsell, 1867.
xxx p., 1 l., 254 p., 1 l.   20½ cm.   (Added t.p.:
New York colonial tracts, no. 3)

25169 [O'Connell, Daniel] 1775-1847.
Address from the people of Ireland to their countrymen
and countrywomen in America. [n.p., 1847]
32 p.   21½ cm.
Caption title.

25170 O'Connell, Daniel, 1775-1847.
The Irish patriot. Daniel O'Connell's legacy to Irish
Americans. Philadelphia, Printed for gratuitous distribution [1863]
cover-title, 32 p.   22½ cm.

25171 O'Connell, Daniel, 1775-1847.
Liberty or slavery? and Reply to O'Connell by Hon. S. P.
Chase. [Cincinnati] Chronicle Print, 1843.
15 p.   23½ cm.
Cover title.

25172 Ogg, Frederic Austin.
Jay's treaty and the slavery interests of the United
States. [Washington, 1902]
273 298 p.   23 cm.
Reprinted from American Historical Association,
Annual report, 1907, vol. 1.

25173 Olive branch - extra. Danville [Ky.] December 24, 1833.
[2] p.   40 cm.
"Constitution and address of the Kentucky Society for
the Gradual Relief of the State from Slavery."

25174 "One idea." [n.p., 1848?]
4 p.   24 cm.
Caption title.
On the Free-soil Party and the presidential candidates.

25175 Onesimus Secundus, pseud.
The true interpretation of the American Civil War, and

of England's cotton difficulty; or, Slavery, from a
different point of view, shewing the relative responsibi-
lities of America and Great Britain. By Onesimus Secundus.
London, Trübner & co., 1863.
iv, [5]-47 p.   20½ cm.

25176 Opinions of the early presidents, and of the fathers of the
republic, upon slavery, and upon Negroes as men and
soldiers. New York, W. C. Bryant & co., printers, 1863.
19, [1] p.   22 cm.   (Loyal Publication Society.
[Pamphlets] no. 18)

25177 Opúsculo. Cuba y Puerto-Rico. Medios de conservar estas
dos Antillas en su estado de esplendor. Por un negrófilo
concienzudo. Madrid, J. Cruzado, 1866.
1 p.l., 157 p., 1 l.   18½ cm.

25178 Orleans (Ter.) Laws, statutes, etc.
Black code. An act prescribing the rules and conduct
to be observed with respect to negroes and other slaves
of this territory. [New Orleans, 1807]
150-213 p.   27½ cm.
Reprinted from Orleans (Ter.) Laws, statutes, etc.
Acts passed at the first session of the First Legislature
of the territory of Orleans... New Orleans, 1807.

25179 Ortiz Fernández, Fernando, 1881-
Hampa afro-cubana. Los negros esclavos; estudio socioló-
gico y de derecho público, por Fernando Ortiz... con 34
figuras. Habana, Revista bimestre cubana, 1916.
viii, 536 p.   front. (port.) illus.   24 cm.

25180 O'Shiell, B   B
Réponses aux objections élevées contre le système colonial
aux Antilles, respectueusement soumises auec autorités
constitutionnelles; par B. B. O'Shiell; suivies d'un
appendice où l'on démontre les vices et les dangers de
l'affranchissement graduel des nègres dans toutes les
colonies occidentales, proposé dernièrement au sein de
la Chambre des communes, en Angleterre, par M. Buxon [!]...
Paris, Grimbert, 1825.
2 p.l., x, 520 p., 1 l.   21½ cm.

25181 Osman, bey, originally Frederick Millingen, 1839?-
Les femmes en Turquie, par Osman-Bey - Major Vladimir
Andrejevich. 2. éd. Paris, Calmann Lévy, 1878.
2 p.l., 361 p.   17½ cm.

25182 Owen, Robert Dale, 1801-1877.
The policy of emancipation: in three letters to the

secretary of war, the President of the United States, and
the secretary of the Treasury. By Robert Dale Owen...
Philadelphia, J. B. Lippincott & co., 1863.
48 p.   18½ cm.

25183   Øxnaes, C   Berg.
Slaverispörgsmaalet, besvaret af C. Berg Øxnaes. Albert
Lea, Minn., Forfatterens forlag, 1878.
11 p.   18 cm.

P

25184   Pacificator, pseud.
The nail hit on the head; or, The two Jonathans agreeing
to settle the slave question with or without more fighting
as the South pleases. By Pacificator. New Haven, T. H.
Pease, 1862.
24 p.   23 cm.
The work has been attributed to Leonard Bacon.

25185   Paddock, Judah.
A narrative of the shipwreck of the ship Oswego, on the
coast of South Barbary, and of the sufferings of the master
and the crew while in bondage among the Arabs; interspersed
with numerous remarks upon the country and its inhabitants,
and concerning the peculiar perils of that coast. By Judah
Paddock, her late master. New-York, Published by Captain
James Riley. J. Seymour, printer... 1818.
1 p.l., [v]-xvi, [17]-332 p.   22½ cm.

25186   Page, Moses B
Speech of Moses B. Page, Esq., of Berwick, in the House
of Representatives of Maine, February 27, 1863, in
opposition to the Emancipation resolutions. Augusta,
Printed by G. Smith, 1863.
16 p.   24 cm.

25187   Page, Thomas Nelson, 1853-1922.
A captured Santa Claus, by Thomas Nelson Page, with
illustrations by W. L. Jacobs. New York, C. Scribner's
sons, 1902.
3 p.l., 81 p.   col. front., col. pl.   20 cm.

25188   Page, Thomas Nelson, 1853-1922.
The negro: the Southerner's problem, by Thomas Nelson
Page. New York, S. S. McClure, 1904.
548-554, 619-626, 96-102 p.   port.   25 cm.
Reprinted from McClure's magazine, v. 22, no. 5, March
1904; no. 6, April 1904; and v. 23, no. 1, May 1904.

25189 Page, Thomas Nelson, 1853-1922.
　　　　Social life in old Virginia before the war, by Thomas
　　　　Nelson Page. With illustrations by the Misses Cowles.
　　　　New York, C. Scribner's sons, 1897.
　　　　　viii, 109 p. incl. front., illus., plates.　　21 cm.

25190 Page, Thomas Nelson, 1853-1922.
　　　　Two little Confederates, by Thomas Nelson Page...
　　　　New York, C. Scribner's sons, 1888.
　　　　　3 p.l., 156 p. incl. plates, front.　　21½ x 17 cm.

25191 Page, Thomas Nelson, 1853-1922.
　　　　Unc' Edinburg; a plantation echo illustrated by B. West
　　　　Clinedinst. New York, Charles Scribner's sons, 1897.
　　　　　3 p.l., 53 p.　　illus.　　22 cm.

25192 Paine, Elijah, 1757-1842.
　　　　A collection of facts in regard to Liberia, by Judge
　　　　Paine, of Vermont; to which is added the correspondence
　　　　of the Rev. Benjamin Tappan, of Maine, and Francis S. Key,
　　　　esquire, of the District of Columbia. Woodstock, Vt.,
　　　　Printed by A. Palmer, 1839.
　　　　　2 p.l., [3]-36 p.　　21½ cm.

25193 Paine, Lewis W　　　　b. 1819.
　　　　Six years in a Georgia prison. Narrative of Lewis W.
　　　　Paine, who suffered imprisonment six years in Georgia, for
　　　　the crime of aiding the escape of a fellow-man from that
　　　　state, after he had fled from slavery. Written by himself.
　　　　New York, Printed for the author, 1851.
　　　　　187 p.　　front. (port.)　　18 cm.

25194 Palfrey, John Gorham, 1796-1881.
　　　　Correspondence between Nathan Appleton and John G. Palfrey
　　　　intended as a supplement to Mr. Palfrey's pamphlet on the
　　　　slave power. Boston, Eastburn's press, 1846.
　　　　　20 p.　　23½ cm.

25195 Palmer, Benjamin Morgan, 1818-1902.
　　　　Thanksgiving sermon, delivered at the First Presbyterian
　　　　church, New Orleans, on Thursday, December 29, 1860, by
　　　　Rev. B. M. Palmer, D. D. New-York, G. F. Nesbitt & co.,
　　　　printers, 1861.
　　　　　20 p.　　23 cm.
　　　　Cover-title: Slavery a divine trust. The duty of the South
　　　to preserve and perpetuate the institution as it now exists.
　　　Date in title corrected in ms. to read: Nov. 29.

25196 Paris. Bibliothèque nationale. Département des imprimés.
　　　　... Catalogue des ouvrages donnés par M. V. Schoelcher,
　　　　sénateur. [Nogent-le-Rotrou, Impr. Daupeley-Gouverneur]
　　　　1884.
　　　　　99 p.　　24½ cm.

25197   Parker, Joel, 1795-1875.
            Personal liberty laws (statutes of Massachusetts) and
        slavery in the territories (case of Dred Scott) By Joel
        Parker. Boston, Wright & Potter, printers, 1861.
            97 p.   24 cm.

25198   Parker, Joel, 1799-1873.
            The discussion between Rev. Joel Parker, and Rev. A.
        Rood, on the question "What are the evils inseparable from
        slavery," which was referred to by Mrs. Stowe, in "Uncle
        Tom's cabin." Reprinted from the Philadelphia Christian
        observer of 1846. New York, S. W. Benedict; Philadelphia,
        H. Hooker, 1852.
            v, [7]-120 p.   18½ cm.
            The discussion was carried on over the signature of "O.
        Meridionus" and "The correspondent of the N. Y. evangelist

25199   Parker, Theodore, 1810-1860.
            The Boston kidnapping: a discourse to commemorate the
        rendition of Thomas Simms, delivered on the first anniver-
        sary thereof, April 12, 1852, before the Committee of
        Vigilance, at the Melodeon in Boston. By Theodore Parker.
        Boston, Crosby, Nichols & company, 1852.
            72 p.   23½ cm.

25200   Parker, Theodore, 1810-1860.
            The law of God and the statutes of men. A sermon,
        preached at the Music Hall, in Boston, on Sunday, June 18,
        1854. By Theodore Parker... Phonographically reported
        by Rufus Leighton. Boston, B. B. Mussey & co., 1854.
            32 p.   23 cm.

25201   Parker, Theodore, 1810-1860.
            The new crime against humanity. A sermon, preached at
        the Music hall, in Boston, on Sunday, June 4, 1854. By
        Theodore Parker... Boston, B. B. Mussey & co., 1854.
            76 p.   22½ cm.

25202   Parker, Theodore, 1810-1860.
            A new lesson for the day: a sermon preached at the
        Music Hall, in Boston, on Sunday, May 25, 1856. By
        Theodore Parker... Phonographically reported by Messrs.
        Yerrinton and Leighton. Boston, B. H. Greene, 1856.
            40 p.   23½ cm.

25203   Patterson, Caleb Perry.
            ... The negro in Tennessee, 1790-1865, by Caleb Perry
        Patterson... Austin, Tex., The University [1922]
            213 p.   22 cm.   (University of Texas bulletin.
        no. 2205: Feb. 1, 1922)

25204 Patterson, Robert Mayne, 1832-1911.
        Our duty. A fast-day discourse. By Robert M. Patterson...
        Published by request. Philadelphia, W. S. & A. Martien,
        1864.
        31 p.   22½ cm.

25205 Patton, William Weston, 1821-1889.
        ... President Lincoln and the Chicago memorial of
        emancipation, a paper read before the Maryland historical
        society December 12th, 1887, by Rev. W. W. Patton...
        Baltimore [Printed by J. Murphy and co.] 1888.
        36 p.   24½ cm.   ([Maryland Historical Society]
        Fund publication, no. 27)
        A narrative of the interview of the writer and Rev. John
        Dempster with President Lincoln.

25206 Patton, William Weston, 1821-1889.
        Slavery and infidelity: or, Slavery in the church
        ensures infidelity in the world. Cincinnati, American
        Reform Book and Tract Society [1856]
        70 p.   14 cm.

25207 Paul, D
        A sermon preached in the United Presbyterian church,
        Mansfield, Ohio, January 24, 1864. By Rev. D. Paul...
        Mansfield, Oh., Printed by G. T. Myers & bro., Mansfield
        herald office, 1864.
        14 p.   21 cm.

25208 Paul, Nathaniel, 1775?-1839.
        An address, delivered on the celebration of the abolition
        of slavery, in the state of New-York, July 5, 1827. By
        Nathaniel Paul, pastor of the First African Baptist
        Society in the city of Albany. Pub. by the trustees for
        the benefit of said Society. Albany, Printed by J. B.
        Van Steenbergh, 1827.
        24 p.   23½ cm.

25209 [Peabody, Ephraim] 1807-1856.
        Slavery in the United States: its evils, alleviations,
        and remedies. Reprinted from the North American review,
        Oct. 1851. Boston, C. C. Little and J. Brown, 1851.
        36 p.   23½ cm.

25210 Pearce, John J   d. 1888.
        Speech of Hon. John J. Pearce, of Pennsylvania, on the
        slavery question. Delivered in the House of Representa-
        tives, August 9, 1856. Washington, Printed at the
        Congressional globe office, 1856.
        8 p.   23½ cm.

25211 [Pearl, Cyril] 1805-1865.
       Remarks on African colonization and the abolition of
       slavery. In two parts. By a citizen of New England.
       Windsor, Vt., Richards & Tracy, 1833.
       47, [1] p.   20½ cm.

25212 Pease, Verne Seth, 1856-
       In the wake of war; a tale of the South under carpet-
       bagger administration, by Verne S. Pease. Chicago, New
       York, G. M. Hill company, 1900.
       440 p.   19½ cm.

25213 Peck, George, 1797-1876.
       Slavery and the Episcopacy: being an examination of
       Dr. Bascom's review of the reply of the majority to the
       protest of the minority of the late General Conference
       of the M. E. church, in the case of Bishop Andrew. By
       George Peck... New-York, G. Lane & C. B. Tippett, 1845.
       139 p.   21½ cm.

25214 Peck, John Mason, 1789-1858.
       The duties of American citizens: a discourse, preached
       in the State-House, Springfield, Illinois, January 26,
       1851, by J. M. Peck... St. Louis, Printed by T. W. Ustick,
       1851.
       24 p.   22 cm.

25215 Peck, Lucius B   1802-1866.
       Slavery in the territories. Speech of Hon. Lucius B.
       Peck, of Vermont, in the House of Representatives, April 23
       1850, in committee of the whole on the state of the Union,
       on the President's message transmitting the constitution
       of California. [Washington, Printed at the Congressional
       globe office, 1850]
       8 p.   24½ cm.
       Caption title.

25216 Pelletan, Eugène i.e. Pierre Clément Eugène, 1813-1884.
       Adresse au Roi Coton. Par Eugène Pelletan. Paris,
       Pagnerre, 1863.
       2 p.l., 43 p.   22½ cm.

25217 Pellow, Thomas, fl. 1738.
       The adventures of Thomas Pellow, of Penryn, mariner,
       three and twenty years in captivity among the Moors.
       Written by himself, and ed. with an introduction and notes
       by Dr. Robert Brown... London, T. F. Unwin; New York,
       Macmillan & co., 1890.
       3 p.l., 379 p.   front. (port.) 8 pl. (2 fold.)
       22 cm.   (Half-title: the adventure series. [4])

25218   Pendleton, James Madison, 1811-1891.
            Reminiscences of a long life. By J. M. Pendleton...
        Louisville, Ky., Press Baptist book concern, 1891.
            vii, 203 p.   front. (port.)   20½ cm.

25219   Pendleton, Louis Beauregard, 1861-1939.
            King Tom and the runaways; the story of what befell
        two boys in a Georgia swamp, by Louis Pendleton... New
        York, D. Appleton and company, 1890.
            4 p.l., 273 p.   front., plates.   20 cm.

25220   Penn, I   Garland.
            The Afro-American press and its editors. Springfield,
        Mass., Willey & co., 1891.
            565 p.   illus.   20½ cm.

25221   [Penniman, Purcell]
            Questions and expositions of slavery, obtained from
        those who have experienced it, by the author. [Boston?
        1856?]
            15 p.   20 x 11 cm.

25222   Pennington, James W   C
            Covenants involving moral wrong are not obligatory upon
        man: a sermon delivered in the Fifth Congregational Church,
        Hartford, on Thanksgiving Day, Nov. 17th, 1842. By J. C. W.
        Pennington... Hartford, J. C. Wells, 1842.
            12 p.   20 cm.

25223   Pennsylvania. General Assembly. House of Representatives.
            Speeches of Messrs. J. S. Van Voorhis, of Washington
        co.; Wareham Warner, of Erie co.; and Simeon B. Chase,
        of Susquehanna co., in the House of Representatives of
        Pennsylvania, on the extension of slavery. Harrisburg,
        George Bergner, 1857.
            15 p.   23½ cm.

25224   Pennsylvania. General Assembly. Senate. Committee on the
        Increase of Slaves in the State.
            Report of the committee appointed in the Senate of
        Pennsylvania, to investigate the cause of an increased
        number of slaves being returned for that commonwealth,
        by the census of 1830, over that of 1820. Read in
        Senate, February 25, 1833. Samuel Breck, chairman.
        Harrisburg, Printed by H. Welsh, 1833.
            7 p.   21 cm.

25225   [Pennsylvania Hall Association, Philadelphia]
            History of Pennsylvania Hall, which was destroyed by a

mob, on the 17th of May, 1838... Philadelphia, Printed by
Merrihew and Gunn, 1838.
200 p.   col. front., pl. $23\frac{1}{2}$ cm.
Authorship attributed to Samuel Webb.

25226 Pennsylvania Society for Promoting the Abolition of Slavery.
Celebration of the ninetieth anniversary of the organization of the Pennsylvania Society for Promoting the Abolition
of Slavery, for the relief of free negroes unlawfully held
in bondage, and for improving the condition of the African
race. Held at Concert hall, fourth month (April) 14, 1865..
Philadelphia, Merrihew & son, printers, 1866.
25 p.   22 cm.

25227 Pennsylvania Society for Promoting the Abolition of Slavery.
Centennial anniversary of the Pennsylvania Society, for
promoting the abolition of slavery, the relief of free
negroes unlawfully held in bondage: and for improving the
condition of the African race. Philadelphia, Grant,
Faires & Rodgers, printers, 1875.
82 p.   23 cm.
Errata slip attached to last page.

25228 Pennsylvania Society for Promoting the Abolition of Slavery.
Constitution and act of incorporation of the Pennsylvania
society, for promoting the abolition of slavery and the
relief of free negroes, unlawfully held in bondage.   And
for improving the condition of the African race. To which
are added, the acts of the General assembly of Pennsylvania
for the gradual abolition of slavery, and the acts of the
Congress of the United States, respecting slaves and the
slave-trade... Philadelphia, Printed by J. Ormrod, 1800.
53 p. $21\frac{1}{2}$ cm.

25229 Pennsylvania Society for Promoting the Abolition of Slavery.
Constitution and act of incorporation of the Pennsylvania
society for promoting the abolition of slavery, and for the
relief of free negroes, unlawfully held in bondage, and
for the improving the condition of the African race. To
which are added abstracts of the laws of the states of
Pennsylvania, New York, New Jersey, Delaware and Maryland,
and of the acts of Congress, respecting slavery and the
slave trade... Philadelphia, Printed for the Society, by
Hall & Atkinson, 53, Market street, 1820.
31 p. $21\frac{1}{2}$ cm.

25230 Pennsylvania Society for Promoting the Abolition of Slavery.
The constitution of the Pennsylvania Society, for
Promoting the Abolition of Slavery, and the relief of free

negroes, unlawfully held in bondage. Begun in the year
1774, and enlarged on the twenty-third of April, 1787.
To which are added, the acts of the General Assembly of
Pennsylvania, for the Gradual Abolition of Slavery...
Philadelphia, Printed by F. Bailey, 1788.
29 p.   19½ cm.

25231 Pennsylvania Society for Promoting the Abolition of Slavery.
An historical memoir of the Pennsylvania society, for
promoting the abolition of slavery; the relief of free
negroes unlawfully held in bondage, and for improving
the condition of the African race. Comp. from the minutes
of the Society and other official documents, by Edward
Needles, and pub. by authority of the Society. Philadelphia, Merrihew and Thompson, printers, 1848.
116 p.   21½ cm.

25232 Pennsylvania Society for Promoting the Abolition of Slavery.
Memorials presented to the Congress of the United States
of America, by the different societies instituted for
promoting the abolition of slavery, &c. &c. in states of
Rhode-Island, Connecticut, New-York, Pennsylvania, Maryland, and Virginia. Published by order of "The Pennsylvania
society for promoting the abolition of slavery, and the
relief of free negroes unlawfully held in bondage, and for
improving the condition of the African race." Philadelphia,
Printed by Francis Bailey, no. 116, High-street, 1792.
2 p.l., 31 p.   18½ cm.

25233 Pennsylvania Society for Promoting the Abolition of Slavery.
The oldest abolition society, being a short story of the
labors of the Pennsylvania society for promoting the
abolition of slavery, the relief of free negroes unlawfully
held in bondage, and for improving the condition of the
African race. Philadelphia, Pa., The Society, 1911.
[16] p.   16½ cm.

25234 Pennsylvania State Anti-slavery Society.
Address to the coloured people of the state of Pennsylvania. Philadelphia, Merrihew and Gunn, printers, 1837.
7 p.   23 cm.
"Signed on behalf and by order of the Convention for
forming the Pennsylvania anti-slavery society, at Harrisburg, the 3d day of the second month (February) 1837.
F. J. Le Moyne, president."

25235 Pennsylvania State Anti-slavery Society.
Proceedings of the Pennsylvania convention, assembled
to organize a state anti-slavery society, at Harrisburg,

on the 31st of January and 1st, 2d and 3d of February
1837. Philadelphia, Printed by Merrihew and Gunn, 1837.
97 p.   23 cm.

25236   [Peoples Party (Massachusetts)]
Proceedings of the convention of the people of Massachusetts, holden at Faneuil Hall, Boston, October 7th, 1862,
in accordance with the call of Joel Parker and others.
Boston, Stereotyped and printed by C. J. Peters, 1862.
31 p.   23 cm.

25237   [Perry, Benjamin Franklin] 1805-1886.
To the democracy of the fifth congressional district in
South Carolina. [Greenville, S. C., G. E. Elford, printer
1860]
13 p.   21 cm.

25238   Petit, Émilien, b. 1713.
Traité sur le gouvernement des esclaves. Par M. Petit,
député des Conseils supérieurs des colonies... Paris,
Knapen, imprimeur, 1777.
2 v.   20 cm.

25239   Pettit, Eber M   b. 1800 or 1801.
Sketches in the history of the Underground Railroad,
comprising many thrilling incidents of the escape of
fugitives from slavery, and the perils of those who aided
them. With introd. by W. McKinstry. Fredonia, N. Y.,
W. McKinstry & son, 1879.
174 p.   23 cm.

25240   Peytraud, Lucien Pierre, 1858-
L'esclavage aux Antilles françaises avant 1789, d'après
des documents inédits des archives coloniales... par
Lucien Peytraud... Paris, Hachette, 1897.
xxii, 472 p.   25 cm.

25241   Pfaff, Ivo, 1864-
Ein Beitrag zur Lehre von favor libertatis von dr.
Ivo Pfaff... Wien, Manz, 1894.
8 p.l., 45 p.   23 cm.

25242   Pfeiffer, G   S[imon] F[riedrich]
The voyages and five years' captivity in Algiers, of
Doctor G. S. F. Pfeiffer: with an appendix, giving a
true description of the customs, manners, and habits
of the different inhabitants of the country of Algiers.
Written by himself. Tr. from the 2d German ed. by I.
Daniel Rupp... Harrisburg, Pa., J. Winebrenner, 1836.
v, 398 p.   16½ cm.

25243   Phelps, Samuel Shethar, 1793-1855.
            Speech of Mr. Phelps, of Vermont, on the subject of
        slavery, &c. In Senate, January 23, 1850. [Washington,
        Gideon & co., printers, 1850]
            16 p.   23½ cm.
            Caption title.

25244   Philadelphia. Anti-slavery Convention, 1833.
            Proceedings of the Anti-slavery Convention, assembled
        at Philadelphia, December 4, 5, and 6, 1833. New-York,
        Printed by Dorr & Butterfield, 1833.
            28 p.   21 cm.
            Formed the American Anti-slavery Society.

25245   Philadelphia. Union League.
            Proceedings of the Union League of Philadelphia, in
        commemoration of the eighty-ninth anniversary of American
        independence, July 4th, 1865. Oration of Charles Gibbons,
        esq. Philadelphia, King & Baird, printers, 1865.
            32 p.   23 cm.

25246   Philadelphia Anti-slavery Society.
            ... Annual report. 1st-   ; 1835-
        Philadelphia, The Society, 1835-
            v.   21½ cm.

25247   Philadelphia Anti-slavery Society.
            Constitution of the Philadelphia Anti-slavery Society.
        Instituted fourth month 30th, 1834. Philadelphia,
        Printed by T. Town, 1834.
            vi, [7]-12 p.   23 cm.

25248   Philadelphia Female Anti-slavery Society.
            ... Extracts from the American slave code. [Philadelphia,
        Philadelphia Female Anti-slavery Society, 1829?]
            4 p.   22 cm.

25249   [Philanthropos] pseud.
            An address to the inhabitants of the state of Delaware.
        [n.p.] 1843.
            24 p.   17 cm.

25250   Philippine Islands. Dept. of the Interior.
            ... Slavery and peonage in the Philippine Islands, by
        Dean C. Worcester, secretary of the interior. Manila,
        Bureau of printing, 1913.
            120 p.   front., pl.   25½ cm.

25251   Philippine Islands. Legislature, 3rd, 2d sess. Philippine
        Assembly. Committee on Slavery and Peonage.

... Resumen de la investigación sobre esclavitud y
peonaje en las Islas Filipinas, por el comité que investig
el asunto. Manila, Bureau of printing, 1914.
     25 p.   23 cm.   (Document no. 3472-A130)
     Signed by Serviliano Platón.

25252 Phillippo, James M[ursell], 1798-1879.
          Jamaica: its past and present state. By James M.
       Phillippo... Philadelphia, J. M. Campbell & co.;
       New York, Saxton & Miles, 1843.
          viii, [9]-176 p.   front., illus.   21 cm.

25253 Phillips, John.
          An appeal to matter of fact & common sense, recommended
       to the serious conideration [!] of the inhabitants of
       Charleston, South Carolina, &c. To which is affixed,
       a letter to the **** By John Phillips... New-York,
       Printed by T. Kirk, 1798.
          vii, [9]-31, [1] p.   21 cm.

25254 Phillips, Ulrich Bonnell, 1877-1934.
          American negro slavery; a survey of the supply, employ-
       ment and control of Negro labor as determined by the
       plantation regime, by Ulrich Bonnell Phillips... New
       York, London, D. Appleton and company, 1918.
          xi, 529 p.   22½ cm.

25255 Phillips, Ulrich Bonnell, 1877-1934.
          The economic cost of slaveholding in the cotton belt.
       [n.p., 1905]
          257-275 p.   table.   22 cm.
          Reprinted from the Political science quarterly, v. 20,
       June 1905.

25256 Phillips, Ulrich Bonnell, 1877-1934.
          A Jamaica slave plantation [by] Ulrich B. Phillips...
       [Washington, 1914]
          cover-title, p. 543-558.   27 cm.
          Reprinted from the American historical review, v. 19,
       1914.

25257 Phillips, Ulrich Bonnell, 1877-1934.
          Racial problems, adjustments and disturbances in the
       antebellum South, by Ulrich B. Phillips... Richmond,
       Va., The Southern Publication Society, 1909.
          1 p.l., [194]-241 p.   23½ cm.
          Reprinted from The South in the building of the nation
       (vol. 4)

25258   Phillips, Ulrich Bonnell, 1877-1934.
        The slavery issue in federal politics, by Ulrich B.
Phillips... Richmond, Va., The Southern publication
society, 1909.
        1 p.l., p. [382]-422.   23½ cm.
        Reprinted from The South in the building of the nation,
v. 4.

25259   Phillips, Ulrich Bonnell, 1877-1934.
        The slave labor problem in the Charleston district, by
Ulrich Bonnell Phillips... Boston, Ginn & company, 1907.
        [1], 416-439 p.   23 cm.
        Reprinted from Political science quarterly, v. 22, 1907.

25260   [Phillips, Wendell] 1811-1884.
        ... Can abolitionists vote or take office under the
United States Constitution?... New York, American anti-
slavery society, 1845.
        39 p.   28½ cm.   (The Anti-slavery examiner, no. 13)

25261   Phillips, Wendell, 1811-1884.
        The lesson of the hour. Lecture of Wendell Phillips
delivered at Brooklyn, N. Y. ... November, 1859. [n.p.,
1859]
        24 p.   15 cm.
        Caption title.

25262   Phillips, Wendell, 1811-1884.
        ... Speech of Wendell Phillips, at the Melodeon,
Thursday evening, Jan. 27, 1853. Phonographically reported
by J. M. W. Yerrinton. [Boston? 1853]
        32, 3, [1] p.   24 cm.
        Caption title.

25263   Phillips, Wendell, 1811-1884.
        Speeches before the Massachusetts Anti-slavery Society,
January, 1852. By Wendell Phillips. Boston, R. F.
Wallcut, 1852.
        24 p.   23 cm.

25264   Philo-Xylon, pseud.
        Letters of Philo-Xylon, first published in the Barbados
gazettes, during the years 1787 and 1788. Containing
the substance of several conversations at sundry times,
for seven years past, on the subject of negro laws, and
negro government, on plantations, in Barbados. Barbados,
Printed by T. W. Perch, 1789.
        4 p.l., [5]-47, [2] p.   21 cm.

25265   [Philpot, Francis]
Facts for white Americans, with a plain hint for dupes,
and a bone to pick for white nigger demagogues and amalgamation abolitionists, including the parentage, brief career
and execution, of amalgamation abolitionism, whose funeral
sermon was preached by Washington on the 7th of February,
1839... Philadelphia, The author, 1839.
62 p.   18½ cm.

25266   Pia opera pel riscatto delle fanciulle more, Genoa.
... Relazione sui progressi della Pia opera pel riscatto
delle fanciulle more... Genova, Stamperia Casamara, 185-
v.   front.   20½ cm.

25267   Pickens, Francis Wilkinson, 1805-1869.
Letter... The crops and conditions of the country. The
interests of labor. Effects of emancipation. The
different races of mankind. Written to a gentleman in
New Orleans. Baltimore, the Printing Office, 1866.
18 p.   23 cm.

25268   Pickens, Francis Wilkinson, 1805-1869.
Speech of Hon. F. W. Pickens, delivered before a
public meeting of the people of the district, held at
Edgefield C. H., S. C., July 7, 1851. Edgefield, S. C.,
Printed at the Advertiser office, 1851.
19 p.   12 cm.

25269   Pickens, Francis Wilkinson, 1805-1869.
Speech of Mr. Pickens, of South Carolina, in the House
of representatives, January 21, 1836, on the abolition
question. Pub. from the notes of Henry Godfrey Wheeler,
rev. and cor. by the author. Washington, Printed by
Gales & Seaton, 1836.
16 p.   23½ cm.

25270   A picture of slavery, drawn from the decisions of southern
courts. [Philadelphia, Crissy & Markley, 1863]
16 p.   21½ cm.
Issued as a campaign document against Judge Woodward,
Democratic candidate for governor.

25271   Pierce, Franklin, pres. U. S., 1804-1869.
Slave and coolie trade, message from the president of
the United States communicating information in regard
to the slave and coolie trade. [Washington, 1856]
159 p.   23½ cm.   (34th Cong. 1st sess. House of
Representatives, Ex. doc. no. 105)

25272　Pilaski, Alphonsus.
　　　　De possessione servi et per servum acquirenda et
　　retinenda...　Berolini, typis Eduardi Krause, 1862.
　　　　2 p.l., 41 p.　　21 cm.
　　　　Inaug.-diss. - Berlin.

25273　Pillsbury, Parker, 1809-1898.
　　　　Acts of the anti-slavery apostles.　By Parker Pillsbury...
　　Concord, N. H., [Clague, Wegman, Schlicht, & co., printers,
　　Rochester, N. Y.] 1883.
　　　　vii, [9]-503 p.　　20 cm.

25274　Pillsbury, Parker, 1809-1898.
　　　　The church as it is:　or, The forlorn hope of slavery.
　　2d ed.　Concord, N. H., Printed by the Republican Press
　　Association, 1885.
　　　　96 p.　　18 cm.

25275　Pillsbury, Parker, 1809-1898.
　　　　... Stephen Symonds Foster.　By Parker Pillsbury.
　　[Concord, N. Y., 1882]
　　　　7 p.　　24½ cm.

25276　Pinckard, George, 1768-1835.
　　　　Notes on the West Indies:　written during the expedition
　　under the command of the late General Sir Ralph Abercromby:
　　including observations on the island of Barbados, and the
　　settlements captured by the British troops, upon the coast
　　of Guiana:　likewise remarks relating to the Creoles and
　　slaves of the western colonies, and the Indians of South
　　America:　with occasional hints, regarding the seasoning,
　　or yellow fever of hot climates.　By George Pinckard...
　　Longdon, Longman, Hurst, Rees, and Orme, 1806.
　　　　3 v.　　21 cm.

25277　[Pinckney, Henry Laurens] 1794-1863.
　　　　Address to the electors of Charleston District, South
　　Carolina, on the subject of the abolition of slavery.
　　Washington, 1836.
　　　　15 p.　　21½ cm.

25278　[Pinckney, Thomas] 1750-1828.
　　　　Reflections, occasioned by the late disturbances in
　　Charleston.　By Achates [pseud.]　Charleston, Printed
　　and sold by A. E. Miller, 1822.
　　　　30 p.　　21½ cm.

25279   Pinkney, William, 1764-1822.
            Speech of William Pinkney, esq., in the House of
        Delegates of Maryland, at their session in November, 1789.
        Philadelphia, Printed by Joseph Crukshank, in Market-
        street, between Second and Third-streets, 1790.
            22 p.   20 cm.

25280   A pioneer emancipator.   Richmond, Ky., Kentucky Register
        Print, 1881.
            6 p.   23 cm.
        On Cassius Marcellus Clay.

25281   A plain statement addressed to all honest Democrats.   By one
        of the people.   Boston, J. P. Jewett & company; Cleveland,
        O., Jewett, Proctor & Worthington; [etc., etc.] 1856.
            43 p.   19½ cm.

25282   Platte County Self-defensive Association, Platte Co., Mo.
            Negro-slavery, no evil; or, The North and the South.
        The effects of negro-slavery, as exhibited in the census,
        by a comparison of the condition of the slaveholding and
        non-slaveholding states.   Considered in a report made to
        the Platte County Self-defensive Association, by a
        committee, through B. F. Stringfellow, chairman.   Pub. by
        order of the association.   St. Louis, Printed by Niedner
        & co., 1854.
            40 p.   23½ cm.

25283   Pleasants, Mary Minta, 1853-
            Which one? and other ante bellum days, by Mary M.
        Pleasants.   Boston, J. H. Earle company [c1910]
            90 p. incl. plates.   20 cm.
            Contents. - Which one? - "My mistis." - How Frank
        Christian got his master's shote. - The passing of
        Mammy Jane.

25284   Plumer, William, 1789-1854.
            Speech of Mr. Plumer, of New-Hampshire, on the
        Missouri question, delivered in the House of Representa-
        tives of the United States, February 21, 1820.
        [Washington? 1820]
            42 p.   18½ cm.

25285   Poems on the abolition of the slave trade, written by James
        Montgomery, James Grahame, and E. Benger.   Embellished
        with engravings from pictures painted by R. Smirke.
        London, Printed for R. Bowyer by T. Bensley, 1809.
            141 p.   plates, ports.   35 cm.
        Apparently compiled by R. Bowyer.

25286   Poetry for the times.   [n.p., 1856?]
            16 p.   13½ cm.
            Caption title.
            Contents. - Henry Ward Beecher. - Mrs. H. B. Stow [!] -
        The Sumner outrage. - An eulogy on Col. Fremont. - A
        description of Col. Fremont's foes. - The Irish appeal. -
        A sermon. - The poets defence. - Sodomites and Balaamites. -
        The New York observer. - On the marriage of Mr. Armstrong
        to Miss Miner.

25287   Political action against slavery.   Cazenovia, N. Y., 1838.
            [1] p.   55 cm.
            Union herald, extra.

25288   Politics and the pulpit: a series of articles which appeared
        in the Journal of commerce and in the Independent, during
        the year 1850.   To which is added an article from the
        Independent of Feb. 21, 1850, entitled "Shall we compro-
        mise?" New York, W. Harned, 1851.
            63 p.   22½ cm.

25289   Pollard, Edward Alfred, 1831-1872.
            The first year of the war. By Edward A. Pollard...
        Corrected and improved ed. Richmond, West & Johnston,
        145 Main Street, 1862. [New York, Charles B. Richardson,
        1863?]
            2 p.l., 368 [i.e. 362] p.   ports. (incl. front.)
        24 cm.
            In spite of the Richmond imprint on the title-page
        (which is like the added title-page in the 1862 New York
        ed.) this appears to be the 1863 N. Y. edition reprinted
        by Charles B. Richardson from the Richmond corrected
        edition of 1862.

25290   Pollard, Edward Alfred, 1831-1872.
            The lost cause; a new southern history of the war of
        the Confederates. Comprising a full and authentic account
        of the rise and progress of the late southern Confederacy -
        the campaigns, battles, incidents, and adventures of the
        most gigantic struggle of the world's history. Drawn
        from official sources, and approved by the most distin-
        guished Confederate leaders. By Edward A. Pollard...
        With numerous splendid steel portraits... New York,
        E. B. Treat & co., Baltimore, Md., L. T. Palmer & co.;
        [etc., etc.] 1866.
            xxx p., 1 l., [33]-752 (i.e. 740) p.   front., ports.
        24½ cm.

25291   Pomeroy, Samuel Clarke, 1816-1891.
            The conflict and triumph. Speech of Hon. S. C. Pomeroy,

(of Kansas) in the Senate of the United States,
March 5th, 1866... [Washington, H. Polkinhorn & son,
printers, 1866]
16 p.   23 cm.

25292   Poor old slave. [n.p., n.d.]
[1] p.   28 cm.
An abolition ballad.

25293   Pope, Samuel, 1826-
The American war: secession and slavery; a lecture
delivered at Tunstall, Staffordshire. Manchester [Eng.]
Manchester Union and Emancipation Society [1863?]
16 p.   17 cm.   (Union and emancipation tracts,
no. 1)
"Reprinted from the 'Staffordshire sentinel,' of
January 17, 1863."

25294   Porter, Albert Gallatin, 1824-1897.
Speech of Hon. Albert G. Porter, of Indiana. Deli-
vered in the House of Representatives, June 4, 1862.
[Washington, L. Towers & co., print, 1862]
8 p.   24½ cm.
Caption title.

25295   Potts, Mrs. Eugenia Dunlap.
Historic papers on the causes of the Civil War, by
Mrs. Eugenia Dunlap Potts... Lexington, Ky., Ashland
printing co. [1909?]
cover-title, [37] p.   22½ cm.

25296   Poussielgue, Achille.
... Homme ou singe; ou, La question de l'esclavage
aux États-Unis, par m. Poussielgue... Paris, E. Dentu,
1861.
24 p.   24 cm.

25297   Powell, Aaron Macy, 1832-1899.
Personal reminiscences of the anti-slavery and other
reforms and reformers. By Aaron M. Powell. Plainfield,
N. J., A. R. Powell; New York, Caulon press, 1899.
xx, 279 p. incl. ports., facsims.   21 cm.

25298   Powell, Lazarus Whitehead, 1812-1867.
Amendments to the Constitution. Speech of Hon. L. W.
Powell, of Ky. in reply to Senators Clarke, Hale, and
Sumner, delivered in the Senate of the United States,
April 8, 1864, on the joint resolution proposing amend-
ments to the Constitution of the United States.
Washington, D. C., Printed at the office of "The Consti-

tutional union," 1864.
     12 p.   22½ cm.

25299   Power, John Hamilton, 1798-1873.
         Review of the lectures of Wm. A. Smith, D. D., on the
         philosophy and practice of slavery, as exhibited in the
         institution of domestic slavery in the United States:
         with the duties of masters to slaves. In a series of
         letters addressed to the author. By Rev. John H. Power,
         D.D. Cincinnati, Swormstedt & Poe, 1859.
         1 p.l., 369 p.   19½ cm.

25300   Practical considerations founded on the Scriptures, relative
         to the slave population of South-Carolina. Respectfully
         dedicated to "The South-Carolina Association." By a
         South-Carolinian. Charleston [S. C.] Printed by A. E.
         Miller, 1823.
         38 p.   20 cm.

25301   [Pratt, Minot]
         A friend of the South in answer to Remarks on Dr. Chan-
         ning's Slavery. Boston, Otis, Broaders and company, 1836.
         19 p.   20 cm.

25302   Prentiss, Samuel, 1782-1857.
         Speech of the Hon. Samuel Prentiss, of Vermont, upon the
         question of reception of the Vermont resolutions, on the
         subject of the admission of Texas, the domestic slave trade,
         and slavery in the District of Columbia. Delivered in the
         Senate U. S., January 16, 1838. Washington, Printed by
         Gales and Seaton, 1838.
         10 p.   23 cm.

25303   Presbyterian Church in the U. S.   Executive Committee of
         Publication.
         The distinctive principles of the Presbyterian Church in
         the United States, commonly called the Southern Presbyte-
         rian Church, as set forth in the formal declarations, and
         illustrated by extracts from proceedings of the General
         Assembly, from 1861-70. To which is added, extracts from
         the proceedings of the O. S. Assembly, from 1861-67.
         Richmond, Presbyterian Committee of Publication [n.d.]
         cover-title, 134 p.   22 cm.

25304   Presbyterian Church in the U. S.   (Old School) Board of
         Publications.
         American slavery, as viewed and acted on by the Presby-
         terian church in the United States of America. Comp. for
         the Board of publication, by the Rev. A. T. McGill...

Philadelphia, Presbyterian board of publication [1865]
72 p.   18 cm.

25305 Presbyterian Church in the U. S.   (Old School)   General
       Assembly.
          Testimony of the General Assembly of the Presbyterian
       Church in the United States of America on the subject of
       slavery.   Philadelphia, Presbyterian Publication Committee,
       1858.
          31 p.   22½ cm.

25306 Presbyterian Church in the U. S.   Synods.   South Carolina.
          Report on the subject of slavery, presented to the
       Synod of South Carolina, at their sessions in Winnsborough,
       November 6, 1851; adopted by them, and published by their
       order.   By J. H. Thornwell.   Columbia, Press of A. S.
       Johnston, 1852.
          16 p.   25 cm.

25307 Presidential document.   [Boston, Distributed by Redding,
       1860?]
          16 p.   19 cm.
          Caption title.

25308 Preston, William Campbell, 1794-1860.
          Speech of the Hon. Mr. Preston, on the abolition question
       Delivered Tuesday March 1, 1836.   [n.p., 1836]
          8 p.   22½ cm.
          Caption title.

25309 Price, Robert.
          The Ohio anti-slavery convention of 1836.   By Robert
       Price.   [Columbus, O., 1936]
          173-188 p.   23 cm.
          Reprinted from Ohio state archaeological and historical
       quarterly, v. 45, 1936.

25310 The price of gold and the presidency.   Considerations for
       the people.   New York, Dodge & Grattan, printers, 1864.
          19 p.   22½ cm.

25311 Priest, Josiah, 1788-1851.
          Bible defence of slavery; and origin, fortunes, and
       history of the negro race.   By Rev. Josiah Priest, A.M.
       5th ed. - stereotyped.   Glasgow, Ky., W. S. Brown, 1852.
          ix, [iii]-xiii, [15]-569 p.   23 cm.

25312 [Priest, Josiah] 1788-1851.
          Slavery, as it relates to the negro, or African race,

examined in the light of circumstances, history and the
Holy Scriptures; with an account of the origin of the
black man's color, causes of his state of servitude and
traces of his character as well in ancient as in modern
times: with strictures on abolitionism... Albany,
Printed by C. van Benthuysen and co., 1843.
   xii, [13]-340 p. incl. pl.   19½ cm.

25313 Prigg, Edward, plaintiff in error.
   Report of the case of Edward Prigg against the Commonwealth of Pennsylvania. Argued and adjudged in the Supreme
Court of the United States, at January term, 1842. In which
it was decided that all the laws of the several states relative to fugitive slaves are unconstitutional and void; and
that Congress have the exclusive power of legislation on the
subject of fugitive slaves escaping into other states. By
Richard Peters, reporter of the decisions of the Supreme
Court of the United States. Philadelphia, Stereotyped by
L. Johnson, 1842.
   140 p.   24½ cm.

25314 Prime, Nathaniel Scudder, 1785-1856.
   The year of jubilee; but not to Africans: a discourse,
delivered July 4th, 1825, being the 49th anniversary of
American independence. By Nathaniel S. Prime... Salem,
N. Y., Printed by Dodd and Stevenson, 1825.
   24 p.   22½ cm.

25315 Prince, Benjamin F   1840-
   The rescue case of 1857. [By] Benj. F. Prince. [Columbus,
   O., 1907]
   292-309 p.   23½ cm.
   Reprinted from Ohio archaeological and historical quarterly,
v. 16, 1907.
   The rescue of Addison White, a fugitive slave from
Kentucky.

25316 [Pringle, Edward J   ]
   Slavery in the southern states. By a Carolinian... 2d ed.
Cambridge, J. Bartlett, 1852.
   2 p.l., [3]-53 p.   20 cm.
   "An answer to the question, What do you think of 'Uncle
Tom's cabin' at the South?"

25317 The privilege and dignity, responsibility and duty of the
   present Congress to emancipate the slaves by law.
   [Washington? 1865]
   [4] p.   28 x 21½ cm.
   Signed: Geo. B. Cheever, Wm. C. Bryant, James A. Hamilton,
John E. Williams, Peter Cooper, Col. James McKaye.

25318   Protest of the state of Louisiana to the Senate of the
        United States... [New Orleans? 1868?]
            8 p.   21½ cm.
        Caption title.

25319   Providence. Citizens.
            Proceedings of a public meeting of the citizens of
        Providence, held in the Beneficent Congregational Church,
        March 7, 1854, to protest against slavery in Nebraska;
        with the addresses of the speakers. Providence,
        Knowles, Anthony & co., printers, 1854.
            32 p.   23½ cm.

25320   Providence Anti-slavery Society.
            The report and proceedings of the first annual meeting
        of the Providence Anti-slavery Society. With a brief
        exposition of the principles and purposes of the aboli-
        tionists. Providence, H. H. Brown, 1833.
            16 p.   21½ cm.

25321   [Providence Society for Abolishing the Slave-trade]
            Constitution of a society for abolishing the slave-
        trade. With several acts of the legislatures of the
        states of Massachusetts, Connecticut and Rhode Island,
        for that purpose. Providence, Printed by J. Carter,
        1789.
            19 p.   21 cm.

25322   Prussing, Eugene Ernst, 1855-
            Chicago's first great lawsuit, by Eugene E. Prussing.
        [Madison, 1915]
            [123]-139 p.   24 cm.   (The State Historical Society
        of Wisconsin, Separate no. 168)
            "From the Proceedings of the Society for 1915."
            The case of Thomas Forsyth and John Kinzie vs. Jeffrey
        Nash, in which the plaintiffs sought to have the defendant
        returned as a runaway slave.

25323   Puerto Rico. Laws, statutes, etc.
            Ordenanza general de emancipados. [n.p., 1859?]
            9 p.   21 cm.
        Caption title.

25324   Pugh, George Ellis, 1822-1876.
            Territorial policy. Speech of Hon. George E. Pugh, of
        Ohio, in reply to Messrs. Iverson and Green, in the Senate
        of the United States, Wednesday, January 11, 1860.
        [Washington] Printed by L. Towers [1860]
            32 p.   23 cm.
        Caption title.

25325　Pullen, William H
　　　　　The blast of a trumpet in Zion, calling upon every son
　　　　and daughter of Wesley, in Great Britain and Ireland, to
　　　　aid their brethren in America in purifying their
　　　　American Zion from slavery.　By William H. Pullen... By
　　　　authority of the anti-slavery societies of Great Britain
　　　　and Ireland...　London, Webb, Millington, & co. [etc.]
　　　　1860
　　　　　48 p.　　21½ cm.

25326　Purviance, Samuel A　　　　b. 1809.
　　　　　Speech of Hon. Samuel A. Purviance, of Pennsylvania, on
　　　　the slavery and presidential questions.　Delivered in the
　　　　House of Representatives, August 4, 1856.　Washington,
　　　　Printed at the Congressional globe office, 1856.
　　　　　14 p.　　24 cm.

25327　Putnam, Mary Burnham.
　　　　　The Baptists and slavery, 1840-1845, by Mary Burnham
　　　　Putnam...　Ann Arbor, Mich., G. Wahr, 1913.
　　　　　96 p.　　19½ cm.

25328　[Putnam, Mrs. Mary (Lowell)]　1810-1898.
　　　　　Tragedy of errors...　Boston, Ticknor and Fields, 1861.
　　　　　5 p.l., [7]-249 p.　　29½ x 23 cm.

25329　[Putnam, Mary (Lowell)] 1810-1898.
　　　　　Tragedy of success...　Boston, Ticknor and Fields, 1862.
　　　　　191 p.　　18 cm.
　　　　　Sequel to her "Tragedy of errors."
　　　　　In verse.

25330　Pye, S
　　　　　Essay on negro emancipation.　Originally published in
　　　　the Long-Island star, under the signature of S. Pye.　Also
　　　　an essay on the phenomena of dreams, by the same.
　　　　Brooklyn, Printed by A. Spooner, 1832.
　　　　　35 p.　　20½ cm.

Q

25331　Quaife, Milo Milton, 1880-
　　　　　... The doctrine of non-intervention with slavery in the
　　　　territories...　Chicago, M. C. Chamberlin co., 1910.
　　　　　150 p.　　24½ cm.
　　　　　Thesis (Ph.D.) - University of Chicago.

25332 Quaw, James E
       The wolf detected; or, Political abolition exposed.
       By James E. Quaw... Detroit, Geiger & Christian, printers,
       1845.
         35, [1] p.   19 cm.

25333 Queal, William G
       The overthrow of American slavery, containing des-
       criptions of important events and sketches of some of the
       prominent actors. By William G. Queal... Printed for the
       author. New York, Phillips & Hunt; Cincinnati, Cranston &
       Stowe, 1885.
         275 p.   19½ cm.
         In verse.

25334 Questions cubaine; l'esclavage et la traite à Cuba. Paris,
       Typ. T. et I. Joseph, 1876.
         x, 30 p.   21 cm.
         Tr. from the Spanish by R. E. Bétancès.

25335 A question in casuistry. [n.p., 1909]
         905-906 p.   23 cm.
         Reprinted from Independent, v. 67, 28 Oct. 1909.

25336 Quincy, Edmund, 1808-1877.
       An examination of the charges of Mr. John Scoble &
       Mr. Lewis Tappan against the American Anti-slavery
       Society. By Edmund Quincy... Dublin, Webb and Chapman;
       [etc., etc.] 1852.
         27, [1] p.   21½ cm.

25337 Quincy, Ill. Anti-slavery Concert for Prayer, 1842.
       Narrative of facts, respecting Alanson Work, Jas. E. Bur:
       & Geo. Thompson prisoners in the Missouri Penitentiary, fo:
       the alleged crime of negro stealing. Prepared by a com-
       mittee. Quincy, Ill., Quincy Whig office, 1842.
         37 p.   21½ cm.

                                 R

25338 Radical Political Abolitionists.
       Proceedings of the convention of Radical Political Abo-
       litionists, held at Syracuse, N. Y., June 26th, 27th, and
       28th, 1855... New-York, The Central Abolition Board, 1855
         68 p.   23 cm.

25339 Radical rule: military outrage in Georgia. Arrest of
       Columbus prisoners: with facts connected with their impri

sonment and release. Louisville, Ky., Printed by J. P. Morton and company, 1868.
   199 p.   23 cm.
   "Proceedings of the Military commission" [for the trial of Elisha J. Kirksey, on a charge of killing George W. Ashburn]: p. [15]-183.

25340   [Ramsay, James] 1733-1789.
   An inquiry into the effects of putting a stop to the African slave trade, and of granting liberty to the slaves in the British sugar colonies. By the author of the Essay on the treatment and conversion of African slaves in the British sugar colonies. London, Printed and sold by J. Phillips, 1784.
   44 p.   18 cm.

25341   Randolph, Peter.
   From slave cabin to the pulpit; the autobiography of Rev. Peter Randolph: the southern question illustrated and sketches of slave life. Boston, J. H. Earle, 1893.
   220 p.   front. (port.)   19½ cm.

25342   Randolph County, Ill. Citizens.
   Memorial of sundry inhabitants of the counties of Randolph and St. Clair, in the Indiana Territory. January 17, 1806. Referred to the committee appointed the 19th ultimo, on a letter from William Henry Harrison, governor of the Indiana Territory. Washington, A. & G. Way, printers, 1806.
   12 p.   23 cm.

25343   Rantoul, Robert, 1805-1852.
   The fugitive slave law. Speech of Hon. Robert Rantoul, jr., of Beverly, Mass., delivered before the grand mass convention of the democratic voters of the Second congressional district of Massachusetts. Holden at Lynn, Thursday, April 3, 1851. Phonographic report by Dr. James W. Stone. [Lynn? Mass., 1851]
   15 p.   23 cm.
   Caption title.

25344   Raphall, Morris Jacob, 1798-1868.
   Bible view of slavery. A discourse, delivered at the Jewish synagogue, "Bnai Jeshurum," New York, on the day of the national fast, Jan. 4, 1861. By the Rev. M. J. Raphall... New York, Rudd & Carleton, 1861.
   2 p.l., [vii]-viii p., 1 l., [11]-41 p.   19 cm.

25345   Ray, William, 1771-1827.
   The American tars in Tripolitan slavery; containing

227

an account of the loss and capture of the United States
frigate Philadelphia; treatment and sufferings of the
prisoners; description of the place; manners, customs, &c.,
of the Tripolitans; public transactions of the United
States with that regency, including Gen. Eaton's expedition,
interspersed with interesting remarks, anecdotes, and
poetry, on various subjects, written during upwards of
nineteen months' imprisonment and vassalage among the Turks;
by William Ray. Troy, Printed by Oliver Lyon for the
author, 1808. New York, Reprinted, W. Abbatt, 1911.
    295 p.   26½ cm.   (On cover: The Magazine of history
with notes and queries, Extra number, no. 14)
    Originally published under title: Horrors of slavery;
or, The American tars in Tripoli.

25346   [Raymond, Henry Jarvis] 1820-1869.
    ... The slavery question in New-York. [Albany? 1850]
    15 p.   24½ cm.
    At head of title: Evening Journal - Extra.

25347   Raymond, James, 1796-1858.
    Prize essay, on the comparative economy of free and
slave labour, in agriculture. By James Raymond...
Frederick [Md.] Printed by J. P. Thomson, 1827.
    20 p.   20½ cm.

25348   Rayner, Kenneth, 1808-1884.
    Speech of Mr. Rayner, of North Carolina, on the question
of the reception of abolition petitions. Delivered in
the House of Representatives of the United States on
Tuesday, June 15, 1841. [Washington? 1841]
    20 p.   24 cm.
    Caption title.

25349   Read, Benjamin Maurice, 1853-
    A short history of slavery in America, by Benjamin M.
Read... St. Louis, Mo., "Amerika" print, 1919.
    cover-title, 7 p.   22½ cm.

25350   Read, John Meredith, 1797-1874.
    Speech of Hon. John M. Read, at the democratic town
meeting in favor of the union and California, held in
the hall of the Chinese Museum, on Wednesday the 13th
March, 1850. [Philadelphia? 1850]
    11 p.   22 cm.

25351   Reagan, John Henninger, 1818-1905.
    Speech of Hon. John H. Reagan, of Texas, in the House
of Representatives, February 29, 1860. [Washington]

T. McGill, printer [1860]
15 p.   23 cm.
Caption title.

25352 The Record of news, history and literature. v. 1; June 18-
       Dec. 10, 1863. Richmond, Va. [West & Johnston] 1863.
       248 p.   31 x 24 cm.
       Caption title.

25353 Reed, John Calvin, 1836-1910.
       The brothers' war, by John C. Reed... Boston, Little,
       Brown, and company, 1905.
       xviii, 456 p., 1 l.   21 cm.

25354 Reeder, Robert S
       A letter from Robert S. Reeder, esq., to Dr. Stouton W.
       Dent, on the colored population of Maryland, and slavery;
       and a speech on the proposition to call a convention, by
       a single act of the legislature, to change the constitu-
       tion, at December session, 1845. Port Tobacco [Md.]
       Printed by E. Wells, 1859.
       58 p.   22 cm.

25355 Reich, Emil, 1854-1910.
       ... Graeco-Roman institutions, from anti-evolutionist
       points of view. Roman law, classical slavery, social
       conditions. Four lectures delivered before the University
       of Oxford, by Emil Reich... London, Parker and co., 1890.
       5 p.l., [3]-100 p.   20½ cm.   (History of civilization.
       [Pre-history and antiquity])

25356 Reid, James.
       King Slavery's council; or, The midnight conclave: a
       poem, by James Reid... Troy, Printed at the Daily Whig
       office, 1844.
       58 p.   17 cm.

25357 The reign of terror in Kanzas [!]: as encouraged by
       President Pierce, and carried out by the southern slave
       power: by which men have been murdered and scalped!
       Women dragged from their homes and violated! Printing
       offices and private houses burned! Ministers of the
       Gospel tarred and feathered! Citizens robbed and driven
       from their homes! And other enormities inflicted on
       free settlers by border ruffians. As related by eye
       witnesses of the events. Boston, C. W. Briggs, 1856.
       1 p.l., [5]-34 p.   illus.   23½ cm.

25358 Reilley, Edward C
       Politico-economic considerations in the Western Reserve's

early slavery controversy. By Edward C. Reilley.
[Columbus, O., 1943]
141-159 p.   23 cm.
Reprinted from Ohio state archaeological and historical
quarterly, v. 52, 1943.

25359 The relation to the pulpit to slavery: Letter to a minister
of the Gospel. Philadelphia, Philadelphia Ladies' Anti-
slavery Society, 1836.
8 p. $21\frac{1}{2}$ cm.

25360 The relative territorial status of the North and the South.
[New Orleans? 1859]
cover-title, 29 p.   22 cm.
A letter addressed to J. D. B. De Bow, esq. Signed:
"Python."

25361 Remarks occasioned by strictures in the Courier and New York
enquirer of December 1852, upon the Stafford-House address.
In a letter to a friend in the United States, by an English-
woman. London, Hamilton, Adams, and co.; [etc., etc.] 1853
42 p.   22 cm.

25362 Remarks on an Address to the members of the new Parliament,
on the proceedings of the Colonial Department, with respect
to the West India question. By a member of the late
Parliament. London, J. Murray, 1826.
1 p.l., 78 p.   1 fold. tab. $20\frac{1}{2}$ cm.

25363 Remarks on "Slavery. By William E. Channing." (First
pub. in the Boston atlas, in a series of numbers) Boston,
J. H. Eastburn, printer, 1836.
61 p.   25 cm.

25364 Remarks on the immediate abolition lecture of Rev. Mr.
Phelps, delivered in the 2d Baptist Church in Taunton,
Sunday evening, May 24, 1835. By a hearer. Taunton
[Mass.] E. Anthony, printer, 1835.
12 p. $24\frac{1}{2}$ cm.

25365 Remarks upon a plan for the total abolition of slavery in
the United States. By a citizen of New-York. New-York,
Printed for the author [1833?]
16 p. $20\frac{1}{2}$ cm.

25366 Remarks upon slavery; occasioned by attempts made to
circulate improper publications in the southern states.
By a citizen of Georgia. Augusta, Printed at the S. R.
sentinel office, 1835.

32 p.   22½ cm.
The name W. J. Hobby, sr., is pencilled on the t.-p.

25367   Remarks upon slavery and the slave-trade, addressed to the
Hon. Henry Clay. [n.p.] 1839.
23 p.   21 cm.
Signed: A slave-holder.
"The authorship has been attributed to Morgan Gibbes." -
Sabin.

25368   Remarks upon the controversy between the commonwealth of
Massachusetts and the state of South Carolina. By a
friend to the union. Boston, W. Crosby & H. P. Nichols,
1845.
21 p.   22½ cm.
S. D. Ward, supposed author.

25369   Renny, Robert.
An history of Jamaica. With observations on the climate,
scenery, trade, productions, negroes, slave trade,
diseases of Europeans, customs, manners, and dispositions
of the inhabitants. To which is added, an illustration of
the advantages, which are likely to result, from the abolition of the slave trade. By Robert Renny, esq. London,
J. Cawthorn, 1807.
xx, 333, [1] p. incl. front. (fold. map)   27½ x 22 cm.

25370   A reply to "Letters to Joseph Sturge, Esq. by William Alers
Hankey, Esq." by the authors of "The West Indies in
1837," with a letter from the Marquis of Sligo also, a
letter to the Directors of the London Missionary Society
by Joseph Sturge. London, Hamilton, Adams, 1838.
24 p.   23 cm.

25371   Republican Party. Illinois. State Central Committee.
Political record of Stephen A. Douglas on the slavery
question. A tract issued by the Illinois Republican
State Central Committee. [n.p., 1860]
16 p.   24½ cm.
Caption title.

25372   The Republican scrap book; containing the platforms, and a
choice selection of extracts, setting forth the real
questions in issue, the opinions of the candidates,
the nature and designs of the slave oligarchy, as shown
by their own writers, and the opinions of Clay, Webster,
Josiah Quincy, and other patriots, on slavery and its
extension. Boston, J. P. Jewett & co., 1856.
80 p.   22½ cm.

25373 Requited Labor Convention, Philadelphia, 1838.
       Minutes of proceedings of the Requited Labor Convention,
       held in Philadelphia, on the 17th and 18th of the Fifth
       month, and by adjournment on the 5th and 6th of the Ninth
       month, 1838. Philadelphia, Printed by Merrihew and Gunn,
       1838.
       36 p.   23 cm.
       Address to abolitionists, signed Lewis C. Gunn: p. 22-36
       Address also published separately.

25374 A review of the decision of the Supreme Court of the United
       States in the Dred Scott case. By a Kentucky lawyer.
       Louisville, Ky., Morton & Griswold, printers, 1857.
       47 p.   21 cm.

25375 A review of the Rev. Dr. Junkin's synodical speech, in
       defence of American slavery; delivered September 19th and
       20th, and published December 1843: with an outline of the
       Bible argument against slavery... Cincinnati, Printed at
       the Daily atlas office, 1844.
       136 p.   21½ cm.

25376 Revocet, Samuel.
       [Letter dated New York, 29 April 1859, to Office of
       Superintendent of Police, 413 Boone Street, corner of Elm,
       New York, regarding finding of a body in the Ohio River.
       New York] 1859.
       2 p.   illus.   41 cm.
       Reprinted from Frank Leslie's Illustrated newspaper,
       no. 179 VII, under caption of "Missing people and
       defaulters. Discovery of the body of Samuel Yeager..."
       Related to the "Oberlin slave kidnapping case".

25377 ... Revolution the only remedy for slavery. [New York,
       American Anti-slavery Society, 1855]
       20 p.   19 cm.   (Anti-slavery tracts, no. 7)
       Caption title.

25378 Reynolds, Elhanan Winchester, 1827-1867.
       The relations of slavery to the war: and the position of
       the clergy at the present time. Three discourses,
       preached at Watertown, N. Y., by Rev. E. W. Reynolds.
       Watertown, N. Y., Sold at the bookstores and at Rand's,
       1861.
       iv, [5]-48 p.   21 cm.

25379 Rhett, Robert Barnwell, 1800-1876.
       Address to the people of Beaufort and Colleton districts,
       upon the subject of abolition, by Robert Barnwell Rhett.

January 15, 1838. [Washington? 1838]
13 p.   21½ cm.

25380   [Rhoads, Samuel]
Considerations on the use of the productions of slavery,
addressed to the Religious Society of Friends. 2d ed.
Philadelphia, Printed by Merrihew and Thompson, 1845.
36 p.   17 cm.

25381   Rhode Island. General Assembly. House of Representatives.
Select Committee to Whom were Referred the Resolutions
of Mr. Wells, on slavery.
Mr. Whipple's report, and Mr. Otis's letter. Boston,
Printed by Cassady and March, 1839.
30 p.   25 cm.
The report of the committee, signed by James F. Simmons:
p. 3-4; minority report signed by John Whipple: p. 4-19.

25382   Rice, David, 1733-1816.
Slavery inconsistent with justice and good policy;
proved by a speech delivered in the convention, held at
Danville, Kentucky. By the Rev. David Rice... Philadelphia
printed, 1792. London, Reprinted and sold by M. Gurney,
1793.
24 p.   18 cm.

25383   Rice, Nathan Lewis, 1807-1877.
Lectures on slavery, delivered in the First Presbyterian
Church, Cincinnati, July first and third, 1845. By Rev.
N. L. Rice... Cincinnati, J. A. James, 1845.
72 p.   18 cm.

25384   [Richardson, Anna H   ]
Anti-slavery memoranda. [Newcastle-upon-Tyne, Printed
by J. G. Forster, 1860?]
12 p.   18 cm.

25385   Richardson, John G
Obedience to human law considered in the light of
divine truth. A discourse delivered in the First Baptist
Meeting House, Lawrence, Mass., July 4, 1852. By John G.
Richardson... Lawrence, Printed by H. A. Cooke, 1852.
18 p.   21 cm.

25386   [Richardson, Nathaniel Smith] 1810-1883.
The Union, the Constitution, and slavery... New York,
1864.
36 p.   22 cm.
From the American quarterly church review, for January,
1864.

25387   Richardson, William Alexander, 1811-1872.
        Speech of Hon. W. A. Richardson, of Illinois, on the
        Admission of California. Delivered in the House of Repre-
        sentatives, April 3, 1850. Washington, Printed at the
        Congressional globe office, 1850.
        7 p.   24½ cm.

25388   Richmond, Legh, 1772-1827.
        The African servant; an authentic narrative. [Andover,
        Printed for the New England Tract Society, 1820]
        16 p.   16½ cm.   (New England Tract Society, no. 53)

25389   Riddell, William Renwick, 1852-
        The slave in Canada, by the Hon. William Renwick Riddell.
        Washington, D. C., The Association for the study of Negro
        life and history, 1920.
        v, 120 p.   25 cm.
        Reprinted from the Journal of Negro history, vo. 5, no. 3,
        July, 1920.

25390   Rider, Sidney Smith, 1833-1917.
        An historical inquiry concerning the attempt to raise a
        regiment of slaves by Rhode Island during the war of the
        revolution. By Sidney S. Rider. With several tables
        prepared by Lt.-Col. Jeremiah Olney, commandant. Provi-
        dence, S. S. Rider, 1880.
        xxii p., 1 l., 86 p. incl. tables.   21 x 16 cm.
        (Added t.-p.: Rhode Island historical tracts, [1st ser.]
        no. 10)
        Memoir of Col. Jeremiah Olney: p. [vii]-xxii.

25391   The right of petition. Remarks of Messrs. Seward, Hale, and
        Chase, with a sketch of the debate in the Senate on various
        petitions and other matters connected with the subject of
        slavery. Washington, Printed by Buell & Blanchard, 1850.
        15 p.   24½ cm.

25392   The right of recognition. A sketch of the present policy
        of the Confederate States. By a recent tourist... London,
        R. Hardwicke, 1862.
        30 p.   21½ cm.

25393   Riland, John, 1778-1863.
        Memoirs of a West-India planter. Published from an
        original ms., with a preface and additional details.
        By the Rev. John Riland... London, Hamilton, Adams, & co.
        [etc.] 1827.
        xxxv, 218 p.   18½ cm.

25394   Riley, James, 1777-1840.
         An authentic narrative of the loss of the American brig
    Commerce, wrecked on the western coast of Africa, in the
    month of August, 1815, with an account of the sufferings
    of the surviving officers and crew, who were enslaved by
    the wandering Arabs, on the African desert, or Zahahrah;
    and observations historical, geographical, &c. made during
    the travels of the author, while a slave to the Arabs, and
    in the empire of Morocco. By James Riley... Preceded by
    a brief sketch of the author's life; and containing a des-
    cription of the famous city Tombuctoo, and of another larger
    city... called Wassanah, narrated to the author at Mogadore,
    by Sidi Hamet, the Arabian merchant. Illustrated and
    embellished with ten copper-plate engravings; rev., and
    his life continued, by the author, in January, 1828.
    Hartford, S. Andrus and son, 1851.
         xiv, [15]-271 p.   front., plates.   19½ cm.
    Edited by Anthony Bleecker.

25395   Riley, James, 1777-1840.
         Sequel to Riley's Narrative; being a sketch of interesting
    incidents in the life, voyages and travels of Capt. James
    Riley, from the period of his return to his native land,
    after his shipwreck, captivity and sufferings among the
    Arabs of the desert, as related in his narrative, until his
    death. Comp. chiefly from the original journal and manus-
    cripts left at his death in possession of his son, W.
    Willshire Riley. Columbus, G. Brewster; Springfield,
    A. R. Wright, 1851.
         xii p., 2 l., [17]-448 p.   front., plates, ports.,
    fold. plan.   23 cm.

25396   Ritter, George.
         A speech, delivered on the 13th. January, 1802, before
    the society, called the Proficuous judicatory; concerning
    the advantages that would be derived from a total abolition
    of slavery. By George Ritter... Philadelphia, Printed
    for the author, 1802.
         iv, [5]-20 p.   23 cm.

25397   Robbins, Archibald, 1792-1865.
         A journal, comprising an account of the loss of the brig
    Commerce, of Hartford, Conn.; James Riley, master: - upon
    the western coast of Africa, August 28th, 1815: also, of
    the slavery and sufferings of the author and the rest of
    the crew, upon the desert Zahara, in the years 1815, 1816,
    1817; with accounts of the manners, customs, and habits of
    the wandering Arabs; aldo a brief historical and geographical
    view of the continent of Africa. By Archibald Robbins.

235

Hartford, S. Andrus & son, 1851.
1 p.l., [v]-vii, [6], [15]-275 p.   19 cm.

25398   Robert, Charles Edwin.
        Negro civilization in the South; educational, social and
        religious advancement of the colored people. A review of
        slavery as a civil and commercial question. The "divine
        sanction of slavery." A glance at African history.
        Ethnological status of the negro, etc. ... By Charles
        Edwin Robert... Nashville, Tenn., Printed by Wheeler bros
        for the author, 1880.
        3 p.l., [5]-172 p.   illus.   23 cm.

25399   Roberts, Robert, 1868-
        Das Familien-, Sklaven- und Erbrecht im Qoran, von Robt.
        Roberts... Leipzig, J. C. Hinrichs, 1908.
        2 p.l., 56 p.   22 cm.   (On cover: Leipziger semi-
        tistische Studien, II, 6)

25400   Robertson, Daniel A   1813-1895.
        The South and the Democratic party. A speech by D. A.
        Robertson, delivered in St. Paul, Wednesday, Sept. 30.
        Saint Paul, Goodrich, Somers, & co., printers, 1857.
        15 p.   22 cm.

25401   Robertson, John, jr., 1787-1873.
        Speech of Mr. Robertson, of Virginia, on his motion to
        recommit the Report and resolutions of the Select Committee
        on the Subject of Abolition. Delivered in the House of
        Representatives, May, 1836. Washington, Printed by D.
        Green, 1836.
        24 p.   22½ cm.

25402   [Robinson, C   H   ]
        The slave trade in the west African hinterland.
        [n.p., 1898]
        698-705 p.   22 cm.
        Reprinted from the Contemporary review, v. 73, May 1898.

25403   [Robinson, Conway] 1805-1884.
        An essay upon the constitutional rights as to slave prop
        erty. Republished from the "Southern literary messenger,"
        for Feb. 1840. Richmond, Printed by T. W. White, 1840.
        20 p.   26½ cm.

25404   Robinson, Rachel Sargent, 1891-
        The size of the slave population at Athens during the
        fifth and fourth centuries before Christ, by Rachel Louisa
        Sargent... [Urbana, Ill, 1924]

3 p.l., 9-136 p.   24 cm.
Thesis (Ph.D.)- University of Illinois, 1923.
Reprinted from the University of Illinois studies in the
social sciences, v. 15, no. 3.

25405 [Robson, W   ] of Warrington, Eng.
Why I have not gone to the South. [New York, American
Anti-slavery Society, 1858]
4 p.   14½ cm.
Caption title.

25406 Roche, Emma Langdon.
Historic sketches of the South, by Emma Langdon Roche;
drawings and photographs by author. New York, The Knicker-
bocker press, 1914.
iii p., 1 l., 148 p.   front., plates, ports.   21 cm.

25407 [Rockwell, John Arnold] 1803-1861.
States vs. territories. A true solution of the territorial question. By an old line Whig. [Washington?]
1860.
cover-title, 20 p.   23½ cm.

25408 Rodgers, G   B
A vision of judgment; an allegorical satire. With an
appendix of notes. By G. B. Rodgers. Conneaut, O.,
The author, 1856.
35 p.   16½ cm.

25409 Rogers, Nathaniel Peabody, 1794-1846.
A collection from the miscellaneous writings of Nathaniel
Peabody Rogers. 2d ed. Manchester, N. H., W. H. Fisk;
[etc., etc.] 1849.
xxiv, 380 p.   front. (port.)   19½ cm.

25410 Roles, John.
Inside views of slavery on southern plantations. By
John Roles, for twenty-five years a resident of the South,
and for ten years an overseer on some of the largest
cotton plantations. With an introduction by Nathan Brown
... New-York, J. A. Gray & Green, printers, 1864.
v, [1], 47 p.   front., illus.   22½ cm.

25411 Rollins, Edward Henry, 1824-1889.
Slavery in the capital of the republic. Speech of Hon.
E. H. Rollins, of New Hampshire, in the House of Representatives, April 11, 1862, on the bill for the release
of certain persons held to service or labor in the District
of Columbia. Washington, D. C., Scammell & co., printers,

1862.
8 p.   24 cm.

25412   Rollins, James Sidney, 1812-1888.
Speech of James S. Rollins, of Boone County, delivered
in joint session of the Senate and House of Representatives
pending the election for United States senator, February 2d
1855. In reply to Mr. Goode, of St. Louis. Jefferson City
Lusk's steam power press, print, 1855.
16, [3] p.   21½ cm.

25413   Rooker, Alfred, 1814-1875.
Does it answer? Slavery in America. A history. By
Alfred Rooker... London, Virtue, brothers, & co.; [etc.,
etc.] 1864.
34 p.   22 cm.

25414   Roper, Moses.
A narrative of the adventures and escape of Moses Roper,
from American slavery; with a preface, by the Rev. T. Price
... 4th ed. London, Harvey and Darton, 1840.
xii, 120 p.   front. (port.)   illus.   15 cm.

25415   Ross, Alexander Milton, 1832-1897.
Memoirs of a reformer, 1832-1892. Toronto, Hunter,
Rose, 1893.
271 p.   illus., ports.   19 cm.

25416   Ross, Alexander Milton, 1832-1897.
Recollections and experiences of an abolitionist; from
1855 to 1865. By A. M. Ross... Toronto, Rowşell and
Hutchinson, 1875.
4 p.l., [xiii]-xv, 224 p.   front., ports.   18½ cm.

25417   Ross, Thomas, d. 1865.
Speech of Hon. Thos. Ross, of Pennsylvania, on the
admission of California, delivered in the House of Representatives, April 10, 1850. Washington, Printed at the
Congressional globe office, 1850.
12 p.   23 cm.

25418   Rowson, Mrs. Susanna (Haswell) 1762-1824.
Slaves in Algiers; or, A struggle for freedom: a play,
interspersed with songs, in three acts. By Mrs. Rowson.
As performed at the new theatres, in Philadelphia and
Baltimore. Philadelphia, Printed for the author, by
Wrigley and Berriman, No. 149, Chestnut-street, 1794.
2 p.l., ii, 72, [2] p.   16½ cm.

25419   Royal African Company of England.
        The fourth charter of the Royal African Company of
        England, September 27, 1672, with prefatory note,
        exhibiting the past relation of Virginia to African
        slavery, by R. A. Brock.   [Richmond, Va., 1887]
        60 p.   25 cm.
        Reprinted from Virginia Historical Society, Collections,
        new ser., v. 6, 1887.

25420   Rozier, Firmin A
        150th celebration of the founding of Ste. Genevieve.
        Address of Hon. Firmin A. Rozier, historian and orator
        selected for the occasion, giving a full history of Ste.
        Genevieve, the first permanent settlement in the United
        States west of the Mississippi River.   Delivered at the
        city of Ste. Genevieve, Mo., July 21, 1885.   [St. Louis,
        G. A. Pierrot & son, printers, 1885]
        1 p.l., 19 p. $25\frac{1}{2}$ cm.

25421   Rubin, Simon.
        Das talmudische Recht auf den verschiedenen Stufen
        seiner Entwicklung mit dem romischen verglichen und
        dargestellt von Lektor dr. Simon Rubin...   Wien, 1920-
        v. $20\frac{1}{2}$ cm.

25422   [Rush, Benjamin] 1745-1813.
        A vindication of the Address, to the inhabitants of the
        British settlements, on the slavery of the Negroes in
        America, in answer to a pamphlet entitled, "Slavery not
        forbidden by Scripture; or, A defence of the West-India
        planters from the aspersions thrown out against them by
        the author of the Address"...   By a Pennsylvanian.
        Philadelphia, Printed by J. Dunlap, 1773.
        54 p. $18\frac{1}{2}$ cm.   (In his An address to the inhabitants
        of the British settlements in America, upon slave-keeping.
        Philadelphia, 1773.   [pt. 2])

25423   [Rush, Caroline E   ]
        The North and South; or, Slavery and its contrasts.
        A tale of real life.   By the author of Way-marks in the
        life of a wanderer, etc. ...   Philadelphia, Crissy &
        Markley, 1852.
        vii, [9]-350 p.   front., plates. $20\frac{1}{2}$ cm.

25424   Rushton, Edward, 1756-1814.
        Expostulatory letter to George Washington, of Mount
        Vernon, in Virginia, on his continuing to be a proprietor
        of slaves.   By Edward Rushton...   Liverpool, printed
        1797.
        24 p. $18\frac{1}{2}$ cm.

25425   Russo, Pasquale.
        Negro slavery; or, Crime of the clergy; a treatise on
chattel and wage slavery, presenting a brief historical
discussion of the Negro problem in America. By Pasquale
Russo. Chicago, Ill., Modern school of pedagogy, 1923.
        55, [1] p.   19 cm.

25426   Ryland, Robert, 1805-1899.
        The American Union. An address, delivered before the
alumni association of the Columbian College, D. C.,
June 23, 1857. By R. Ryland... Richmond, Printed by
H. K. Ellyson, 1857.
        23 p.   23 cm.

                                S

25427   Sackett, William Augustus, 1812-1895.
        Shall slavery be extended? Speech of Hon. W. A.
Sackett, of New York, in the House of Representatives,
March 4, 1850, in committee of the whole on the state of
the Union, on the President's message communicating the
constitution of California. [Washington, Printed at the
Congressional globe office, 1850]
        8 p.   22 cm.
        Caption title.

25428   Saco, José Antonio, 1797-1879.
        L'esclavage à Cuba et la révolution d'Espagne, par J. A.
Saco; traduction et préface de Montluc (Léon-Pierre-Adrien
de)... 2. éd. Paris, E. Dentu, 1869.
        23 p.   23½ cm.

25429   Sage, Russell, 1816-1906.
        Speech of Hon. Russell Sage, of New York, on the pro-
fessions and acts of the President of the United States;
the repeal of the Missouri Compromise; the outrages in
Kansas; and the sectional influence and aggressions of
the slave power. Delivered in the House of Representatives, August 6, 1856. Washington, 1856.
        21 p.   22 cm.

25430   St. Bo', Theodore.
        ... Wilfrid and Mary; or, Father and daughter. A do-
mestic comedy illustrative of American slave life. By
Theodore St. Bo'... Edinburgh, M. Macphail; New York,
Appleton; [etc., etc.] 1861.
        2 p.l., vi p., 1 l., 72 p.   17 cm.

25431   St. Landry Parish, La.
        An ordinance organizing and establishing patrols for
        the police of slaves in the parish of St. Landry.
        Opelousas [La.] Printed at the office of the Opelousas
        patriot, 1863.
        29 p.   19½ cm.

25432   St. Paul, Henry.
        Our home and foreign policy. November, 1863. [Mobile,
        Ala.] Printed at the Office of the Daily register and
        advertiser, 1863.
        23 p.   21 cm.

25433   St. Vincent. Governor, 1809-1829 (Bristane)
        A communication from Sir Charles Brisbane... governor
        of Saint Vincent, to the House of Assembly of that colony,
        enclosing Lord Bathurst's dispatch of the 9th of July,
        with the joint reply of the Council and Assembly; and a
        letter depicting the alarm and danger excited by the
        insurrection in Demerara. London, Printed by C. M. Willich,
        1823.
        74 p.   20½ cm.

25434   Salkowki, Karl, 1838-1899.
        Zur Lehre vom Sklavenerwerb. Ein Beitrag zur Dogmatik
        des römischen Privatrechts. Von dr. Carl Salkowki...
        Leipzig, B. Tauchnitz, 1891.
        4 p.l., 256 p.   23 cm.

25435   [Salontha,   de]
        Précis de deux lettres avec une réflexion général sur
        l'état present de la colonie de Surinam. [Nimmegue, Impr.
        de I. van Campen, 1778]
        29, [1] p.   19 cm.

5436   Sampson, Marmaduke Blake, d. 1876.
        Slavery in the United States. A letter to the Hon.
        Daniel Webster. By M. B. Sampson. London, S. Highley,
        1845.
        vi p., 1 l., 88 p.   23 cm.

5437   [Samson, George Whitefield] 1819-1896.
        Outlines of the history of ethics, by a teacher.
        Washington, M'Gill & Witherow, 1861.
        54, 36 p.   19 cm.

5438   Sanborn, Franklin Benjamin, 1831-1917.
        Recollections of seventy years, by F. B. Sanborn, of
        Concord... Boston, R. G. Badger, 1909.
        2 v.   fronts., plates, ports., facsims.   22½ cm.

25439   Sanromá, Joaquín María, 1828-1895.
        La esclavitud en Cuba; discurso pronunciado en la
tercera Conferencia abolicionista de 1872, por Don
Joaquín María Sanromá... Madrid, Impr. de T. Fortanet,
1872.
        24 p.   22 cm.

25440   Sargent, Fitzwilliam, 1820-1889.
        England, the United States, and the Southern Confederacy
By F. W. Sargent... 2d ed. rev. and amended... London,
Hamilton, Adams, and co., 1864.
        viii, 184 p.   21½ cm.

25441   Sargent, Fitzwilliam, 1820-1889.
        Les États Confédérés et l'esclavage par F. W. Sargent...
Paris, L. Hachette et cie., 1864.
        3 p.l., [3]-176 p., 2 l.   22½ cm.
        A free translation of the author's "England, the United
States and the Southern Confederacy."

25442   Sartorius von Waltershausen, August, freiherr, 1852-
        Die Arbeits-verfassung der englischen Kolonien in
Nord-amerika. Von A. Sartorius Freiherrn von Waltershausen... Strassburg, K. J. Trübner, 1894.
        xi, 232 p.   23 cm.

25443   Savage, William Sherman.
        The origin of the Giddings resolutions. By W. Sherman
Savage. [Columbus, O., 1938]
        20-39 p.   23 cm.
        Reprinted from Ohio state archaeological and historical
quarterly, v. 47, 1938.

25444   Sawyer, George S
        Southern institutes; or, An inquiry into the origin and
early prevalence of slavery and the slave-trade: with an
analysis of the laws, history, and government of the
institution in the principal nations, ancient and modern,
from the earliest ages down to the present time. With
notes and comments in defence of the southern institution
By George S. Sawyer... Philadelphia, J. B. Lippincott &
co., 1858.
        xii, 13-393 p.   23 cm.

25445   Scales, Thomas, 1786-1860.
        Paper presented to the General Anti-slavery Convention.
By the Rev. Thomas Scales... [London, Johnston & Barrett
printers, 1840]
        4 p.   20½ cm.
        Caption title.

25446   Schaff, Philip, 1819-1893.
            Slavery and the Bible. A tract for the times, by Rev.
        Philip Schaff... Chambersburg, Pa., M. Kieffer & co's
        caloric printing press, 1861.
            32 p.   23 cm.

25447   Schaub, Friedrich.
            Studien zur Geschichte der Sklaverei im Frühmittel-
        alter. Von dr. Friedrich Schaub. Berlin und Leipzig,
        W. Rothschild, 1913.
            6 p.l., 116 p.   24 cm.   (Added t.-p.: Abhandlungen
        zur mittleren und neueren Geschichte... Lift. 44)

25448   Schevichaven, Herman Diederik Johan van, 1827-1918.
            ... Slavernij en dienstbaarheid, hoofdzakelijk in de
        vroege middeleeuwen, door H. D. J. van Schevichaven.
        Arnhem, S. Gouda Quint, 1924.
            4 p.l., 104 p.   24½ cm.   (Added t.-p.: Werken, uitg.
        door Gelre. Vereeniging tot beoefening van Geldersche
        geschiedenis, oudheidkunde en recht, no. 15)

25449   La schiavitù e la guerra negli Stati Uniti d'America.
        [Roma? 1864?]
            62 p.   21½ cm.
        Translation of an article which appeared in the Dublin
        review for April, 1864.

25450   Schilling, John L
            Burst asunder! Rich results from what to the human
        comprehension appeared an inhuman wrong. By Jno. L.
        Schilling. [Bellaire, O., The Bellaire herald job print,
        c1892]
            31 p.   13½ cm.

25451   Schilling, John L
            ... The story of John Brown's raid and capture, and the
        founding of historic Harper's Ferry. Also: Will slavery
        in the United States be instrumental in redeeming Africa?
        ... By John L. Schilling... Toledo, O. [c1895]
            cover-title, 10 numb. 1., 1 1., 2 numb. 1.   port.
        21 x 35 cm.

25452   Schmidt, Karl Adolf, 1815-1903.
            Das Pflichttheilsrecht des Patronus und des parens
        manumissor. Eine rechtsgeschichtliche Abhandlung von dr.
        Adolf Schmidt... Heidelberg, Bangel & Schmitt, 1868.
            2 p.l., 170 p., 1 1.   22 cm.

25453   Schoelcher, Victor, 1804-1893.
            Abolition de l'esclavage; examen critique du préjugé

contre la couleur des Africains et des sang-mêlés; par
V. Schoelcher. Paris, Pagnerre, 1840.
    187 p.   13½ cm.

25454 Schoelcher, Victor, 1804-1893.
       Colonies étrangères et Haiti, résultats de l'émancipa-
       tion anglaise; par Victor Schoelcher... Paris, Pagnerre,
       1843.
       2 v.   22 cm.
       Contents. - v. 1. Colonies anglaises. Iles espagnoles.
       Quelques mots sur la traite et sur son origine. - v. 2.
       Colonies danoises. Haiti. Du droit de visite. Coup-
       d'oeil sur l'état de la question d'affranchissement.

25455 Schoolcraft, Mary (Howard) "Mrs. H. R. Schoolcraft"
       The black gauntlet: a tale of plantation life in
       South Carolina. By Mrs. Henry R. Schoolcraft... Phila-
       delphia, J. B. Lippincott & co., 1860.
       x, 11-569 p.   18½ cm.

25456 [Schoolcraft, Mary (Howard)] "Mrs. H. R. Schoolcraft"
       Letters on the condition of the African race in the
       United States. By a southern lady. Philadelphia, T. K.
       and P. G. Collins, printers, 1852.
       34 p.   23 cm.
       Four letters to the writer's brother, Gen. John H. Howard
       dated Washington, Sept. 15-Nov. 20, 1851.

25457 Schulz, Frits, 1826-1905.
       Die Haftung für das Verschulden der Angestellten im
       klassischen römischen Recht. Von dr. Fritz Schulz...
       Wien, A. Hölder, 1911.
       1 p.l., 46 p.   22 cm.
       "Separat-abdruck aus der von... prof. Grünhut heraus-
       gegebenen Zeitschrift für das privat- und öffentliche
       recht der Gegenwart, XXXVIII. bd."

25458 Schurz, Carl, 1829-1906.
       The great issue of American politics. Speech of Carl
       Schurz, of Wisconsin, at Verandah hall, St. Louis,
       Missouri, August 1, 1860. [Washington, Republican Party,
       Congressional committee, 1860]
       14 p., 1 l.   24½ cm.
       Caption title.

25459 Scoble, John.
       British Guiana. Speech delivered at the anti-slavery
       meeting in Exeter Hall, on Wednesday, the 4th of April,
       1838, by John Scoble, esq., the Marquis of Clanricarde,

in the chair. London, Central Negro Emancipation
Committee, 1838.
35 p.   21 cm.

25460   Scoble, John.
Texas: its claims to be recognized as an independent
power, by Great Britain; examined in a series of letters,
by John Scoble. London, Harvey and Darton [etc.] 1839.
56 p.   20½ cm.

25461   Scott, John, 1785-1861.
Mr. Scott's speech on the Missouri question, in the
House of Representatives of the United States. Washington,
Printed by Davis and Force, 1820.
39 p.   18½ cm.

25462   Scott, Orange, 1800-1847.
Address to the General Conference of the Methodist
Episcopal Church... presented during its session in
Cincinnati, Ohio, May 19, 1836. To which is added the
speech of the Rev. Mr. Scott delivered on the floor of
the General Conference, May 27th, 1836. New York, H. R.
Piercy, 1836.
24 p.   21½ cm.

25463   Scott, Robert Eden, 1808-1862.
Speech of R. E. Scott of Fauquier, on certain resolutions touching the action of Congress on the subject of
slavery. Delivered in the House of Delegates of Virginia,
on the 11th day of January 1849. Richmond, Printed by
Shepherd and Colin, 1849.
24 p.   24½ cm.

25464   Scoville, Joseph Alfred, 1815-1864.
What shall be done with the confiscated negroes? The
question discussed and a policy proposed in a letter to
Hon. Abraham Lincoln, Gen. Winfield Scott, Hon. William H.
Seward... and all other patriots. [n.p., 1862?]
15 p.   22 cm.

25465   Scribner, Isaac W   d. 1864.
Review of the Rev. U. C. Burnap's sermon on Bible
servitude. By I. W. Scribner... Pub. by request of the
friends of the slave in Lowell. [Lowell?] Printed by
J. G. Pillsbury, 1844.
22 p.   21½ cm.

25466   The Scripture doctrine with regard to slavery. By a clergyman of the Protestant Episcopal church. Pottsville [Pa.]

B. Bannan, printer, 1854.
    10 p.   24 cm.
    "The authorship has been attributed to Wm. M. Peyton." -
Sabin, Bibl. Amer.

25467   Scripture the friend of freedom; exemplified by a refutation
    of the arguments offered in defence of slavery, in a tract
    entitled Scriptural researches on the licitness of the
    slave trade... London, Printed by W. Smith; sold by J.
    Phillips [etc.] 1789.
        vi, [1], 79 p. $19\frac{1}{2}$ cm.
        The "Scriptural researches", by Raymond Harris.

25468   [Seabrook, Whitemarsh Benjamin] 1795-1855.
        An appeal to the people of the northern and eastern states
    on the subject of negro slavery in South Carolina. By a
    South Carolinian...   New-York, 1834.
        27 p. $22\frac{1}{2}$ cm.

25469   Seabrook, Whitemarsh Benjamin, 1795-1855.
        A concise view of the critical situation, and future
    prospects of the slave-holding states, in relation to
    their coloured population. By Whitemarsh B. Seabrook:
    read before the "Agricultural Society of St. John's
    Colleton," on the 14th of September, 1825, and published
    at their request. 2d ed. Charleston, Printed by A. E.
    Miller, 1825.
        31 p.   23 cm.

25470   Seaman, Ezra Champion, 1805-1880.
        Commentaries on the constitutions and laws, peoples and
    history, of the United States; and upon the great
    rebellion and its causes. By Ezra C. Seaman... Ann Arbor,
    Printed for the author, at the Journal office, 1863.
        vii, 287 p. $22\frac{1}{2}$ cm.

25471   Searle, Mrs. L   C
        Washington, our example. The father of a nation will
    restore it to peace. By Mrs. L. C. Searle... Philadelphia,
    J. Challen & son, 1865.
        121 p.   23 cm.

25472   [Sears, David] 1787-1871.
        Contrabands and vagrants. [Newport? R. I., 1861]
        43 p.   17 cm.
        Caption title.

25473   Sears, David, 1787-1871.
        Hon. David Sears' plan for emancipation. [New York, 1857]

12 p.   18½ cm.
Caption title.

25474 Sears, Edmund Hamilton, 1810-1876.
       Revolution or reform. A discourse occasioned by the
       present crisis. Preached at Wayland, Mass., Sunday,
       June 15, 1856. By Edmund H. Sears. [Washington, D. C.,
       Buell & Blanchard, printers, 1856]
       8 p.   23 cm.

25475 [Sedgwick, Theodore] 1780-1839.
       The practicability of the abolition of slavery: a
       lecture, delivered at the Lyceum in Stockbridge, Massa-
       chusetts, February, 1831... New York, Printed by J.
       Seymour, 1831.
       48 p.   22½ cm.

25476 Seebohm, Frederic, 1833-1912.
       The crisis of emancipation in America; being a review of
       the history of emancipation, from the beginning of the
       American war to the assassination of President Lincoln.
       By F. Seebohm... London, A. W. Bennett, 1865.
       cover-title, 40 p. incl. map.   21½ cm.

25477 Segar, Joseph E   1804-1885.
       ... Letter of Jos. Segar, esq., to Gen. Dix. [Washington,
       D. C., W. H. Moore, printer, 1861]
       9 p.   21½ cm.
       Caption title.

25478 [Senior, Bernard Martin]
       Jamaica, as it was, as it is, and as it may be: compris-
       ing interesting topics for absent proprietors, merchants,
       &c., and valuable hints to persons intending to emigrate
       to the island: also, an authentic narrative of the
       negro insurrection in 1831; with a faithful detail of the
       manners, customs and habits of the colonists, and a
       description of the country, climate, productions, &c.,
       including an abridgment of the slave law. By a retired
       military officer... London, T. Hurst; [etc., etc.] 1835.
       vii, 311, 309-313, [1] p., 1 l.   fold. front.   19½ cm.

25479 Senior, Nassau William, 1790-1864.
       American slavery: a reprint of an article on "Uncle
       Tom's cabin," of which a portion was inserted in the
       206th number of the "Edinburgh review"; and of Mr.
       Sumner's speech of the 19th and 20th of May, 1856. With
       a notice of the events which followed that speech. By
       Nassau W. Senior, esq. London, T. Fellows [1862]
       iv, 164 p.   22 cm.

25480   Sergeant, John, 1779-1852.
            Speech of Mr. Sergeant, on the Missouri question.   In
        the House of Representatives of the United States...
        [n.p., 1820]
            48 p.   21 cm.
            Caption title.

25481   Seward, William Henry, 1801-1872.
            Immigrant white free labor, or imported black African
        slave labor.   Speech of William H. Seward, at Oswego,
        New York, November 3, 1856.   [Washington, Republican
        Association of Washington, 1857]
            7, [1] p.   23 cm.
            Caption title.

25482   Seward, William Henry, 1801-1872.
            The slaveholding class dominant in the republic.   Speech
        of William H. Seward, at Detroit, October 2, 1856.
        Washington, D. C., The Republican Association of Washington
        1857.
            14 p. $24\frac{1}{2}$ cm.

25483   Seward, William Henry, 1801-1872.
            Speech of William H. Seward, on emancipation in the
        District of Columbia.   Delivered in the Senate of the
        United States, September 11, 1850.   Washington, Printed
        and for sale by Buell & Blanchard, 1850.
            8 p.   22 cm.

25484   Seward, William Henry, 1801-1872.
            ... Speeches of Hon. William H. Seward, and Hon. Lewis
        Cass, on the subject of slavery.   Delivered in the
        Senate of the United States, March, 1850.   New York,
        Stringer & Townsend, 1850.
            cover-title, 32 p.   22 cm.
            On the admission of California.

25485   Seward, William Henry, 1801-1872.
            The usurpations of slavery.   Speech of William H. Seward,
        in the Senate of the United States, on the bill to protect
        officers of the United States.   February 23, 1855.
        [Washington, Buell & Blanchard, printers, 1855]
            7 p. $23\frac{1}{2}$ cm.
            Caption title.

25486   Shaffner, Taliaferro Preston, 1818-1881.
            The war in America: being an historical and political
        account of the southern and northern states: showing the
        origin and cause of the present secession war.   With a

large map of the United States, engraved on steel. By
Colonel Tal. P. Shaffner... London, Hamilton, Adams, and
co. [1862]
vi, 418 p.   front. (fold. map)   18½ cm.

25487 Shanafelt, J   R
The end to the slavery controversy. By the Rev. J. R.
Shanafelt... Pittston, Luzerne Co., Pennsylvania, 1864.
cover-title, 16 p.   22 cm.

25488 [Shannon, James] 1799-1859.
An address delivered before the Pro-slavery convention
of the State of Missouri, held in Lexington, July 13, 1855,
on domestic slavery, as examined in the light of Scripture,
of natural rights, of civil government, and the constitutional power of Congress. Pub. by order of the convention.
St. Louis, Mo., Printed at the Republican book and job
office, 1855.
vi, [7]-32 p.   22½ cm.

25489 Sharp, Granville, 1735-1813.
An essay on slavery, proving from Scripture its inconsistency with humanity and religion; in answer to a late
publication, entitled, "The African trade for negro
slaves shewn to be consistent with principles of humanity,
and with the laws of revealed religion". By Granville
Sharp, esq. With an introductory preface, containing the
sentiments of the Monthly reviewers on that publication;
and the opinion of several eminent writers on the subject.
To which is added, An Elegy on the miserable state of an
African slave, by the celebrated and ingenious William
Shenstone, esq. ... Burlington, Printed and Sold by
Isaac Collins, 1773.
xvi, 17-28 p.   19½ cm.

25490 [Sharp, Granville] 1735--1813.
Extract of a letter to a gentleman in Maryland; wherein
is demonstrated the extreme wickedness of tolerating the
slave trade, in order to favour the illegalities of our
colonies, where the two first foundations of English law
(two witnesses of God), are supplanted by opposite (and,
of course, illegal) ordinances, which occasions a civil
death of the English constitution, so that these two
witnesses may be said to lie dead in all the West India
islands! Originally printed in America. First printed
in London in 1793. 3d ed. London, Printed by J. Phillips
and son, 1797.
14 p.   17 cm.

25491   Sharp, Granville, 1735-1813.
        Letter from Granville Sharp, esq., of London, to the
Maryland Society for Promoting the Abolition of Slavery,
and the Relief of Free Negroes and Others, Unlawfully Held
in Bondage. Published by order of the Society. Baltimore,
Printed by D. Graham, L. Yundt, and W. Patton, in Calvert-
street, near the Court-house, 1793.
        11 p.   21 cm.

25492   Sharp, Granville, 1735-1813.
        "The system of colonial law" compared with the eternal
laws of God; and with the indispensable principles of the
English constitution. By Granville Sharp. London, Printed
by Richard Edwards, 1807.
        20 p.   16½ cm.

25493   Sheldon, George, 1818-1916.
        Negro slavery in old Deerfield. By George Sheldon.
[Boston? 1893?]
        [49]-60 p.   23½ cm.
        Caption title.
        Reprinted from New England magazine of March, 1893.

25494   [Sheppard, Moses]
        African slave trade in Jamaica, and comparative treatment
of slaves. Read before the Maryland Historical Society,
October, 1854. [Baltimore] Printed for the Maryland
Historical Society, by J. D. Toy, 1854.
        14 p.   22 cm.   [Maryland Historical Society.
Publications. v. 3, no. 9]

25495   Sherman, John, 1823-1900.
        Slaves and slavery: how affected by the war. Remarks
of Hon. John Sherman, of Ohio, in the Senate of the
United States, april 2, 1862. [Washington, D. C., Scammell
& co., printers, 1862]
        15 p.   24 cm.
        Caption title.

25496   Shipherd, Jacob R   comp.
        History of the Oberlin-Wellington rescue... Comp. by
Jacob R. Shipherd. With an introduction by Prof. Henry E.
Peck and Hon. Ralph Plumb. Boston, J. P. Jewett and
company; New York, Sheldon and company; [etc., etc.] 1859.
        viii, 280 p.   1 illus.   23 cm.

25497   A short journey in the West Indies, in which are interspersed, curious anecdotes and characters... London,
Printed for the author, 1790.
        2 v.   16 cm.

25498 A short history and description of the Ojibbeway Indians
       now on a visit to England... London [Vizetelly brothers
       and co., printers] 1844.
           1 p.l., [5]-30 p.   17½ cm.
           An adventure in Canada. An illustration of slavery in
       America [the rescue of a fugitive slave from Kentucky,
       by Arthur Rankin in Cleveland, O., narrated by C. Stuart]:
       p. 21-30.

25499 Shorter, Eli Sims, 1823-1879.
           Speech of Hon. Eli S. Shorter, of Alabama, on the Massa-
       chusetts personal liberty bill and the constitutional
       rights of the South. Delivered in the House of Represen-
       tatives April 9, 1856. Washington, Printed at the Union
       office, 1856.
           16 p.   24½ cm.

25500 Sibley, Guy C
           Pay for the slaves under a sixteenth amendment. By Guy
       C. Sibley... Mobile, Ala., Graham & Delchamps, printers,
       1896.
           30 p.   16 cm.

25501 Siebert, Wilbur Henry, 1866-
           The underground railroad for the liberation of fugitive
       slaves. [Washington, 1895]
           395-402 p.   23 cm.
           Reprinted from American Historical Association, Annual
       report for 1895, 1896.

25502 Sihler, Wilhelm, 1801-1885.
           Die Sklaverei im Lichte der Heiligen Schrift betrachtet.
       Von Professor dr. Sihler. Mit Genehmigung hrsg. von
       A. Schlitt. Baltimore, 1863.
           34 p.   23 cm.

25503 Silva Mafra, Manuel da, b. 1831.
           Promptuario das leis de manumissão; ou, Indice alpha-
       betico das disposições da Lei n. 2040 de 28 de setembro
       de 1871, regulamentos n. 4835 de 1.º de dezembro de 1872,
       n. 4960 de 8 de março de 1872, n. 6341 de 20 de setembro
       de 1876, e avisos do Ministerio da agricultura, commercio
       e obras publicas, e da jurisprudencia do Conselho de estado,
       dos tribunaes das Relações e Supremo tribunal de justiça,
       por Manoel da Silva Mafra... Rio de Janeiro, Typographia
       nacional, 1877.
           vii, 394 p.   forms (part fold.)   21 cm.

25504 [Simmons, George Frederick] 1814-1855.
           Review of the Remarks on Dr. Channing's Slavery, by a

citizen of Massachusetts. Boston, J. Munroe and company, 1836.
48 p. 23½ cm.

25505 Simmons, George Frederick, 1814-1855.
Two sermons on the kind treatment and on the emancipation of slaves. Preached at Mobile, on Sunday the 10th, and Sunday the 17th of May, 1840. With a prefatory statement. By Geo. F. Simmons. Boston, W. Crosby and company, 1840.
viii, [9]-30 p. 24 cm.

25506 Simpson, John Hawkins.
Horrors of the Virginian slave trade and of the slave-rearing plantations. The true story of Dinah, an escaped Virginian slave, now in London, on whose body are eleven scars left by tortures which were inflicted by her master, her own father. Together with extracts from the laws of Virginia, showing that against these barbarities the law gives not the smallest protection to the slave, but the reverse. By John Hawkins Simpson... London, A. W. Bennett 1863.
vii, [1], 64 p. 16½ cm.

25507 Sinclair, Peter.
... Freedom or slavery in the United States, being facts and testimonies for the consideration of the British people. By Peter Sinclair. 2d ed. London, J. Caudwell; [etc., etc., 1862]
cover-title, 160 p. 21½ cm.

25508 Sipkins, Henry.
An oration on the abolition of the slave trade; delivered in the African Church, in the city of New-York, January 2, 1809. By Henry Sipkins, a descendant of Africa. New-York, Printed by J. C. Totten, 1809.
1 p.l., 21 p. 22 cm.

25509 La situación de Puerto-Rico, las falacias de los conservadores y los compromisos del partido radical, por un puerto-riqueño. Madrid, Impr. de J. Noguera á cargo de M. Martinez, 1873.
79 p. 22½ cm. (On cover: [Sociedad abolicionista española] Propaganda reformista)

25510 ... The six species of men, with cuts representing the types of the Caucasian, Mongol, Malay, Indian, Esquimaux and negro. With their general physical and mental qualities, laws of organization, relations of civilization, &c.

252

New York, Van Evrie, Horton & company, 1868.
31 p.   illus.   22½ cm.   (Anti-abolition tracts, no. 5)

25511   Sketches and recollections of the West Indies. By a resident... London, Smith, Elder, & co., 1828.
2 p.l., [vii]-xii, 330 p.   20 cm.

25512   Das Sklavenwesen in den Vereinigten Staaten von Nordamerika. [Leipzig, 1862]
27-68, 101-137p.   23 cm.
Caption title.
Reprinted from Unsere Zeit, v. 6.

25513   Slade, William, 1786-1859.
Speech of Mr. Slade, of Vermont, on the subject of the abolition of slavery and the slave trade within the District of Columbia. Delivered in the House of Representatives, December 23, 1835. [Washington] National intelligencer office, 1836.
11 p.   26½ cm.

25514   Slaughter, Philip, 1808-1890.
The Virginian history of African colonization. By Rev. P. Slaughter... Richmond, Macfarlane & Ferguson, 1855.
xx, 116 p.   25 cm.

25515   Slave holding piety illustrated. [Edinburgh, Reprinted by the Edinburgh Ladies' Emancipation Society, 1857]
8 p.   16 cm.
Caption title.

25516   Slave market of America. [n.p.] William S. Dorr [n.d.]
Broadside with woodcuts.
Includes the vote of Congress on slavery in the District of Columbia.

25517   Slavery. A treatise, showing that slavery is neither a moral, political, nor social evil. Penfield, Ga., Printed by B. Brantly, 1844.
40 p.   23 cm.

25518   Slavery. By a Marylander. Its institution and origin. Its status under the law and under the gospel. Its agricultural, commercial and financial, aspects.
[Baltimore, J. P. Des Forges, 1860]
8 p.   22 cm.
Caption title.

25519   Slavery, con. and pro. or, A sermon and its answer. By
        Amor patriae... Washington, H. Polkinhorn, printer,
        1858.
            44 p.   22½ cm.
            On t.-p.: This publication is intended especially for
        the North.
            The sermon was by Rev. J. P. Thompson, pub. under title
        "Teachings of the New Testament on slavery."

25520   Slavery and its prospects in the United States. Cambridge
        [Mass.] Metcalf and company, printers, 1857.
            28 p.   23 cm.
            Attributed by Cushing (Anonyms) doubtfully, to S. A.
        Eliot.

25521   Slavery and serfdom considered... Boston, T. R. Marvin &
        son, 1861.
            24 p.   23 cm.

25522   The slavery question. Dred Scott decision. To the free
        voters of Ohio. [n.p., n.d.]
            16 p.   21½ cm.

25523   Slight, William Willcocks, b. 1796.
            Abolitionism exposed! Proving that the principles of
        abolitionism are injurious to the slaves themselves,
        destructive to this nation, and contrary to the express
        commands of God; with strong evidence that some of the
        principal champions of abolitionism are inveterate
        enemies to this country, and are taking advantage of
        the 'antislavery war-whoop' to dissever, and break up,
        the nation... By W. W. Sleigh... Philadelphia, D.
        Schneck, 1838.
            93 p.   20½ cm.

25524   [Sligo, Howe Peter Browne, 2d Marquess of] 1788-1845.
            Jamaica under the apprenticeship system. By a proprie-
        tor... London, J. Andrews, 1838.
            2 p.l., xx, 111, [cxiii]-cxlvii p.   22½ cm.

25525   Sloane, James Renwick Wilson, 1823-1886.
            Life and work of J. R. W. Sloane, D.D., professor of
        theology in the Reformed Presbyterian Seminary at
        Allegheny City, Penn. 1868-1886 and pastor of the Third
        Reformed Presbyterian Church, New York, 1856-1868.
        Edited by his son. New York, A. C. Armstrong and son,
        1888.
            2 p.l., 3-440 p.   front. (port.)   22½ cm.

25526   Sloane, James Renwick Wilson, 1823-1886.
        Review of Rev. Henry J. Van Dyke's discourse on "The
   character and influence of abolitionism," a sermon
   preached in the Third Reformed Presbyterian Church,
   Twenty-third street, New York, on Sabbath evening,
   December 23, 1860, by Rev. J. R. W. Sloane, pastor.
   Also, by special request, in the Church of the Puritans
   (Rev. Dr. Cheever's) on Sabbath evening, January 6, 1861.
   New York, W. Erving, 1861.
        40 p.   22 cm.

25527   Slocum, William Neill, 1828-
        The war, and how to end it. By William N. Slocum...
   3d ed., rev. San Francisco, 1861.
        48 p.   22½ cm.

25528   Small, Jonathan.
        An inquiry into the nature and character of ancient and
   modern slavery. To which is added a brief review of a
   book entitled, Testimony of God against slavery, by Rev.
   La Roy Sunderland... By J. Small, M. D. [n.p.] 1836
        2 p.l., 122 p., 1 l.   19 cm.

25529   [Smith, Charles Henry] 1826-1903.
        Bill Arp, so called. A side show of the southern side
   of the war... Illustrated by M. A. Sullivan. New York,
   Metropolitan record office, 1866.
        2 p.l., [3]-204 p.   front. (port.) plates.   18 cm.

25530   Smith, Edward Dunlap, 1802-1883.
        Our country, and our country's constitution and laws.
   A discourse delivered on Thanksgiving day, December 12th,
   1850, in the Chelsea Presbyterian Church, New York, by
   Edward Dunlap Smith, D.D. Published by request. New
   York, R. Carter & brothers, 1851.
        59 p.   22 cm.

25531   Smith, Elihu Hubbard, 1771-1798.
        A discourse, delivered April 11, 1798, at the request
   of and before the New-York Society for Promoting the
   Manumission of Slaves, and protecting such of them as have
   been or may be liberated. By E. H. Smith, a member of
   the Society. New-York, Printed by T. & J. Swords,
   1798.
        30 p.   21 cm.

25532   Smith, Gerrit, 1797-1874.
        Letter of Gerrit Smith to S. P. Chase, on the unconsti-
   tutionality of every part of American slavery. Albany,

S. W. Green, 1847.
12 p.   14½ cm.

25533   Smith, Gerrit, 1797-1874.
A letter to Elizabeth C. Stanton.   Peterboro [N.Y.] 1855
[4] p.   31½ cm.

25534   Smith, Gerrit, 1797-1874.
A letter to Hon. Stephen C. Phillips, of Salem, Mass.
Peterboro [N. Y.] 1846.
[2] p.   31½ cm.

25535   Smith, Gerrit, 1797-1874.
Letters of Gerrit Smith to Hon. Gulian C. Verplanck.
Whitesboro [N.Y.] Press of the Friend of Man, 1837.
18 p.   20½ cm.

25536   Smith, Gerrit, 1797-1874.
Slanders refuted! [n.p.] 1838.
[1] p.   41 cm.
Union herald, extra.

25537   Smith, Goldwin, 1823-1910.
Does the Bible sanction American slavery? By Goldwin
Smith. Oxford and London, J. Henry and J. Parker, 1863.
v, 128 p.   18½ cm.

25538   [Smith, James]
Slavery. [New York, 1845?]
6 p.   21 cm.
Caption title.
A notice of "Domestic slavery considered as a scriptural
institution in a correspondence between the Rev. Richard
Fuller... and the Rev. Francis Wayland.

25539   Smith, James Lindsay.
Autobiography, including also reminiscences of slave
life, recollections of the war, education of freedmen,
causes of the exodus, etc. 2d ed. Norwich [Conn.]
Press of the Bulletin Co., 1882.
xiii, 150 p.   plates, port.   20 cm.

25540   Smith, Jeremiah, 1805-1874.
Is slavery sinful? being partial discussions of the
proposition, Slavery is sinful, between Ovid Butler,
esq., a bishop of the Christian Church, at Indianapolis,
Ind., and Jeremiah Smith, esq., late judge of the 11th
and 13th judicial circuits, Ind.; and between Elder
Thomas Wiley, late pastor of the Christian Church, at
Union City, Ind., and Jeremiah Smith, late judge of the

11th and 13th judicial circuits, Indiana; with an introduction, episode, and conclusion of the discussion. By
Jeremiah Smith. Indianapolis, H. H. Dodd & co., printers,
1863.
396 p.   20 cm.

25541 Smith, Joseph Tate.
Address on the acts and deliverances of the General
Assembly of the Old School Presbyterian Church, during
the past five years, on the state of the country. By
Rev. Joseph T. Smith, D.D. Delivered by request, in the
Central Presbyterian Church, Baltimore, on Thursday
evening, June 21, 1866. Baltimore, W. K. Boyle, printer,
1866.
36 p.   22½ cm.

25542 Smith, L   M
The great American crisis: or, Cause and cure of the
rebellion: embracing phrenological characters and pen-
and-ink portraits of the President, his leading generals
and cabinet officers; together with an appendix on the
slavery controversy, in which is submitted a novel plan
for the full and final adjustment of this vexed question.
By L. M. Smith, practical phrenologist. Cincinnati, O.,
Johnson, Stephens & co., printers, 1862.
36 p.   diagrs.   21½ cm.

25543 Smith, Theodore Clarke, 1870-
The Liberty and Free Soil Parties in the Northwest.
Toppan prize essay of 1896; by Theodore Clarke Smith...
New York [etc.] Longmans, Green, and co., 1897.
xi, 351 p. incl. maps.   23 cm.   (Added t.-p.:
Harvard historical studies, v. 6)

25544 Smith, Theodore Clarke, 1870-
... Parties and slavery, 1850-1859, by Theodore Clarke
Smith... New York and London, Harper & brothers, 1906.
xvi, 341 p.   front. (port.) maps (part double)
21½ cm.   (Half-title: The American nation: a history...
ed. by A. B. Hart... v. 18)

25545 Smith, Venture, 1729-1805.
A narrative of the life and adventures of Venture, a
native of Africa, but resident above sixty years in the
United States of America. Related by himself, New London:
Printed in 1798. Reprinted A.D. 1835, and published by a
descendant of Venture. Rev. and republished with tradi-
tions by H. M. Selden, Haddam, Conn., 1896. Middletown,
Conn., J. S. Stewart, printer, 1897.
iv, [5]-41 p.   23½ cm.

25546   Smith, William Henry, 1833-1896.
        ... The first fugitive slave case of record in Ohio,
        by Hon. William Henry Smith...   Washington, 1894
        91-100 p.   24½ cm.
        Reprinted from American Historical Association, Annual
        report for the year 1893, 1894.

25547   Smith, William Henry, 1833-1896.
        A political history of slavery; being an account of
        the slavery controversy from the earliest agitations in
        the eighteenth century to the close of the reconstruction
        period in America, by William Henry Smith... with an
        introduction by Whitelaw Reid...   New York and London,
        G. P. Putnam's sons, 1903.
        2 v.   front. (port.)   23½ cm.

25548   Smith, William Nathan Harrell, 1812-1889.
        The crisis, its responsibilities and perils.   Speech
        of the Hon. William N. H. Smith, of North Carolina.
        Delivered in the House of Representatives, February 8,
        1861. [Washington, W. H. Moore, printer, 1861]
        16 p.   22½ cm.

25549   Smith, William Nathan Harrell, 1812-1889.
        Slavery restriction in conflict with judicial authority.
        Speech of Hon. William N. H. Smith, of North Carolina.
        Delivered in the House of Representatives, May 2, 1860.
        [Washington, Printed by L. Towers, 1860]
        16 p.   21½ cm.
        Caption title.

25550   Smith, William Russell, 1815-1896.
        The history and debates of the Convention of the people
        of Alabama, begun and held in the city of Montgomery,
        on the seventh day of January, 1861; in which is pre-
        served the speeches of the secret sessions and many
        valuable state papers.   By William R. Smith, one of the
        delegates from Tuscaloosa.   Montgomery, White, Pfister &
        co.; Atlanta, Wood, Hanleiter, Rice & co. [etc., etc.]
        1861.
        v p., 1 l., [9]-464, xii p.   22 cm.

25551   Smith, Zachariah Frederick, 1827-1911.
        The history of Kentucky.   From its earliest discovery
        and settlement, to the present date... its military
        events and achievements, and biographic mention of its
        historic characters.   By Hon. Z. F. Smith...   Louisville,
        Courier-journal job printing company, 1886.
        xxvi, 824 p.   front., illus., plates, ports., fold.
        maps.   24½ cm.

25552 Smithers, Nathaniel Barratt, 1818-1896.
        Speech of Hon. N. B. Smithers, of Delaware, on the
proposed amendment to the Constitution of the United
States, delivered in the House of Representatives,
January 11th, 1865. Washington, Printed by L. Towers,
1865.
        8 p.   22½ cm.

25553 Smyth, Alexander, 1765-1830.
        Speech of Mr. Smyth, on the restriction of slavery in
Missouri. Delivered in the House of Representatives...
January 28, 1820. [Washington, 1820]
        36 p.   18½ cm.

25554 Sneed, William C
        A report on the history and mode of management of the
Kentucky penitentiary, from its origin, in 1798, to March
1, 1860. Prepared by William C. Sneed... Frankfort,
Ky., J. B. Major, state printer, 1860.
        viii, 614 p.   front., illus., plates, ports.   24 cm.

25555 Sociedad abolicionista española, Madrid.
        ... La abolición de la esclavitud en Puerto-Rico.
Reunión celebrada en el Teatro nacional de la opera por la
Sociedad abolicionista española, el dia 23 de enero de
1873. Presidencia: Sr. D. Fernando de Castro. -
Oradores: Señores Carrasco, Labra, Alonso (J. B.) y
Rodriguez (G.) Madrid, Sociedad abolicionista española,
1873.
        53 p.   21½ cm.

25556 Société des amis noirs, Paris.
        Adresse de la Société des amis des noirs à l'Assemblée
nationale, a toutes les villes de commerce, à toutes les
manufactures, aux colonies, à toutes les sociétés des amis
de la Constitution; adresse dans laquelle on approfondit
les rélations politiques et commerciales entre la Métropole
et les colonies, etc. Rédigée par E. Claviere. 2. éd.,
rev. et corr. Paris, Desenne, 1791.
        xxviii, 318 (i.e. 268) p.   21 cm.
        Pages 241-290 omitted in numbering. Other errors in
pagination.

25557 Society for Mitigating and Gradually Abolishing the State
        of Slavery throughout the British Dominions.
        The new slave laws of Jamaica and St. Christopher's
examined; with an especial reference to the eulogies
recently pronounced upon them in Parliament. London,
The Society for the Mitigation and Gradual Abolition of
Slavery throughout the British Dominions, 1828.
        24 p.   20½ cm.

25558   Society for Mitigating and Gradually Abolishing the State of
        Slavery throughout the British Dominions.
            The slave colonies of Great Britain; or, A picture of
        negro slavery drawn by the colonists themselves: being
        an abstract of the various papers recently laid before
        Parliament on that subject... London, Printed by
        Ellerton and Henderson, for the Society, 1825.
            2 p.l., 164 p.   22 cm.   [With Gt. Brit. Parliament
        1823. House of commons. Substance of the debate in the
        House of commons, on the 15th May, 1823... London, 1823]

25559   Solazzi, Siro, 1875-
            ... L'actio de peculio annalis contro gli eredi.
        Torino, Frantelli Bocca; [etc., etc.] 1905.
            48 p.   24 cm.
        "Estratto dagli Studi senesi in onore di Luigi Moriani."

25560   Solazzi, Siro, 1875-
            "Jus deductionis" et "condemnatio cum deductione" nell'
        "actio de peculio". Memoria di Siro Solazzi... Napoli,
        Stab. tip. L. Pierro e figlio, 1905.
            17 p.   25 cm.
        "Estratto dagli Studi in onore di Carlo Fadda". - p. [2]

25561   Solazzi, Siro, 1875-
            Peculio e 'in rem versio' nel diritto classico. Memoria
        di Siro Solazzi... Palermo, Stab. tip. ditta L. Gaipa,
        1910.
            cover-title, 27 p.   25 cm.
        "Estratto dagli 'Studi in onore di Biagio Brugi."

25562   Solazzi, Siro, 1875-
            ... Studi sull' "actio de peculio". Roma, Istituto di
        diritto romano, 1908.
            1 p.l., [5]-111 p., 1 l.   25 cm.
        "Estratto dal Bulletino dell' Istituto di diritto romano
        anno XVII, fasc. IV-VI.

25563   Solazzi, Siro, 1875-
            ... Sulla "condicio emancipationis". Modena, Società
        tip. modenese, 1921.
            57 p.   23 cm.
        Reprinted from Archivio giuridico, v. 86, fasc. 2 (ser.
        4, v. 2, fasc. 2)

25564   Soleau, Alexandre, b. 1804?
            Notes sur les Guyanes française, hollandaise, anglaise,
        et sur les Antilles françaises (Cayenne, Surinam,
        Demerary, la Martinique, la Guadeloupe); par A. Soleau...

Paris, Imprimerie royale, 1835.
88 p.   illus.   23½ cm.
"Extrait des Annales maritimes... 1835."

25565   South Carolina. Convention, 1860-1862.
The address of the people of South Carolina assembled
in convention, to the people of the slaveholding states of
the United States. Printed by order of the Convention.
Charleston, Evans & Cogswell, 1860.
16 p.   23 cm.

25566   South Carolina. General Assembly. House of Representatives.
Special Committee on Slavery and the Slave-trade.
Report of the minority of the Special Committee of
Seven, to whom was referred so much of Gov. Adams' message,
no. 1, as relates to slavery and the slave trade.
Charleston, Harper & Calvo, printers, 1858.
40 p.   22 cm.

25567   South Carolina. General Assembly. Senate.
Report of a special committee of the Senate of South
Carolina, on the resolutions submitted by Mr. Ramsay, on
the subject of state rights. Washington, Printed by Duff
Green, 1828.
19 p.   22 cm.

25568   South Carolina. Governor, 1834-1836 (George McDuffie)
... Governor McDuffie's message on the slavery question.
1835. New York, A. Lovell & co., 1893.
13 p.   18 cm.   (American history leaflets, ed. by
A. B. Hart and E. Channing, no. 10, July, 1893)
Caption title.

25569   South Middlesex Conference of Churches.
The political duties of Christians. A report adopted at
the spring meeting of the South Middlesex Conference of
Churches, April 18, 1848. Boston, Printed by Andrews &
Prentiss, 1848.
40 p.   21½ cm.

25570   Southard, Nathaniel.
Why work for the slave? Addressed to the treasurers and
collectors in the anti-slavery cent-a-week societies by
Nath'l Southard... New-York, American Anti-slavery
Society, 1838.
cover-title, 12 p.   18 cm.

25571   Southern and Western Liberty Convention, Cincinnati, 1845.
The address of the Southern and Western Liberty Convention

held at Cincinnati, June 11 & 12, 1845, to the people of
the United States. With notes by a citizen of Pennsylvania. [Philadelphia, Office of the American citizen, 1845]
15, [1] p.   22½ cm.
Caption title.

25572 Southern Commercial Convention, Vicksburg, Miss., 1859.
A report on the African apprenticeship system, read at
the Southern Commercial Convention, by Henry Hughes.
Held at Vicksburg, May 10th, 1859. [Vicksburg, 1859]
cover-title, 15 p.   21½ cm.

25573 Southern slavery considered on general principles; or,
A grapple with abstractionists. By a North Carolinian.
New York, D. Murphy's son, printer, 1861.
24 p.   21½ cm.

25574 Southern state rights, free trade and anti-abolition tract
no. 1. Contents. Letter of the Hon. Langdon Cheves.
Speech of the Hon. Daniel Webster at Fanieul [!] hall,
1820. Bancroft's speech in New-York. Jackson's letter
on Texas. Address of the Democratic Association at
Washington. John Quincy Adams' disunion letter.
Charleston, Walker & Burke, printers, 1844.
1 p.l., 40 p.   23 cm.

25575 Southerne, Thomas.
Oroonoko; a tragedy... As performed at the Theatre
Royal, Covent Garden. Printed under the authority of the
managers from the prompt book; with remarks by Mrs. Inch-
bald. London, Longman, Hurd, Rees and Orme [18--?]
68 p.   front.   16 cm.

25576 Spain. Cortes, 1879-1880.
[Discursos de la ley de abolición de la esclavitud en
la isla de Cuba. Madrid, 1879-80]
[412] p.   33 cm.
Extracts from "Diario de las sesiones".

25577 Spain. Junta informativa de ultramar, 1866-1867.
... Interrogatorio sobre la manera de reglamentar el
trabajo de la población de color y asiática y los medios
de facilitar la inmigración que sea mas conveniente en
las provincias de Cuba y Puerto-Rico. Madrid, Imprenta
nacional, 1866.
8 p.   21 cm.

25578 Spatafora, Bartolomeo, fl. 1554.
Qvattro orationi di M. Bartolomeo Spathaphòra di Moncata.

L'vna in morte del Serenissimo Marc' Antonio Triuisano.
L'altra nella creatione del Serenissimo Francesco Veniero
principe di Venetia, et una in defesa della seruitù. L'
altra in difesa della discordia... In Venetia, P.
Pietrasanta, 1554.
   1 p.l., 120 p.   20 cm.

25579 Spears, John R[andolph] 1850-1936.
   The American slave-trade; an account of its origin,
growth and suppression... illustrated by W. A. Clark.
New York, C. Scribner's sons, 1900.
   232 p.   illus.   23 cm.

25580 Speed, James, 1866-
   James Speed, a personality, by James Speed, his grandson.
Louisville, Ky., Press of J. P. Morton & company, incorpo-
rated, 1914.
   4 p.l., 136 p., 1 l.   front., plates, ports. 22 cm.

25581 [Speed, Joseph J   ]
   A letter from a gentleman of Baltimore, to his friend in
the state of New York, on the subject of slavery. 3d ed.
Baltimore, Sherwood & co., printers, 1842.
   16 p.   18½ cm.

25582 Spencer, Charles S
   An appeal for freedom, made in the Assembly of the state
of New York, March 7th, 1859. By Hon. Charles S. Spencer
... Albany, Weed, Parsons & company, 1859.
   21 p.   22 cm.

25583 Spermaceti for inward bruises, with prescriptions from the
saddle-bags of Drs. Franklin and Jefferson, revised and
amended for the use of modern politico, theologico,
valetudinarians... Syracuse, Printed at the Journal
office, 1851.
   32 p.   19½ cm.

25584 Sperry, Earl Evelyn, 1875-
   The Jerry rescue, October 1, 1851, by Earl E. Sperry...
delivered before the Onondaga Historical Association,
October, 1921... Additional Jerry rescue documents and
rescue of Harriet Powell in Syracuse, September, 1839.
Collected and edited by Franklin H. Chase... Syracuse,
N. Y., Onondaga Historical Association, 1924.
   69, [5] p.   front., plates, ports. 23½ cm.

25585 [Spindler, Adeline B   ]
   The slavery question during the terms of office of John

Whitehill and Robert Jenkins, congressmen from Lancaster
County from 1803 to 1807 and 1807 to 1811, respectively.
[Lancaster, Pa., 1911]
   253-265 p.   23 cm.
Reprinted from Lancaster County Historical Society,
Historical papers and addresses, v. 15, 1911.

25586   [Stacy, George W   ] comp.
   Anti-slavery hymns, designed to aid the cause of human
rights. Containing original hymns written by Abby H. Price,
and others of Hopedale Community, with a choice selection
from other authors... Hopedale, Mass., Community press,
1844.
   36 p. $14\frac{1}{2}$ cm.

25587   Stanley, Sir Henry Morton, 1841-1904.
   Slavery and the slave trade in Africa, by Henry M. Stanley
... New York, Harper & brothers, 1893.
   2 p.l., 86 p.   front., plates. $13\frac{1}{2}$ cm.

25588   Stanley, Jacob.
   Mr. Borthwick's description of slavery, and his discussions with the Rev. Edward Dewdney, A. M. and the Rev.
Messrs. Price and Knibb, at ... Bath, examined, and his
sophistry exposed... Bath, G. Wood, 1833.
   16 p.   19 cm.
Cover-title.

25589   Stanly, Edward, 1810-1872.
   Letter from Mr. Stanly, of N. C. to Mr. Botts, of
Virginia. [Washington, 1840]
   7 p.   23 cm.
Caption title.

25590   Stanly, Edward, 1808-1872.
   Speech of Edw. Stanly, of North Carolina, establishing
proofs that the abolitionists are opposed to Gen.
Harrison, and that Gen. Harrison is opposed to their
"unconstitutional efforts." Delivered in the House of
Representatives, April 13, 1840. [Washington? 1840]
   24 p.   24 cm.
Caption title.

25591   Stanton, Mrs. Elizabeth (Cady) 1815-1902.
   The slave's appeal. By E. Cady Stanton. Pub. at the
anti-slavery depository, 15 Steuben street, Albany.
Albany, Weed, Parsons and company, printers, 1860.
   7 p.   19 cm.

25592   Stanton, Frederick P
          The frauds in Kansas illustrated. Speech of Hon.
        Frederick P. Stanton, late acting Governor of Kansas, at
        the Chinese Assembly Rooms, New York, February 17, 1858.
        [Washington, D. C., Buell & Blanchard, 1858]
          16 p.   21½ cm.

25593   Stanton, Robert Livingston, 1810-1885.
          The church and the rebellion: a consideration of the
        rebellion against the government of the United States;
        and the agency of the church, north and south, in relation
        thereto. By R. L. Stanton... New York, Derby & Miller,
        1864.
          xiv, 562 p.   19½ cm.

25594   [Stanton, Robert Livingston] 1810-1885.
          Vindication of the General Assembly of the Presbyterian
        church (O. S.), of 1866, from the aspersions of Rev.
        William Brown, D. D. [Cincinnati? 1876?]
          16 p.   22½ cm.
          Caption title.

25595   Staples, Nahor Augustus, 1830-1864.
          A sermon on the "irrepressible conflict," preached by
        Rev. N. A. Staples, on Thanksgiving Day, Nov. 24th, 1859...
        Milwaukee, Strickland & co., 1859.
          22 p.   22 cm.

25596   The star of freedom.   New-York [W. S. Dorr, printer, 184-?]
          96 p.   11 cm.

25597   Starke, Peter B
          Communication from the Hon. Peter B. Starke, as
        Commissioner to Virginia, to His Excellency, J. J. Pettus,
        with accompanying documents. Jackson, E. Barksdale, 1860.
          22 p.   24 cm.

25598   Starr, Frederick, jr., 1826-1867.
          What shall be done with the people of color in the
        United States? A discourse delivered in the First Pres-
        byterian Church of Penn Yan, New York, November 2d, 1862.
        By Rev. Frederick Starr, jr. ... Albany, Weed, Parsons
        and company, printers, 1862.
          30 p.   23 cm.

25599   Stearns, Charles.
          The way to abolish slavery. By Charles Stearns...
        Boston, The author, 1849.
          iv, [5]-36 p.   18 cm.

25600   Stearns, Edward Josiah, 1810-1890.
        Notes on Uncle Tom's cabin: being a logical answer to
        its allegations and inferences against slavery as an insti-
        tution. With a supplementary note on the key, and an
        appendix of authorities. By the Rev. E. J. Stearns...
        Philadelphia, Lippincott, Grambo & co., 1853.
        vi, 7-314 p.   19 cm.

25601   Stearns, Frank Preston, 1846-1917.
        The life and public services of George Luther Stearns,
        by Frank Preston Stearns... Philadelphia & London, J. B.
        Lippincott company, 1907.
        vii, [1] p., 2 l., 13-401, [1] p.   3 pl., 11 port.
        (incl. front.)   21½ cm.

25602   Stearns, Isaac.
        Right and wrong, in Mansfield, Mass. Or, an account
        of the pro-slavery mob of October 10th, 1836: when an
        anti-slavery lecturer [Charles C. Burleigh] was silenced
        by the beat of drums, &c., with some reasoning in favor
        of emancipation. By Isaac Stearns. Appendix, containing
        a list of officers and members of the Mansfield Anti-
        slavery Society. Pawtucket, Mass., R. Sherman, printer,
        1837.
        1 p.l., 61 p.   22 cm.

25603   Stedman, John Gabriel, 1744-1797.
        Capitain Johan Stedmans dagbok öfwer sina fälttåg i
        Surinam, jämte beskrifning om detta nybygges inwånare och
        öfriga märkwärdigheter. Sammandrag. Stockholm, Tryckt i
        Kongl. Ordens boktryckeriet hos J. Pfeiffer, 1800.
        3 p.l., 306, 15 p.   18 cm.
        An abridged translation, by Samuel L. Odmann, of the
        author's "Narrative, of a five years' expedition, against
        the revolted negroes of Surinam... from the year 1772, to
        1777," London, 1796.

25604   Stedman, John Gabriel, 1744-1797.
        Reize naar Surinamen, en door de binnensje gedeelten
        van Guiana; door den capitain John Gabriël Stedman...
        Naar het engelsch... Amsterdam, J. Allart, 1799-1800.
        4 v.   XLII pl. (incl. front. (port.) plates (1 fold.)
        fold. maps, plans)   22½ cm.

25605   Steele, John Benedict, 1814-1866.
        Speech of Hon. John B. Steele, of New York, on the
        question of slavery. Delivered in the House of Repre-
        sentatives, Jan. 20, 1862. [Washington, D. C., Printed
        by L. Towers & co., 1862]

8 p.   23 cm.
Caption title.

25606   Steiner, Bernard Christian, 1867-1926.
... History of slavery in Connecticut; by Bernard C.
Steiner, Ph.D. Baltimore, The Johns Hopkins press, 1893.
84 p.   24½ cm.   (Johns Hopkins University studies
in historical and political science... 11th ser., 9-10)
With bibliographical list and foot-notes.

25607   Steinthal, S   Alfred.
American slavery. A sermon, preached at Christ Church
Chapel, Bridgwater, on Sunday, May the first, 1853, by
the Rev. S. Alfred Steinthal. Bridgwater [Eng.] Printed
by J. Whitby [1853]
26 p.   18 cm.

25608   [Stephen, James] 1758-1832.
The crisis of the sugar colonies; or, An enquiry into
the objects and probable effects of the French expedition
to the West Indies; and their connection with the colonial
interests of the British empire. To which are subjoined,
sketches of a plan for settling the vacant lands of
Trinidada. In four letters to the Right Hon. Henry
Addington... London, Printed for J. Hatchard, 1802.
vii, 222 p.   21½ cm.

25609   Stephen, James, 1758-1832.
The slavery of the British West India colonies deline-
ated, as it exists both in law and practice, and compared
with the slavery of other countries, antient and modern.
By James Stephen... London, J. Butterworth and son
etc. 1824-30.
2 v.   22½-23½ cm.

25610   Stephens, Alexander Hamilton, 1812-1883.
Carpenter's picture, Lincoln and emancipation. Speech of
the Hon. Alexander H. Stephens, of Georgia, in the House
of Representatives, 12th of February, 1878. [Washington,
Darby & Duvall, printers, 1878]
4 p.   24 cm.
Caption title.

25611   Stephens, Alexander Hamilton, 1812-1883.
A constitutional view of the late war between the states;
its causes, character, conduct and results. Presented in a
series of colloquies at Liberty hall. By Alexander H.
Stephens... Philadelphia [etc.] National publishing
company; Chicago [etc.] Zeigler, McCurdy & co., 1868-70.
3 v.   front., ports., facsim.   24 cm.

25612   Stephens, Alexander Hamilton, 1812-1883.
         The reviewers reviewed; a supplement to the "War between
         the states," etc., with an appendix in review of "recon-
         struction," so called. By Alexander H. Stephens. New
         York, D. Appleton and company, 1872.
         273 p.   24 cm.

25613   Sterret, James.
         The Black republican, by James Sterret, the American
         cosmopolite... Harrisonburg, Va., Printed at the "Register"
         office, 1856.
         36 p.   18 cm.

25614   Steuart, Richard Sprigg, 1797-1876.
         Letter to John L. Carey, on the subject of slavery. By
         Dr. R. S. Steuart. Baltimore, Printed by J. Murphy, 1845.
         12 p.   20 cm.

25615   Stevens, Thaddeus, 1792-1868.
         Speech of Hon. T. Stevens, in reply to the attack on
         Gen. Hunter's letter. [n.p., 1862]
         15 p.   24 cm.
         Caption title.
         European Catholic opinion of slavery [signed Felix,
         bishop of Orleans]: p. 9-15.

25616   Stevens, William.
         The slave in history; his sorrows and his emancipation,
         by William Stevens... With portraits, and with illus-
         trations by J. Finnemore. London, The Religious Tract
         Society, 1904.
         3 p.l., [v]-vi p., 1 l., 9-379 p.   front., plates,
         ports.   20½ cm.

25617   Stewart, Alvan, 1790-1849.
         A legal argument before the Supreme court of the state
         of New Jersey, at the May term, 1845, at Trenton, for the
         deliverance of four thousand persons from bondage. By
         Alvan Stewart... New York, Finch & Weed, 1845.
         52 p.   23 cm.

25618   Stewart, James Augustus, 1808-1879.
         Powers of the government of the United States - federal,
         state, and territorial. Speech of Hon. James A. Stewart,
         of Maryland, on African slavery, its status - natural,
         moral, social, legal and constitutional... Delivered in
         the House of Representatives, July 23, 1856. Washington,
         Printed at the Congressional globe office, 1856.
         24 p.   22½ cm.

25619 [Stewart, John] of Jamaica.
       An account of Jamaica, and its inhabitants. By a gentle-
       man, long resident in the West Indies. 2d ed. Kingston,
       Jamaica, 1809.
       viii, [9]-213 p.   front.   19½ cm.

25620 Stewart, John, of Jamaica.
       A view of the past and present state of the island of
       Jamaica; with remarks on the moral and physical condition
       of the slaves, and on the abolition of slavery in the
       colonies. By J. Stewart... Edinburgh, Oliver & Boyd;
       [etc., etc.] 1823.
       xiii p., 1 l., 363, [1] p.   21 cm.

25621 Stiles, William Henry, 1808-1865.
       An address, delivered before the Georgia Democratic State
       Convention, held at Milledgeville, July 4th, 1856, by Hon.
       William H. Stiles... Atlanta, Ga., Printed at the
       "Examiner" office, 1856.
       35 p.   21 cm.

25622 Still, William, 1821-1902.
       The Underground Railroad. A record of facts, authentic
       narratives, letters, &c., narrating the hardships, hair-
       breadth escapes and death struggles of the slaves in
       their efforts for freedom, as related by themselves and
       others, or witnessed by the author; together with sketches
       of some of the largest stockholders, and most liberal
       aiders and advisers, of the road. By William Still...
       Philadelphia, Porter & Coates, 1872.
       2 p.l., 780 p.   front., illus., pl., ports.   23 cm.

25623 Stone, Alfred Holt, 1870-
       The early slave laws of Mississippi. Being some brief
       observations thereon, in a paper read before the Mississippi
       Historical Society, at a meeting held in the city of
       Natchez, April 20th-21st, 1899. By Alfred H. Stone...
       [Oxford? Miss., 1899?]
       cover-title, p. [133]-145.   22 cm.
       Reprinted from the Publication of the Mississippi
       Historical Society for 1899.

25624 Stone, Jacob L
       Slavery and the Bible; or, Slavery as seen in its
       punishment. By J. L. Stone... San Francisco, Printed by
       B. F. Sterett, 1863.
       48 p.   23½ cm.

25625 Storrs, George, 1796-1879?
       Mob, under pretense of law, or, The arrest and trial

of Rev. George Storrs at Northfield, N. H., with the circumstances connected with that affair and remarks thereon. Concord, E. G. Chase, printer, 1835.
    22, 2 p.   18½ cm.

25626 Storrs, Richard Salter, 1787-1873.
    American slavery, and the means of its removal. A sermon, preached in the First Congregational Church, Braintree, April 4, 1844. By Richard S. Storrs... Boston, Press of T. R. Marvin, 1844.
    31 p.   22½ cm.

25627 Stowe, Harriet Elizabeth (Beecher) 1811-1896.
    A key to Uncle Tom's cabin; presenting the original facts and documents upon which the story was founded. Together with corroborative statements verifying the truth of the work. Boston, John Jewett & co. [etc. etc.] 1853.
    262 p.   25½ cm.

25628 Stowe, Harriet Elizabeth (Beecher) 1811-1896.
    Life of Harriet Beecher Stowe, comp. from her letters and journals, by her son Charles Edward Stowe. Boston and New York, Houghton Mifflin and company, 1889.
    xii, 530 p.   front., illus., plates, ports., facsims. (1 fold.)   23 cm.

25629 Stowe, Harriet Elizabeth (Beecher) 1811-1896.
    Mrs. H. B. Stowe on Dr. Monod and the American tract society; considered in relation to American slavery... [Edinburgh? Reprinted for the Edinburgh ladies' emancipation society, 1858]
    8 p.   17½ cm.
    Caption title.

25630 Stowe, Harriet Elizabeth (Beecher) 1811-1896.
    A reply to "The affectionate and Christian address of many thousands of women of Great Britain and Ireland, to their sisters, the women of the United States of America." By Mrs. Harriet Beecher Stowe, in behalf of many thousands of American women. London, S. Low, son, and co., 1863.
    3 p.l., [3]-63 p.   17 cm.

25631 Stowe, Harriet Elizabeth (Beecher) 1811-1896.
    Uncle Tom's cabin; or, Life among the lowly. By Harriet Beecher Stowe. New ed., with illustrations, and a bibliography of the work, by George Bullen... Together with an introductory account of the work. Boston, Houghton, Osgood and company, 1879.
    1 p.l., lxvii, 529 p.   front., illus.   20½ cm.

25632   Stringfellow, Thornton.
         A brief examination of Scripture testimony on the insti-
         tution of slavery, in an essay, first published in the
         Religious herald and republished by request: with remarks
         on a review of the essay. By Thornton Stringfellow.
         Richmond, Printed at the office of the Religious herald,
         1841.
         40 p.   22 cm.
         An examination of Elder Galusha's reply to the preceding
         essay: p. 28-40.

25633   Strohal, Emil, 1844-1914.
         Über relative Unwirksamkeit. Von dr. Emil Strohal...
         Wien, Manz, 1911.
         1 p.l., 72 p.   27 cm.
         "Sonderabdruck aus der Festschrift zur Jahrhundertfeier
         des osterreichschen Allgemeinen bürgerlichen Gesetzbuches."

25634   Stroud, George McDowell, 1795-1875.
         Ein Abriss der Gesetze betreffend die Sklaverei in ver-
         schiedenen Staaten der Vereinigten Staaten von Amerika;
         von George M. Stroud. 2. bedeutend verm. und abgeanderte
         Ausg. Philadelphia, 1856.
         116 p.   18½ cm.
         Translation of the author's A sketch of the laws relating
         to slavery.

25635   Stroud, George McDowell, 1795-1875.
         Southern slavery and the Christian religion. Communica-
         tion from Judge Stroud. [Philadelphia, 1863]
         4 p.   18½ cm.
         Caption title.

25636   Stroyer, Jacob, 1849-
         My life in the South. By Jacob Stroyer. 4th ed.
         Salem, Newcomb & Grause, printers, 1898.
         100 p.   19 cm.

25637   Stuart, Charles, 1783?-1865.
         Immediate emancipation safe and profitable for masters -
         happy for slaves - right in government - advantageous to
         the nation - would interfere with no feelings but such as
         are destructive - cannot be postponed without continually
         increasing danger. At outline for it, and remarks on
         compensation. By Charles Steward [!] Reprinted from the
         (Eng.) Quarterly magazine and review, for April, 1832.
         2d American ed. Newburyport, C. Whipple, 1838.
         35 p.   22 cm.

25638 [Stuart, Moses] 1780-1852.
       Civil government. Reprinted from the Princeton review,
    for January, 1851. Princeton, N. J., 1851.
       47 p.   22½ cm.

25639 Stuart, Mrs. Ruth (McEnery) 1856-1917.
       Napoleon Jackson, the gentleman of the plush rocker,
    by Ruth McEnery Stuart; with pictures by Edward Potthast.
    New York, The Century co., 1902.
       3 p.l., 132 p. incl. pl. front.   18 cm.

25640 [Sturge, Edmund] 1808-1893.
       West India "compensation" to the owners of slaves...
    Its history and its results. Gloucester, J. Bellows [1893]
       23 p.   22 cm.

25641 Sturges, Joseph.
       An address, delivered before the citizens of Becket,
    Mass. January 18, 1839. Upon the subject of slavery, by
    Joseph Sturges... Lee [Mass.] Printed by E. J. Bull, 1839.
       24 p.   17½ cm.

25642 Sturgis, C   F
       Melville letters; or, The duties of masters to their
    servants. By Rev. C. F. Sturgis. Charleston, S. C.,
    Southern Baptist publication society, 1851.
       47-128 p.   16½ cm.
       Reprinted from Holland N. McTyeire. Duties of masters
    to servants. 1851.

25643 Sudan. Governor-general, 1927-1933 (Maffey)
       ... Despatch from the governor-general of the Sudan to
    the secretary-general of the League of Nations relating
    to slavery in the Sudan... London, H. M. Stationery
    off., 1927.
       4 p.   24½ cm.   ([Gt. Brit. Foreign Office] Sudan
    no. 1 (1927))
       Gt. Brit. Parliament. Papers by command. Cmd. 2872.

25644 Sullivan, Thomas Russell, 1799-1862.
       Letters against the immediate abolition of slavery;
    addressed to the free blacks of the non-slave-holding
    states. By T. R. Sullivan. Comprising a legal opinion
    on the power of legislatures in non-slave-holding states
    to prevent measures tending to immediate and general
    emancipation; in a letter to the author from William
    Sullivan, L.L.D. Published with his permission.
       The whole first printed in the Boston courier. Boston,
    Hilliard, Gray and co., 1835.
       2 p.l., 51 p.   18½ cm.

25645 Sullivan, Thomas Russell, 1799–1862.
        The limits of responsibility in reforms. By T. R.
    Sullivan. Boston, A. Williams and company, 1861.
        32 p.   19 cm.

25646 Sumner, Charles, 1811–1874.
        The demands of freedom. Speech of Hon. Charles Sumner,
    in the Senate of the United States, on his motion to
    repeal the fugitive slave bill. February 23, 1855.
    [Washington, D. C., Buell & Blanchard, printers, 1855]
        8 p.   22½ cm.
    Caption title.

25647 Sumner, Charles, 1811–1874.
        Duties of Massachusetts at this crisis. A speech of
    Hon. Charles Sumner, delivered at the Republican conven-
    tion at Worcester, Sept. 7, 1854. [n.p., 1854]
        8 p.   24½ cm.
    Caption title.

25848 Sumner, Charles, 1811–1874.
        Immediate emancipation a war measure! Speech of Hon.
    Charles Sumner, of Massachusetts, on the bill providing
    for emancipation in Missouri. In the Senate of the
    United States, February 12th, 1863. [Washington, H.
    Polkinhorn, printer, 1863]
        3 p.   22 cm.
    Caption title.

25849 Sumner, Charles, 1811–1874.
        ... No property in man. Speech of Hon. Charles Sumner,
    on the proposed amendment of the Constitution abolishing
    slavery through the United States. In the Senate of the
    United States, April 8th, 1864. New York, Loyal Publica-
    tion Society, 1864.
        23, [1] p.   22 cm.   (Loyal Publication Society...
    [Pamphlets] no. 51)

25850 Sumner, Charles, 1811–1874.
        Ransom of slaves at the national capital. Speech of
    Hon. Charles Sumner, of Massachusetts, on the bill for
    the abolition of slavery in the District of Columbia, in the
    Senate of the United States, March 31, 1862. Washington,
    Printed at the Congressional globe office, 1862.
        13 p.   22½ cm.

25651 Sumner, Charles, 1811–1874.
        The rebellion: its origin and mainspring. An oration
    delivered... under the auspices of the Young Men's Repu-

blican Union, 1861.
    16 p.   front. (port.)   25½ cm.

25652   Sumner, Charles, 1811-1874.
    The Republican party; its origin, necessity and per-
manence. Speech of Hon. Charles Sumner, before the
Young Men's Republican Union of New York, July 11th,
1860. New-York, J. A. H. Hasbrouck & co., printers,
1860.
    cover-title, 16 p.   23½ cm.

25653   Sumner, Charles, 1811-1874.
    Slavery and the rebellion, one and inseparable. Speech
of Hon. Charles Sumner, before the New York Young men's
Republican Union, at Cooper Institute, New York, on the
afternoon of November 5, 1864. Boston, Wright & Potter,
printers, 1864.
    30 p.   21½ cm.

25654   Sumner, Charles, 1811-1874.
    Universal emancipation without compensation... Speech
of Hon. Charles Sumner, on the proposed amendment of the
Constitution abolishing slavery through the United States,
in the Senate of the United States, April 8, 1864.
[Washington, H. Polkinhorn, printer, 1864]
    16 p.   22 cm.

25655   Sumner, Charles, 1811-1874.
    Usurpation of the Senate. Two speeches of Hon. Charles
Sumner, on the imprisonment of Thaddeus Hyatt. In the
Senate of the United States, 12th March and 15th June,
1860. [Washington, D. C., Buell & Blanchard, 1860]
    8 p.   22 cm.

25656   Supplement to an Address to the members of the new Parliament, on the proceedings of the Colonial Department on
the West India question. [n.p., 182-?]
    1 p.l., 5 p.   20½ cm.

25657   The suppressed book about slavery! Prepared for publication
in 1857 - never published until the present time. New
York, Carleton, 1864.
    432 p.   8 pl. (incl. front.)   19 cm.

25658   Swain, B
    Why work for the slave? [n.p., 1835]
    12 p.   17½ cm.

25659   Swan, Charles Albert.
    The slavery of to-day; or, The present position of the

open sore of Africa, Glasgow, Pickering & Inglis; New
York, D. T. Bass [1909?]
202 p.   plates.   19 cm.

25660   Swift, Morrison I[saac]
Human submission. By Morrison I. Swift. Philadelphia,
The Liberty press, 1905-
pt.   19½ cm.

25661   Swift, Zephaniah, 1759-1823.
An oration on domestic slavery. Delivered at the North
meeting-house in Hartford, on the 12th day of May, A.D.
1791. At the meeting of the Connecticut Society for the
Promotion of Freedom, and the Relief of Persons Unlawfully
Holden in Bondage. By Zephaniah Swift, esquire. Hartford,
Printed and sold by Hudson and Goodwin, 1791.
23 p.   21 cm.

25662   Sydnor, Charles Sackett, 1898-
... Slavery in Missippi, by Charles Sackett Snydor...
New York, London, D. Appleton-Century company, incor-
porated [c1933]
xiii, 270 p. incl. front. (map)   23 cm.
At head of title: The American historical association.

25663   Sylvain, Benito.
Du sort des indigenes dans les colonies d'exploitation;
par Benito Sylvain... Paris, L. Boyer, 1901.
528 p., 1 l. incl. port.   22½ cm.

25664   Symmes, Elmore.
Aunt Eliza and her slaves. [n.p., 1847]
528-537 p.   music.   21 cm.
Reprinted from New England magazine, v. 15, Jan. 1897.

25665   Sypesteyn, Cornelis Ascanius van, 1823-1892.
Afschaffing der slavernij in de Nederlandsche West-
Indische kolonien, uit officiële bronnen zamensgesteld.
['s-Gravenhage] 1866.
100 p.   25 cm.

T

25666   Talbot, Thomas Hammond, 1823-1907.
The constitutional provision respecting fugitives from
service or labor, and the act of Congress, of September 18,
1850. By Thomas H. Talbot... Boston, B. Marsh, 1852.
128 p.   21½ cm.

25667   Tallmadge, James, 1778-1853.
        Speech of the Hon. James Tallmadge, of Duchess County,
        New York, in the House of Representatives of the United
        States, on slavery. Boston, Printed by Ticknor &
        company, 1849.
        vii, [9]-24 p.   23½ cm.

25868   Tangorra-Milano, Angelo.
        ... Gli ultimi schiavi, con note e illustrazioni dello
        stesso autore... New York [Saitta press co.] 1924.
        243 p., 2 l.   illus.   22½ cm.

25669   Tappan, Lewis, 1788-1873.
        Important intelligence from Liberia [a letter] New
        York, Nov. 24, 1838, and to Lewis Tappan, Esq., New York,
        U. S. America, via London [a letter in reply] by Louis
        Sheridan, Edina, Liberia, 16th July, 1838. [n.p., 1838?]
        [4] p.   32 cm.
        Caption title.

25670   [Tappan, Lewis] 1788-1873.
        Letters respecting a book "dropped from the catalogue"
        of the American Sunday School Union in compliance with
        the dictation of the slave power. New York, American
        and Foreign Anti-slavery Society, 1848.
        36 p.   18 cm.

25671   [Tappan, Lewis] 1788-1873.
        The life of Arthur Tappan... New York, Hurd and
        Houghton, 1870.
        432 p.   front. (port.)   19½ cm.

25672   Taylor, Hannis.
        The Lincoln-Douglas debates and their application to
        the present problems. [n.p., 1909]
        161-173 p.   21 cm.
        Reprinted from North American review, v. 189, Feb.
        1909.

25673   Taylor, Richard.
        Destruction and reconstruction: personal experiences
        of the late war. By Richard Taylor... New York,
        D. Appleton and company, 1879.
        274 p.   23 cc.

25674   Tee-total anti-slavery pledge. [n.p., n.d.]
        [1] p.   11 cm.

25675   Teenstra, Marten Douwes, 1795-1864.
        De negerslaven in de kolonie Suriname en de uitbrei-
        ding van het Christendom onder de heidensche bevolking,
        door M. D. Teenstra. Dordrecht, H. Lagerweij, 1842.
        xviii, 380 p.   front., fold. plan.   23 cm.

25676   Teissier, Georges, 1862-
        ... Des affranchissements par acte de dernière volonté...
        De la condition des navires dans les rapports inter-
        nationaux... Par Georges Teissier... Paris, A. Rousseau,
        1886.
            268 p., 1 l.   25 cm.
            Thèse - Faculté de droit de Paris.

25677   Terrell, Robert Heberton, 1857-1925.
            A glance at the past and present of the negro; an
        address by Robert H. Terrell, delivered at Church's
        auditorium before the Citizen's Industrial League of
        Memphis, Tennessee, September 22, 1903. Washington,
        Press of R. L. Pendleton, 1903.
            16 p.   22 cm.

25678   ... The territorial question. By a volunteer... [Washington,
        1860]
            33 p.   23 cm.   (National Democratic Volunteers.
        Document no. 2)
            Caption title.

25679   Thayer, Eli, 1819-1899.
            The suicide of slavery. Speech of Hon. Eli Thayer,
        of Mass. Delivered in the House of Representatives,
        March 25, 1858. [Washington, Buell & Blanchard, printers,
        1858]
            8 p.   24 cm.
            Caption title.

25680   [Thomas, Abel Charles] 1807-1880.
            The gospel of slavery: a primer of freedom. By Iron
        Gray [pseud.]... New York, T. W. Strong [c1864]
            [28] p.   illus.   17 cm.
            In verse.

25681   Thomas, E
            A concise view of the slavery of the people of colour
        in the United States; exhibiting some of the most
        affecting cases of cruel and barbarous treatment of the
        slaves by their most inhuman and brutal masters; not
        heretofore published: and also showing the absolute
        necessity for the most speedy abolition of slavery, with
        an endeavour to point out the best means of effecting
        it. To which is added, A short address to the free
        people of colour. With a selection of hymns, &c. &c.
        By E. Thomas. Philadelphia, E. Thomas, 1834.
            v, [iii]-iv, [7]-178 p.   front., pl. $14\frac{1}{2}$ cm.

25682   Thomas, Thomas Ebenezer, 1812-1875.
         Correspondence of Thomas Ebenezer Thomas, mainly re-
         lating to the anti-slavery conflict in Ohio, especially in
         the Presbyterian Church. Pub. by his son. [Dayton? O.]
         1909.
         8 p.l., 137 p.   23½ cm.

25683   [Thomas, William] d. 1836?
         The enemies of the Constitution discovered, or, An
         inquiry into the origin and tendency of popular violence.
         Containing a complete and circumstantial account of the
         unlawful proceedings at the city of Utica, October 21st,
         1835; the dispersion of the state anti-slavery convention
         by the agitators, the destruction of a democratic press,
         and of the causes which led thereto. Together with a
         concise treatise on the practice of the court of His Honor
         Judge Lynch... accompanied with numerous highly inte-
         resting and important documents. By Defensor [pseud.]
         New-York, Leavitt, Lord, & co.; Utica, G. Tracy, 1835.
         xii, [9]-183 p.   18 cm.

25884   Thompson, George, 1804-1878.
         ... The Free Church of Scotland and American slavery.
         Substance of speeches delivered in the Music hall, Edin-
         burgh, during May and June 1846, by George Thompson, esq.
         and the Rev. Henry C. Wright. With an appendix, containing
         the deliverances of the Free Church on the subject of
         slavery, 1844, 1845, and 1846, and other valuable docu-
         ments. Edinburgh, T. & W. M'Dowall; [etc., etc.] 1846.
         104 p.   21½ cm.

25685   Thompson, George, 1804-1878.
         Lectures of George Thompson, with a full report of the
         discussion between Mr. Thompson and Mr. Borthwick, the
         pro-slavery agent, held at the Royal Amphitheatre, Liver-
         pool, Eng., and which continued for six evenings with
         unabated interest, comp. from various English editions.
         Also, a brief history of his connection with the anti-
         slavery cause in England, by Wm. Lloyd Garrison. Boston,
         I. Knapp, 1836.
         190 p.   20 cm.

25686   Thompson, George, 1804-1878.
         The substance of Mr. Thompson's lecture on slavery,
         delivered in the Wesleyan chapel, Irwell street, Salford,
         Manchester (Eng.) Manchester, Printed by S. Wheeler and
         son; Boston, Re-printed by I. Knapp, 1836.
         24 p.   18 cm.

25887   Thompson, Joseph Parrish, 1819-1879.
         The fugitive slave law; tried by the Old and New Testa-
         ments. By Joseph P. Thompson... New York, M. H. Newman &
         co., 1850.
            35 p.   22 cm.
         Reprinted from the New Englander for Nov., 1850.

25688   Thompson, Richard Wigginton, 1809-1900.
         Speech of R. W. Thompson, of Indiana, on the slavery
         question. Delivered in the House of Representatives,
         January 25, 1849. [Washington] Towers, printer [1849]
            16 p.   23 cm.
         Caption title.

25689   [Thomson, Mortimer] 1832-1875.
         Great auction sale of slaves, at Savannah, Georgia,
         March 2d and 3d, 1859. Reported for the Tribune. New
         York, American Anti-slavery Society [1859]
            28 p.   14½ cm.

25690   Thoreau, Henry David, 1817-1862.
         A Yankee in Canada, with Anti-slavery and reform papers,
         by Henry D. Thoreau... Boston, Ticknor & Fields, 1866.
            3 p.l., [3]-286 p.   18½ cm.
         Contents. - A Yankee in Canada. - Anti-slavery and
         reform papers: Slavery in Massachusetts. - Prayers. -
         Civil disobedience. - A plea for Captain John Brown. -
         Paradise (to be) regained. - Herald of freedom. - Thomas
         Carlyle and his works. - Life without principle. -
         Wendell Phillips before the Concord Lyceum. - The last
         days of John Brown.

25691   Thorne, James A
         Prayer for the oppressed. A premium tract. By Rev.
         James A. Thorne... Boston, American Tract Society [1859]
            24 p.   18½ cm.   [American Tract Society, Boston,
         Publications, no. 38]

25692   Thornton, Thomas C   1794-1860.
         An inquiry into the history of slavery; its introduction
         into the United States; causes of its continuance; and
         remarks upon the abolition tracts of William E. Channing,
         D.D. By Rev. T. C. Thornton... Washington, W. M.
         Morrison, 1841.
            2 p.l., [3]-345 p.   19 cm.

25693   Thornton, William, 1761-1828.
         Political economy: founded in justice and humanity.
         In a letter to a friend. By W. T., Washington. City of

Washington, Printed by S. H. Smith, 1804.
24 p.   23 cm.
On slavery.

25694 [Thorpe, Thomas Bangs] 1814-1878, supposed author.
The master's house; a tale of Southern life. By Logan
[pseud.]... New York, T. L. McElrath & co.; [etc., etc.]
1854.
391 p.   front., plates.   19½ cm.

25695 Thoughts in a series of letters, in answer to a question
respecting the division of the states. By a Massachusetts
farmer. [n.p., 1813]
24 p.   24 cm.

25696 Thoughts on American slavery, and its proposed remedies. By
a northerner. Hartford, H. Benton, 1838.
82 p.   15 cm.

25697 Thoughts on British Guiana. By a planter [pseud.]   2d ed.,
rev. and cor., with an appendix... Demerara, Printed at
the Royal gazette office, 1847.
42 p.   23½ cm.

25698 Thoughts on the slavery of the negroes. London, Printed and
sold by James Phillips, 1784.
32 p.   18 cm.

25699 Thrasher, John B
Slavery a divine institution. By J. B. Thrasher, of
Port Gibson. A speech, made before the Breckinridge and
Lane Club, November 5th, 1860. Port Gibson, Miss.,
Southern reveille book and job office, 1861.
22 p.   20½ cm.

25700 ... Three unlike speeches, by William Lloyd Garrison, of
Massachusetts, Garrett Davis, of Kentucky, Alexander H.
Stephens, of Georgia. The abolitionists, and their
relations to the war. The war not for emancipation.
African slavery, the corner-stone of the southern
confederacy. New York, E. D. Barker; [etc., etc.] 1862.
cover-title, [31]-78 p.   20 cm.   (The Pulpit and
rostrum, no. 26-27)

25701 Tiffany, Mrs. Nina (Moore)
Sanuem E. Sewall; a memoir, by Nina Moore Tiffany.
Boston and New York, Houghton, Mifflin and company, 1898.
4 p.l., 175, [1] p.   front., port.   19½ cm.

25702 Tijdschrift, uitg. van wege der Nederlandsche maatschap-
          pij ter bevordering van de afschaffing der slavernij...
          [1.]-8. jaarg.; Apr. 1855-Nov. 1862. 's Gravenhage,
          M. Nijhoff [1855-62]
             8 v.   22½ cm.
          From Apr. 1855 to Mar. 1856 title reads: Maaandblad,
          uitg. van wege de Nederlandsche maatschappij ter bevor-
          dering van de afschaffing der slavernij.

25703 Tilden, Daniel R
          Speech of Hon. Daniel R. Tilden, of Ohio, on the Mexican
          war and slavery. Delivered in the House of Representatives,
          February 4, 1847. Washington, Printed at the office of
          Blair and Rives, 1847.
             12 p.   24 cm.

25704 Tilmon, Levin, 1807-1863.
          A brief miscellaneous narrative of the more early part
          of the life of L. Tilmon, pastor of a colored Methodist
          Congregational church in the city of New York. Written
          by himself. Jersey City, W. W. & L. A. Pratt, printers,
          1853.
             1 p.l., 97 p.   17 cm.

25705 Tisserant, Charles.
          Ce que j'ai connu de l'esclavage en Oubangui-Chari.
          Paris, Société antiesclavagiste de France [n.d.]
             vi, 112 p.   illus., fold. map.   21 cm.

25706 To the citizens of the United States. A plea for the gospel
          scheme for the abolition of slavery.
             4 p.   22½ cm.

25707 To the Presbyterian clergy of the United States. [n.p.,
          1836?]
             20 p.   21½ cm.
          Contains a letter by David Nelson on slavery.

25708 Tobie, Edward Parsons, 1838-
          Personal recollections of General Sheridan. By Edward
          P. Tobie... Providence, The Society, 1889.
             40 p.   20½ x 16 cm.   (Series t.-p.: Personal
          narratives of events in the war of the rebellion, being
          papers read before the Rhode Island Soldiers and Sailors
          Historical Society, 4th ser., no. 5)

25709 Toombs, Robert Augustus, 1810-1885.
          An oration, delivered before the Few and Phi Gamma
          Societies, of Emory College, at Oxford, Ga., July, 1853,

by Hon. Robert Toombs. Slavery in the United States; its consistency with republican institutions, and its effect upon the slave and society. Augusta, Ga., Steam power press of Chronicle & sentinel, 1853.
26 p.   22 cm.

25710 Torres Campos, Rafael, 1853-1904.
Estudios geográficos, por Rafael Torres Campos... con un prólogo del Excmo. Sr. D. Francisco Coello... Madrid, Est. tip. de Fortanet, 1895.
xvi, 475 p.   25 cm.

25711 T[orres] Texugo, F
A letter on the slave trade still carried on along the eastern coast of Africa, called the province of Mosambique, showing the little importance those possessions are of to Portugal, in a commercial point of view, and suggesting improvements. Addressed (by permission) to T. Powell Buxton, esquire. By F. T. Texugo... London, J. Hatchard & son [etc.] 1839.
62 p., 1 l., liii p. $23\frac{1}{2}$ cm.

25712 Torrey, Jesse, fl. 1787-1834.
American slave trade; or, An account of the manner in which the slave dealers take free people from some of the United States of America, and carry them away, and sell them as slaves in other of the states; and of the horrible cruelties practised in the carrying on of this most infamous traffic: with reflections on the project for forming a colony of American blacks in Africa, and certain documents respecting that project. By Jesse Torrey, jun., physician. With five plates. London, Reprinted by C. Clement and published by J. M. Cobbett, 1822.
xvi, [17]-119 p.   5 pl. (incl. front.) $18\frac{1}{2}$ cm.

25713 Tourgée, Albion Winegar, 1838-1905.
A fool's errand, by one of the fools; the famous romance of American history. New, enl., and illustrated ed. To which is added, by the same author, part II. The invisible empire: a concise review of the epoch on which the tale is based. With many thrilling personal narratives and startling facts of life at the South never before narrated for the general reader... By Albion W. Tourgée... New York, Fords, Howard, & Hulbert; Boston, W. H. Thompson & co.; [etc., etc., 1880]
1 p.l., vii-x, 521 p.   front., 15 pl.   20 cm.

25714 [Townsend, John] fl. 1860.
The doom of slavery in the Union: its safety out of it.

2d ed. ... Charleston, S. C., Printed by Evans & Cogswell,
1860.
39, [1] p.   22½ cm.

25715 [Townsend, John] fl. 1860.
... The South alone, should govern the South. And
African slavery should be controlled by those only, who
are freindly to it. 3d ed. ... Charleston, Steam-power
presses of Evans & Cogswell, 1860.
62 p., 1 l.   22 cm.   (Tract, no. 1)

25716 Train, George Francis, 1829-1904.
The facts; or, At whose door does the sin (?) lie?
Who profits by slave labor? Who initiated the slave trade?
What have the philanthropists done? These questions
answered, by Geo. Francis Train... New York, R. M. De Witt;
London, Trübner & co.; [etc., etc.] 1860.
144 p.   19½ cm.

25717 Train, George Francis, 1829-1904.
Train's speeches in England, on slavery and emancipation.
Delivered in London, on March 12th, and 19th, 1862. Also
his great speech on the "Pardoning of traitors." By
George Francis Train... [Authorized American ed.] Philadelphia, T. B. Peterson & brothers [1862]
1 p.l., [19]-32 p.   24½ cm.

25718 A treatise on slavery, by an unknown author, of Virginia.
[n.p., 183-?]
40 p.   18½ cm.
Caption title.

25719 Tremain, Mary.
... Slavery in the District of Columbia; the policy of
Congress and the struggle for abolition, by Mary Tremain,
M.A. New York [etc.] G. P. Putnam's sons, 1892.
iv, 100 p.   24 cm.   (University of Nebraska.
Departments of History and Economics. Seminary papers,
no. 2. April, 1892)

25720 Trescot, William Henry, 1822-1898.
The position and course of the South. By Wm. H. Trescot.
Charleston [S.C.] Steam Power Press of Walker & James,
1850.
20 p.   26 cm.

25721 Trexler, Harrison Anthony, 1883-
... Slavery in Missouri, 1804-1865, by Harrison Anthony
Trexler... Baltimore, The Johns Hopkins press, 1914.

viii, 9-259 p.   25 cm.   (Johnn Hopkins University studies in historical and political science... Ser. XXXII, no. 2)
Published also as thesis (Ph.D.) Johns Hopkins University, 1914.

25722 Trimble, Robert.
Popular fallacies relating to the American question. A lecture, delivered in November, 1863. By Robert Trimble. London, Whittaker & co.; [etc., etc.] 1863.
36 p.   21 cm.

25723 Trollope, Frances (Milton) 1780-1863.
The life and adventures of Jonathan Jefferson Whitlaw; or, Scenes on the Mississippi. With fifteen engravings. London, R. Bentley, 1836.
3 v.   15 pl.   19 cm.

25724 Trotter, William B
A history and defense of African slavery. By William B. Trotter... [Quitman? Miss.] Pub. for the author, 1861.
vii, 9-204 p.   plates. $19\frac{1}{2}$ cm.

25725 Trow, John Fowler, 1810-1886, pub.
Alton trials: of Winthrop S. Gilman, who was indicted with Enoch Long, Amos B. Roff, George H. Walworth, George H. Whitney, William Harned, John S. Noble, James Morss, jr., Henry Tanner, Royal Weller, Reuben Gerry, and Thaddeus B. Hurlbut: for the crime of riot, committed on the night of the 7th of November, 1837, while engaged in defending a printing press, from an attack made on it at that time, by an armed mob. Written out from notes of the trial, taken at the time, by a member of the bar of the Alton Municipal Court. Also, the trial of John Solomon, Levi Palmer, Horace Beall, Josiah Nutter, Jacob Smith, David Butler, William Carrn, and James M. Rock, indicted... for a riot committed in Alton, on the night of the 7th of November, 1837, in unlawfully and forcibly entering the warehouse of Godfrey, Gilman & co., and breaking up and destroying a printing press. Written out from notes taken at the time of trial, by William S. Lincoln... New-York, J. F. Trow, 1838.
158 p.   front.   18 cm.

25726 Trowbridge, John Townsend, 1827-1916.
Cudjo's cave. Boston, J. E. Tilton and company, 1864.
504 p.   19 cm.

25727 Trumbull, Lyman, 1813-1896.
The campaign in Illinois. Speech of Senator Trumbull,

at Chicago. His private opinion of Douglas publicity
expressed... [Chicago, 1860]
   10 p.   23½ cm.
Caption title.

25728   Trumbull, Lyman, 1813-1896.
The constitutionality and expediency of confiscation
vindicated. Speech of Hon. Lyman Trumbull, of Illinois,
on the bill to confiscate the property and free the
slaves of rebels; delivered in the Senate of the United
States, April 7, 1862. Washington, Printed at the
Congressional globe office, 1862.
   15 p.   24 cm.

25729   Trumbull, Lyman, 1813-1896.
Speech of Hon. Lyman Trumbull, of Illinois, on amending
the Constitution to prohibit slavery. Delivered in the
Senate of the United States, March 28, 1864. [Washington,
Printed by L. Towers for the Union Congressional Committee,
1864]
   8 p.   22½ cm.
Caption title.

25730   Tucker, George, 1775-1861.
Speech of Mr. Tucker, of Virginia, on the restriction
of slavery in Missouri. Delivered in the House of
Representatives of the United States, February 25, 1820.
[Washington? 1820]
   20 p.   18½ cm.
Caption title.

25731   Tucker, St. George, 1752-1827.
Queries respecting the slavery and emancipation of
negroes in Massachusetts and answered by Dr. Belknap,
1795. [Boston, 1795]
   191-211 p.   22 cm.
Reprinted from Massachusetts Historical Society,
Collections, v. 4, 1745.

25732   Tuckerman, Bayard, 1855-1923.
William Jay and the constitutional movement for the
abolition of slavery, by Bayard Tuckerman, with a preface
by John Jay. New-York, Dodd, Mead & company, 1894.
   xxii, 183 p.   4 port. (incl. front.)   23 cm.

25733   Tufts, Samuel N
Slavery, and the death of John Brown. A sermon
preached in Auburn hall, Auburn, Sabbath afternoon,
Dec. 11th, 1859. By Rev. Samuel N. Tufts, pastor of

the Auburn Free Baptist Church. Lewiston [Me.] Printed
at the Journal office, 1859.
    20 p.   18 cm.

25734 Turnbull, David.
       Travels in the West. Cuba; with notices of Porto Rico,
and the slave trade. By David Turnbull... London,
Printed for Longman, Orme, Brown, Green, and Longmans,
1840.
       2 p.l., [iii]-xvi, 574 p.   front. (map)   22 cm.

25735 Turner, Edward Raymond, 1881-
       The first abolition society in the United States, by
Edward Raymond Turner... [Philadelphia] Printed by
J. B. Lippincott company [1912?]
       cover-title, 93-110 p.   illus. (facsims.)   25½ cm.
       Reprinted from The Pennsylvania magazine of history
and biography, for January, 1912.

25736 Turner, Edward Raymond, 1881-
       Slavery in Pennsylvania... by Edward Raymond Turner...
Baltimore, The Lord Baltimore press, 1911.
       1 p.l., 88 p.   19½ cm.
       Thesis (Ph.D.) - Johns Hopkins University, 1910.

25737 Turner, Jonathan Baldwin, 1805-1898.
       The three great races of men; their origin, character,
history and destiny, with special regard to the present
condition and future destiny of the black race in the
United States. By J. B. Turner. Springfield [Ill.]
Bailhache & Baker, printers, 1861.
       v p., 1 l., 112 p.   21 cm.

25738 Turner, Nat, 1800?-1831.
       The confession, trial and execution of Nat Turner,
the negro insurrectionist; also, a list of persons
murdered in the insurrection in Southampton County,
Virginia, on the 21st and 22nd of August, 1831, with
introductory remarks. By T. R. Gray. Petersburg, Va.,
J. B. Ege, printer, 1881.
       23 p.   21 cm.

25739 [Tussac, Fr   Richard de]
       Cri des colons contre un ouvrage de m. l'éveque et
sénateur Grégoire, ayant pour titre De la littératures
des nègres, ou réfutation des inculpations calomnieuses
faites aux colons par l'auteur, et par els autres
philosophes négrophiles, tels que Raynal, Valmont de
Bomare, etc. Conduite atroce des nègres et des mulatres

qui ont joue les premiers roles dans les scènes tragiques
de S. Domingue, et dont l'évêque Grégoire préconise les
qualités morales et sociales. Dissertation sur l'esclavage... Paris, Chez les marchands de nouveautés, 1810.
2 p.l., 312 p.   20½ cm.

25740 Twelvetrees, Harper, 1823-1881, ed.
        The story of the life of John Anderson, the fugitive
        slave. Ed. by Harper Twelvetrees, M.A., chairman of the
        John Anderson committee. London, W. Tweedie, 1863.
        xv, 182 p.   front. (port.)   19½ cm.

25741 $2,500 reward... St. Louis, Mo., 1852.
        [1] p.   46 cm.

25742 Tyng, Dudley Atkins, 1825-1858.
        Our country's troubles, no. II. Or, National sins
        and national retribution. A sermon preached in the
        Church of the Covenant, Philadelphia, July 5, 1857.
        By the Rev. Dudley A. Tyng, rector. Philadelphia,
        W. S. & A. Martien, 1864.
        24 p.   22½ cm.

25743 Tyson, J   Washington.
        The doctrines of the "abolitionists" refuted, in a
        letter from J. Washington Tyson, the Democratic Harrison
        candidate for Congress, in the first district, of
        Pennsylvania. Philadelphia, 1840.
        8 p.   23 cm.

25744 Tyson, Job Roberts, 1803-1858.
        Speech of Hon. J. R. Tyson, of Pennsylvania, on the
        fugitive slave laws and compromise measures of 1850;
        delivered in the House of Representatives, February 28,
        1857. Washington, Printed at the office of the
        Congressional globe, 1857.
        19 p.   24½ cm.

U

25745 Uncle Ned's cabin, by a son of the South... New Orleans,
        La., E. S. Upton printing co. [1922]
        2 p.l., 3-61 p.   16½ cm.

25746 The Uncle Tom's cabin almanack; or, Abolitionist memento.
        For 1853. London, J. Cassell [1852]
        70 p.   front., illus.   26 cm.

25747   Underwood, John Cox, 1840&

          Speech, at Alexandria, Va., July 4, 1863. Washington,
        McGill & Witherow, printers, 1863.
          11 p.   22 cm.

25748   Underwood, Joseph Rogers, 1791-1876.
          An address delivered to the Colonization Society of
        Kentucky, at Frankfort, Jan. 15, 1835. By the Hon.
        Joseph R. Underwood. Frankfort, Printed by A. G.
        Hodges, 1835.
          24 p.   21 cm.

25749   Underwood, Joseph Rogers, 1791-1876.
          Speech of Mr. J. R. Underwood, upon the resolution
        proposing to censure John Quincy Adams for presenting
        to the House of Representatives a petition praying for
        the dissolution of the union. Delivered in the House
        of Representatives, on the 27th of January, 1842.
        Washington, Printed at the National intelligencer
        office, 1842.
          15 p. $24\frac{1}{2}$ cm.

25750   Underwood, T   H
          Our flag. A poem in four cantos. By T. H. Underwood.
        New York, Carleton, 1862.
          41 p.   1 illus. $18\frac{1}{2}$ cm.

25751   The Union: being a condemnation of Mr. Helper's scheme,
        with a plan for the settlement of the "irrepressible
        conflict." By one who has considered both sides of the
        question... New York, F. A. Brady [1857?]
          32 p.   22 cm.

25752   Union and Emancipation Society, Manchester.
          The working men of Manchester and President Lincoln.
        [Manchester, Smith and Barnes, printers, 1863?]
          4 p. $21\frac{1}{2}$ cm.   (Union and emancipation tracts,
        no. 2)

25753   The union must be preserved! Four crisis letters to the
        ladies, proposing the speedy formation of the Martha
        Washington Society. Published by Friends of the move-
        ment... New York, J. H. Duyckinck, printer [1860]
          11 p. $21\frac{1}{2}$ cm.
          Signed: Spectator.

25754   Union Safety Committee.
          Selections from the speeches and writings of prominent
        men in the United States, on the subject of abolition
        and agitation, and in favor of the compromise measures

of the last session of Congress, addressed to the
people of the state of New-York, by the Union Safety
Committee. New-York, Printed by J. P. Wright, 1851.
69 p.   22 cm.

25755 United Nations. Secretary-General, 1946-1953 (Lie)
The suppression of slavery, memorandum submitted by
the Secretary General. New York, United Nations Economic and Social Council, Ad Hoc Committee on Slavery,
1951.
iv, 83 p.   23 cm.   (United Nations. [Document]
ST/SOA/4. 11 July 1951)
"United Nations publications. Sales no.: 1951.XIV.2."

25756 United Nations. Secretary-General, 1946-1953 (Lie)
Slavery, the slave trade, and other forms of servitude.
[New York] 1953.
83 p.   28 cm.   (United Nations. [Document] E/2357)

25757 United Nations. Secretary-General, 1953-1961 (Hammarskjöld)
Slavery; supplementary report. [New York] 1954.
93 p.   28 cm.   (United Nations. [Document] E/2548)
Accompanied by corrigendum.

25758 U. S. American Freedmen's Inquiry Commission.
Preliminary report touching the condition and manage-
ment of emancipated refugees; made to the Secretary of
war, by the American Freedmen's Inquiry Commission,
June 30, 1863. [Publication authorized by the Secretary
of war] New York, J. F. Trow, printer, 1863.
40 p.   22½ cm.

25759 U. S. Circuit Court (1st Circuit)
A charge delivered to the grand juries of the Circuit
court, at October term, 1819, in Boston, and at November
term, 1819, in Providence, and published at their unanimous request. By the Hon. Joseph Story. [Boston?
1819]
8 p.   24 cm.
Caption title.

25760 U. S. 20th Cong., 2d sess., 1828-1829. House.
Powers of the general government - Right of the States.
Report of a committee, and resolutions of the legislature
of Georgia, upon certain resolutions of the states of
South Carolina and Ohio. [Washington, D. C., Gales &
Seaton, Printers to House of Representatives] 1829.
3 p.   22 cm.

25761 U. S. 31st Cong., 1st sess., 1849-1850. Senate.
Proceedings of the United States Senate, on the fugi-

tive slave bill - the abolition of the slave-trade in
the District of Columbia - and the imprisonment of free
colored seamen in the southern ports: with the speeches
of Messrs. Davis, Winthrop and others. [Washington]
Press of T. R. Marvin [1850]
cover-title, 68 p. 22½ cm.

25762 U. S. 34th Cong., 1st sess., 1855-1856. House.
Slavery in the territories. Debate on the power of
Congress to establish or prohibit slavery in the territories of the United States; in the House of Representatives, January 17, 1856. Washington, Printed at the
Congressional globe office, 1856.
15 p. 24 cm.

25763 U. S. 34th Cong., 1st sess., 1855-1856. Senate.
The spurious Kansas memorial. Debate in the Senate
of the United States, on the memorial of James H. Lane,
praying that the Senate receive and grant the prayer
of the memorial presented by General Cass, and afterwards
withdrawn; embracing the speeches of Senators Douglas,
Pugh, Butler, Toucey, Rusk, &c. Washington, Printed
at the Union office, 1856.
32 p. 23 cm.

25764 U. S. Congress. House. Committee on Military Affairs.
Report of the minority of the Committee on Military
Affairs, on the petition of the legal representatives
of Antonio Pacheco, praying compensation for a slave.
[Washington, 1848]
16 p. 24 cm. (30th Cong., 1st sess. House.
Rep. 187)

25765 U. S. Congress. House. Select Committee on Slavery
in the District of Columbia.
Report of the Select committee upon the subject of
slavery in the District of Columbia, made by Hon. H. L.
Pinckney, to the House of Representatives, May 18, 1836.
To which is appended the votes in the House of Representatives upon the several resolutions with which the
report concludes. Washington, Blair and Rives, printers,
1836.
16 p. 23 cm.

25766 U. S. Congress. House. Select Committee on Slavery in
the District of Columbia.
... Slavery in the District of Columbia... Washington
Blair & Rives, printers [1836]
24 p. 23 cm. (24th Cong., 1st sess. House.
Rep. 691)
Submitted by Mr. Pinckney.

25767 U. S. Congress. House. Select Committee to Whom Were Referred the Memorial of the American Society for Colonizing the Free People of Color of the United States.
Slave trade, to accompany bill H. R. no. 412. [Washington] 1830.
293 p. 23½ cm. (21st Cong. 1st sess. Report no. 348)

25768 U. S. Congress. Joint Select Committee on the Condition of Affairs in the Late Insurrectionary States.
[Report of the Joint Select Committee appointed to inquire into the condition of affairs in the late insurrectionary states, so far as regards the execution of laws, and the safety of the lives and property of the citizens of the United States and Testimony taken. Washington, Govt. print. off., 1872]
13 v. 23½ cm. (42d Cong., 2d sess. House, Rept. 22)
Issued also as Senate rept. 41, 42d Cong., 2d sess.
Luke P. Poland, chairman on the part of the House.
John Scott, chairman on the part of the Senate.

25769 U. S. Congress. Senate. Select Committee on Circulation of Abolition Literature.
... Report, with Senate bill no. 122. The Select Committee to whom was referred that portion of the President's message which relates to the attempts to circulate, through the mail, inflammatory appeals, to excite the slaves to insurrection, submit the following report. [Washington] Gales & Seaton, print [1836]
12 p. 24½ cm. (24th Cong., 1st sess. [Senate. Rept.] (118))

25770 U. S. Congress. Senate. Select Committee on Slavery and the Treatment of Freedmen.
... Report. To accompany bill S. no. 141. [Washington, Govt. print. off., 1864]
34 p. 24½ cm. (38th Cong., 1st sess. Senate. Rept. 24)

25771 U. S. Dept. of State.
... Message of the President of the United States communicating, in compliance with the resolution of the Senate of the 8th instant, information in relation to the emancipation of slaves in Cuba... July 13, 1870. [Washington, 1870]
24 p. 22½ cm. (41st Cong., 2d sess. Senate. Ex. doc. 113)

25772   U. S.   Dept. of State.
        ... Slavery in Peru. Message from the President of
        the United States, transmitting report of the secretary
        of state, with accompanying papers, concerning the
        alleged existence of slavery in Peru... Washington,
        Govt. print. off., 1913.
          443 p.   23 cm.   (62d Cong., 3d sess. House.
        Doc. 1366)
          Contains reports of Stuart J. Fuller, American consul
        at Iquitos, Charles C. Eberhardt, and Rómulo Paredes.

25773   U. S.   Laws, statutes, etc.
        ... An act to provide for the valuation of lands
        and dwelling-houses, and the enumeration of slaves
        within the United States. Trenton, Printed by Matthias
        Day, 1798.
          22 p.   22½ cm.
          Caption title.

25774   U. S.   Laws, statutes, etc.
        Laws of the United States, relative to the slave-
        trade. Washington, Printed by Davis and Force, 1823.
          43 p.   15 cm.

25775   U. S.   Laws, statutes, etc.
        Revision of the United States statutes. 1. Slave
        trade. 2. Flag and seal. 3. Militia. 4. Seal [i.e.
        seat] of government, including public buildings and
        grounds. 5. Arms, armories, and arsenals. As drafted
        by the commissioners appointed for that purpose.
        Washington, Govt. print. off., 1871.
          cover-title, 50 p.   27 cm.

25776   U. S.   Laws, statutes, etc.
        The slavery code of the District of Columbia, together
        with notes and judicial decisions explanatory of the
        same. By a member of the Washington bar. Washington,
        L. Towers & co., printers, 1862.
          38 p.   22 cm.

25777   U. S.   Laws, statutes, etc., 1849-1850 (31st Cong., 1st
        sess.)
        The Fugitive slave bill. Enacted by the United States
        Congress, and approved by the President, Millard Fill-
        more, September 18, 1850. Boston, Printed and for sale
        at 145 Hanover street, 1854.
          7, [1] p.   illus.   23 cm.

25778   U. S.   Navy Dept.
        Letter from the Secretary of the Navy, transmitting

copies of the instructions, which have been issued to naval commanders, upon the subject of the importation of slaves, made in pursuance of a resolution of the House of Representatives, of the Fourth January, instant. Washington [D.C.] Printed by E. De Krafft, 1819.
    10 p.   21½ cm.

25779 U. S. President, 1829-1837 (Jackson)
    ... Message from the President of the United States, in compliance with a resolution of the Senate, transmitting copies of orders given to the military and naval commander at the Charleston station, &c. Feb. 12, 1833. [Washington, 1833]
    11 p.   (22d Cong., 2d sess. [Senate. Doc.] 71)

25780 U. S. President, 1861-1865 (Lincoln)
    Message communicating, in answer to a resolution of the Senate of the 26th of February, correspondence with the workingmen of England. [Washington, 1863]
    6 p.   23 cm.   (37th Cong., 3d sess. Senate. Ex. doc. no. 49)
    Caption title.

25781 U. S. Treasury Dept.
    ... Emancipation in the District of Columbia. Letter from the secretary of the Treasury, in answer to a resolution of the House of Representatives, of the 11th of January, transmitting the report and tabular statements of the commissioners appointed in relation to emancipated slaves in the District of Columbia. February 17, 1864... [Washington, 1864]
    79 p.   24 cm.   (38th Cong., 1st sess. House. Ex. doc. no. 42)

25782 U. S. War Dept.
    ... Human slavery in the Philippines. Letter from the secretary of war, relating to the question of human slavery in the Philippine Islands. [Washington, Govt. print. off., 1913]
    3 p.   24 cm.   (63d Cong., 1st sess. Senate. Doc. 22)
    Lindley M. Garrison, secretary of war.

25783 Upham, Charles Wentworth, 1802-1875.
    Speech of Charles W. Upham, of Salem, in the House of Representatives of Massachusetts, on the compromises of the Constitution: with an appendix, containing the ordinance of 1787. Salem, Printed at the Tri-weekly gazette office, 1849.
    40 p.   22½ cm.

25784   Utley, H   T
        The history of slavery and emancipation. Speech deli-
        vered by H. T. Utley, before the Democratic Association
        in Dubuque, Iowa, February 12th, 1863. Pub. by request.
        Philadelphia, J. Campbell, 1863.
           31 p.   22 cm.

                                    V

25785   Vail, Eugène A
        Réponse à quelques imputations contre les États-Unis,
        énoncées dans des écrits et journaux récens, par Eugène
        A. Vail... Paris, Delaunay, 1837.
           36 p.   22 cm.

25786   Vail, Stephen Montford, 1818-1880.
        The church and the slave power. A sermon preached
        before the students of the Methodist Biblical Institute,
        Concord, N. H., February 23, 1860. By Rev. S. M. Vail,
        D.D. Pub. by the students. Concord, Fogg, Hadley & co.,
        printers, 1860.
           23 p.   21½ cm.

25787   Valiente, Porfirio.
        Réformes dans les îles de Cuba et de Porto-Rico, par
        Porfirio Valiente; avec une préface par Édouard Laboulaye
        ... Paris, A. Chaix et cie, 1869.
           2 p.l., xx, 412 p.   24 cm.
        A history of the work of the "Junta informativa de
        ultramar de 1866-67" and the attempted reforms of that
        period.

25788   Valladão, Alfredo, 1873-
        Joaquim Nabuco, o evangelista da abolição.   [Conferência]
        Rio de Janeiro, 1950.
           40 p.   24 cm.

25789   Valle Moré, José G   del, 1892-
        Cisneros y las leyes de Indias... por José del Valle
        Moré... con prólogo del dr. José Antolín del Cueto...
        Habana, Librería "Cervantes," 1918.
           116 p., 2 l.   20½ cm.

25790   Van Buren, Martin, pres. U. S., 1782-1862.
        Opinions of Martin Van Buren, vice president of the
        United States, upon the powers and duties of Congress,
        in reference to the abolition of slavery either in the
        slave-holding states or in the District of Columbia.

To which are added sundry documents showing his sentiments upon other subjects. Washington, Blair & Rives,
printers, 1836.
32 p.   22 cm.

25791 Van Dyke, Henry Jackson, 1822-1891.
The spirituality and independence of the church. A
speech delivered in the Synod of New York, October 18th,
1864. By Henry J. Van Dyke... New York, 1864.
40 p. $22\frac{1}{2}$ cm.

25792 Van Dyke, John, 1807-1878.
"Slaveholding not sinful": a reply to the argument of
Rev. Dr. How. By John Van Dyke, esq. New-Brunswick,
N. J., Printed at the Fredonian and Daily New-Brunswicker
office, 1856.
16 p.   22 cm.

25793 Van Dyke, John, 1807-1878.
Speech of Mr. John Van Dyke, of New Jersey, delivered
in the House of Representatives of the United States,
March 4, 1850, on the subject of slavery, and in vindication of the North from the charges brought against it
by the South. Washington, Gideon and co., printers, 1850.
14 p.   23 cm.

25794 Van Dyke, Nicholas, 1769-1826.
Speech of Mr. Van Dyke, on the amendment offered to a
bill for the admission of Missouri into the Union, prescribing the restriction of slavery as an irrevocable
principle of the state constitution. Delivered in the
Senate of the United States, January 28, 1820.
[Washington? 1820]
14 p. $18\frac{1}{2}$ cm.
Caption title.

25795 Van Horne, John Douglass.
Concerning a full understanding of the southern attitude toward slavery, by John Douglass Van Horne...
[Sewanne, Tenn., 1921]
31 p.   24 cm.
Reprinted from the July number of the Sewanee review,
1921.

25796 Van Evrie, John H   1814-1896.
White supremacy and Negro subordination; or, Negroes
a subordinate race, and (so-called) slavery its normal
condition, with an appendix, showing the past and present
condition of the countries south of us. By J. H. Van
Evrie... 2d ed. New York, Van Evrie, Horton & co.,

1870.
xvi, [17]-339, 60 p.   front., col. plates.   19 cm.

25797   Van Meter, Benjamin Franklin, 1834-
A dead issue and the live one, by B. F. Van Meter, sr.
... Louisville, Ky., Printed by the Bradley & Gilbert
co., 1913.
103 p.   23½ cm.

25798   Van Rensselaer, Cortlandt, 1808-1860.
God glorified by Africa. An address delivered on
December 31, 1856, at the opening of the Ashmun Institute,
near Oxford, Pennsylvania. By C. Van Rensselaer...
Philadelphia, J. M. Wilson, 1859.
48 p.   23 cm.

25799   Van Wyck, Charles Henry, 1824-1895.
Now and then. Speech of the Hon. Charles H. Van Wyck,
of New York, upon the report of the committee of thirty-
three upon the state of the Union. Delivered in the
House of Representatives, January 29, 1861. [Washington,
D. C., W. H. Moore, printer, 1861]
8 p.   24½ cm.
Caption title.

25800   Venable, Abraham Watkins, 1799-1876.
Slavery in the territories. Speech of Hon. A. W. Venable,
of N. Carolina, in the House of Representatives, June 1,
1848, in committee of the whole, upon the power of
Congress to legislate upon the subject of slavery in the
territories. [Washington, Printed at the Congressional
globe office, 1848]
8 p.   24 cm.
Caption title.

25801   [Venable, William Henry] 1836-1920.
Down South before the war. [Columbus, Ohio state
archaeological and historical society, 1889]
[28] p.   24 cm.
Reprinted from Ohio archaeological and historical
quarterly, vol. 2, no. 4.

25802   Venezuela. Laws, statutes, etc.
Ley y reglamento sobre abolición de la esclavitud en
Venezuela. Caracas, Imprenta republicana de E. Ortiz,
1854.
16, [4] p.   21½ cm.

25803   Vermont. General Assembly. Senate.
Reports of select committees of the Senate on slavery

and the condition of Kansas, and on the outrage on the freedom of debate in Congress. Burlington, Free Press Print, 1856.
8, 6, 6 p.   23 cm.

25804 Verot, Augustine, bp., 1804-1876.
A tract for the times. Slavery & abolitionism, being the substance of a sermon, preached in the Church of St. Augustine, Florida, on the 4th day of January, 1861, day of public humiliation, fasting and prayer. By the Right Rev. A. Verot... [St. Augustine? 1861?]
14 p.   24 cm.

25805 [Viger, Jacques] 1787-1858.
De l'esclavage en Canada. [Montreal, 1859]
63 p.   25½ cm.
Reprinted from Société historique de Montréal, Mémoires, 1. livr., 1959.
"Commencé par M. J. Viger et complété par Sir L. H. Lafontaine."

25806 Vigornius, pseud.
Essays on slavery; republished from the Boston Recorder & telegraph, for 1825. By Vigornius, and others.
Amherst, Mass., M. H. Newman, 1826.
iv, 5 -83 p.   20½ cm.
Of these essays six numbers are by Vigornius, one by a Carolinian, one by Philo, and nine by Hieronymus. Entered under "Palmer, Dr. (?)" in Alice D. Adams' The neglected period of anti-slavery in America, p. 283.

25807 Villiot, Jean de, pseud.
... En Virginie, épisode de la guerre de sécession, précédé d'une étude sur l'esclavage et les punitions corporelles en Amérique. Paris, C. Carrington, 1901.
xxxvi, 343, [1] p.   front., plates.   23 cm.

25808 Vindex, pseud.
Vindex on the liability of the abolitionists to criminal punishment, and on the duty of the non-slave-holding states to suppress their efforts. Charleston, Printed by A. E. Miller, 1835.
31 p.   22½ cm.

25809 [Vingut, Mrs. Gertrude (Fairfield)]
Our unity as a nation. From the "New Englander" for January, 1862. [New Haven, 1862]
p. [1], 98-114.   23 cm.

25810   Virginia. General Assembly. House of Delegates.
        ... Report of the select committee appointed under a
        resolution of the House to enquire into the existing
        legislation of Congress upon the subject of fugitive
        slaves, and to suggest such additional legislation as
        may be proper. [Richmond, 1848]
            20 p.   25½ cm.   (Virginia. General Assembly,
        1848-49. [House of Delegates] Doc. 50)
            Caption title.
            Submitted by Mr. Faulkner.

25811   Vliet, Leonard van.
            Rapport van den Gouverneur van Suriname omtrent de ont-
        worpen Nederlandsche West-Indische ontginning- en handel-
        maatschappij, met de Memorie van beantwoording.   's Graven-
        hage, A. Belinfante, 1858.
            xii, 53 p.   23 cm.

                                    W

25812   Wade, Edward, 1803-1862.
            Slavery question. Speech of Hon. Edward Wade, of Ohio,
        in the House of Representatives, August 2, 1856.
        Washington, D. C., Buell & Blanchard, printers, 1856.
            14 p.   23 cm.

25813   Waldron, Henry, b. 1819.
            Modern Democracy against the Union, the Constitution,
        the policy of our fathers, and the rights of free labor.
        Speech of Hon. Henry Waldron, of Michigan. Delivered
        in the House of Representatives April 26, 1860.
        [Washington, Republican Executive Congressional Committee,
        1860]
            7, [1] p.   22½ cm.

25814   Walker, David, 1785-1830.
            Walker's appeal, in four articles; together with a
        preamble, to the coloured citizens of the world, but in
        particular, and very expressly, to those of the United
        States of America, written in Boston, state of Massa-
        chusetts, September 28, 1829. 2d and last ed., with
        additional notes, corrections, &c. Boston, D. Walker,
        1830.
            88 p.   21½ nm.

25815   Walker, David, 1785-1830.
            Walker's appeal, with a brief sketch of his life. By

                                   298

Henry Highland Garnet. And also Garnet's Address to the slaves of the United States of America. New-York, Printed by J. H. Tobitt, 1848.
vii p., 1 l., [11]-96 p.   pl.   20½ cm.

25816   Walker, George Leon, 1830-1900.
The material and the spiritual in our national life, and their present mutual relations. A sermon preached in State Street Church, Portland, November 24, 1859, by Rev. Geo. Leon Walker... Portland [Me.] Printed by B. Thurston, 1859.
30 p.   21 cm.

25817   Walker, James, of the Berbice Commission.
Letters on the West Indies. By James Walker. London, Printed for R. Fenner, 1818.
2 p.l., [vii]-xvi, 268 p.   21 cm.

25818   [Walker, Jonathan] 1799-1878.
A picture of slavery, for youth. By the author of "The branded hand" and "Chattelized humanity"... Boston, J. Walker and W. R. Bliss [184-?]
36 p.   illus.   18½ cm.

25819   Walker, Robert James, 1801-1869.
Argument of Robert J. Walker, esq., before the Supreme Court of the United States, on the Mississippi slave question, at January term, 1841. Involving the power of Congress and of the states to prohibit the inter-state slave trade. Philadelphia, Printed by J. C. Clark, 1841.
1 p.l., lxxxviii p.   22 cm.
Argument for Moses Groves in the case of Groves et al. v. Slaughter.

25820   Wall, Garret Dorset, 1783-1850.
Speech of Mr. Wall, of New Jersey, on the memorial of the Caln Quarterly Meeting of the Society of Friends, of Lancaster County, Pennsylvania, praying for the abolition of slavery and the slave trade in the District of Columbia. In Senate, February 29, 1836. Washington, Blair and Rives, printers, 1836.
7 p.   25 cm.

25821   Wall, James Walter, 1820-1872.
Speech of Hon. James W. Wall, of N. J., on the Missouri emancipation bill, delivered in the United States Senate, February 7th, 1863. Washington, M'Gill & Witherow, printers, 1863.
16 p.   23 cm.

25822   Wallace, Daniel, d. 1859.
            The slavery question. Speech of Hon. Daniel Wallace,
        of South Carolina, in the House of Representatives,
        April 8, 1850, in Committee of the whole on the state
        of the Union, on the President's message communicating
        the constitution of California. [Washington, Printed at
        the Congressional globe office, 1850]
            7 p.   23 cm.
            Caption title.

25823   Wallace, Susan Elston.
            The chain of the last slave. An incident of the War
        of the Rebellion. [n.p., 1892]
            340-343 p.   20 cm.
            Reprinted from Arena, v. 6, Aug. 1892.

25824   Waller, James B[reckinridge] 1817-
            The true doctrine of state rights, with an examination
        of the record of the Democratic and Republican parties
        in connection with slavery. By James B. Waller.
        Chicago, Jameson & Morse, printers, 1880.
            83 p.   22½ cm.

25825   Wallon, Henry Alexandre, 1812-1904.
            Histoire de l'esclavage dans l'antiquité, par H. Wallon
        ... 2. éd. Paris, Hachette et c^{ie}, 1879.
            3 v.   23 cm.

25826   Wanderley, João Mauricio, barão de Cotegipe, 1815-1889.
            Discussão da lei de abolição no Senado. Discurso
        proferido na sessão de 12 de maio de 1888 pelo exm. sr.
        barão de Cotegipe. Bahia, Typographia da "Gazeta da
        Bahia," 1888.
            29 p.   17½ cm.

25827   Ward, Jonathan, 1769-1860.
            American slavery, and the means of its abolition. By
        Rev. Jonathan Ward... Boston, Printed by Perkins &
        Marvin, 1840.
            26 p.   18½ cm.

25828   Ward, Jonathan, 1769-1860.
            Father Ward's letter to Professor Stuart. [Newbury-
        port? Mass., C. Whippe? 1837]
            10 p.   17 cm.
            Caption title.

25829   Warner, Harry B
            The poor old slave, or Plantation life before the war.

A dramatic sketch, by Harry B. Warner...   San Francisco,
Warner & co., printers, 1872.
12 p.   17 cm.

25830   Warner, Hiram, 1802-1881.
Slavery in the territories. Speech of Hon. Hiram Warner,
of Georgia, delivered in the House of Representatives,
April 1, 1856, on the power of the general government
to exclude slave property from the territories. [Washing-
ton, Printed at the office of the Congressional globe,
1856]
7 p.   23½ cm.
Caption title.

25831   [Warner, Samuel]
Authentic and impartial narrative of the tragical scene
which was witnessed in Southampton County (Virginia)
on Monday the 22d of August last, when fifty-five of its
inhabitants (mostly women and children) were inhumanly
massacred by the blacks! Communicated by those who were
eye witnesses of the bloody scene, and confirmed by the
confessions of several of the blacks while under sentence
of death. [New York] Printed for Warner & West, 1831.
1 p.l., [5]-38 p.   fold. pl.   18 cm.

25832   Warnshuis, Abbe Levingston, 1877-1958.
... The slavery convention of Geneva, September 25, 1926,
by A. L. Warnshuis, Joseph P. Chamberlain and Quincy
Wright; text of the General act for the repression of
African slave trade, July 2, 1890...   Worcester, Mass.,
New York city, Carnegie Endowment for International Peace.
Division of Intercourse and Education [1928]
3 p.l., 5-69 p.   19½ cm.   (International concilia-
tion, January, 1928, no. 236)

23833   Washburn, Cadwallader Colden, 1818-1882.
The slavery question. Speech of Hon. C. C. Washburn,
of Wisconsin. Delivered in the U. S. House of Representatives, April 26, 1860. [n.p., n.d.]
14 p.   22½ cm.

25834   Washburn, Emory, 1800-1877.
The extinction of slavery in Massachusetts, a paper
read before the Massachusetts Historical Society,
April, 1857. Boston, 1858.
333-346 p.   22 cm.
Reprinted from Collections of the Massachusetts Historical Society, Ser. 4, v. 4, 1858.

25835   Washburne, Elihu Benjamin, 1816-1887.
Sketch of Edward Coles, second governor of Illinois,

301

and of the slavery struggle of 1823-4.   Prepared for the
Chicago Historical Society, by E. B. Washburne...
Chicago, Jansen, McClurg & company, 1882.
253 p.   front. (port.)   facsims.   21½ cm.

25836   Washington, Booker Taliaferro, 1859?-1915.
An address on Abraham Lincoln, delivered before the
Republican Club of New York City on the night of February
twelfth, 1909. [Tuskegee? Ala., 1909]
12 p.   port.   23 cm.

25837   Washington, Booker Taliaferro, 1859?-1915.
... The story of slavery, by Booker T. Washington...
with biographical sketch. Dansville, N. Y., F. A. Owen
pub. co.; Chicago, Ill., Hall & McCreary [c1913]
31 p.   1 illus. (port.)   18½ cm.   (Instructor
literature series [no. 286])

25838   Waterman, Arba Nelson, 1836-1917.
A century of caste. Chicago, M. A. Donohue [1901]
85 p.   19 cm.

25839   Watkins, James, b. 1821?
Narrative of the life of James Watkins, formerly a
"chattel" in Maryland, U. S.; containing an account of
his escape from slavery, together with an appeal on behalf
of three millions of such "pieces of property," still
held under the standard of the eagle... Boston, Kenyon
and Abbatt, printers, 1852.
vi, [7]-48 p.   illus.   16 cm.

25840   Watson, John Henry, 1851-
Address by Hon. John W. Watson, chief justice of the
Supreme court of Vermont, delivered before the Vermont
Bar Association January 4, 1921. Montpelier, 1921.
[225]-256 p.   23 cm.
Reprinted from Vermont Historical Society, Proceedings,
1919-20, 1921.

25841   Webb, James Watson, 1802-1884.
Great mass meeting on the battle ground of Tippecanoe.
60,000 freemen in council! Speech of General J. Watson
Webb... [New York, 1856]
20 p.   24 cm.
Caption title.

25842   Webb, Richard Davis.
The national anti-slavery societies in England and the
United States; or, Strictures on "A reply to certain

302

charges brought against the American and Foreign Anti-slavery Society, etc., etc.; by Lewis Tappan of New York, United States: with an introduction, by John Scoble." By Richard D. Webb... Dublin, C. Hedgelong, 1852.
　　56 p.　　21 cm.

25843　Webb, William.
　　The history of William Webb, composed by himself. Detroit, E. Hoekstra, printer, 1873.
　　77 p.　　illus. (ports.)　　22 cm.

25844　Webster, Daniel, 1782-1852.
　　Letter from citizens of Newburyport, Mass., to Mr. Webster, in relation to his speech delivered in the Senate of the United States on the 7th March, 1850, and Mr. Webster's reply. Washington, Printed by Gideon and co., 1850.
　　16 p.　　23 cm.

25845　Webster, Daniel, 1782-1852.
　　Mr. Webster's speech at Marshfield, Mass., delivered September 1, 1848, and his speech on the Oregon bill, delivered in the United States Senate, August 12, 1848. Boston, Press of T. R. Marvin, 1848.
　　24 p.　　23 cm.

25846　Webster, Daniel, 1782-1852.
　　... Remarks of Mr. Webster on the following resolution, moved by Mr. Clay, as a substitute for the 5th of Mr. Calhoun's resolutions, viz: "Resolved, That the interference, by the citizens of any of the states, with the view to the abolition of slavery in this District, is endangering the rights and security of the people of this District; and that any act or measure of Congress, designed to abolish slavery in this District, would be a violation of the faith implied in the cessions by the states of Virginia and Maryland; a just cause of alarm to the people of the slave-holding states, and have a direct and inevitable tendency to disturb and endanger the Union." [Washington, 1838]
　　8 p.　　$24\frac{1}{2}$ cm.
　　Caption title.

25847　Webster, Daniel, 1782-1852.
　　Speech of the Hon. Daniel Webster, in the Senate of the United States, on the subject of slavery. Delivered March 7, 1850. New York, 1850.
　　[13]-32 p.　　23 cm.
　　Reprinted from Calhoun, John C. Speeches. New York, 1850.

25848 Weeks, Stephen Beauregard, 1865-1918.
       ... Anti-slavery sentiment in the South; with unpu-
       blished letters from John Stuart Mill and Mrs. Stowe.
       By Stephen B. Weeks, Ph.D. [Washington, 1898]
          87-130 p.   24 cm.
       Reprinted from Southern History Association, Publica-
       tions, v. 2, 1898.

25849 Weeks, Stephen Beauregard, 1865-1918.
       Southern Quakers and slavery: a study in institutional
       history, by Stephen B. Weeks... Baltimore, The Johns
       Hopkins press, 1896.
          xiv, 400 p.   fold. map. $23\frac{1}{2}$ cm.   (Half-title:
       Johns Hopkins University studies in historical and poli-
       tical science... Extra vol. XI)

25850 Weidner, Fritz.
       ... Die Haussklaverei in Ostafrika. Geschichtlich und
       politisch dargestellt von dr. Fritz Weidner. Mit 1
       Kurve im text. Jena, G. Fischer, 1915.
          xxiv, 209, 1 p.   diagr. $23\frac{1}{2}$ cm.   ([Germany.
       Kolonialamt] Veröffentlichungen, nr. 7)

25851 Weiss, Oscar.
       De personis, quibus servorum stipulationes acquiruntur
       ... Auctor Oscar Weiss... Berolini, typis expressit
       G. Schade, 1862.
          2 p.l., 77, [1] p. $19\frac{1}{2}$ cm.
       Inaug.-diss.-Berlin.

25852 Weissmann, Konrad Maximilian Heinrich, 1888-
       De servi currentis persona apud comicos romanos...
       Gissae, typis officinae aulicae et academicae O. Kindt,
       1911.
          47, [1] p.   23 cm.
       Inaug.-diss.-Giessen.

25853 Welling, James Clarke.
       Slavery in the territories. [Washington, 1892]
          133-160 p.   23 cm.
       Reprinted from American Historical Association, Annual
       report for 1891, 1892.

25854 Wells, Alfred 1814-1867.
       To the people of the 27th congressional district of
       the state of New York. [Washington, H. Polkinhorn,
       printer, 1861]
          15 p. $22\frac{1}{2}$ cm.
       Caption title.

25855 West, Gerald Montgomery.
       The status of the negro in Virginia during the colonial
       period... New York, W. R. Jenkins [1889?]
       iv, 76 p.   24 cm.
       Thesis (Ph.D.) - Columbia College.

25856 West Brookfield Anti-slavery Society.
       An exposition of difficulties in West Brookfield, con-
       nected with anti-slavery operations, together with a
       reply to some statements in a pamphlet put forth by
       "Moses Chase, pastor of the church," purporting to be a
       "Statement of facts in the case of Deacon Henshaw." By
       the Board of Managers of the W. B. Anti-slavery Society.
       West Brookfield, Mass., The Anti-slavery society, 1844.
       59 p.   24 cm.
       Signed: John M. Fisk.

25857 West India Association, Glasgow.
       Case of the British West Indies stated. By the West
       India Association of Glasgow. Glasgow, Printed by the
       Glasgow courier company, 1852.
       14 p.   20½ cm.

25858 West Randolph, Vt. Anti-slavery convention, 1858.
       Proceedings of the Anti-slavery Convention held at
       West Randolph, Vermont, August 24th and 25th, 1858. New
       York, American Anti-slavery Society, 1858.
       24 p.   15½ cm.

25859 What shall be done? [Philadelphia, W. F. Geddes, printer,
       186-?]
       4 p.   19½ cm.

25860 What the North said to the South. [n.p., 1860?]
       cover-title, [3]-7 p.   22 cm.
       Signed: A Union man in search of the Union.

25861 [Wheat, Marvin T   ]
       Progress and intelligence of Americans, whether in the
       northern, central, or southern portion of the continent,
       founded upon the normal and absolute servitude of inferior
       animates to mankind, as indicated by the order of nature
       and by the acts of creation, as laid down in the Bible:
       progress of that servitude south and southwest, as new
       territory may be acquired, either by purchase, or by
       national immergence of Mexico and Central America into
       the United States, through the vindication of the Monroe
       doctrine in becoming their protectorate. Advantages
       enumerated and explained. By Alonzo Alvarez... [pseud.]

n.p. Tr., printed and pub. by the author, 1865.
2 p.l., [iii]-iv, [5]-595, xvii p.   23 cm.

25862   Wheaton, Nathaniel Sheldon, 1792-1862.
A discourse on St. Paul's epistle to Philemon; exhibiting
the duty of citizens of the northern states in regard to
the institution of slavery; delivered in Christ Church,
Hartford; Dec. 22, 1850; by N. S. Wheaton, D.D. Hartford,
Press of Case, Tiffany and company, 1851.
30 p.   24 cm.

25863   [Whipple, Charles King] 1808-1900.
The American Tract Society, Boston. Boston, Mass.
A[nti] s[lavery] society, 1859.
24 p.   16 cm.
Signed: C. K. W.

25864   Whipple, Charles King, 1808-1900.
The Methodist Church and slavery. By Charles K.
Whipple. New York, American Anti-slavery Society;
Boston, 1859.
31 p.   14 cm.

25865   Whipple, Charles King, 1808-1900.
The non-resistance principle: with particular application to the help of slaves by abolitionists. By Charles
K. Whipple. Boston, R. F. Wallcut, 1860.
24 p.   17½ cm.

25866   [Whipple, Charles King] 1808-1900.
To the friends of the A. B. C. F. M. [Boston, 1857]
18 p.   14 cm.
Caption title.

25867   Whipple, Phila M
Negro neighbors, bond and free; lessons in history and
humanity. Boston, Woman's American Baptist Home Mission
Society, 1907.
143 p., [1] l.   plates, ports.   20 cm.

25868   [White, Lucy] d. 1894.
Our nation; by Mary [pseud.]... Bangor, Printed by
S. S. Smith, 1860.
2 p.l., 3-14 p.   15½ cm.

25869   ... White slavery in the United States. [New York,
American Anti-slavery Society, 1855]
8 p.   18½ cm.   (Anti-slavery tracts, no. 2)
Caption title.

25870   Whitefield, George, 1714-1770.
        Three letters from the Reverend Mr. G. Whitefield;
        viz. Letter I. To a friend in London, concerning Arch-
        bishop Tillotson. Letter II. To the same, on the same
        subject. Letter III. To the inhabitants of Maryland,
        Virginia, North and South-Carolina, concerning their
        negroes. [Ornament] Philadelphia, Printed and sold by
        B. Franklin, at the New printing-office near the market,
        1740.
        16 p.   19 cm.

25871   Whiteley, Henry.
        ... Three months in Jamaica, in 1832; comprising a
        residence of seven weeks on a sugar plantation. By Henry
        Whiteley. Newcastle, Printed for the Anti-slavery
        Society, by J. Blackwell & co. [18-]
        24 p.   19½ cm.
        Caption title.

25872   [Whiteman, Susan Godfred (Hooker)] 1838-1928.
        Wakefield Standley. A story of the flag.   Carrollton,
        Mo., Carroll record, 1888.
        3 p.l., [11]-190 p.   20½ cm.
        In verse.

25873   Whitman, Albert Allson, 1851-1901.
        Not a man, and yet a man: by A. A. Whitman.   Spring-
        field, O., Republic printing company, 1877.
        254 p.   front. (port.)   19½ cm.
        Poems.

25874   [Whitson, Thomas]
        ... The early abolitionists of Lancaster County...
        Lancaster, Pa., 1911.
        2 p.l., 69-89 p.   23 cm.   (Papers read before the
        Lancaster County Historical Society, March 3, 1911...
        vol. XV, no. 3)

25875   Whittier, John Greenleaf, 1807-1892.
        ... Justice and expediency; or, Slavery considered
        with a view to its rightful and effectual remedy,
        abolition. By John G. Whittier... New-York, 1833.
        [49]-63 p.   23½ cm.   (In Anti-slavery reporter,
        v. 1, no. 4)

25876   [Whittier, John Greenleaf] 1807-1892, ed.
        The north star: the poetry of freedom, by her
        friends... Philadelphia, Merrihew and Thompson, 1840.
        vi, [7]-117, [1] p.   16 cm.

25877   Whittier, John Greenleaf, 1807-1892.
         Poems written during the progress of the abolition
         question in the United States, between the years 1830
         and 1838. By John G. Whittier. Boston, I. Knapp, 1837.
         x p., 3 l., [17]-103 p. incl. illus., pl.   17 cm.

25878   Why work for the slave? [n.p., 1838?]
         12 p.   18½ cm.
         Caption title.

25879   Wick, William W   . 1796-1868.
         Speech of Mr. W. W. Wick of Indiana, on the privilege
         of members and the subject of slavery. Delivered in the
         House of Representatives April 25, 1848. Washington,
         Towers, printer, 1848.
         16 p.   24½ cm.
         Caption title.

25880   Wicksteed, Charles.
         The Englishman's duty to the free and the enslaved
         American. A lecture, twice delivered at Leeds, in
         January, 1853. By the Rev. Charles Wicksteed, B. A.
         London, W. & F. G. Cash; [etc., etc.] 1853.
         24 p.   17½ cm.   (Leeds anti-slavery series, no. 44)

25881   Wieczorek, Rudolph.
         To the 38th Congress of the United States of America.
         An open letter from Dr. Rudolph Wieczorek... [New York,
         1864]
         12 p.   20 cm.
         Caption title.

25882   Wiggins, John H
         A review of an anti-abolition sermon, preached at
         Pleasant Valley, N. Y., by Rev. Benjamin F. Wile,
         August, 1838. By John H. Wiggins. Whitesboro, Press
         of the Oneida institute, 1838.
         60 p.   22½ cm.
         Extracts from Mr. Wile's sermon included.

25883   Wikoff, Henry, 1813-1884.
         A letter to Viscount Palmerston, K. C., prime minister
         of England, on American slavery. By Henry Wikoff...
         New York, Ross & Tousey, 1861.
         84 p.   23 cm.

25884   Wilberforce, Edward, 1834-
         Brazil viewed through a naval glass: with notes on
         slavery and the slave trade. By Edward Wilberforce...

London, Longman, Brown, Green, and Longmans, 1856.
x p., 1 l., 236 p.   18 cm.   [Traveller's library, pt. 88]

25885 Wilberforce, William, 1759-1833.
An appeal to the religion, justice, and humanity of the inhabitants of the British empire, in behalf of the negro slaves in the West Indies. By Wm. Wilberforce... New ed. London, Printed for J. Hatchard and son, 1823.
56 p.   21½ cm.

25886 Wilberforce, William, 1759-1833.
The correspondence of William Wilberforce. Edited by his sons, Robert Isaac Wilberforce... and Samuel Wilberforce... London, J. Murray, 1840.
2 v.   19 cm.

25887 Wilbur, Henry Watson, 1851-1914.
President Lincoln's attitude towards slavery and emancipation, with a review of events before and since the civil war, by Henry W. Wilbur. Philadelphia, Pa., W. H. Jenkins, 1914.
220 p.   20 cm.

25888 Wilcox, Andrew Jackson, 1835-1870.
The powers of the federal government over slavery! By Andrew J. Wilcox. Baltimore, 1862.
23 p.   22 cm.

25889 Wilcox, Andrew Jackson, 1835-1870.
A remedy for the defects of the Constitution. By Andrew J. Wilcox... [Baltimore, 1862]
40 p.   22½ cm.

25890 Wilkinson, Thomas, d. 1836.
An appeal to England, on behalf of the abused Africans, a poem. By T. Wilkinson. London, Printed and sold by J. Phillips, 1789.
v, [7]-34 p.   24 cm.

25891 [Willard, Mrs. Emma (Hart)] 1787-1876.
The African in America. To find his true position, and place him in it, the via media on which the north and south might meet in a permanent and happy settlement. [Baltimore? 1862]
10 p., 1 l.   20 cm.
Caption title.

25892 Willey, Austin, 1806-1896.
The history of the antislavery cause in state and

nation. By Rev. Austin Willey... Portland, Me., B.
Thurston [etc.] 1886.
   xii, 503 p.   front., ports.   20 cm.

25893 Williams, Carl O
         Thraldom in ancient Iceland, by Carl O. Williams.
       Chicago, Ill., The University of Chicago press [1937]
         xxv, 168, [1] p.   22 cm.

25894 Williams, Isaac D   b. 1821?
         Sunshine and shadow of slave life. Reminiscences as
       told by Isaac D. Williams to "Tege" [pseud.] East Sagi-
       naw, Mich., Evening news printing and binding house,
       1885.
         91 p.   port.   22 cm.

25895 Williams, James, 1796-1869.
         Letters on slavery from the Old World: written during
       the canvass for the presidency of the United States in
       1860. To which are added a letter to Lord Brougham on
       the John Brown raid; and a brief reference to the result
       of the presidential contest and its consequences. By
       James Williams... Nashville, Tenn., Southern Methodist
       publishing house, 1861.
         x, 9-321 p.   19 cm.

25896 Williams, James, b. 1825.
         Life and adventures of James Williams, a fugitive
       slave, with a full description of the Underground Rail-
       road. 5th ed. Philadelphia, A. H. Sickler & co., 1893.
         130 p. incl. 3 pl.   pl.   23 cm.
         Preface signed: John Thomas Evans (formerly) now
       James Williams.

25897 Williamson, Passmore, respondent.
         Case of Passmore Williamson. Report of the proceedings
       on the writ of habeas corpus, issued by the Hon. John K.
       Kane, judge of the District Court of the United States
       for the Eastern District of Pennsylvania, in the case
       of the United States of America ex rel. John H. Wheeler
       vs. Passmore Williamson, including the several opinions
       delivered; and the arguments of counsel, reported by
       Arthur Cannon, esq. ... Philadelphia, U. Hunt & son,
       1856.
         191 p.   23½ cm.

25898 Willson, Edmund Burke, 1820-1895.
         The proclamation of freedom. A sermon preached in the
       North Church, Salem, January 4, 1863. By Edmund B.

Willson... Salem, T. J. Hutchinson, printer, 1863.
16 p.   22½ cm.

25899   Willson, James Renwick, 1780-1853.
Tokens of the divine displeasure, in the late confla-
grations in New-York, & other judgments, illustrated...
By James R. Willson... Newburgh [N. Y.] Printed by C. U.
Cushman, 1836.
46 p.   20½ cm.

25900   Wilmot, David, 1814-1868.
Slavery in the territories. Speech of Hon. D. Wilmot,
of Pennsylvania, in the House of Representatives, May 3,
1850, in committee of the whole on the state of the
Union, on the President's message transmitting the
constitution of California. [Washington, Printed at the
Congressional globe office, 1850]
8 p.   24 cm.
Caption title.

25901   Wilmot-Horton, Sir Robert John, bart., 1784-1841.
First letter to the freeholders of the county of York,
on negro slavery: being an inquiry into the claims of
the West Indians for equitable compensation. By the
Right Hon. R. Wilmot-Horton... London, E. Lloyd, 1830.
112 p.   23 cm.

25902   Wilson, Calvin Dill, 1857-
Black masters: a side-light on slavery. [n.p., 1905]
685-698 p.   21 cm.
Reprinted from North American review, v. 181, Nov.
1905.

25903   Wilson, Calvin Dill, 1857-
Negroes who owned slaves, by Calvin D. Wilson...
[New York? 1912]
cover-title, p. [483]-494.   25 cm.
Reprinted from the Popular science monthly, November,
1912.

25904   [Wilson, Henry] 1812-1875.
Are working-men "slaves?" Speech in reply to the
Hon. J. H. Hammond, of South Carolina, in the Senate,
March 20, 1858, on the bill to admit Kansas under the
Lecompton constitution. [Washington, Buell & Blanchard,
printers, 1858]
16 p.   24½ cm.
Caption title.

25905   Wilson, Henry, 1812-1875.
        History of the antislavery measures of the Thirty-
    seventh and Thirty-eighth United-States Congresses,
    1861-64. By Henry Wilson. Boston, Walker, Wise, and
    company, 1864.
        xv, 384 p.   19½ cm.

25906   Wilson, Henry, 1812-1875.
        The position of John Bell and his supporters. Speech
    of Hon. Henry Wilson, at Myrick's, September 18, 1860.
    From the verbatim report in the Daily atlas and bee.
    Boston, Bee printing co.   1860
        8 p.   22½ cm.
        Caption title.

25907   Wilson, Henry, 1812-1875.
        Speech of Hon. Henry Wilson, of Mass., in the Senate,
    March 27th, 1862, on the bill to abolish slavery in
    the District of Columbia, introduced by him December 16th,
    1861, referred to the District Committee, and reported
    back with amendments by Mr. Morrill. [Washington, D. C.,
    Scammell, 1862]
        8 p.   22 cm.

25908   Wilson, Joseph Thomas.
        Emancipation: its course and progress, from 1841 B.C.
    to A.D. 1875, with a review of President Lincoln's pro-
    clamations, the XIII amendment, and the progress of the
    freed people since emancipation; with a history of the
    emancipation monument. By Jos. T. Wilson. Hampton, Va.,
    Normal sccool steam power press print, 1882.
        242 p.   front. (port.)   22½ cm.

25909   Wilson, William Dexter, 1816-1900.
        A discourse on slavery: delivered before the anti-
    slavery society of Littleton, N. H., February 22, 1839,
    being the anniversary of the birth of Washington. By
    W. D. Wilson... Concord, Printed by A. McFarland, 1839.
        51 p.   24 cm.

25910   Winn, T   S
        A speedy end to slavery in our West India colonies, by
    safe, effectual, and equitable means, for the benefit of
    all parties concerned... By T. S. Winn... London, Sold
    by W. Phillips [etc.] 1825.
        2 p.l., 123 p.   22½ cm.
        -- Supplement to A speedy end to slavery, by T. S. Winn,
    1827... London, Sold by W. Phillips [etc.] 1827.
        1 p.l., 32 p.   22½ cm.

25911 Wisconsin. Supreme Court.
            Unconstitutionality of the Fugitive slave act. Deci-
       sions of the Supreme court of Wisconsin in the cases of
       Booth and Rycraft. Milwaukee, R. King & co., printers,
       1855.
            iv, 218 p.   24 cm.

25912 Wisconsin State Historical Society. Library.
            ... Catalogue of books on the war of the rebellion, and
       slavery, in the library of the State Historical Society
       of Wisconsin. Madison, Democrat printing company, 1887.
            1 p.l., 61 p.   22½ cm.   (Class list, no. 1:
       April 30, 1887)

25913 Wise, Henry Alexander, 1806-1976.
            Territorial government, and the admission of new states
       into the Union. A historical and constitutional treatise.
       By Henry A. Wise... [Richmond? 1859]
            cover-title, 157 p.   fold. map.   22½ cm.

25914 Wisner, William Carpenter, 1808-1880.
            The Biblical argument on slavery. Being principally
       a review of T. D. Weld's "Bible against slavery." By
       Rev. William C. Wisner... New-York, Leavitt, Trow, &
       co., 1844.
            40 p.   24 cm.

25915 Wood, Bradford Ripley, 1800-1889.
            Speech of Mr. Wood, of New York, on the three million
       appropriation bill, and the Wilmot proviso. Delivered in
       the House of Representatives of the U. S., Feb. 10,
       1847. Washington, Printed by J. & G. S. Gideon, 1847.
            14 p.   23½ cm.

25916 Wood, Frank Hoyt.
            Ursprung und Entwickelung der Sklaverei in den ursprüng-
       lich von Frankreich und Spanien besessenen Teilen der
       Vereinigten Staaten und Canadas. Leipzig, B. Zechel,
       1900.
            59, [1] p.   20 cm.

25917 Wood, Norman Barton, 1857-
            The white side of a black subject; enlarged and
       brought down to date. A vindication of the Afro-American
       race. From the landing of slaves at St. Augustine,
       Florida, in 1565, to the present time. By Rev. Norman
       B. Wood... Cincinnati, O., W. H. Ferguson company [c1899]
            2 p.l., 7-408 p.   front., plates, ports.   20½ cm.

25918 Woodburn, James Albert, 1856-
       The attitude of Thaddeus Stevens toward the conduct
       of the civil war, by James Albert Woodburn... [Washington,
       1908]
           211-231 p.   24½ cm.
       Reprinted from American Historical Association, Annual
       report for the year 1906, 1908.

25919 Woodward, A
       A review of Uncle Tom!s cabin; or, An essay on slavery.
       By A. Woodward, M.D. Cincinnati, Applegate & co., 1853.
           vi, [7]-216 p.   19 cm.

25920 [Woodward, George Washington] 1809-1875.
       Opinions of a man who wishes to be governor of Pennsyl-
       vania. [Philadelphia, Printed by C. Sherman son & co.,
       1863]
           7 p.   22½ cm.

25921 Woodward, Joseph Addison, 1806-1885.
       Speech of Mr. J. A. Woodward, of S. C., on the
       relations between the United States and their territorial
       districts: delivered in the House of Representatives
       of the U. S., July 3, 1848. Washington, J. and G. S.
       Gideon, printers, 1848.
           14 p.   23 cm.

25922 Woolman, John, 1720-1772.
       A journal of the life, gospel labours, and Christian
       experiences of that faithful minister of Jesus Christ...
       To which are added, his works, containing his last
       epistle and other writings. Dublin, Printed by R. M.
       Jackson, 1794.
           464 p.   20½ cm.

25923 Wright, Elizur, 1804-1885.
       An eye opener for the wide awakes. By Elizur Wright.
       A Union-saving, constitutional, conservative... aboli-
       tionist. Boston, Thayer & Eldridge, 1860.
           59 p.   18½ cm.

25924 [Wright, Elizur] 1804-1885.
       Myron Holley; and what he did for liberty and true
       religion... Boston, Printed for the author, 1882.
           328 p.   front. (port.)   19 cm.

25925 Wright, Elizur, 1804-1855, ed.
       Perforations in the "Latter-day pamphlets," by one
       of the "eighteen millions of bores. Edited by Elizur

Wright. No. 1. Universal suffrage. Capital punishment.
Slavery. Boston, Phillips, Sampson, and company, 1850.
48 p.   20 cm.

25926   [Wright, Elizur] 1804-1885.
The programme of peace. By a Democrat of the old
school. Boston, Ticknor & Fields, 1862.
22 p.   22 cm.

25927   Wright, Henry Clarke, 1797-1870.
Ballot box and battle field. To voters under the
United States government. By H. C. Wright... Boston,
Dow & Jackson's press, 1842.
1 p.l., 20 p.   16 cm.

25928   [Wright, Henry Clarke] 1797-1870.
Christian communion with slaveholders: Will the
Alliance sanction it? Letters to Rev. John Angell James,
D.D., and Rev. Ralph Wardlaw, D.D., shewing their
position in the Alliance. 3d thousand. Rochdale, J.
Hall, 1846.
12 p.   18½ cm.

25929   Wright, Henry Clarke, 1797-1870.
Manstealers: will the Free church of Scotland hold
Christian fellowship with them? An address, by Henry
C. Wright... Glasgow, The Glasgow Emancipation Society,
1845.
16 p.   23 cm.

25930   [Wright, Henry Clarke] 1797-1870.
Self-convicted violators of principle. [n.p., 184-?]
8 p.   17½ cm.
Caption title.

25931   Wright, James Martin, 1879-
... The free Negro in Maryland, 1634-1860, by James M.
Wright... New York, Columbia University; [etc., etc.]
1921.
362 p.   22½ cm.   (Studies in history, economics
and public law, ed. by the Faculty of Political Science
of Columbia University, v. 97, no. 3; whole no. 222)

25932   Wright, James Martin, 1879-
History of the Bahama Islands, with a special study of
the abolition of slavery in the colony, by James Martin
Wright... [Baltimore, The Friedenwald company] 1905.
3 p.l., [419]-583, [1] p.   pl.   26 cm.

25933   Wright, John.
         A refutation of the sophisms, gross misrepresentations,
         and erroneous quotations contained in "An American's
         Letter to the Edinburgh reviewers"; or, Slavery inimical
         to the character of the great Father of all, unsupported
         by divine revelation, a violation of natural justice, and
         hostile to the fundamental principles of American inde-
         pendence. By John Wright... Washington, D. C., Printed
         for the author, 1820.
           viii, [9]-52 p.   22½ cm.

25934   Wright, John Stephen, 1815-1874.
         Civil war from an absurdity. The South wrong in this
         war. The North wrong with regard to slavery and as to
         the principles of our government. The United States
         neither monster nor mongrel, but a pure federal republic.
         A plea from the young West, the giant offspring of Union,
         for that Union and for our federal government as insti-
         tuted by our honored fathers. By J. S. Wright...
         Chicago, 1862.
           23, [1] p.   24 cm.

                              X

25935   Xavier de Brito, José Joaquim.
         ... Organisation et recrutement de la main d'oeuvre
         dans la province de St. Thomé et Prince; rapport pré-
         senté par José Joaquim Xavier de Brito... Lisbonne,
         Impr. "A Editora limitada," 1914.
           30 p.   26 cm.
         At head of title: III° Congrès international d'agri-
         culture tropicale, Londres - 1914.

                              Y

25936   Yancey, William Lowndes, 1814-1863.
         Six speeches. [n.p., 1861?]
           1 v. (various pagings)   22½ cm.

25937   Yancey, William Lowndes, 1814-1863.
         Speech of Hon. W. L. Yancey, delivered in the Democratic
         State Convention, of the State of Alabama, held at
         Montgomery, on the 11th, 12th, 13th & 14th January,
         1860. Montgomery, Advertiser Book and Job Steam Press,
         1860.
           31 p.   22 cm.

25938　The Yankee slave-dealer; or, An abolitionist down South.
A tale for the times. By a Texan... Nashville, Tenn.,
The author, 1860.
vi, 7-368 p.　19 cm.

25939　Yates, Edward, 1829-1864.
A letter to the women of England, on slavery in the
southern states of America; considered especially in
reference to the condition of the female slaves, most
of the facts from the observation of the author while
travelling in the South. By Edward Yates... New York,
C. Blanchard, 1863.
68 p.　21 cm.

25940　Yates, Richard, 1818-1873.
Speech of Hon. Richard Yates, of Illinois, on the bill
to organize territorial governments in Nebraska and
Kansas, and opposing the repeal of the Missouri Compromise. House of Representatives, March 28, 1854.
Washington, Printed at the Congressional Globe Office,
1854.
16 p.　22½ cm.

25941　Yates, William, 1767-1857.
Rights of colored men to suffrage, citizenship and
trial by jury: being a book of facts, arguments and
authorities, historical notices and sketches of debates -
with notes. By William Yates. Philadelphia, Printed by
Merrihew and Gunn, 1838.
viii, [9]-104 p.　21 cm.

25942　Yeadon, Richard.
The amenability of northern incendiaries, as well to
southern as to northern laws, without prejudice to the
right of free discussion; to which is added an inquiry
into the lawfulness of slavery, under the Jewish and
Christian dispensations, together with other views of
the same subject, being a series of essays, originally
published in the Charleston courier, by Richard Yeadon,
one of the editors. Charleston, Printed by T. A. Hayden...
1835. [Charleston] Re-printed, with additions, by
J. B. Nixon, 1853.
48 p.　24 cm.

25943　Young, J　　H
Map of the west coast of Africa, from Sierra Leone to
Cape Palmas; including the colony of Liberia. Compiled
chiefly from the surveys and observations of the late
Rev. J. Ashmun. Published by A. Finley... Philadelphia,

1831.
    col. map.   21 x 29 cm.
    Scale ca. 1:2,400,000.
    Insets: "Remarks." - "Plan of the town of Monrovia."

                            Z

25944   Zaborowski-Moindron, Sigismond, 1851-
        Ancient Greece and its slave population. By S. Zaborow-
        ski... [Washington, 1913]
            597-608 p.   23½ cm.
        Reprinted from Smithsonian Institution, Annual report,
        1912, 1913.
        "Translated... from Revue anthropologique, Paris, vol.
        21, 1911, p. 245-258.

25945   Zabriskie, James C
        Speech of Col. Jas. C. Zabriskie, on the subject of
        slavery, and in reply to the address of the Pittsburgh
        convention, and Geo. C. Bates, esq., delivered at
        Sacramento, Cal., on the 10th day of May, A.D. 1856.
        Sacramento, Printed at the Democratic state journal
        office [1856]
            14 p.   24 cm.

25946   Zoltowski, Joseph Johann Maria von, 1847-
        De pignore rei frugiferae... publice defendet auctor
        Josephus a Zoltowski, Posnaniensis... Berolini, typis
        expressit G. Schade [1870]
            44, [2] p.   23 cm.

                            318

This volume is based on the Lost Cause Press' microfiche collection on slavery. The numbers of titles in this collection which have been described in earlier volumes are:

14	1556	3199	5314	10787	14026
17	1584	3303	5318	10861	14052
89	1597	3370	5330	10903	14123
98	1699	3412	5363	11036	14124
110	1781	3425	5442	11100	14247
146	1794	3426	5464	11207	14288
154	1823	3427	5638	11255	14516
172	1831	3479	5831	11280	14843
206	1872	3526	6089	11324	14960
256	1889	3532	6636	11357	15016
291	1890	3610	6919	11372	15187
299	1929	3611	6934	11437	15351
387	1950	3689	7137	11439	15708
393	2002	3782	7293	11565	15714
429	2019	3884	7497	11635	15727
443	2094	3906	7898	11719	16219
451	2104	3967	8046	11737	17145
470	2121	4013	8138	11740	17552
471	2133	4076	8460	11754	
534	2257	4105	8472	11783	
580	2282	4148	8672	11798	
639	2300	4154	8803	11868	
646	2457	4220	8849	11885	
655	2545	4283	8929	11890	
693	2598	4389	8932	11918	
799	2718	4411	9103	12422	
948	2719	4413	9245	12522	
977	2793	4445	9338	12843	
1043	2822	4451	9457	12953	
1048	2831	4618	9494	13122	
1126	2834	4706	9622	13147	
1153	2835	4723	9623	13168	
1213	2850	4812	9665	13216	
1339	2851	4814	9666	13490	
1341	2969	4817	9748	13525	
1359	2974	4821	9833	13842	
1381	3023	4911	9851	13866	
1429	3025	4920	9971	13867	
1459	3026	5003	9982	13881	
1490	3030	5039	10008	13885	
1491	3098	5187	10142	13892	
1499	3138	5196	10509	13925	
1512	3153	5282	10630	13928	
1527	3175	5285	10785	13984